⪡ CATO ⪢
SUPREME COURT
REVIEW

2019 — 2020

❦ CATO ❦
SUPREME COURT
REVIEW

2019 — 2020

ILYA SHAPIRO
Publisher

ROGER PILON
Founder

TREVOR BURRUS
Editor in Chief

ROBERT A. LEVY
Associate Editor

CLARK NEILY
Associate Editor

WALTER OLSON
Associate Editor

JAY SCHWEIKERT
Associate Editor

WILL YEATMAN
Associate Editor

ROBERT A. LEVY
CENTER FOR CONSTITUTIONAL STUDIES

CATO
INSTITUTE
Washington, D.C.

THE CATO SUPREME COURT REVIEW (ISBN 978-1-952223-11-2) is published annually at the close of each Supreme Court term by the Cato Institute, 1000 Massachusetts Ave., N.W., Washington, D.C. 20001-5403.

CORRESPONDENCE. Correspondence regarding subscriptions, changes of address, procurement of back issues, advertising and marketing matters, and so forth, should be addressed to:

Publications Department
The Cato Institute
1000 Massachusetts Ave., N.W.
Washington, D.C. 20001

All other correspondence, including requests to quote or reproduce material, should be addressed to the editor.

CITATIONS: Citation to this volume of the Review should conform to the following style: 2019-2020 Cato Sup. Ct. Rev. (2020).

INTERNET ADDRESS. Articles from past editions are available to the general public, free of charge, at www.cato.org/pubs/scr.

978-1-952223-11-2 (print)
978-1-952223-12-9 (digital)

Printed in the United States of America.

Cato Institute
1000 Massachusetts Ave., N.W.
Washington, D.C. 20001
www.cato.org

Published through the generosity of George M. Yeager

Contents

CONTENTS

FOREWORD

The Roberts Court

Ilya Shapiro[*]

The Cato Institute's Robert A. Levy Center for Constitutional Studies is pleased to publish this 19th volume of the *Cato Supreme Court Review*, an annual critique of the Court's most important decisions from the term just ended plus a look at the term ahead. We are the first such journal to be released, and the only one that approaches its task from a classical liberal, Madisonian perspective, grounded in the nation's first principles, liberty through constitutionally limited government. We release this volume each year at Cato's annual Constitution Day symposium on September 17—which this year also coincides with the release of my new book, *Supreme Disorder: Judicial Nominations and the Politics of America's Highest Court.*

Of course, this year is unusual in that our Constitution Day symposium, like so many other annual events that mark the rhythms of Cato's, Washington's, and the legal community's calendar, is virtual. Those of us fortunate enough to be able to continue gainful employment during the COVID-19 pandemic, at vocations that allow relatively uninterrupted remote work, have had to adjust to a new way of doing business.

That includes the Supreme Court. After canceling the March and April oral arguments, the Court set a rare May argument session, while also pushing a dozen cases into next term. The Court's ten arguments that month were the first time since 1997 that the court heard arguments so late—and the most May arguments since 1961. These arguments, like so much else these days, relied on technology rather than in-person meetings, albeit as 20th-century teleconferences instead of 21st-century videoconferences.

[*] Director, Robert A. Levy Center for Constitutional Studies; publisher, *Cato Supreme Court Review*. This foreword in part adapts my article "Roberts Rules." Wash. Examiner, July 28, 2020, at 12.

Chief Justice John Roberts, soon after presiding over Donald Trump's impeachment trial—remember that?—choreographed what turned out to be genteel hearings, with the justices asking questions one at a time by seniority, not the traditional free-for-all where advocates have a hard time getting a word in edgewise. It turns out that the Supreme Court's teleconferences are just like ours, with flushing toilets and participants' forgetting to unmute.

The argument delays and cancellations left the Court with just 53 signed opinions, the lowest number since the Civil War. Many of those opinions came down in July, as the Court pushed into the second week of that month for the first time in recent memory. Of course, like the rest of us, this year the justices had nowhere else to be.

More importantly, for the substance of the Court's work, John Roberts emerged in the majority more than any of his colleagues, including in all but one of the 5-4 decisions. Although Justice Brett Kavanaugh was in the majority in just three fewer cases than Roberts, and Justice Neil Gorsuch in just two fewer than that—that trio is the Court's nucleus—this is the year it really became the Roberts Court.

To put a finer point on it, Roberts was in the majority in 58 of 60 cases, a 97-percent win rate. The only other justice who participated in at least 50 cases in a term and was in the majority that much since Roberts joined the Court in 2005 was Anthony Kennedy, who did it three times. Before Kennedy, the most recent justice to be in the majority that much was William Brennan in the 1968-69 term. The last chief justice to do it was Fred Vinson in 1949-50.

Now, Roberts isn't a true "swing" vote, even though this term he went with the progressives in 5-4 rulings more than any other conservative—twice, with Gorsuch the only other "defector," in the Indian law case on the last day of term (*McGirt v. Oklahoma*). Instead, he's the Court's "driver," steering the institution where he wants to go. Or the "anchor" justice, as SCOTUSblog's Adam Feldman put it, because of his tendency to vote in the Court's majority.

Most notably, Roberts shocked court-watchers by joining the liberals on three key cases decided at the end of June, involving LGBTQ rights (*Bostock v. Clayton County*), immigration (*DHS v. Regents of the University of California*), and abortion (*June Medical Center v. Russo*). That, plus Gorsuch's writing the opinion in *Bostock*, which had a

6-3 margin, set off a circular firing squad on the right, as so-called common-good constitutionalists—more interested in conservative results than neutral methods—went after originalists and textualists. That outrage tamped down a bit a few weeks later, when the Court issued three key religious-liberty rulings, two of them by 7-2 margins (*Little Sisters of the Poor v. Pennsylvania* and *Our Lady of Guadalupe School v. Morrissey-Berru*) and the other an emphatic rejection of any unequal treatment of religious schools in school-choice programs (*Espinoza v. Montana Department of Revenue*), written by the chief justice himself.

Moreover, when you look at the numbers, it was a pretty good term for conservatives. Of the thirteen 5-4 decisions, nine had the conservative justices together, and only three had a conservative defection. (The other was a quixotic copyright case with a heterodox alignment.) Compare that to the previous term, when there were eight 5-4 cases where a conservative justice joined the liberals and only seven where conservatives stuck together. Losses in high-profile cases sting, but this is by no means a left-wing court—which is why progressives breathed sighs of relief but aren't treating Roberts as the second coming of Anthony Kennedy, let alone David Souter.

Roberts has gone out of his way not to rock the boat, to maintain the status quo, and to try to extricate the Court from the larger political narrative. He strives mightily to defy political—and especially partisan—expectations. The chief justice is acutely aware that it's historically unusual to have all the Court's conservatives appointed by Republican presidents and all its liberals by Democrats, and yet that's where we are, at a time of maximum polarization and toxic public discourse.

That's why Roberts made several important moves this term that frustrated those of us who want clarity and the development of legal doctrine from the Court rather than the avoidance of potentially controversial decisions. In April, he led the Court to dismiss as moot *New York State Rifle and Pistol Association v. City of New York*, the first Second Amendment case the Court had taken up in more than a decade. Justice Brett Kavanaugh concurred in that 6-3 decision not to decide but urged the Court to "address that issue soon." Alas, Roberts's maneuvering apparently scared off Justice Gorsuch or Justice Samuel Alito—or he explicitly warned them off—because six weeks later, the Court lacked the four votes necessary to grant *any* of the 10 pending Second Amendment petitions for review, over a dissent by Justices Kavanaugh and Clarence Thomas.

The same day as those denials—and further denials in a slew of qualified-immunity cases, with Justice Thomas again dissenting—the Court decided *Bostock*, which found that Title VII of the Civil Rights Act of 1964 protected against employment discrimination based on sexual orientation and gender identity. This was a textualist decision, interpreting "based on sex" to include those categories, not progressive cant about the meaning of words changing over time or finding contrived legislative history that trumped statutory text. Justice Kavanaugh had the better of the argument in dissent, explaining that Gorsuch was being too literal and that, even in 2020, we wouldn't say that someone fired for being gay was fired "based on sex." But regardless, Roberts wasn't the deciding vote, instead sliding over to make the Court look more united and achieve a popular result.

Then in *DHS v. Regents*, Roberts wrote an opinion saying that the Trump administration didn't properly explain why it rescinded DACA, the Obama-era program that allowed people who entered the country illegally as children to stay and receive certain benefits. There are many problems with that ruling—including requiring the government to maintain a potentially unconstitutional program without examining whether President Obama had the authority to create it in the first place—but Roberts again deferred to the political process. If President Trump is reelected, he can try rescission again to force Congress to fix our broken immigration system, but otherwise another popular policy remains in force. Regardless, Roberts's opinion here serves as a roadmap for evermore ratcheting up executive power.

June Medical was perhaps Roberts's most strategic, and most cynical, move. Here he joined the liberals' invalidation of a Louisiana abortion regulation, but only on *stare decisis* grounds—the idea that sometimes we preserve erroneous precedent because it would be more disruptive to get it right. Roberts maintained his disagreement with a four-year-old case involving a similar Texas law *where he himself dissented*, but felt bound by that ruling. It was an unprincipled application of a doctrine that didn't stop him from overturning more longstanding precedents in *Citizens United v. FEC* (2010), *Janus v. AFSCME* (2018), and *Knick v. Township of Scott* (2019). It also didn't prevent his vote in *Gonzales v. Carhart* (2007), which upheld a federal ban on partial-birth abortion seven years after the Court invalidated a similar Nebraska ban in *Stenberg v. Carhart* (2000).

Finally, the last day of the term brought John Roberts's finest hour, perhaps because constitutional principle coincided with his strategic machinations. In *Trump v. Vance*, the Court held that the president doesn't have absolute immunity from state grand jury subpoenas seeking his financial records. In *Trump v. Mazars*, it held that Congress doesn't have carte blanche to engage in a fishing expedition against the president. It was a split decision—President Trump won one and lost one—but both cases ended up 7-2, with Roberts writing both majority opinions. The chief justice assembled strong coalitions for balancing state-federal relations and checking both the legislative and executive branches. Equally important to his own purposes, both cases will now continue in the lower courts, with no final resolution until after the election.

Those "Trump tax" rulings hearkened to the end of the previous term, the first in the post-Kennedy era. June 2019 saw Roberts write the controlling opinions in decisions to (1) remove federal courts from policing partisan gerrymandering; and (2) reject a question regarding citizenship for the 2020 census while allowing the Commerce Department to try again with a better rationale.

All of these rulings show that Chief Justice Roberts is acting politically, not in the partisan sense or even to curry favor with the progressives who control elite institutions, but in thinking about how to best to position his beloved Court. That's nothing new: he's always had a strong belief in the judiciary's independence, but he's also always been cautious.

All that was evident 15 years ago, when George W. Bush named him to replace Sandra Day O'Connor. Roberts had an underwhelming interview with Vice President Dick Cheney and senior White House officials, playing his cards close to the vest and not admitting to any overarching legal theories. Speculation was rampant that others had the edge, with movement types pushing Fourth Circuit Judge Michael Luttig, who was a clear and unabashed legal conservative.

President Bush went with Roberts because of a gut instinct for what a justice was like. Then, when Chief Justice William Rehnquist died, picking Roberts for chief avoided the sort of fight that would've attended the nomination of someone with a longer record of originalist jurisprudence—including the possible elevation of Justice Antonin Scalia—at a time when Bush was politically weakened by his Iraq policy and the government's response to Hurricane Katrina.

Roberts put on a clinic at his hearing, emphasizing his dedication to precedent, restraint, and a limited role for the judiciary. Judicial "modesty" became his watchword, likening the role of a judge to a baseball umpire, to "call balls and strikes and not to pitch or bat." And this wasn't some "confirmation conversion": memos from his time in the Reagan White House showed that he was critical of the Court's intervention in too many cases. There was speculation about Roberts's membership in the Federalist Society, the conservative/libertarian legal network, but he disclaimed the association. That's telling.

Roberts became the youngest chief justice since his hero John Marshall. It didn't take long for a man who had planned for this moment seemingly all his life to settle in. And it didn't take long for him to make his mark; to the extent that Roberts's project is to have the Court speak more with one voice, his first term, 2005–06 saw a marked increase in unanimous decisions: 45 percent, up from a five-year average of just over 25 percent.

The Roberts Court hasn't hit that level of agreement every term—this past year it was at 36 percent—and some "bipolar" terms have seen high rates of both unanimity and 5-4 decisions. But the statistics bear out the fact that, if you go beyond the cases that trend on Twitter, this Court is more united now than it has been since the days of FDR. The 2013–14 term, for example, saw a record two-thirds of the cases decided unanimously in the judgment, although many of those had strident concurrences that were dissents in all but name.

It's readily apparent that the chief justice has a conservative judicial philosophy, but it's a conservatism of restraint and minimalism. "If it is not necessary to decide more to a case, then in my view it is necessary not to decide more to a case," he explained in a speech toward the end of his first term. "Division should not be artificially suppressed, but the rule of law benefits from a broader agreement." Chief Justice Roberts practices what he preaches, writing fewer opinions than all of his colleagues—and he has *never* issued a solo dissent.

In other words, the Court will only go as far and as fast on any particular issue as the chief justice wants. That's typically not very far and not very fast.

Where he has supported "big" changes in the law, those have been preceded by small moves in that direction. *Citizens United*, which threw out the restriction on using corporate and union funds for independent political speech, was preceded by several campaign-finance cases rejecting justifications for various other parts of the 2002 Bipartisan Campaign Reform Act (also known as "McCain-Feingold"). *Shelby County v. Holder* (2013), which invalidated the "coverage formula" for determining which jurisdictions had to "preclear" their electoral rules under Section 5 of the Voting Rights Act, was preceded by *Northwest Austin Municipal Utility District No. 1 v. Holder* (2010), in which Roberts essentially warned Congress and the American people that Section 5 stood on dubious constitutional ground.

Of course, Roberts is most famous (or infamous) for his role in upholding the Affordable Care Act, first against constitutional attack in *NFIB v. Sebelius* (2012), and then statutory attack in *King v. Burwell* (2015). In both cases, he attempted to show judicial restraint or even "modesty" by tweaking Congress's work rather than invalidating it.

Unfortunately, he failed on his own terms. As the four *NFIB* dissenters wrote, "The Court regards its strained statutory interpretation as judicial modesty. It is not. It amounts instead to a vast judicial overreaching. It creates a debilitated, inoperable version of healthcare regulation that Congress did not enact and the public does not expect." The chief's judicial passivism, combined with the activism of the four liberal justices who saw no judicially enforceable limits on federal power, created a Frankenstein's monster. Justifying a mandate with accompanying penalty for noncompliance under the taxing power doesn't rehabilitate the statute's constitutional abuses. And by letting Obamacare survive in such a dubious manner, Roberts undermined the trust people have that the justices act as impartial arbiters, not politicians.

Ironically, the chief didn't have to do what he did to "save the Court." For one thing, Obamacare was highly unpopular—particularly its individual mandate, which even a majority of Democrats thought was unconstitutional. For another, Roberts damaged his own reputation by doing what he did only after warnings from pundits and politicians that striking down the law would be "conservative judicial activism." Had the Court sent Obamacare back to the drawing board, it would have been just the sort of thing for which the Court needs its institutional gravitas. Instead, we had a strategic decision dressed up in legal robes, judicially enacting a new law and feeding public cynicism.

Nor did the ruling legitimate President Obama's health care reform; eight years after *NFIB* and over a decade since the ACA was enacted, litigation continues. After Congress in 2017 zeroed out the "tax" for not purchasing a complying insurance policy—seemingly eliminating Roberts's taxing-power justification—the Supreme Court next term faces déjà vu all over again in *California v. Texas*.

In any case, with Justice Kennedy's retirement in June 2018, Roberts became the first chief justice to be the median vote in half a century and the first to be the deciding vote since Charles Evans Hughes in the 1930s. It's a very different Court than what we would've seen had Luttig been picked instead of Roberts in 2005—whether as chief justice or with Scalia elevated and Alito in Scalia's place. While it's possible that Roberts might be voting differently had he become an associate justice instead of the chief, he was never a Scalia or Thomas (or Gorsuch) to begin with.

Meanwhile, anyone can judge the success of Chief Justice Roberts's project to depoliticize the judiciary: tacking left and right while issuing narrow decisions, even if marginally improving public perception, does nothing to address an underlying dynamic that's driven by irreconcilable interpretive theories.

While Chief Justice Roberts now has even more incentive to indulge his minimalist fantasies, he is a surer vote for conservatives—if not libertarians—than Justice Kennedy was. What that means in the long term only time will tell, though of course Roberts will only remain in the middle of the Court if a Democratic president gets to replace Justices Ruth Bader Ginsburg and Stephen Breyer. If it's President Trump making one or both of those appointments, we'll all start talking about the Kavanaugh Court.

Introduction

*Trevor Burrus**

This is the 19th volume of the *Cato Supreme Court Review*, the nation's first in-depth critique of the Supreme Court term just ended, plus a look at the term ahead. Things changed a bit in my second year as editor in chief. In response to the COVID-19 pandemic, Cato employees have been working remotely since March. Like the Supreme Court, which heard oral arguments over the phone for the first time in history, the pandemic has disrupted the normal flow of life and challenged us to find new ways to work, socialize, and just live life.

The pandemic changed a lot, but it hasn't changed the *Cato Supreme Court Review*. We release the *Review* every year in conjunction with our annual Constitution Day symposium—which is virtual this year, of course—less than three months after the previous term ends and two weeks before the next term begins. It would be difficult to produce a law journal faster, even under normal conditions. The Court generally likes to hold big decisions until the end of June, but in this crazy year, due to delays in oral arguments (and no pressing European vacations for the justices), the Court's last decision was issued on July 9. Normally, authors would have little more than a month to produce their articles. This year, for some of our authors, it was less than that. I'm thankful that they (mostly) met their deadlines and, in some cases, even submitted early, which, trust me, became Christmas in July for the *Review*'s editor.

We're proud that this isn't a typical law review, filled with long, esoteric articles on, say, the influence of Immanuel Kant on evidentiary approaches in 18th-century Bulgaria.[1] Instead, this is a book

* Research fellow in constitutional studies, Cato Institute, and editor in chief, *Cato Supreme Court Review*

[1] Chief Justice John Roberts once opined on the uselessness of law reviews: "Pick up a copy of any law review that you see and the first article is likely to be, you know, the influence of Immanuel Kant on evidentiary approaches in 18th-century Bulgaria, or something, which I'm sure was of great interest to the academic that wrote it, but isn't

of essays on law intended for everyone from lawyers and judges to educated laymen and interested citizens. Despite some authors' attachment to them, we try to keep footnotes relatively low in number and length, and we don't make our authors provide cites for sentences like "the Internet exploded in the late 90s" (as once happened to me). There's more than enough esoteric legal scholarship out there, and the workings of the Supreme Court should be, as much as possible, publicly accessible and understandable to average citizens. In the end, the Constitution is sustained by Americans' belief in it, and every year the Supreme Court justices write thousands of words explaining and expounding on our founding document. This review provides a deeper look into a few of the most important decisions.

And we're happy to confess our bias: It's the same bias that infected Thomas Jefferson when he drafted the Declaration of Independence and James Madison as he contemplated a new government. After discarding ideas like the divine right of kings and other theories by which rulers are said to be imbued with a monopoly on the legitimate use of force in a geographic area, Enlightenment thinkers, most prominently John Locke, properly concluded that governments don't inherently have any power whatsoever. Like a pile of stones found in the woods, a government, by itself, is not a moral agent or an object of moral concern. Yet if someone takes those stones and turns them into a house, that pile of stones becomes an object of moral concern—a piece of property—via the actions of the primary moral agent: a rights-holding person. Governments don't have rights, they have powers. People have rights and they can sometimes delegate to a government the power to secure those rights. Or, as was once said by a much wiser person: "That to secure these rights, Governments are instituted among Men, deriving their just powers from the consent of the governed."

Individual liberty is protected and secured by a government of delegated, enumerated, separated, and thus limited powers. Through the ratification process, the People created a federal government

---

of much help to the bar." Remarks at the Annual Fourth Circuit Court of Appeals Judicial Conference 28:45–32:05 (June 25, 2011), https://cs.pn/30QsLpx. See also Orin S. Kerr, The Influence of Immanuel Kant Evidentiary Approaches in Eighteenth-Century Bulgaria, 18 Green Bag 2d 251, 251 (2015) ("This Article fills the gap in the literature by exploring Kant's influence on evidentiary approaches in 18th-century Bulgaria. It concludes that Kant's influence, in all likelihood, was none.").

bound by the strictures of the Constitution. A government that acts beyond those powers is not just unconstitutional, it is fundamentally immoral and illegitimate. It is pure force without reason or justification.

The delicate balance of powers within the government is partially maintained by a judiciary that enforces the Constitution according to its original public meaning, which sometimes means going against the "will of the people" and striking down popularly enacted legislation. The Constitution is not an authorization for "good ideas." Everyone who cares about the Constitution should be able to think of something that they believe is a good idea but is unconstitutional, as well as something that is a bad idea but is constitutionally authorized. If you can't think of either, then you don't really believe in the Constitution, you just believe in your good ideas. That's fine if you're a member of Congress—although they also take an oath to support and defend the Constitution—but judges are obligated to think beyond their preferences and enforce the law.

This has been a difficult year for the U.S. Constitution, as it has been for nearly everything else. A pandemic, protests in the streets over police violence, an erratic and divisive president, and a presidential election have combined to make things seem quite dire. Some argue for a radical restructuring of our government, possibly even throwing out or heavily amending the Constitution. That document, the argument goes, is irrevocably tainted by slaveholding signatories and its countenancing of America's original sin. But while the absolute evil of slavery should never be forgotten and the lasting effects of racial discrimination must not be ignored, going after the Constitution is targeting the wrong suspect. At the Founding, slavery tainted the new republic. Any governing document produced by and with people who held others in bondage would inevitably protect an institution that would eventually require a vicious war and 750,000 lives to formally abolish. Even after the war, the South clung to its old ways like a man clinging to a life raft, with decades of peonage laws, Black Codes, Jim Crow, lynchings, and state-condoned (if not encouraged) violence.

There never would've been a union of free and slaveholding states without accommodating slavery, so the Founding generation left it to its successors to resolve that contradiction. In a sense, then, the Constitution wasn't "completed" until the adoption of the Thirteenth,

Fourteenth, and Fifteenth Amendments. Those amendments did something that couldn't have been done at the Framing: establish a human-rights floor below which states were not allowed to go that could be enforced by federal courts. Southern states would have walked out of the Constitutional Convention if the proposed constitution meddled with slavery. The likely result would have been two countries, with a proto-confederacy having even fewer reasons to change its ways.

All of this history should be common knowledge to Americans. Yet, given the well-known decrepit state of American civics education, it's worth a reminder. I have seen more than one person on social media or interviewed at a protest saying something remarkably ignorant about the Constitution. One masked protester told a reporter, "the Constitution didn't abolish slavery, so it's worthless."

It has never been more important for Americans to understand what the Constitution is and what it can and can't do. It was created with the hope that a fledgling nation with a vast, still-unknown amount of territory would have the power and energy to address issues of common concern. Yet it was well known, even then, that the nation was large and diverse, with many clashing values and ideals. Aside from slavery, New Yorkers viewed South Carolinians as essentially citizens of a foreign nation, and vice versa. They could join forces on questions that concerned all states—foreign policy, defense, interstate trade, and a few others—but there was no way they could agree on issues like education and religion. There is thus no federal power to administer education, and the First Amendment prohibits Congress from meddling in religion.

The Framers knew that giving powers over important local matters to a central government was impractical and unworkable. Some critics of the Constitution, today called the anti-federalists, thought that the Constitution as written gave far too much power to the federal government. The result would be chaos and hatred within the nation. The pseudonymous "Brutus"—probably Robert Yates of New York, an anti-federalist who actually attended the Constitutional Convention until July 5, when he left in disgust because the convention had decided to scrap rather than amend the Articles of Confederation—penned one of the first essays opposing the Constitution. That essay, usually termed "Brutus 1," published on

October 18, 1787, a month after the Constitution was signed, contains one of the anti-federalists' most prescient critiques:

> The territory of the United States is of vast extent; it now contains near three millions of souls, and is capable of containing much more than ten times that number. Is it practicable for a country, so large and so numerous as they will soon become, to elect a representation, that will speak their sentiments, without their becoming so numerous as to be incapable of transacting public business? It certainly is not.
>
> In a republic, the manners, sentiments, and interests of the people should be similar. If this be not the case, there will be a constant clashing of opinions; and the representatives of one part will be continually striving against those of the other. This will retard the operations of government, and prevent such conclusions as will promote the public good. If we apply this remark to the condition of the United States, we shall be convinced that it forbids that we should be one government. The United States includes a variety of climates. The productions of the different parts of the union are very variant, and their interests, of consequence, diverse. Their manners and habits differ as much as their climates and productions; and their sentiments are by no means coincident. The laws and customs of the several states are, in many respects, very diverse, and in some opposite; each would be in favor of its own interests and customs, and, of consequence, a legislature, formed of representatives from the respective parts, would not only be too numerous to act with any care or decision, but would be composed of such heterogeneous and discordant principles, as would constantly be contending with each other.

The territory of the United States certainly is now "of vast extent," and we contain more than one hundred times the three million souls of Yates's time, but everything else in that passage is stunningly prophetic. He could be describing our current situation, in which half the country hates the other half and each party is viewed as an existential threat by the other. Presidential elections have become apocalyptic events, partially because the executive is the only effective policymaking branch of government. Congress doesn't pass laws anymore; it has already empowered administrative agencies to legislate so much that the executive branch essentially runs the entire government.

For the foreseeable future we will whip back and forth between different regulatory regimes. A Republican president will rescind some environmental and labor regulations, and four or eight years later they will be put back in place by a Democratic president. President Donald Trump, like all recent presidents, has raised (lowered?) the bar for unilateral and constitutionally dubious presidential actions. Future presidents will thus have a new arrow in their quiver: the "national emergency" executive action. A President Joe Biden or Kamala Harris could declare a national emergency on gun violence or health care or climate change. Meanwhile Congress bickers away, the only purely democratic branch reduced to people of such "heterogeneous and discordant principles," that they are "constantly [] contending with each other."

This bickering and stagnation are directly related to how much power the federal government has over our daily lives and our deepest values. By expanding the powers of the federal government to extend to just about every aspect of our lives, we compromised the Framers' vision of a diverse federal structure that would allow diverse people to live together cooperatively rather than combatively. As in 1787, South Carolinians don't want to be governed like New Yorkers, but rather than follow the guiding principle of federalism—good fences make good neighbors—we continually try to cram unwanted forms of government onto unwilling states. The spate of recent state-led lawsuits against federal actions highlights this fact. Twenty-six states sued to stop Obamacare. Dozens of sanctuary states and cities are still fighting the Trump administration over its attempt to coerce cooperation on immigration enforcement.

This is unsustainable. Our constitutional system, if it isn't broken already, is getting there fast. For decades, critics like myself and my colleagues at Cato have been emphasizing the importance of maintaining the critical aspects of constitutional governance, such as the separation of powers, federalism, and the nondelegation of legislative power. That was not persnickety carping about tedious details, as opponents often claimed, but attempts to protect vital constitutional guardrails. We will continue to do that, because hopefully it is not too late. We still have a republic, if we can keep it.

* * *

Turning to the *Review* and the Supreme Court term itself, it was another big year. Some long-percolating issues returned (executive power over immigration, Obamacare's contraceptive mandate), and some new ground was forged on questions of presidential power and the administrative state. We saw a strange abortion ruling in which the chief justice did perhaps the most John Roberts thing ever and went against his own dissent from a four-year-old ruling because he felt bound by that precedent. And we saw a major ruling that extended Title VII protections against sex discrimination to cover sexual orientation and gender identity.

Oh, and the chief justice presided over the third presidential impeachment trial in American history. Wait, did that happen?

The *Review* kicks off, as always, with the annual B. Kenneth Simon Lecture, delivered at last year's Constitution Day symposium by Judge Thomas Hardiman of the Third Circuit. Hardiman gives a stirring reminder of not only the importance of an independent judiciary but also the fact that, despite many claims to the contrary, we have one. The Supreme Court is routinely lambasted as a partisan institution, usually by those who don't follow the Court's work closely, but also occasionally by those who should know better. Yes, the justices have their particular judicial philosophies that can produce predictable results, but, for an independent judiciary that is freed from political controls, those results often diverge from simplistic "conservative" or "liberal" outcomes. Hardiman shows how the current Court is actually composed of nine independent justices, not simply blocks of "conservative" or "liberal" ones.

Next, Jonathan Adler of Case Western Reserve University School of Law (and the *Review*'s editorial board) discusses the Trump subpoena cases in the cleverly titled article, "All the President's Papers." Litigation against President Trump is by this point not new, but, in the subpoena cases, the Court decided important questions on the scope of presidential immunity to state and congressional subpoenas. Because the Court was refereeing a dispute between two branches of government, Chief Justice Roberts unsurprisingly wrote both opinions. In the end, writes Adler, "the Court reaffirmed two fundamental constitutional values: No person is above the law and the powers of Congress are limited. In the process, the Court also demonstrated an ability to resolve important constitutional questions without descending into the political polarization that engulfs the body politic in 2020."

For history aficionados, Princeton's Keith Whittington contributed a fascinating and informative article on the Electoral College cases.

The Electoral College is probably one of the Framers' biggest oversights. Yes, it performs a valuable role in raising the importance of small states in presidential campaigns, requiring broad-based support across different regions to be elected, but that wasn't how it was envisioned. The Framers left many questions concerning the presidency until the final weeks of the convention. They extensively debated the method for choosing the president, and the same rivalries—big states versus small states, northern versus southern—formed the contours of the debate. Allowing Congress to choose the president would create too much dependency between the two branches, and a popular vote was certain to fail because average voters were thought to be too ignorant and provincial to choose the best candidate. The Electoral College was the compromise, but it was quickly subsumed by partisanship and political machines. Now, even though most Americans are generally aware of the Electoral College, they're often unaware that, technically speaking, they're not voting for the president but rather for electors who will vote for their candidate when the Electoral College convenes in December. But what happens if a pledged elector breaks his or her pledge, as happened seven times in 2016? Can a state punish that so-called faithless elector? In the Court's decision, all "justices agreed that states could adopt measures to discourage faithless electors, but they disagreed on the source of that authority." Many questions were left unanswered, however, and the Court may one day have to address whether, as Whittington asks, states can "require electors to vote only for presidential candidates who have released their tax returns."

Paul Larkin of the Heritage Foundation returns to the pages of the *Review* for the second straight year with an article on a fascinating and somewhat overlooked case, *Kahler v. Kansas*. In *Kahler*, the Court was asked whether a state can alter its insanity defense via statute. Traditionally, the insanity defense lets a defendant attempt to show either that (1) he didn't know what he was doing or (2) that he didn't know that what he was doing was wrong. Kansas changed its law to essentially eliminate the second option, although it can be raised at the sentencing stage. Ultimately, a defendant could plead insanity if he shot someone he truly thought was the devil. If, however, he said the devil told him to shoot someone, the defense would not be available. The Court was asked to declare this change unconstitutional and it declined. This was a rare Supreme Court case on substantive, rather than procedural, criminal law. Substantive criminal law—such as the definition of crimes and the defenses available—is almost always left to the states. Larkin praises the Court for continuing that doctrine. "The states and Congress remain free to decide how best to reconcile the need to deter crime," he writes, "as well as punish the people who disregard society's rules, with the need to define the rules of the road in a way that respects our fundamental beliefs about not holding parties accountable for conduct they truly believed was legal or lawful."

Peter Margulies of Roger Williams University School of Law writes on the Deferred Action for Childhood Arrivals (DACA) cases, which challenged the Trump administration's rescinding of President Obama's DACA program. DACA allowed people who were brought to the country illegally as children to stay and receive certain benefits, at least under some circumstances. Through a series of memoranda, Trump administration officials announced that DACA would be wound down, causing potentially great harm to its beneficiaries. "Consider a DACA recipient who enrolled in a four-year college in September 2016 and whose two-year DACA period of participation was due to end on March 6, 2018," writes Margulies. Such considerations formed an important part of Chief Justice Roberts's opinion. Much like in the census case the previous term, in which the chief justice joined with the "liberal" justices to stop an immigration-status question from being added to the census due to a defect in administrative procedure, the chief justice "defected" here, writing for the Court on a sensitive political issue. It was classic John Roberts, diplomatically charting his Court down a precarious middle path. The agency didn't think through the consequences of rescinding the program, and "in ending the program, Roberts explained, an agency had to at least address the interests of stakeholders as part of 'the agency's job' and its 'responsibility.'"

Next, Ilan Wurman of the Sandra Day O'Connor College of Law at Arizona State University dives deep into the president's removal power in his article on *Seila Law v. Consumer Financial Protection Bureau* (CFPB). For some time, constitutional scholars in the originalist camp have been complaining about a 1935 case called *Humphrey's Executor v. United States*, which limited the president's ability to remove appointees to independent agencies. Rather than being able to remove someone for any reason whatsoever, *Humphrey's* said that

Congress can limit a president's removal power to only "for cause" dismissal. This has been used to create various "independent" agencies, like the CFPB. In *Seila Law*, the Court ruled that the CFPB's structure, with a single director, removable only for cause, violates the separation of powers. The Court didn't go so far as to overrule *Humphrey's*, however, leaving many constitutional law scholars waiting for the other shoe to drop. Wurman's article goes deep into the debate over the removal power and past cases that helped shape the doctrine today. "It may be better in the future to recognize that the reasoning of *Humphrey's* has been abandoned," he concludes. But it will take a future case to overrule *Humphrey's*.

Jennifer Schulp, Cato's new director of financial regulation studies, uses her considerable expertise in the area to comment on *Liu v. SEC*. To extract ill-gotten gains from wrongdoers, the SEC has long used a remedy called "disgorgement." While it's easy enough to say, "someone shouldn't unduly gain from violations of securities laws," in practice it's difficult to figure out exactly what gains are ill-gotten and who should receive recompense. As Schulp writes, "[a]s a practical matter, SEC disgorgement often penalizes by leaving the defendant worse off, and it routinely fails to return disgorged funds as restitution to those harmed by the wrongdoer." In *Liu*, the Court was asked "whether the SEC is authorized to seek, and district courts are empowered to grant, disgorgement by statutory authority providing for 'any equitable relief that may be appropriate or necessary for the benefit of investors.'" The Court's answer seems obvious: "a disgorgement award [must not] exceed a wrongdoer's net profits and [must be] awarded for victims." While many questions remain, writes Schulp, *Liu's* "immediate effects are welcome, and include increased scrutiny of SEC requests for disgorgement, more frequent return of disgorged funds to victims, and increased transparency and consistency in the application of SEC remedies."

The saga of the Little Sisters of the Poor has been going on since the Obama administration. Tanner J. Bean of the firm Fabian VanCott and Robin Fretwell Wilson of the University of Illinois College of Law recount the saga, explain the Catholic nuns' ultimate victory at the Court, and explain why that victory is probably fleeting. The Affordable Care Act did many things, but one of the most controversial, and most litigated, has been the so-called contraception mandate. Employers of a certain size are required to provide qualifying health care plans for their employees. Via regulations, "qualifying plans" were defined as covering the full range of contraception and fertility treatments for women. For those who object to contraception or view some types of contraception as abortifacients—by preventing a fertilized egg from implanting in the uterus—the mandate clashed with their core values. In the most high-profile case, Hobby Lobby Stores sued, winning at the Supreme Court an exemption from the mandate as a closely held corporation run on Christian values. Little Sisters of the Poor qualified for an accommodation to the mandate but "rejected its mechanics." *Little Sisters of the Poor v. Pennsylvania,* however, was ultimately about whether the Trump administration could rescind Obama-era regulations and pass broader employer exemptions. The Court ruled it could, but the truce will last only until the next Democratic president changes those regulations. Echoing my concerns voiced earlier in this introduction, Bean and Wilson write, "Just as *Little Sisters of the Poor* will not lay to rest conflicting claims over the coverage mandate, the holding that broad delegation by Congress supports virtually any agency action (that is not arbitrary or capricious) almost certainly means that administrative whiplash will become commonplace for culture-war clashes."

Stephen Vladeck of the University of Texas School of Law writes about a case that he argued before the Court, *Hernández v. Mesa.* Arising from a tragic cross-border shooting incident in which a 15-year-old Mexican boy standing on Mexican soil was shot by a U.S. border agent standing in the United States, this was the second time *Hernández* has been at the Court. This time the question was whether the once somewhat notorious but now basically toothless *Bivens v. Six Unknown Federal Narcotics Agents* (1971) could be used to provide an implied federal cause of action in this cross-border shooting case. The Court declined to extend *Bivens.* "In *Bivens,* the Supreme Court recognized at least some circumstances in which federal courts can and should fashion a judge-made damages remedy for constitutional violations by federal officers," writes Vladeck. In the ensuing decades, however, conservatives have attacked *Bivens* as an illegitimate "usurpation of the legislative power," and called for it to be overturned. The problem with that position, Vladeck argues, is that court-fashioned remedies like the one in *Bivens* have a longer pedigree than conservatives admit. Moreover, if understood in context of the federal Westfall Act, which preempts all state tort claims against federal officers acting within the scope of their employment, then curtailing *Bivens* often means the victims will have no avenue to try to remedy constitutional violations. Because of this, even if the Court reached the right result in *Hernández*, "it certainly shouldn't have been that easy."

Arizona Supreme Court Justice Clint Bolick, who delivered the 2016 B. Kenneth Simon Lecture, returns to the *Review* to comment on a case near to his heart, *Espinoza v. Montana Department of Revenue*. *Espinoza* was brought by our friends at the Institute for Justice (IJ). Justice Bolick co-founded IJ and litigated school-choice cases there for many years. One problem that such litigation often encounters are states with so-called "Blaine amendments" in their constitutions—named after anti-Catholic Senator James G. Blaine, who ran for president in 1884. Under Blaine's influence, more than 30 states added amendments to their constitutions to prohibit any public money going to "sectarian" schools, which basically meant Catholic schools. As more states create school-choice programs, opponents have used Blaine amendments to prevent vouchers or even tax-creditable donations from going to any religious school. *Espinoza* arose from the Montana Supreme Court's decision to invalidate an entire tax-credit program because the "program allowed public funds to flow to religious schools, a result incompatible with the state's Blaine amendment." The Supreme Court ruled that "the Montana Constitution discriminates based on religious status," thus neutering Blaine amendments around the country. Bolick writes, "*Espinoza*, in a very important sense, is the culmination of a long journey meant to make America safe for school choice." While there are still questions to be resolved, "school-choice advocates have a victory to cherish."

The final article looking back at last term is by Nicholas Mosvick, former Cato legal associate and current senior fellow at the National Constitution Center, and his brother Mitchell, a lawyer in England. They cover *Ramos v. Louisiana*, a fascinating case that asked whether it violates the right to trial by jury to allow nonunanimous verdicts in criminal cases. The Court, in an opinion by Justice Neil Gorsuch, ruled that Evangelisto Ramos's Louisiana conviction violated the Sixth Amendment because it was achieved by a 10-2 vote. "Trial by jury" can't mean just anything, Gorsuch argues, and he reviewed historical sources to argue that it means, among other things, a unanimous verdict. The Mosvick brothers take issue with

Gorsuch's analysis. A good originalist would have found that jury trials at the Founding and before had many characteristics, including some that would appall modern sensibilities. Sometimes unanimity was required, but sometimes not. Sometimes unanimity was seen as harmful because it led to coercion of juries—literally locking up and starving jurors until they all agreed. "*Ramos* risks damaging 'original public meaning' as an interpretive method," the Mosvicks write, "making it seem reducible to a process of finding historical evidence for a common view at the time of ratification."

This volume concludes with our annual "looking ahead" essay, this time written by former Cato legal associate and now Pacific Legal Foundation senior attorney, Anastasia Boden. Anastasia takes a look at a coming term that is quite interesting, although maybe not yet as interesting as last term. John Roberts's chickens are coming home to roost as a result of his taxing decision in *NFIB v. Sebelius*—holding that the individual mandate to purchase health insurance was constitutional if construed as an exercise of Congress's taxing powers. Since Congress has now lowered the ~~penalty~~ tax to where people without health insurance have to pay $0, the Court in *California v. Texas* will answer whether the individual mandate can still be maintained, and, if not, how much of the rest of the Affordable Care Act must fall. The Court will also hear a challenge to one of religious-freedom advocates' more reviled cases, *Employment Division v. Smith*, which held that the Free Exercise Clause doesn't require religious exemptions from laws of neutral applicability. The case, *Fulton v. City of Philadelphia*, which involves Philadelphia's decision not to work with Catholic agencies in placing children for fostering and adoption, will be one of the most watched of the term. The Court will also hear another high-profile interbranch dispute, *Department of Justice v. House Committee on the Judiciary*, which came out of the House Judiciary Committee's attempt to get the full, unredacted Mueller Report from the Justice Department. And there will, of course, be more cases taken up when the justices return from summer break.

*   *   *

This is the second volume of the *Cato Supreme Court Review* I've edited, and I could not have done so without a lot of help. I'd like to thank Ilya Shapiro for being an excellent director of the Robert A. Levy Center for Constitutional Studies and Roger Pilon for supplying the vision for the department and leadership for so many years. I'd also like to thank the authors, without whom there would be nothing to edit or read. They're often given a difficult task—to write an 8–12,000-word article in four or five weeks—and this year it was even more difficult given the pandemic and the Court's extended term.

Thanks also to my colleagues Bob Levy (even though the department is named after him and he's chairman of the Cato Institute, he still likes to get his hands dirty), Clark Neily, Walter Olson, Jay Schweikert, Will Yeatman, and (again) Ilya for helping to edit the articles, and legal associates Michael T. Collins, Dennis Garcia, James T. Knight, Christian Townsend, and Mallory Reader for helping with the thankless but essential tasks of cite-checking and proofreading. Legal interns Brandon Beyer and Wentao Zhai were also quite helpful in these tasks, despite the unfortunate fact that their entire internship was remote. Special thanks again go to legal associate Sam Spiegelman, who stepped up and did an exceptional job with all the nuts and bolts of putting out the *Review*, as well as a significant amount of editing. Sam was indispensable.

I hope that this collection of essays will secure and advance the Madisonian first principles of our Constitution, giving renewed voice to the Framers' fervent wish that we have a government of laws and not of men. Our Constitution was written in secret but ratified by the People in one of the most extraordinary acts of popular governance ever undertaken. During that ratification process, ordinary people debated the pros and cons of the document, and, in so doing, helped turn the Constitution into a type of American DNA, belonging to no one but part of all of us. Those of the Founding generation shared many of our concerns today. They fretted over the possibility of rule by elites. They wished to ensure prosperity throughout the country. They worried that self-interested rulers would ignore the law and collect power. The Constitution is their best attempt at creating an energetic yet restrained government. It reflects and protects the natural rights of life, liberty, and property, and serves as a bulwark against government abuses. In this schismatic time, it's more important than ever to remember our proud roots in the Enlightenment tradition.

We hope that you enjoy this 19th volume of the *Cato Supreme Court Review*.

Judicial Independence and the Roberts Court

*Judge Thomas M. Hardiman**

Thank you, Ilya Shapiro, for that generous introduction. Roger Pilon may be the only one here who appreciates just how honored I am to have been invited to give the B. Kenneth Simon Lecture on this Constitution Day. Roger was kind enough to travel to Pittsburgh to honor Ken at the memorial celebration after his passing. And as Roger knows, I had the privilege of knowing Ken personally. We met in the summer of 2000 in Pittsburgh and I was immediately drawn to the man's energy, intellect, and love of liberty. I don't know what Ken saw in me, but we became fast friends even though he was 42 years my senior.

Ken and I enjoyed many wonderful lunches together. No subject was off limits. He taught me about history, business, and even law, though he wasn't a lawyer. One particularly fond memory involved Ken's profound disappointment upon learning that I had never read *The Law* by Frederic Bastiat. Ken was so distressed by this lacuna in my Great Books education that he refused to have lunch again until I read Bastiat. Fortunately, the brevity of that work enabled me to complete the homework assignment, and our lunches quickly resumed.

It's hard to believe Ken left us over 16 years ago. I hope he would be pleased with my remarks today. One thing's for sure: Ken would have opinions—and thoughtful criticisms—to offer.

I would like to speak to you today about judicial independence and the Roberts Court. Alexander Hamilton wrote in Federalist 78: "[T]here is no liberty, if the power of judging be not separated from the legislative and executive powers. . . . [Since] liberty can have

---

*Judge, U.S. Court of Appeals for the Third Circuit. This is a slightly revised version of the 18th annual B. Kenneth Simon Lecture in Constitutional Thought, delivered at the Cato Institute on September 17, 2019.

nothing to fear from the judiciary alone, but would have every thing to fear from its union with either of the other departments . . . [t]he complete independence of the courts of justice is . . . essential."[1]

Hamilton viewed an independent judiciary as a "citadel of the public justice and the public security." But he knew the judicial branch—which he regarded as "the weakest of the three departments" and "least dangerous to the political rights of the Constitution"—required greater autonomy than colonial courts enjoyed. For federal courts to be "bulwarks" of liberty, judges needed *more* than an "independent spirit." They needed structural protections to bolster their "firmness and independence" in faithfully performing "so arduous a duty." So what were Hamilton's "indispensable ingredients" for an independent judiciary? "[P]ermanency in office" and tenure "during good behavior."

I see the wisdom in Hamilton's insistence upon permanency in office. But my affinity for life tenure has nothing to do with comfort and security. Some may consider a federal judgeship a sinecure, but that is the corruption of life tenure. Properly understood, life tenure is a necessary, but not a sufficient, condition for judicial independence. And judicial independence is essential to ensure that everyone who comes before the court is heard "without respect to persons," so we can "do equal right to the poor and to the rich," and "faithfully and impartially discharge and perform all the duties incumbent upon [us] . . . under the Constitution and laws of the United States."[2] We judges protect liberty by our fidelity to the oath of office, which includes the timeless principles I just mentioned. And for over two centuries, judicial independence has made the discharge of that oath a reality.

Court watchers and commentators alike have spent the summer wrapping their minds around what they have called the "shifting alliances" and "surprise votes" that marked the end of the last term.[3] How do those regarded as the Supreme Court's liberal justices prevail in

---

[1] The Federalist No. 78 (Hamilton). The quotations in the following paragraph also come from this source.

[2] Oaths of Justices and Judges, 28 U.S.C. § 453.

[3] Adam Liptak & Alicia Parlapiano, "A Supreme Court Term Marked by Shifting Alliances and Surprise Votes," N.Y. Times, June 29, 2019, https://www.nytimes.com/2019/06/29/us/supreme-court-decisions.html.

almost half of the cases decided 5-4? Why have Justices Neil Gorsuch and Brett Kavanaugh disagreed in nearly half of those rulings? For those of us who have served as judges for a number of years, there's nothing surprising at all about this. It's simply a function of nine *independent* justices.

Whether you are pleased or displeased with recent decisions of the Court, one conclusion seems indisputable: The Roberts Court practices and embraces the judicial independence fundamental to our founding. Hamilton believed that tenure "during good behavior" was "the best expedient . . . to secure a steady, upright, and impartial administration of the laws."[4] And he hoped that independent judges would be "an essential safeguard against the effects of [society's] occasional ill humours."[5] After more than 230 years, our federal judiciary continues to vindicate Hamilton's aspiration.

The idea of an independent judiciary arose within a broader conversation about separation of powers prior to the American Revolution. Hamilton and fellow delegates brought to the Philadelphia Convention of 1787 an informed perspective on English and American judicial precedents, as well as insights from Locke and Montesquieu. More poignantly, they brought their experience as colonists under the British Crown.

Until 1701, English judicial officers served at the pleasure of the king.[6] Even jurists appointed during good behavior—who effectively possessed a judicial life estate—could be forced to forfeit their office for misconduct, whether real or manufactured. That appointment practice went unchallenged until 1628, when Charles I ordered Sir John Walter to surrender his post as chief baron of the court of the exchequer.[7] Walter's offense? He defied King Charles's call for the dissolution of Parliament. When his court sanctioned members of Parliament for conspiring to resist dissolution of the Commons, Walter dissented. King Charles deemed that dissent treasonous, and he wanted Walter gone.

---

[4] The Federalist No. 78.

[5] *Id.*

[6] Joseph H. Smith, An Independent Judiciary: The Colonial Background, 124 U. Pa. L. Rev. 1104, 1105 (1976).

[7] *Id.* at 1106 n.11; J.M. Rigg, Walter, John, 59 Dictionary of National Biography (Sidney Lee ed., 1899).

Walter challenged the king. Unlike English jurists removed before him, Walter insisted that his tenure was based on good behavior, so he could be removed only if the King's Bench found he had misbehaved.[8] Charles begrudgingly allowed Walter to remain in his post, although Charles later dismissed several judges before ultimately accepting Parliament's petition for judicial tenure *quam diu se bene gesserint*, "during good behavior."[9] And while English monarchs continued to dismiss judges intermittently, the governing commitment generally remained. Judges enjoyed tenure during good behavior, independent from the pleasure of England's Crown. With Parliament's 1701 Act of Settlement, tenure during good behavior became part of English law.[10]

But the rules were different in the American colonies. Early colonial judges served overwhelmingly at the pleasure of their royal governors. And other than Pennsylvania's, no colonial assembly could impeach a despotic royal governor.[11] England wanted it that way—because the colonial bench was deemed so mediocre. Colonial bars lacked competent men for the bench, so Westminster's Colonial Office begged the best English lawyers to serve in America—to no avail. King George III established tenure at royal pleasure in 1761 because the "state of learning in the colonies" was ostensibly too low.[12]

George III not only distrusted the colonial bar, he distrusted the colonies themselves—especially in the run up to Lexington and Concord. Attempting to assert ever greater control, in 1772 George established a fixed salary for superior court judges in Massachusetts, effectively preventing them from receiving grants from local governments.[13] That's why the Declaration of Independence charged, "[The king] has made judges dependent upon his good will alone, for the tenure of their offices, and the amount and

[8] Raoul Berger, Impeachment of Judges and "Good Behavior" Tenure, 79 Yale L.J. 1475, 1480–81 (1970).

[9] Smith, *supra* note 6, at 1106–09.

[10] *Id.* at 1110–11.

[11] *Id.* at 1113–14.

[12] William Seal Carpenter, Judicial Tenure in the United States: With Special Reference to the Tenure of Federal Judges 2–3 (1918).

[13] *Id.* at 3.

payment of their salaries."[14] To whom would judges be beholden, London or their local constituents? So frustrated were the colonists by the Crown's refusal to grant judicial tenure during good behavior that it became a feature of nearly every state constitution drafted after 1776.

Although state constitutions varied in their models for selecting judges and granting tenure, judicial independence was ubiquitous. The 1780 Massachusetts Bill of Rights offers one example, stating:

> It is essential to the preservation of the rights of every individual, his life, liberty, property, and character, that there be an impartial interpretation of the laws, and administration of justice. It is the right of every citizen to be tried by judges as free, impartial and independent as the lot of humanity will admit. It is therefore not only the best policy, but for the security of the rights of the people, and of every citizen, that judges hold their office as long as they behave themselves well; and that they should have honourable salaries ascertained and established by standing laws.[15]

"Impartial interpretation of the laws" and "administration of justice" struck particular chords in Philadelphia in the summer of 1787. Before the Revolutionary War, Parliament was paramount— whatever it said *was* law. This absolute sovereignty insulated legislative error from review, so English citizens had no recourse but for Parliament to correct itself. Pamphleteers wrote about this dynamic in America, suggesting that an independent judiciary could correct the legislature. Delegates in Philadelphia took that proposition one step further: An independent judiciary could invalidate legislation that contravened the Constitution.[16] This form of separation of powers—our "checks and balances"—did not meet the strict separation championed by Montesquieu.[17] But, as James Madison argued in Federalist 47, such overlapping separation at least precluded the "accumulation of all powers, legislative, executive and judiciary, in

---

[14] The Declaration of Independence, Grievance 9 (U.S. 1776).

[15] Mass. Const. art. XXIX.

[16] Carpenter, *supra* note 12, at 24–25.

[17] Sam J. Ervin Jr., Separation of Powers: Judicial Independence, 35 Law & Contemp. Probs. 108, 108–109 (Winter 1970).

the same hands, whether of one, a few, or many . . . the very definition of tyranny."[18]

At the Constitutional Convention of 1787, John Randolph of Virginia proposed that "indispensable ingredient"[19] for an independent judiciary, calling for judges to "hold their offices during good behavior."[20] Charles Pinckney of South Carolina and Hamilton likewise submitted proposals calling for judicial tenure during good behavior.[21] Only John Dickinson of Delaware suggested keeping Parliament's practice of legislative "address," allowing Congress to remove judges for less-than-impeachable, noncriminal misconduct.[22] Unsurprisingly, Dickinson was voted down seven-to-one. Randolph thought legislative address would "weaken[] too much the independence of judges,"[23] while Gouverneur Morris—whose own grandfather had been removed as chief justice of New York after displeasing royal Governor William Cosby—found the removal of tenured judges without trial a "contradiction in terms."[24] And so we find in the Constitution's Article III, Section 1: "The Judges, both of the supreme and inferior Courts, shall hold their Offices during good Behaviour, and shall, at stated Times, receive for their Services, a Compensation, which shall not be diminished during their Continuance in Office." The Framers thus constitutionalized an independent judiciary.

So after two centuries of experience, has the framework secured an independent judiciary? Chief Justice John Roberts assumed office right before the October 2005 term.[25] And although the Supreme Court is often known by the name of the chief justice—think Warren Court, Burger Court, Rehnquist Court—for the first 13 years of Chief Justice Roberts's tenure, the Court was often

[18] The Federalist No. 47 (Madison).

[19] The Federalist No. 30 (Hamilton).

[20] Carpenter, *supra* note 12, at 23.

[21] *Id.* at 24–25, 30.

[22] John T. Nugent, Note, Removal of Judges by Legislative Action, 6 J. Legis. 140, 144 (1979).

[23] Carpenter, *supra* note 12, at 30.

[24] *Id.* at 29.

[25] Chief Justice John G. Roberts, Jr., The Supreme Court Historical Society, https:// supremecourthistory.org/history-of-the-court/the-current-court/chief-justice-john -roberts-jr.

called the "Kennedy Court." During those years, Justice Anthony Kennedy was in the majority a striking 70 percent of the time when the Court split 5-4.[26]

Immediately following Justice Kennedy's retirement, a host of commentators made dire predictions about what it would mean for judicial independence. Similar concerns were voiced following Justice Antonin Scalia's death, but they took on an apocalyptic tone with the Kennedy vacancy. Some criticisms were undoubtedly fueled by antipathy for President Trump. But they went beyond critique of the White House, pointing at the Supreme Court itself. Here's just a sampling of what we heard last summer:

From an op-ed in the *Washington Post* on June 27: "[Justice Kennedy] and the court have served as a bulwark for the rule of law in a world often set against it. As a result, his retirement will spark chaos. . . . Things will get ugly—very ugly. [The] court's very legitimacy is now up for grabs."[27]

Then an op-ed in the *New York Times*: "For the first time in living memory, the court will be seen by the public as a party-dominated institution, one whose votes on controversial issues are essentially determined by the party affiliation of recent presidents."[28]

As summer 2018 turned into fall, the headlines told an increasingly desperate story. Powerful news corporations told us: "The Supreme Court is coming apart."[29] "Stop pretending everything is okay."[30]

[26] Andrew Nolan et al., Justice Anthony Kennedy: His Jurisprudence and the Future of the Court, Cong. Research Serv. 31–33 (2018); Alicia Parlapiano & Jugal K. Patel, "With Kennedy's Retirement, the Supreme Court Loses Its Center," N.Y. Times, June 27, 2018, https://www.nytimes.com/interactive/2018/06/27/us/politics/kennedy-retirement-supreme-court-median.html.

[27] Joshua Matz, "The Supreme Court Will Now Fall into Chaos," Wash. Post, June 27, 2018, https://www.washingtonpost.com/opinions/with-anthony-kennedys-departure-the-supreme-court-will-fall-to-chaos/2018/06/27/a052dfde-5a01-11e7-a9f6-7c3296387341_story.html.

[28] Lee Epstein & Eric Posner, "If the Supreme Court Is Nakedly Political, Can It Be Just?" N.Y. Times, July 9, 2018, https://www.nytimes.com/2018/07/09/opinion/supreme-court-nominee-trump.html.

[29] David Leonhardt, "The Supreme Court Is Coming Apart," N.Y. Times, Sept. 23, 2018, https://www.nytimes.com/2018/09/23/opinion/columnists/supreme-court-brett-kavanaugh-partisan-republicans.html.

[30] Molly Roberts, "Stop Pretending Everything Is Okay," Wash. Post, Oct. 11, 2018, https://www.washingtonpost.com/blogs/post-partisan/wp/2018/10/11/the-supreme-court-celebrates-its-own-corruption.

"President Trump's nominee would bring a virus of illegitimacy and partisanship to the Supreme Court."[31] "The Supreme Court was America's least-damaged institution—until now."[32]

In his dystopian "Requiem for the Supreme Court," one *Atlantic* contributor captured the emotion thus:

> Critically, skeptically, but deeply, I loved that Supreme Court. Where is it? Where is the Court that claimed it was at least striving to transcend partisan politics? That Court is gone forever. We will spend at least the rest of my lifetime fighting over its rotting corpse. No prating about civility can change that fact. The fight is upon us now, and the party that shirks it will be destroyed.[33]

Have these concerns proved justified? Let's review the Roberts Court during the past two years. But first, let me offer a disclaimer. I reject the labels "conservative" and "liberal" as valid descriptors of judges. I agree with Justice Gorsuch that they are reductionist and fail to capture the judicial enterprise. I will use those labels here only as a reluctant concession to their widespread adoption in the academy and the media.

During the October 2017 term, Justice Kennedy's final year, nearly 75 percent of the Court's 5-4 decisions divided along supposedly ideological lines, and all 14 of them were conservative majorities.[34] The following term, with Justice Kennedy absent for the first time, only a third of those 5-4 or 5-3 decisions went that way (7 of 21).[35]

---

[31] Ronald Brownstein, "Brett Kavanaugh Is Patient Zero: President Trump's Nominee Would Bring a Virus of Illegitimacy and Partisanship to the Supreme Court," The Atlantic, Oct. 1, 2018, https://www.theatlantic.com/politics/archive/2018/10/kavanaughs-partisanship-threatens-supreme-court/571702.

[32] George F. Will, "The Supreme Court Was America's Least-Damaged Institution—Until Now," Wash. Post, Sept. 21, 2018, https://www.washingtonpost.com/opinions/the-supreme-court-was-americas-least-damaged-institution—until-now/2018/09/21/7600e14e-bdc0-11e8-8792-78719177250f_story.html.

[33] Garrett Epps, "Requiem for the Supreme Court," The Atlantic, Oct. 7, 2018, https://www.theatlantic.com/ideas/archive/2018/10/supreme-court-loses-its-special-status/572416.

[34] Adam Feldman, "Changes Are Afoot: Evidence from 5-4 Decisions during the 2018 Term and What This Tells Us about the Supreme Court Moving Forward," Empirical SCOTUS, July 7, 2019, https://empiricalscotus.com/2019/07/07/changes-are-afoot.

[35] *Id.*

And that's not the half of it. *Ten* of last term's 21 5-4 or 5-3 decisions involved four liberal justices joined by one conservative.[36] Let me say that again: Last term nearly half of what has been called a "conservative" Supreme Court's closest cases were decided by "liberal" majorities.

And while Justice Gorsuch provided the "swing vote" more often than any other justice in the 2018–2019 term—voting four times with his liberal colleagues, on questions of criminal and tribal law—he was far from alone in showing an independent streak. *All five* of the Court's conservative justices joined at least one 5-4 decision when the liberal justices voted together. That's a first in the 13 years since Chief Justice Roberts joined the Court.[37]

But there's more. As I noted earlier, this is a two-way street. Not only did the Court's conservative justices join liberal majorities, but each of the four liberal justices—who generally stay together more than their conservative colleagues[38]—in turn joined conservative majorities. And, as always, there were mixed alignments that defy ideological explanation.

As Court watchers have noted, there were 10 different alignments in the 5-4 decisions during the 2018 term.[39] *Ten.* Three more than any previous Roberts Court term. Twice as many as we saw during Justice Kennedy's final term. Justice Gorsuch voted with the majority most frequently this past term, in 62 percent of all 5-4 or 5-3 decisions.[40] Justice Kavanaugh was close behind at 58 percent, with Chief Justice Roberts at 57 percent.[41] But even Justices Samuel Alito, Sonia Sotomayor, and Elena Kagan, who were least frequently in the majority that term, still voted with the majority in more than half of all 5-4 decisions.[42] To put that in perspective: The 2017 term produced

[36] *Id.*

[37] *Id.*; Adam Feldman, "SCOTUSBlog Stat Pack 2018," Empirical SCOTUS, July 1, 2019, https://empiricalscotus.com/2019/07/01/scotusblog-stat-pack-2018.

[38] See Ilya Shapiro, "Liberal Supreme Court Justices Vote in Lockstep, Not the Conservative Justices," USA Today, Sept. 10, 2019, https://www.usatoday.com/story/opinion/2019/09/10/liberal-supreme-court-justices-vote-in-lockstep-not-the-conservative-justices-column/2028450001.

[39] Feldman, *supra* note 34.

[40] *Id.*

[41] *Id.*

[42] *Id.*

19 5-4 decisions—two fewer than the following term—and Justice Kagan voted with the majority in only 17 percent of those decisions. Chief Justice Roberts? 89 percent.[43]

To what can we ascribe this state of affairs, which seems to be the polar opposite of so many pundits' dire predictions? Let's take a look at some of the most notable cases that account for those statistics.

A criminal case likely to affect legions of the accused and the already convicted is *United States v. Davis*.[44] In that case, the Court held unconstitutionally vague Section 924(c)(3)(B) of Title 18, which defines "crime of violence" as a felony "that by its nature, involves a substantial risk that physical force against the person or property of another may be used in the course of committing the offense."[45] Justice Gorsuch—joined by Justices Ruth Bader Ginsburg, Stephen Breyer, Sotomayor, and Kagan—began his opinion for the Court by stating: "A vague law is no law at all."[46] Justice Kavanaugh, in a dissent joined by the chief justice and Justices Clarence Thomas and Alito, noted that tens of thousands of cases have been prosecuted under Section 924(c).[47] In their view, the statute could have been saved by the doctrine of constitutional avoidance.

In another case involving criminal law, *United States v. Haymond*, Justice Gorsuch wrote for a plurality that included Justices Ginsburg, Sotomayor, and Kagan.[48] At issue in *Haymond* was the punishment to be imposed on certain violators of their conditions of supervised release. According to the plurality, Section 3583(k) of Title 18 violates the Fifth and Sixth Amendments because it imposes a mandatory minimum punishment when the district judge finds by a preponderance of the evidence that the defendant engaged in certain criminal conduct.[49] Justice Breyer concurred only in the judgment, saying that he agreed with much of the dissent and that because supervised

---

[43] Epps, *supra* note 33; Adam Feldman, "Final Stat Pack for October Term 2018," SCOTUSblog, June 28, 2019, https://www.scotusblog.com/2019/06/final-stat-pack-for-october-term-2018.

[44] United States v. Davis, 139 S. Ct. 2319 (2019).

[45] *Id.* at 2323–24.

[46] *Id.* at 2323.

[47] *Id.* at 2337 (Kavanaugh, J., dissenting).

[48] United States v. Haymond, 139 S. Ct. 2369 (2019) (plurality op.).

[49] *Id.* at 2373–75.

release is like parole, the *Apprendi* line of cases (requiring juries to find all elements of a crime that enhance punishments) does not apply.[50] Justice Breyer's opinion was especially significant to Justice Alito, who authored a dissent joined by Chief Justice Roberts and Justices Thomas and Kavanaugh. According to Justice Alito, Justice Breyer's concurrence "saved our jurisprudence from the consequences of the plurality opinion, which is not based on the original meaning of the Sixth Amendment, is irreconcilable with precedent, and sports rhetoric with potentially revolutionary implications."[51] In the view of the dissenters, the Sixth Amendment applies only to criminal prosecutions, so it doesn't apply in supervised release revocation proceedings. Don't be surprised by future spirited disagreements over the original public meaning of constitutional guarantees.

Justice Gorsuch joined his liberal colleagues in two other closely divided cases that involve the rights of Native Americans. In *Herrera v. Wyoming*, the Court held that Wyoming's admission to the Union did not abrogate the Crow Tribe of Indians' 1868 federal treaty right to hunt on the "unoccupied lands of the United States."[52] In *Washington State Department of Licensing v. Cougar Den*, the Court held that the "right to travel" provision of the Yakama Treaty of 1855 preempts the state's fuel tax as applied to Cougar Den's importation of fuel by public highway for sale within the Yakama Indian Reservation.[53] Justice Gorsuch concurred in the judgment in that case.[54] In his separate opinion joined by Justice Ginsburg, Justice Gorsuch criticized the state of Washington for trying to get more from the Yakama than it had initially bargained for. It remains to be seen whether these cases—along with Justice Gorsuch's votes the previous year in *Upper Skagit Indian Tribe v. Lundgren* and *Patchak v. Zinke*[55]—portend a particular solicitude for the rights of Native Americans. More broadly, it's worth watching whether Justice Gorsuch's Colorado roots influence his thinking on cases involving

---

[50] *Id.* at 2386 (Breyer, J., concurring in the judgment).

[51] *Id.* (Alito, J., dissenting).

[52] Herrera v. Wyoming, 139 S. Ct. 1686 (2019).

[53] Wash. State Dep't of Licensing v. Cougar Den, Inc., 139 S. Ct. 1000 (2019).

[54] *Id.* at 1016–21 (Gorsuch, J., concurring).

[55] Upper Skagit Indian Tribe v. Lundgren, 138 S. Ct. 1649 (2018); Patchak v. Zinke, 138 S. Ct. 897 (2018).

not just Native Americans but also other Western concerns involving water rights and land use.

As I noted previously, Justice Gorsuch was not the only conservative justice to join with the four liberals to form a majority. In *Gundy v. United States* it was Justice Alito's turn. That case involved the Sex Offender Registration and Notification Act (SORNA), in which Congress delegated to the attorney general the power to issue regulations establishing registration requirements for sex offenders convicted before SORNA was enacted.[56] Justice Gorsuch dissented, joined by the chief justice and Justice Thomas, deeming SORNA an unconstitutional delegation of authority from Congress to the executive branch. In his concurrence, Justice Alito didn't think *Gundy* was the right case to reconsider the Court's nondelegation doctrine but expressed a willingness to do so in a later case.[57]

In a highly anticipated commercial case, *Apple v. Pepper,* Justice Kavanaugh joined his liberal colleagues to hold that consumers have standing to sue Apple for antitrust harm caused by prices set by app developers who sell their product on Apple devices.[58]

In a less newsworthy civil procedure case, *Home Depot U.S.A. v. Jackson,* Justice Thomas wrote an opinion joined only by the four liberal justices.[59] The Court held that Section 1441(a) of Title 28 does not permit a third-party counterclaim defendant to remove a case to federal court. Justice Thomas also joined the majority in a Voting Rights Act case, *Virginia House of Delegates v. Bethune-Hill,* where Justice Ginsburg authored the majority opinion joined by Justices Sotomayor, Kagan, and Gorsuch.[60]

And last, but certainly not least, Chief Justice Roberts joined his liberal colleagues in one of the term's most significant cases, *Department of Commerce v. New York.*[61] In that expedited matter, which bypassed review by the Second Circuit "because the case involved an issue of imperative public importance,"[62] the Court prevented the

---

[56] Gundy v. United States, 139 S. Ct. 2116 (2019).

[57] *Id.* at 2131 (Alito, J., concurring in the judgment).

[58] Apple v. Pepper, 139 S. Ct. 1515 (2019).

[59] Home Depot, U.S.A., Inc. v. Jackson, 139 S. Ct. 1743 (2019).

[60] Va. House of Delegates v. Bethune-Hill, 139 S. Ct. 1945 (2019).

[61] Dep't of Commerce v. New York, 139 S. Ct. 2551 (2019).

[62] *Id.* at 2565.

Department of Commerce from including a citizenship question on the 2020 census questionnaire.

As the brief summaries I just described show, all five of the conservative justices joined liberal colleagues to form majorities. But this was not a one-way street, as the liberal justices did just the same.

Consider the 5-4 decision in *Mont v. United States,* in which the Court held that pretrial detention later credited as time served for a new conviction tolls a supervised-release term under 18 U.S.C. §3624(e).[63] Justice Ginsburg provided an essential vote in support of Justice Thomas's opinion for the Court, which was joined by the chief justice and Justices Alito and Kavanaugh.

In a patent case, *Return Mail, Inc. v. U.S. Postal Service,* Justice Sotomayor broke ranks from Justices Ginsburg, Breyer, and Kagan to author an opinion for the Court holding that the federal government is not a "person" capable of petitioning the Patent Trial and Appeal Board to institute patent review proceedings.[64]

And in another 5-4 decision, Justice Breyer, along with Justices Alito, Gorsuch, and Kavanaugh, joined Justice Thomas's opinion in *Stokeling v. United States.* In that case, the Court held that a state robbery offense that includes "as an element" the common-law requirement of overcoming "victim resistance" is categorically a "violent felony" under the Armed Career Criminal Act, 18 U.S.C. § 924(e)(2)(b)(i).[65]

Another interesting line of division appears when we compare the votes of Justices Gorsuch and Kavanaugh, who disagreed in nine cases. In addition to the *Davis* and *Cougar Den* cases I already mentioned:

- They parted ways in a *Batson* case (racial discrimination in jury selection) called *Flowers v. Mississippi.*[66]
- They disagreed about the presumption of prejudice to establish ineffective assistance of counsel in *Garza v. Idaho.*[67]

---

[63] Mont v. United States, 139 S. Ct. 1826, 1829 (2019).

[64] Return Mail, Inc. v. U.S. Postal Service, 139 S. Ct. 1853 (2019).

[65] Stokeling v. United States, 139 S. Ct. 544, 548–55 (2019).

[66] Flowers v. Mississippi, 139 S. Ct. 222 (2019).

[67] Garza v. Idaho, 139 S. Ct. 738 (2019).

- They disagreed in *Tennessee Wine and Spirits Retailers Association v. Thomas*, which involved the dormant Commerce Clause and the Twenty-first Amendment.[68]
- They were on opposite sides in *Gamble v. United States*, where the Court upheld its "separate sovereigns" exception to the Double Jeopardy Clause.[69]
- They did the same with *Mitchell v. Wisconsin*, involving the administration of a warrantless blood test.[70]
- They disagreed in *Biestek v. Berryhill*, a case involving evidence in Social Security appeals.[71]
- And they disagreed in a bankruptcy case involving the debtor's rejection of a license agreement in *Mission Product Holdings, Inc. v. Tempnology, LLC*.[72]

And there are perennial cases where the voting patterns of the justices defy any ideological classification. For example, following on the heels of the *Matal v. Tam* case about the registrability of allegedly disparaging trademarks,[73] the Court in *Iancu v. Brunetti* held that the Lanham Act's prohibition on the federal registration of "immoral" or "scandalous" marks also violates the Free Speech Clause of the First Amendment.[74] Justice Kagan wrote for the Court, joined by Justices Thomas, Ginsburg, Alito, Gorsuch, and Kavanaugh. Dissents were filed by each of Chief Justice Roberts and Justices Breyer and Sotomayor.

In the *Gamble* case, seven justices joined the opinion of the Court, with only Justices Ginsburg and Gorsuch dissenting—the first and only time we've seen that alignment.[75] Similarly, *Biestek*—the Social Security case—was a 6-3 decision with Justices Ginsburg, Sotomayor, and Gorsuch in dissent.[76]

---

[68] Tenn. Wine & Spirits Retailers Ass'n v. Thomas, 139 S. Ct. 2449 (2019).

[69] Gamble v. United States, 139 S. Ct. 1960 (2019).

[70] Mitchell v. Wisconsin, 139 S. Ct. 2525 (2019).

[71] Biestek v. Berryhill, 139 S. Ct. 1148 (2019).

[72] Mission Prod. Holdings, Inc. v. Tempnology, LLC, 139 S. Ct. 1652 (2019).

[73] Matal v. Tam, 137 S. Ct. 1744 (2017).

[74] Iancu v. Brunetti, 139 S. Ct. 2294, 2297 (2019).

[75] Gamble, 139 S. Ct. 1960.

[76] Biestek, 139 S. Ct. 1148.

Finally, in *American Legion v. American Humanist Association*, Justices Breyer and Kagan joined Justice Alito's opinion for the Court, upholding display of the World War I Peace Cross in Bladensburg, Maryland.[77]

In highlighting these variable voting patterns, I do not suggest a randomness to the judicial process. Judicial philosophy influences the work of each justice and the most astute Court watchers can offer thoughtful predictions as to how each justice might rule. With less than one term as a guide, it is too early to predict how Justice Kavanaugh will decide cases. Although Justice Gorsuch has been on the Court for just two years, his approach to criminal procedure cases has often earned the votes of Justices Ginsburg, Sotomayor, and Kagan. Those alignments are reminiscent of Justice Scalia's Confrontation Clause jurisprudence, as reflected in his opinions in *Crawford v. Washington*[78] and *Melendez-Diaz v. Massachusetts*,[79] and in his votes in *Bullcoming v. New Mexico*[80] and *Williams v. Illinois*.[81] Does Justice Gorsuch's vote for privacy in *Collins v. Virginia*[82] portend future votes echoing Justice Scalia's opinion for the Court in *United States v. Jones*[83] or his dissents in *Navarette v. California*[84] and

---

[77] Am. Legion v. Am. Humanist Ass'n, 139 S. Ct. 2067 (2019).

[78] Crawford v. Washington, 541 U.S. 36 (2004) (holding that the state violated the Confrontation Clause because, where testimonial statements are at issue, the only indicium of reliability sufficient to satisfy constitutional demands is confrontation).

[79] Melendez-Diaz v. Massachusetts, 557 U.S. 305 (2009) (holding that it was a violation of the Confrontation Clause to submit a chemical drug test report without the testimony of the person who performed the test).

[80] Bullcoming v. New Mexico, 564 U.S. 647 (2011) (holding that a surrogate analyst could not testify about the testimonial statements in the forensic report of the certifying analyst).

[81] Williams v. Illinois, 567 U.S. 50 (2012) (allowing expert testimony about DNA evidence the analysis of which the expert herself did not perform; Justice Scalia dissented).

[82] Collins v. Virginia, 138 S. Ct. 1663 (2019) (holding that the automobile exception to the Fourth Amendment's warrant requirement does not apply to vehicles parked within the curtilage of a private home).

[83] United States v. Jones, 565 U.S. 499 (2012) (holding that installing a GPS on a suspect's car without a warrant violated the Fourth Amendment).

[84] Navarette v. California, 572 U.S. 393, 404 (2014) (Scalia, J., dissenting from a holding that officers need not personally observe criminal activity when acting upon information provided by an anonymous 911 call).

Maryland v. King?[85] We shall see. But perhaps the most significant question for the future is whether the chief justice will anchor the middle of the Roberts Court as many commentators have suggested, or will Justice Gorsuch continue in the majority more than any other justice? Only time will answer that question.

* * *

The Supreme Court's October 2018 term reflects the constitutional structure perfectly designed for all nine justices to exercise independent judgment. And judicial independence is hardly unique to The Nine. After more than 12 years as an appellate judge, I have had the privilege of serving with dozens of judges and hearing thousands of cases. And I can tell you that in every single one of those cases, the judges with whom I served, and I myself, *always* exercised independent judgment.

Cloaked with life tenure and salary protection, we owe fealty to no man or woman, just the law. Our duty is straightforward. We must adhere to the judicial oath and with the utmost solemnity honor our promise to "administer justice without respect to persons, and to do equal right to the poor and to the rich, and [to] faithfully and impartially discharge and perform [our] duties . . . under the Constitution and laws of the United States."[86] I have every confidence that the justices of the Supreme Court, the judges of the United States Courts of Appeals, and the judges of the United States District Courts will continue to do just that.

---

[85] Maryland v. King, 569 U.S. 435, 466 (2013) (Scalia, J., dissenting from a holding that DNA-swabbing an arrestee's cheek is comparable to fingerprinting and thus a reasonable booking procedure under the Fourth Amendment).

[86] Oaths of Justices and Judges, 28 U.S.C. § 453.

All the President's Papers

*Jonathan H. Adler**

No president has been quite like Donald Trump. No president has entered the Oval Office with the same degree of ongoing financial interests and potential entanglements.[1] No president's financial holdings have spurred as many accusations of malfeasance or provoked the same degree of hostile congressional oversight and investigation.[2] No president has so thoroughly resisted transparency and disentanglement with potential conflicts of interest.[3] As a candidate, Donald Trump refused to release copies of his tax returns, as all major party presidential candidates had done for decades.[4] As president, his financial holdings and business relationships raise

*Johan Verheij Memorial Professor of Law, Case Western Reserve University School of Law. I would like to thank Andy Grewal, Erik Jensen, and participants in a workshop at the Case Western Reserve University School of Law for comments and suggestions, as well as Kathleen Lynch for her research assistance. Any errors or inanities are mine alone.

[1] See "Donald Trump: A List of Potential Conflicts of Interest," BBC News, Apr. 18, 2017, https://bbc.in/2XBHhQ7.

[2] See Alex Moe, "House Investigations of Trump and His Administration: The Full List," NBC News, May 27, 2019, https://nbcnews.to/2DGcDhd (noting then-ongoing investigations by 14 separate House committees).

[3] See, e.g., Robert Costa, et al., "Trump Says He Is Opposed to White House Aides Testifying to Congress, Deepening Power Struggle with Hill," Wash. Post, Apr. 23, 2019; Antia Kumar & Andrew Desiderio, "Trump Showdown with House Democrats Ignites into All-Out War," Politico, Apr. 23 2019, (noting White House resistance to Congressional oversight); Jennifer Wang, "Why Trump Won't Use a Blind Trust and What His Predecessors Did with Their Assets," Forbes, Nov. 15, 2016, https://bit.ly/2XBHsef (noting how prior presidents sought to resolve conflicts of interest).

[4] See Daniel Hemel, "Trump Lost at the Supreme Court, But We Still Won't See His Taxes by November," Wash. Post, July 10, 2020, https://wapo.st/33Bbv9r ("[T]he three Republican and three Democratic presidents before Trump released their returns.").

concerns about constitutionally forbidden emoluments,[5] foreign influence,[6] and cronyism,[7] all while accusations of corporate malfeasance[8] and personal misconduct[9] accumulate.

So perhaps it was inevitable that a Trump presidency would require the Supreme Court to consider the extent to which a president may claim immunity from investigation. This seems to be the history with scandal-ridden presidents. Just as the Watergate investigation prompted the Court to identify presidential immunity[10] and clarify the limits of executive privilege,[11] and the Whitewater investigation and subsequent sexual misconduct allegations prompted courts to identify

[5] See, e.g., Blumenthal v. Trump, 373 F. Supp. 3d 191, 194 (D.D.C. 2018), vacated as moot, 949 F.3d 14 (D.C. Cir. 2020) ("Plaintiffs have alleged that the President has accepted a variety of Emoluments from foreign governments—intellectual property rights, payments for hotel rooms and events, payments derived from real estate holdings, licensing fees for 'The Apprentice,' and regulatory benefits—without seeking and obtaining the consent of Congress."); see also Erik M. Jensen, The Foreign Emoluments Clause, 10 Elon L. Rev. 73 (2018) (advocating an expansive interpretation of the clause); Amandeep S. Grewal, The Foreign Emoluments Clause and the Chief Executive, 102 Minn. L. Rev. 639, 639–41 (2017) (advocating a narrower view).

[6] See, e.g., Michael Hirsh, "How Russian Money Helped Save Trump's Business," Foreign Policy, Dec. 21, 2018, https://bit.ly/30DZjDf. While most of the popular focus has been on potential connections to Russia, some have argued the Trump organization's financial ties to Turkey may be more worrisome. See Tim Miller, "Trump's Turkey Corruption Is Way Worse than You Realize," The Bulwark, Nov. 26, 2019, https://bit.ly/3fA9VHd.

[7] See Nomi Prins, "The Magnitude of Trump's Cronyism Is Off the Charts—Even for Washington," The Nation, Dec. 9, 2016, https://bit.ly/3gPM08t; Aaron Blake, "Ivanka Trump and Jared Kushner Are a Case Study in Why Nepotism Is Problematic," Wash. Post, Mar. 12, 2019, https://wapo.st/2DN4tDC.

[8] See Heather Vogell, "Never-Before-Seen Trump Tax Documents Show Major Inconsistencies," ProPublica, Oct. 16 , 2019, https://bit.ly/3gCmeEz; Doug Criss, "A Judge Has Finalized a $25 Million Settlement for Students Who Claim They Were Defrauded by Trump University," CNN, Apr. 10, 2018, https://cnn.it/2C883bh (regarding the settlement of Trump University litigation, "Trump repeatedly denied the fraud claims and said that he could have won at trial, but he said that as President he did not have time because he wanted to focus on the country").

[9] See Zervos v. Trump, 171 A.D.3d 110 (N.Y. App. Div. 2018); Johnson v. Trump for President, Inc., No. 8:19-CV-00475-T-02SPF, 2019 WL 2492122 (M.D. Fla. 2019); Eliza Relman, "The 25 Women Who Have Accused Trump of Sexual Misconduct," Business Insider, May 1, 2020, https://bit.ly/2C5RxZ9.

[10] Nixon v. Fitzgerald, 457 U.S. 731 (1982).

[11] United States v. Nixon, 418 U.S. 683 (1974).

limits on presidential privilege[12] and immunity from civil litigation,[13] the investigations into alleged financial improprieties and potential foreign influence eventually made their way in to federal court.

In a pair of cases, the Supreme Court revisited the questions of presidential immunity and susceptibility to oversight.[14] In two opinions by Chief Justice John Roberts, *Trump v. Vance* and *Trump v. Mazars*, the Court reaffirmed two fundamental constitutional values: No person is above the law and the powers of Congress are limited. In the process, the Court also demonstrated an ability to resolve important constitutional questions without descending into the political polarization that engulfs the body politic in 2020.

I. The Subpoenas

For the first two years of his presidency, Donald Trump largely escaped meaningful oversight or investigation from Congress.[15] That changed in 2019 as the Democratic Party regained control of the House of Representatives. Almost immediately, congressional leaders announced their intent to engage in wide-ranging oversight and investigation of the president, his administration, and his finances.[16]

---

[12] See In re Sealed Case, 148 F.3d 1073, 1074 (D.C. Cir. 1998) (rejecting the notion that the "protective function privilege" can shield members of the Secret Service from having to testify before a federal grand jury).

[13] Clinton v. Jones, 520 U.S. 681 (1997).

[14] As the Supreme Court issued two opinions, this article refers to a "pair" of cases. As a technical matter, these are actually three cases, as *Trump v. Mazars* was consolidated with *Trump v. Deutsche Bank* for argument and decision.

[15] The Trump campaign was, however, subject to an extensive investigation as a consequence of the May 2017 appointment of Robert Mueller as special counsel to investigate Russian interference in the 2016 presidential campaign and related matters. Special Counsel Robert S. Mueller, III, U.S. Dep't. of Justice, Report on the Investigation into Russian Interference in the 2016 Presidential Election (2019). Trump was also the subject of multiple lawsuits alleging financial improprieties, including violations of the Emoluments Clauses and federal government rules concerning property management. Blumenthal v. Trump, 949 F.3d 14 (D.C. Cir. 2020); Citizens for Responsibility & Ethics in Wash. v. Trump, 939 F.3d 131 (2d Cir. 2019); In re Trump, 958 F.3d 274 (4th Cir. 2020); Am. Oversight v. U.S. Gen. Servs. Admin., 311 F. Supp. 3d 327 (D.D.C. 2018).

[16] See Jonathan Martin and Alexander Burns, "Democrats Capture Control of House; G.O.P. Holds Senate," N.Y. Times, Nov. 6, 2018, https://nyti.ms/31v3eBf; Sonam Sheth and Joe Perticone, "Democrats Just Flipped the House of Representatives—Here's How They Plan to Make Trump's Life a Living Hell," Business Insider, Nov. 7, 2018, https://bit.ly/2F221di ("Democrats plan to tighten the screws by mounting an investigative blitz against the White House and Russian interests"); see also Moe, *supra* note 2.

In April 2019, three separate House committees issued subpoenas to third parties for the financial records of the Trump family and the Trump Organization.[17] On April 11, the House Committee on Financial Services and the House Permanent Select Committee on Intelligence each issued subpoenas to banks that handle financial matters for Trump and his businesses. These two committees issued identical subpoenas to Deutsche Bank, demanding "the financial information of the President, his children, their immediate family members, and several affiliated business entities," including (but not limited to) all account activity and business statements from 2010 to the present.[18] The Financial Services Committee issued a similar subpoena to Capital One, demanding equivalent information concerning numerous business entities related to the Trump Organization, from 2016 to the present.[19] On April 15, the House Committee on Oversight and Reform issued a similar subpoena to Trump's accounting firm, Mazars USA, LLP, demanding financial information concerning the president and several affiliated business entities for the period from 2011 to 2018, as well as all "engagement agreements" and contracts related to Mazars's work for the Trumps and affiliated businesses.[20]

As befits three committees with differing jurisdictions, each committee offered a different rationale for its subpoena. The Financial Services Committee claimed its subpoenas were authorized by its jurisdiction over existing banking regulations, as well as by House Resolution 206, which authorized committee investigations to support legislation "to close loopholes that allow corruption, terrorism, and money laundering to infiltrate our country's financial system."[21] According to the committee, the Trump family and business's

---

[17] Trump v. Mazars USA, LLP, 140 S. Ct. 2019 (2020). It is worth noting that the House Committee on Ways & Means separately sought to subpoena Trump's tax returns from the Department of the Treasury and Internal Revenue Service. See Nicholas Fandos, "House Ways and Means Chairman Subpoenas Trump Tax Returns," N.Y. Times, May 10, 2019, https://nyti.ms/2XER6MZ. This subpoena also resulted in litigation. Comm. on Ways & Means v. Dep't of the Treasury, No. 1:19-CV-01974 (TNM), 2019 WL 4094563 (D.D.C. Aug. 29, 2019).

[18] Mazars, 140 S. Ct. at 2027.

[19] Id.

[20] Id. at 2028.

[21] H.R. Res. 206, 116th Cong. (2019).

financial dealings could serve as a "case study" on how "illicit money, including from Russian oligarchs," enters the United States and evades existing regulatory controls.[22]

The Intelligence Committee, while issuing a Deutsche Bank subpoena identical to that of the Financial Services Committee, cited its authority to investigate "efforts by Russia and other foreign entities to influence the U.S. political process during and since the 2016 U.S. election," and "the counterintelligence threat arising from any links or coordination between U.S. persons and the Russian government and/or other foreign entities, including any financial or other leverage such foreign actors may possess."[23] Such an investigation, the committee's chairman explained, required investigating potential connections to the Trump campaign and the president's family members and business entities, so as to identify whether "President Trump, his family, or his associates are or were at any time at heightened risk of, or vulnerable to, foreign exploitation, inducement, manipulation, pressure, or coercion, or have sought to influence U.S. government policy in service of foreign interests."[24] The committee further cited plans "to develop legislation and policy reforms to ensure the U.S. government is better positioned to counter future efforts to undermine our political process and national security."[25]

The Oversight Committee issued a memorandum citing recent testimony by Trump's former lawyer Michael Cohen and various news reports[26] alleging financial irregularities by Donald Trump and his businesses, including the filing of false or misleading financial statements.[27] According to Cohen, Trump-related entities would alter financial statements so as to inflate or deflate valuations in an effort to

---

[22] *Id.*

[23] Press Release, H. Permanent Select Comm. on Intelligence, "Chairman Schiff Statement on House Intelligence Committee Investigation" (Feb. 6, 2019), https://bit.ly/2F1STp3.

[24] *Id.*

[25] *Id.*

[26] See Steve Benen, "Trump's Alleged Financial Fraud Creates an Important New Vulnerability," MSNBC, Mar. 1, 2019, https://on.msnbc.com/3iicCyX; David A. Fahrenthold and Jonathan O'Connell, "How Donald Trump Inflated His Net Worth to Lenders and Investors," Wash. Post, Mar. 28, 2019, https://wapo.st/33DCdhY.

[27] Memorandum from Chairman Elijah E. Cummings to Members of the Committee on Oversight and Reform 1 (Apr. 12, 2019) [hereinafter Cummings Memo], https://politi.co/2PxtuWb.

mislead investors, lenders, and perhaps even government officials.[28] Cohen's allegations provided the House Oversight Committee with reason to demand financial records from Trump and his businesses. As the Cummings Memo explained,

> The Committee has full authority to investigate whether the President may have engaged in illegal conduct before and during his tenure in office, to determine whether he has undisclosed conflicts of interest that may impair his ability to make impartial policy decisions, to assess whether he is complying with the Emoluments Clauses of the Constitution, and to review whether he has accurately reported his finances to the Office of Government Ethics and other federal entities.[29]

The memo further stated that the subpoenaed information would inform the committee's "review of multiple laws and legislative proposals" within the committee's jurisdiction.[30]

Deutsche Bank, Capital One, and Mazars USA all indicated that they would comply with the congressional subpoenas.[31] This prompted legal action by Trump, in his personal capacity, in an effort to quash the subpoenas and prevent their enforcement.[32]

---

[28] Hearing with Michael Cohen, Former Attorney to President Donald Trump, Before the H. Comm. on Oversight and Reform, 116 Cong. 13, 161 (2019), https://bit.ly/3gHsJ8Y ("It was my experience that Mr. Trump inflated his total assets when it served his purposes"; and explaining that, to avoid paying taxes, Trump's strategy was to "deflate the value of the asset, and then you put in a request to the tax department for a deduction.").

[29] Cummings Memo, *supra* note 27, at 4.

[30] *Id.*

[31] See Tr. of Oral Argument at 30, Trump v. Mazars USA, LLP, 140 S. Ct. 2019 (2020) (No. 19-715) [hereinafter Mazars Oral Argument] (Trump's lawyer said "the recipients of these subpoenas have indicated that they consider it to be a dispute between the President and the House of Representatives, . . . and absent some sort of court order regarding its validity, they feel obligated to comply.").

[32] In *Deutsche Bank*, Trump was joined on the complaint by his three eldest children, The Trump Organization, Inc., and several related business entities: the Donald J. Trump Revocable Trust, Trump Organization LLC, DJT Holdings LLC, DJT Holdings Managing Member LLC, Trump Acquisition LLC, and Trump Acquisition Corp. Trump v. Deutsche Bank AG, 943 F.3d 627, 633 n.2 (2nd Cir. 2019). In the *Mazars* case, Trump was joined by The Trump Organization, Inc., Trump Organization LLC, The Trump Corporation, DJT Holdings LLC, the Donald J. Trump Revocable Trust, and Trump Old Post Office LLC. Trump v. Comm. on Oversight and Reform, 380 F. Supp. 3d 76, 88 n.19 (D.D.C. 2019).

Congress was not alone in investigating potential wrongdoing by Donald Trump. In 2018, the New York County District Attorney's Office (NYCDA) began an investigation into potentially illegal activities related to the Trump Organization and affiliated individuals. Although the precise scope of these investigations remains unclear,[33] one subject of investigation was the alleged "hush money" payments made to two women, Stormy Daniels and Karen McDougal, with whom Trump is alleged to have had extramarital affairs.[34] According to various news reports, the release of the infamous *Access Hollywood* tape in the midst of the 2016 presidential campaign prompted an effort by Michael Cohen to pay Daniels and McDougal to keep quiet about their relations with Trump.[35] Cohen subsequently pleaded guilty to campaign finance violations related to these payments, alleging that he made the payments at Trump's behest, as well as to making false statements to Congress.[36]

According to the NYCDA, local prosecutors agreed to forestall further investigation of Cohen's allegations and the potential involvement of other individuals related to the Trump Organization until the completion of any federal investigation. This investigation concluded in July 2019, prompting the NYCDA to renew its own investigations into the alleged hush money payments and financial improprieties related to the Trump Organization and affiliated individuals. As part of the investigation, the NYCDA obtained a grand jury subpoena seeking financial records and related communications from the Trump Organization, including tax returns.[37] The Trump Organization provided the grand jury with some of the

---

[33] According to the briefs filed by NYCDA, the investigations are detailed in a redacted declaration filed under seal. See, e.g., Brief of Respondent at 2 n.2, Trump v. Vance, 140 S. Ct. 2412 (2020) (No. 19-635) [hereinafter Brief of Respondent].

[34] See William K. Rashbaum & Ben Protess, "8 Years of Trump Tax Returns Are Subpoenaed by Manhattan D.A.," N.Y. Times, Sept. 16, 2019, https://nyti.ms/3gEPOZT.

[35] See Kristine Phillips et al., "FBI Tied Donald Trump and Top Aides to 2016 Effort to Silence a Porn Star, New Court Files Show," USA Today, July 18, 2019, https://bit.ly/30BnFNN.

[36] Press Release, U.S. Att'y Off., S.D.N.Y., "Michael Cohen Pleads Guilty in Manhattan Federal Court to Eight Counts, Including Criminal Tax Evasion and Campaign Finance Violations" (Aug. 21, 2018), https://bit.ly/31n6WwI.

[37] See Trump v. Vance, 395 F. Supp. 3d 283, 291 (S.D.N.Y. 2019).

relevant materials, but did not turn over tax returns, prompting the NYCDA to change its strategy.[38]

On August 29, 2019, the NYCDA served a grand jury subpoena on Mazars, seeking various financial records of the Trump Organization and related individuals, including relevant tax returns, from January 2011 to the present.[39] As the NYCDA acknowledges, this subpoena was "largely patterned" on the Mazars subpoena issued by the House Oversight Committee.[40] Although this subpoena was not served directly on the Trump Organization, as with the congressional subpoenas, Trump sought to block its enforcement and the production of any responsive documents.

II. The Proceedings Below

President Trump, in his personal capacity, filed legal actions in federal district court to enjoin each of the subpoenas for financial records.[41] Suits against the NYCDA grand jury subpoena and the House Financial Services and Intelligence subpoenas were filed in New York. A suit seeking to enjoin the House Oversight Committee was filed in the District of Columbia.

In challenging the House committees' extensive document demands, Trump argued that the subpoenas violated separation-of-powers principles and lacked legitimate legislative purposes. No court below was persuaded by any of these arguments. Neither the U.S. District Court for the District of Columbia nor the U.S. District Court for the Southern District of New York found Trump's concerns remotely persuasive.[42] In the U.S. Courts of Appeals, however, both cases produced divisions of opinion.

[38] Brief of Respondent, *supra* note 33, at 4.

[39] Vance, 395 F. Supp. 3d at 291.

[40] Brief of Respondent, *supra* note 33, at 4. The NYCDA copied the Oversight Committee's subpoena "with the aim of minimizing the burden on Mazars and facilitating expeditious production of responsive documents." *Id.* See also Tr. of Oral Argument at 82, Trump v. Vance, 140 S. Ct. 2412 (2020) (No. 19-635) ("[O]nce the House subpoena became public, it's not unusual for an office like ours to model our subpoena language on that which has already been made public from a different source, when it's going to the same recipient. It makes it easier on the recipient in the process.").

[41] In the cases involving congressional subpoenas, Trump was also joined by various business enterprises and, in one of the suits, by his oldest children. See *supra* note 32.

[42] See Trump v. Mazars USA, LLP, 380 F. Supp. 3d 76 (D.D.C. 2019); Trump v. Deutsche Bank AG, 2019 WL 2204898 (S.D.N.Y. May 22, 2019).

The U.S. Court of Appeals for the D.C. Circuit was the first to rule on the propriety of congressional subpoenas to third parties seeking the financial records of President Trump, his family, and their businesses.[43] In a 2-1 decision, the court concluded that the House had broad and expansive constitutional authority to investigate "topics on which it could legislate," and that such authority readily encompassed the subpoena to Mazars.[44] The court's majority found little merit in the arguments raised by Trump as well as those made by the U.S. Department of Justice, which had filed an amicus brief at the invitation of the court.[45]

In the court's view, the subpoena presented "no direct inter-branch dispute," because it was served upon a third-party custodian, rather than the president himself.[46] Although "separation-of-powers concerns still linger in the air," the court concluded that the subpoena served a valid legislative purpose, even though the committee acknowledged a particular interest in uncovering potentially illegal activity.[47] As Judge David Tatel explained in his opinion (joined by Judge Patricia Millett), the committee's "interest in past illegality can be wholly consistent with an intent to enact remedial legislation."[48] By identifying past illegal conduct, the committee could determine how to revise and reform existing statutes and develop new legislative proposals.

Judge Neomi Rao dissented at length, arguing the committee's focus on identifying and uncovering illegal conduct disqualified any reliance upon legislative power. According to Judge Rao, the Constitution's text and structure provided only one mechanism through which to investigate presidential misconduct: impeachment. "Investigations of impeachable offenses simply are not, and never have been, within Congress's legislative power," she wrote, citing historical practice dating back to the Founding period.[49]

---

[43] Trump v. Mazars USA, LLP, 940 F.3d 710, 748 (D.C. Cir. 2019).

[44] *Id.* at 723.

[45] *Id.* at 718 ("After oral argument, and at the court's invitation, the Department of Justice filed an amicus brief.").

[46] *Id.* at 726.

[47] *Id.*

[48] *Id.* at 728.

[49] *Id.* at 784 (Rao, J., dissenting).

"Allowing Congress to investigate impeachable officials for suspicions of criminality pursuant to the legislative power has serious consequences for the separation of powers because it allows Congress to escape the responsibility and accountability inherent in impeachment proceedings," Judge Rao warned.[50]

Trump filed a petition for rehearing en banc, which was promptly denied.[51] Three judges noted their dissent: Judges Karen Henderson, Gregory Katsas, and Rao. Judges Katsas and Rao published dissents from the denial, emphasizing the important and under-explored issues raised by the case. *Mazars* was only the second time "an Article III court has undertaken to enforce a congressional subpoena for the records of a sitting president," Katsas noted.[52] The first was *Senate Select Committee on Presidential Campaign Activities v. Nixon*, in which the D.C. Circuit, sitting en banc, had declined to enforce a committee subpoena for presidential records.[53] That fact alone would have seemed to make *Mazars* en banc-worthy, though additional review would have further delayed Congress's ability to obtain Trump's financial records. Katsas also emphasized the inherent conflict between the congressional and executive interests. Failing to consider the threat that extensive document demands could pose to "presidential autonomy and independence," Katsas warned, would subject presidential disclosure to "the whim of Congress—the President's constitutional rival for political power."[54] Judge Rao also dissented, reiterating the points of her panel dissent and noting that, although the House had finally authorized the opening of an impeachment inquiry, House Resolution 660 did "not even purport to ratify previously issued subpoenas," and the House Oversight Committee "relied consistently and exclusively on the legislative power to justify this subpoena."[55]

At the other end of the Acela corridor, the U.S. Court of Appeals for the Second Circuit split over the propriety of the other House

---

[50] *Id.* at 783.

[51] Trump v. Mazars USA, LLP, 941 F.3d 1180 (D.C. Cir. 2019) (denying petition for reh'g en banc).

[52] *Id.* at 1180 (Katsas, J., dissenting from denial of reh'g en banc).

[53] 498 F.2d 725, 731–33 (D.C. Cir. 1974) (en banc).

[54] Mazars, 941 F.3d at 1181.

[55] *Id.* at 1182 (Rao, J., dissenting from denial of reh'g en banc).

committee subpoenas. The majority opinion, by Judge Jon Newman (joined by Judge Peter Hall), concluded that both the Intelligence Committee and the Financial Services Committee subpoenas were sufficiently related to valid legislative purposes within their respective jurisdictions.[56] It was perfectly appropriate, according to the court, for Congress to use the president and his family as a "case study" of financial improprieties and foreign influence that could inform remedial legislation.[57] While instructing the district court to protect against the disclosure of "sensitive personal details (such as payments for medical procedures and the like),[58] the Second Circuit disclaimed any separation-of-powers concerns at all.[59]

Judge Debra Ann Livingston wrote separately, concurring in part and dissenting in part, expressing her disagreement with the panel's resolution of the constitutional questions.[60] Judge Livingston could not accept the majority's conclusions that "'this case does not concern separation of powers,'" and rejected its assumption that allowing Congress to issue broad subpoenas for a president's records posed no threat to a president's ability to discharge his constitutional duties.[61] Previewing how these cases would be viewed on One First Street, Judge Livingston urged a remand for the committees to "clearly articulate . . . the legislative purpose that supports disclosure *and* the pertinence of such information to that purpose."[62]

Trump's attempts to quash the NYCDA grand jury subpoena were no more successful in the lower courts than his attempts to block the congressional subpoenas. In September 2019, Trump filed suit in the Southern District of New York seeking to enjoin enforcement of the grand jury subpoena on the grounds that the president enjoys a temporary absolute immunity from all state court criminal proceedings while in office, even insofar as state criminal proceedings seek the production of personal documents from third-party custodians

---

[56] Deutsche Bank AG, 943 F.3d 627.

[57] *Id.* at 662–63 n.67.

[58] *Id.* at 632.

[59] *Id.* at 669.

[60] *Id.* at 676 (Livingston, J., concurring in part and dissenting in part).

[61] *Id.* at 678.

[62] *Id.* at 679.

to a grand jury.[63] He argued further that allowing state or local prosecutors to investigate the president would interfere with federal supremacy. Unlike in the congressional subpoena cases, where the Department of Justice filed amicus curiae briefs at the invitation of the circuit court panels, the department was involved in this litigation from the start, largely supporting Trump's efforts to have the subpoenas quashed.[64]

The district court was reluctant to rule on the president's motion, concluding that the doctrine of "*Younger* abstention" counseled refraining from exercising jurisdiction over the dispute and allowing the state proceedings to continue without federal court interference.[65] In the alternative, the district court rejected the president's arguments of immunity, finding them "repugnant to the nation's governmental structure and constitutional values."[66] As the district court noted, such "special dispensation from the criminal law's purview and judicial inquiry" would, in effect, erect a protective shield around not only the president, but also his family members and business associates, and compromise the "fair and effective administration of justice."[67] While acknowledging the possibility that some criminal proceedings could "impermissibly interfere" with the president's ability to discharge his constitutional obligations, third-party compliance with a grand jury subpoena for personal financial records posed no such risk.[68] On this basis the district court rejected any claim of absolute immunity in favor of a "case-by-case" evaluation of specific objections to specific document requests.[69]

The Second Circuit reversed the district court on *Younger* abstention but affirmed the district court's refusal to grant an injunction

---

[63] See Trump v. Vance, 395 F. Supp. 3d 283 (S.D.N.Y. 2019).

[64] *Id.* at 291–92 (noting department filings).

[65] *Id.* at 301. *Younger* abstention is based upon Younger v. Harris, 401 U.S. 37 (1971); see also Middlesex County Ethics Comm. v. Garden State Bar Ass'n, 457 U.S. 423 (1982) (identifying a set of conditions for the application of *Younger* abstention).

[66] Vance, 395 F. Supp. 3d at 290.

[67] *Id.* at 288–89, 311.

[68] *Id.* at 289. The court also rejected the argument that the NYCDA grand jury subpoena was pursued in bad faith or constituted "harassment" of the president. *Id.* at 298–99.

[69] *Id.* at 315.

against the subpoena.[70] Relying on *United States v. Nixon*[71] and *Clinton v. Jones*,[72] the Second Circuit recognized it was "long-settled" that "'the President is subject to judicial process in appropriate circumstances.'"[73] If, as Judge Robert Katzmann explained, "documents exposing the President's confidential, official conversations may properly be obtained by subpoena" under the right circumstances, there is no argument that "a President's *private* and *non-privileged* documents may be absolutely shielded from judicial scrutiny."[74] On this basis, the Second Circuit rejected the president's claim of immunity and remanded the case back to the district court.

Disappointed in all of the rulings below, Trump filed petitions for certiorari which the Supreme Court granted in December 2019. All three cases—the two consolidated congressional subpoena cases and the NYCDA grand jury subpoena case—were scheduled for argument in March, but that was not to be. Due to the COVID-19 pandemic, the Supreme Court temporarily suspended oral arguments.[75] Consequently, *Trump v. Mazars* and *Trump v. Vance* had to be argued via teleconference in May and would not be decided before the end of June, when the Court's term traditionally ends. The two opinions would be handed down on July 9, the last opinions to be issued on the last day of the term.

III. *Trump v. Vance*

In *Trump v. Vance*, the Supreme Court ruled in favor of the NYCDA, resoundingly rejecting the claims of presidential immunity from state investigation.[76] The Court was unanimous in rejecting Trump's claim of even temporary absolute immunity from state criminal process and voted 7-2 to affirm the judgment of the Second Circuit. Chief Justice Roberts wrote the opinion for the Court, joined by the Court's liberals, Justices Ruth Bader Ginsburg, Stephen Breyer, Sonia

---

[70] Trump v. Vance, 941 F.3d 631 (2d Cir. 2019).

[71] 418 U.S. 683 (1974).

[72] 520 U.S. 681 (1997).

[73] Vance, 941 F.3d at 640 (quoting Jones, 520 U.S. at 703).

[74] *Id.* at 641 (citing Jones, 520 U.S. at 693–94).

[75] Press Release, U.S. Sup. Ct., "Postponement of March Oral Arguments" (Mar. 16, 2020), https://bit.ly/2Dl81xp.

[76] Trump v. Vance, 140 S. Ct. 2412 (2020).

Sotomayor, and Elena Kagan. Justice Brett Kavanaugh concurred in the judgment, joined by the Court's other Trump appointee, Justice Neil Gorsuch. Justices Clarence Thomas and Samuel Alito each filed a dissenting opinion.

The case's outcome was clear from the opening lines of Chief Justice Roberts's opinion for the Court: "In our judicial system, 'the public has a right to every man's evidence.' Since the earliest days of the Republic 'every man' has included the President of the United States."[77] Resting on this principle, and its historical application in the United States, the chief justice concluded that neither Article II nor the Supremacy Clause barred a state grand jury from issuing a subpoena "to a sitting President," nor did either require the application of a heightened standard of review.[78] Justices Kavanaugh and Gorsuch agreed with the chief justice's bottom line, voting to affirm the Second Circuit, albeit advocating a more protective standard for review of subpoenas for a president's documents.

The chief justice grounded his decision on the 200-year history of presidents complying with demands for documents in criminal proceedings,[79] with a heavy emphasis on Chief Justice John Marshall's handling of the Burr trial while sitting as a circuit justice for Virginia.[80] As Roberts recounted, Aaron Burr sought to subpoena documents from President Thomas Jefferson.[81] Although the prosecution resisted these efforts, Marshall concluded that presidential prerogative could not stand in the way of a criminal defendant's right to obtain potentially exculpatory evidence.[82]

---

[77] *Id.* at 2420. The Court attributes the maxim "the public has a right to every man's evidence" to Lord High Chancellor Hardwicke in 1742. See *id.* (citing 12 Parliamentary History of England 693 (1812)).

[78] Vance, 1405. Ct. at 2420.

[79] *Id.* ("Beginning with Jefferson and carrying on through Clinton, Presidents have uniformly testified or produced documents in criminal proceedings when called upon by federal courts."); *id.* at 2423 ("In the two centuries since the Burr trial, successive Presidents have accepted Marshall's ruling that the Chief Executive is subject to subpoena.").

[80] See Josh Blackman, "Symposium: It Must Be Nice to Have John Marshall on Your Side," SCOTUSblog, July 10, 2020, https://bit.ly/3gCezWx.

[81] Vance, 140 S. Ct. at 2422–23. For a more detailed discussion of the haggling over documents at the Burr trial, see Josh Blackman, Presidential Subpoenas during the Burr Trials, SSRN, July 9, 2020, https://bit.ly/3kiILbL.

[82] Vance, 140 S. Ct. at 2422 (citing United States v. Burr, 25 F. Cas. 30, 33–34 (C.C. Va. 1807)).

At common law, only the king was exempt from a duty to provide evidence, and the president was "of the people," not a member of royalty.[83] Unless the president could identify how compliance with an evidentiary demand would interfere with his constitutional duties, he was as subject to the demands of the law as anyone else.[84] The demands of public safety or national security—concerns at the heart of executive privilege—could justify withholding documents. The president's status as head of the executive branch, standing alone, could not. Roberts noted that Marshall's conclusions in the Burr trial have been followed for centuries, most notably in *United States v. Nixon*, where the Court "unequivocally and emphatically" endorsed the conclusion that presidents are subject to subpoena.[85]

The additional wrinkle in *Vance* was that the proceedings arose in state court, whereas all of the relevant precedents involved federal proceedings. Even *Clinton v. Jones*, in which then-president Bill Clinton was sued by Paula Jones alleging sexual harassment while he was the governor of Arkansas, was brought in federal court. "Here we are confronted for the first time with a subpoena issued to the President by a local grand jury operating under the supervision of *state* courts," Roberts observed.[86] This presented at least the possibility of state interference with federal supremacy, as the *Jones* Court had acknowledged, expressly reserving the question whether a president would have a stronger claim for immunity in the case of state-court proceedings.[87]

In *McCulloch v. Maryland*, the Court concluded that allowing a state to levy and collect taxes on a federally chartered bank risked allowing a state to "defeat the legitimate operations" of the federal government.[88] By extension, Trump's attorneys argued, allowing state criminal proceedings to ensnare the president could interfere

---

[83] *Id.*

[84] *Id.*

[85] See Jones, 520 U.S. at 704 (citing Nixon, 418 U.S. 683).

[86] Vance, 140 S. Ct. at 2425.

[87] Jones, 520 U.S. at 691 ("[B]ecause the claim of immunity is asserted in a federal court and relies heavily on the doctrine of separation of powers that restrains each of the three branches of the Federal Government from encroaching on the domain of the other two, it is not necessary to consider or decide whether a comparable claim might succeed in a state tribunal.") (citation omitted).

[88] 17 U.S. (4 Wheat.) 316, 427 (1819).

with Article II.[89] If, as *McCulloch* counseled, "the States have no power" to "retard, impede, burden, or in any manner control" the operations of the federal government,[90] how could states subject a president to criminal process?

Accepting the possibility that state criminal process could conceivably interfere with the performance of some presidential duties, at least in some instances, Roberts explained that such concerns could, at most, justify limitations on state proceedings, such as the tailoring of document demands, but could not justify absolute immunity. As Roberts noted, Trump's attorneys made no argument that this particular subpoena was unduly burdensome. They rather sought to claim that *any* such subpoena impermissibly interferes with the president's work. That was a bridge too far for the Court to cross.

Chief Justice Roberts examined the premises of Trump's claims and found them wanting. Insofar as a subpoena might be distracting, the Court had already rejected such a basis for immunity in *Clinton v. Jones*, a civil case, where the equities in favor of evidence production are less pronounced. If a "properly managed" civil suit could proceed without interfering with a president's ability to perform his duties, "a properly tailored criminal subpoena" would not interfere either.[91] Nor could claims of reputational harms justify preventing properly founded legal investigations from proceeding.[92] If the speculative threat of harassing litigation was no basis for providing immunity in *Clinton v. Jones*, the prospect of local prosecutors attempting to target a sitting president could not justify immunity here.[93] Indeed, as the chief justice noted, not a single justice accepted claims of absolute immunity on these bases.[94]

Although the precise question presented to the Court was whether a state grand jury could issue a criminal subpoena for a president's personal financial records from third parties, the language of the

---

[89] Brief for Petitioner at 23–24, Trump v. Vance, 140 S. Ct. 2412 (2020) (No. 19-635); accord Brief for the United States as Amicus Curiae Supporting Petitioner at 12, Trump v. Vance, 140 S. Ct. 2412 (2020) (No. 19-635).

[90] McCulloch, 17 U.S. at 426, 436.

[91] Vance, 140 S. Ct. at 2426.

[92] *Id.* at 2427.

[93] *Id.*

[94] *Id.* at 2429 ("Our dissenting colleagues agree.").

Court's opinion spoke more broadly. As framed by the chief justice, the question was simply whether the Constitution precludes, or requires a heightened standard for, "the issuance of a state criminal subpoena to a sitting President."[95] As in *Mazars*, the Court did not place significant weight on the fact that another entity, in this case an accounting firm, has possession of the documents sought, for they were still the president's documents and "Mazars is merely the custodian."[96] In this respect, the Court's conclusion is broader than might have been necessary to resolve the case, and certainly broader than we have come to expect in the chief justice's opinions.[97] It nonetheless recognized that a consequence of accepting Trump's argument for immunity would erect a protective shield around all those covered by the subpoena, not merely the president, and could thereby compromise the administration of justice in criminal matters beyond those involving the president himself, a concern the Court had found particularly compelling in *United States v. Nixon*.[98]

The Court also rejected the solicitor general's argument that a state grand jury subpoena seeking the president's private financial records must satisfy a "heightened need" standard. Such a standard, Chief Justice Roberts noted, was appropriate for official documents, particularly those potentially covered by executive privilege, as such documents relate to the president's ability to perform his official duties. No such argument could be made about personal documents with no relation to the president's office. As Marshall noted in the *Burr* case, "If there be a paper in the possession of the executive,

---

[95] *Id.* at 2420.

[96] *Id.* at 2425 n.5.

[97] See Jonathan H. Adler, "This Is the Real John Roberts," N.Y. Times, July 7, 2020, https://nyti.ms/3gCnUxR (discussing the chief justice's minimalist jurisprudence).

[98] Nixon, 418 U.S. at 707 ("The impediment that an absolute, unqualified privilege would place in the way of the primary constitutional duty of the Judicial Branch to do justice in criminal prosecutions would plainly conflict with the function of the courts under Art. III."); Vance, 140 S. Ct. at 2430 ("[E]ven assuming the evidence withheld under that standard were preserved until the conclusion of a President's term, in the interim the State would be deprived of investigative leads that the evidence might yield, allowing memories to fade and documents to disappear. This could frustrate the identification, investigation, and indictment of third parties (for whom applicable statutes of limitations might lapse). More troubling, it could prejudice the *innocent* by depriving the grand jury of exculpatory evidence.") (emphasis original).

which is not of an official nature, he must stand, as respects that paper, in nearly the same situation with any other individual."[99]

While rejecting the arguments for immunity or a "heightened need" to obtain a president's personal financial records, the Court emphasized that "grand juries are prohibited from engaging in 'arbitrary fishing expeditions.'"[100] Nothing in the opinion could be read to excuse the issuance of truly "harassing" subpoenas, or to bar a president from seeking relief from such harassment.[101] To the contrary, Chief Justice Roberts noted, "a President would be entitled to the protection of federal courts" in the case of actual harassment that meaningfully threatened "the independence or effectiveness of the Executive."[102] Indeed, the existence of such "safeguards" made any grant of immunity unnecessary.[103]

Justices Kavanaugh and Gorsuch likewise rejected the claims of absolute immunity, but only concurred in the judgment as they concluded that criminal subpoenas for a president's records should be subject to a higher standard—the "demonstrated, specific need" standard of *United States v. Nixon*—even where the documents sought are of an unofficial nature.[104] The Court's newest justices were not as quick to dismiss concerns about "harassment or diversion" that could interfere with the president's duties.[105] Stressing the qualifications in the language of the majority opinion, such as the need for "high respect" of the president's office and a "particularly meticulous" review of document requests, Kavanaugh predicted lower courts would still need to "delv[e] into why the State wants the information," how much it is needed, and whether it could be obtained in other ways.[106]

Justice Alito agreed with Kavanaugh and Gorsuch that a higher standard should apply to subpoenas for a president's records, but concluded this required reversing the Second Circuit's decision.

[99] Burr, 25 F. Cas. at 191.
[100] Vance, 140 S. Ct. at 2428.
[101] *Id.*
[102] *Id.*
[103] *Id.* at 2429.
[104] *Id.* at 2432 (Kavanaugh, J., concurring in the judgment).
[105] *Id.*
[106] *Id.* at 2433.

Though joining the rest of the Court in rejecting Trump's plea for immunity, Justice Alito largely accepted the more modest position urged by the solicitor general. Relying heavily on *McCulloch,* Alito argued for greater vigilance in protecting the president from state interference, lest he be besieged by demands from hundreds of local prosecutors itching to sink their teeth into the president's hide.[107] Accordingly, Alito argued for a more demanding test before a subpoena for the president's records could be enforced, placing the burden squarely on the NYCDA to meet a "heightened standard" of need.[108] Among other things, Justice Alito would have required the NYCDA to provide greater detail about the offenses under investigation, why the documents were necessary for such an investigation, and why production could not be postponed until the president leaves office,[109] but no other justice joined in this approach. "For all practical purposes," Justice Alito warned, "the Court's decision places a sitting President in the same unenviable position as any other person whose records are subpoenaed by a grand jury."[110] Indeed, the majority could well have responded, that is precisely the point.

Justice Thomas agreed with the majority that the president lacks absolute immunity and that a subpoena for his financial records may issue, though he based this conclusion on the Constitution's text and Founding era materials rather than the history of proceedings since.[111] Despite this conclusion, and despite his rejection of any claim that the NYCDA had to make a showing of heightened need,[112] Justice Thomas concluded the president "may be entitled to relief against [the subpoena's] *enforcement.*"[113]

---

[107] *Id.* at 2452 (Alito, J., dissenting) ("the Court's decision threatens to impair the functioning of the Presidency and provides no real protection against the use of the subpoena power by the Nation's 2,300+ local prosecutors").

[108] *Id.* at 2448.

[109] *Id.* at 2449.

[110] *Id.* at 2451.

[111] *Id.* at 2434 (Thomas, J., dissenting) ("Unlike the majority, however, I do not reach this conclusion based on a primarily functionalist analysis. Instead, I reach it based on the text of the Constitution, which, as understood by the ratifying public and incorporated into an early circuit opinion by Chief Justice Marshall, does not support the President's claim of absolute immunity.").

[112] *Id.* at 2439 n.3.

[113] *Id.* at 2434 (emphasis original).

Although the Constitution expressly provides for legislative immunity, Justice Thomas noted, there is nothing in the text suggesting executive immunity.[114] Nor is there much evidence for any such doctrine in Founding era materials. Nonetheless, Thomas dissented on the grounds that the judiciary is obligated to be particularly deferential to the executive branch's claims of interference. While Thomas would apply the standard articulated by Marshall in *Burr*—a president must produce evidence unless it interferes with his official duties—he would also "take pains to respect the demands on the President's time."[115] And should a president claim that enforcement of a subpoena would compromise his ability to perform his duties, even if only due to "mental burden," courts should "recognize their own limitations" and be hesitant to overrule that determination.[116] On this basis, Justice Thomas would have vacated the Second Circuit's decision and remanded the case to the district court to consider whether "'the President's 'duties as chief magistrate demand his whole time for national objects.'"[117] Though Justice Thomas's formulation is exceedingly deferential, it is not entirely clear why the test he proposes would be of particular help to this president given the apparent lax demands on his time.[118]

The *Vance* decision did not end legal wrangling over the NYCDA grand jury subpoena, as the Court remanded the case to the lower

---

[114] *Id.* As Justice Thomas noted in a footnote, this view could call *Nixon v. Fitzgerald* into question. *Id.* at n.1. This is consistent with Justice Thomas's desire to reconsider the doctrine of qualified immunity. Ziglar v. Abbasi, 137 S. Ct. 1843, 1872 (2017) (Thomas, J., concurring in part and concurring in the judgment) (noting "[i]n an appropriate case, we should reconsider our qualified immunity jurisprudence"); Baxter v. Bracey, 140 S. Ct. 1862 (2020) (Thomas, J., dissenting from denial of certiorari) ("I have previously expressed my doubts about our qualified immunity jurisprudence. Because our §1983 qualified immunity doctrine appears to stray from the statutory text, I would grant this petition.") (citation omitted).

[115] Vance, 140 S. Ct. at 2437.

[116] *Id.* at 2438.

[117] *Id.* at 2439 (quoting Burr, 25 F. Cas. at 34).

[118] See, e.g., Maggie Haberman et al., "Inside Trump's Hour-by-Hour Battle for Self-Preservation," N.Y. Times, Dec. 9, 2017, https://nyti.ms/3kn4vmQ (reporting that Trump watches between four and eight hours of television every day); Daniel Dale & Holmes Lybrand, "Fact Check: Trump Has Spent Far More Time at Golf Clubs than Obama Had at Same Point," CNN, May 25, 2020, https://cnn.it/33AS1BW (reporting that, as of May 2020, Trump had spent all or part of over 200 days golfing during his presidency).

courts for further proceedings, including the consideration of specific objections Trump may have to aspects of the subpoena.[119] As noted above, the Court emphasized that such subpoenas could not be allowed to interfere with the president's performance of his constitutional duties, and that a president is entitled to raise the same constitutional and state law objections to a subpoena's breadth or intrusiveness as any other person.[120] Further, the president remains able to "raise subpoena-specific constitutional challenges, in either a state or federal forum."[121] The Court also declined to address whether local prosecutors could do more than investigate a president through a grand jury. *Vance* should not be read to support the proposition that state officials may indict or attempt to prosecute a sitting president, and there are serious arguments that no such prosecution could be had until a president leaves office.[122]

While the federal district court already rejected any claims of bad faith or presidential harassment on the part of the NYCDA,[123] it is possible that Trump could successfully oppose the production of particular documents or materials in further proceedings. Such objections are likely to be considered quickly. On July 17, Chief Justice Roberts granted the NYCDA's unopposed request for immediate issuance of the Court's judgment, forgoing the traditional 25-day period specified in the Supreme Court's rules.[124] As of this writing, renewed proceedings in the district court are already underway.[125]

---

[119] Vance, 140 S. Ct. at 2431 n.6 (majority op.); *id.* at 2433 (Kavanaugh, J., concurring in the judgment).

[120] *Id.* at 2430–31 (majority op.).

[121] *Id.* at 2430.

[122] See A Sitting President's Amenability to Indictment and Criminal Prosecution, 24 Op. Off. Leg. Couns. 236–37 (2000), https://bit.ly/2XCMyXk ("[T]he constitutional structure permits a sitting President to be subject to criminal process only after he leaves office or is removed therefrom through the impeachment process.").

[123] See Vance, 395 F. Supp. 3d. at 298–300.

[124] See Vance v. Trump, 2020 U.S. LEXIS 3581 (July 17, 2020) (order to issue the judgment forthwith to the U.S. Court of Appeals for the Second Circuit). President Trump consented to this motion.

[125] See Adam Klasfeld, "Trump and Vance Face Off in First Court Hearing since SCOTUS Ruling," Courthouse News Service, July 16, 2020, https://bit.ly/2PuNCIw.

IV. *Trump v. Mazars*

Chief Justice Roberts also wrote for the Court in *Trump v. Mazars*, and this decision was also 7-2, albeit without any concurrences.[126] The chief justice was again joined by the Court's liberal justices (Ginsburg, Breyer, Sotomayor, and Kagan) and both of President Trump's appointees to the Court (Kavanaugh and Gorsuch). As in *Vance*, Justices Thomas and Alito both wrote dissenting opinions. Also, as in *Vance*, each accepted aspects of the majority's analysis.

In *Mazars*, the Court rejected the claims of both sides, reaffirming congressional authority to conduct oversight, but roundly rejecting the claims put forward by the House of Representatives and vacating both of the circuit court opinions. In many respects, the *Mazars* opinion evinces a skepticism of Congress evident in other Roberts Court opinions. Notably, not a single justice on the Court indicated agreement with the holdings and analyses of the circuit courts below, and not a single justice embraced the expansive conception of congressional oversight pressed by the House of Representatives and embraced by most legal commentators.[127]

At the outset, Chief Justice Roberts's opinion stressed the unprecedented nature of the case. While the Court had previously considered efforts to obtain presidential documents, beginning with the Burr trial, and had considered challenges to congressional oversight, it had "never addressed a congressional subpoena for the

---

[126] 140 S. Ct. 2019.

[127] See, e.g., Cass Sunstein, "Trump Tax Case Is an Easy Call," MetroWest Daily News (Framingham, Mass.), Nov. 13, 2019 ("[T]he case is so simple and straightforward that it wouldn't be terribly surprising if the justices decline to consider it at all."); Roger Parloff, "Behind the Bitter Legal Clash between Congress and the White House. Who Might Win?" Newsweek, July 5, 2019 (quoting Brianne Gorod: "These should be easy cases for the courts of appeals"); Paul Waldman, "The Wall of Concealment Trump Built around His Finances Is Beginning to Crumble," Wash. Post, May 23, 2019, https://wapo.st/3a94gqz (suggesting it takes "spectacular chutzpah" to claim Congress cannot investigate alleged illegality of president's financial dealings); Marty Lederman, "Understanding the Two Mazars Subpoena Cases Pending in the Supreme Court," Balkinization (blog), Nov. 25, 2019, https://bit.ly/33G2LyX (characterizing objections to subpoenas as "so weak"); Victoria Bassetti & Tim Lau, "Trump's Troubling Rebuke of Congressional Oversight," Brennan Center, May 7, 2019, https://bit.ly/3fBKXr2 ("the long line of precedent—regarding executive privilege and the scope of Congress' power to request documents and for people to appear—is largely in Congress' favor").

President's information."[128] Most prior subpoenas of presidential records concerned official documents, and most such document demands were resolved outside of court. There was more guidance to be had in the historical practice of interbranch confrontation and accommodation than in judicial precedent.

As in *Vance*, the chief justice canvassed the history of congressional efforts to obtain presidential documents, beginning with a House committee's 1792 demand for documents related to General Arthur St. Clair's campaign against Native Americans in the Northwest Territory.[129] President George Washington's cabinet concluded that Congress has the authority to "call for papers," but the president maintained the "discretion" to withhold documents where necessary to safeguard the public interest.[130] This approach was followed by Washington's successors, producing a practice of seeking to obtain documents without resorting to the courts.[131] As the Court noted, the only other instance in which a dispute over a congressional subpoena directed toward the president reached an appellate court was in *Senate Select Committee on Presidential Campaign Activities v. Nixon*,[132] in which the D.C. Circuit denied enforcement, relying in part on claims of executive privilege, and the Senate dropped the case (assuredly because a separate impeachment inquiry had begun).[133] While this litigation was of limited relevance for the issues in *Mazars*, it did support the proposition that "executive privilege claims are stronger against Congress than they are against criminal process," which is hardly a ringing endorsement of Congress's legislative oversight authority.[134]

For over 200 years, when Congress has sought information or materials from the president, it has pressed its claims directly, prompting negotiation between the two branches, resolving the matter through what then–assistant attorney general Antonin Scalia

[128] Mazars, 140 S. Ct. at 2026.

[129] *Id.* at 2029.

[130] *Id.*

[131] *Id.* at 2030.

[132] 498 F.2d 725.

[133] *Id.* at 732 (noting any need for information was "merely cumulative" given the House Judiciary Committee's impeachment inquiry).

[134] See Josh Chafetz, Congress's Constitution 183 (2017).

called the "hurly-burly, the give-and-take of the political process."[135] There were few cases considering the scope of Congress's subpoena power because such cases were rarely litigated. It was generally unclear whether Congress itself has standing to sue,[136] and those subject to subpoenas, or held in contempt for violating them, rarely brought challenges of their own into court.[137] Here, however, the requests were not made to the president directly, but to third parties. This both eliminated the opportunity for direct negotiation between the president and Congress, leaving Trump with no recourse other than to seek relief in federal court. Intentionally or not, the House's strategy of bypassing the president thrust the Court into a fray of a sort that it had long been able to avoid.[138]

Just because Congress had not made a practice of seeking to enforce subpoenas in court did not mean Congress lacked the power to do so.[139] To the contrary, in *Mazars* the Court reaffirmed that each House of Congress "has power 'to secure needed information' in order to legislate."[140] Although not enumerated in Article I (or anywhere else in the Constitution), the Court reaffirmed that Congress possessed an investigative power "as an adjunct to the legislative process."[141] This "power of inquiry—with process to

---

[135] Mazars, 140 S. Ct. at 2029 (citing Hearings on S. 2170 et al. before the Subcomm. on Intergovernmental Relations of the S. Comm. on Government Operations, 94th Cong. (1975) (A. Scalia, Assistant Attorney General, Office of Legal Counsel)).

[136] One of the first court decisions expressly holding that Congress had standing to enforce a subpoena arose in the George W. Bush administration. See Comm. on Judiciary v. Miers, 558 F. Supp. 2d 53 (D.D.C. 2008). See also Comm. on Judiciary v. McGahn, 951 F.3d 510 (D.C. Cir. 2020), reh'g en banc granted, opinion vacated sub nom. U.S. House of Representatives v. Mnuchin, No. 19-5176, 2020 WL 1228477 (D.C. Cir. 2020), rev'd sub nom. Comm. on Judiciary of U.S. House of Representatives v. McGahn, No. 19-5331, 2020 WL 4556761 (D.C. Cir. Aug. 7, 2020) (holding that the committee does have Article III standing).

[137] See generally Amandeep S. Grewal, Congressional Subpoenas in Court, 98 N.C. L. Rev. 1044 (2020); Louis Fisher, Cong. Res. Serv., Congressional Investigations: Subpoenas and Contempt Power (2003).

[138] Mazars, 140 S. Ct. at 2029 ("Historically, disputes over congressional demands for presidential documents have not ended up in court.").

[139] See McGahn, 951 F.3d 510. Standing questions are beyond the scope of this article.

[140] Mazars, 140 S. Ct. at 2031 (citing McGrain v. Daugherty, 273 U.S. 135, 161 (1927)).

[141] Id. (quoting Watkins v. United States, 354 U.S. 178, 197 (1957)).

enforce it—is an essential and appropriate auxiliary to the legislative function."[142]

While casting no doubt on the existence of Congress's investigatory power, the Court stressed its limit as an "adjunct" or "auxiliary" power. Congress has no power to investigate for investigation's sake, nor to conduct oversight for the purpose of public disclosure,[143] let alone to exact punishment of "'try[ing]' someone 'before [a] committee for any crime or wrongdoing.'"[144] Rather, congressional subpoenas are valid only insofar as they are "related to, and in furtherance of, a legitimate task of the Congress."[145] More generally, congressional subpoenas must serve "a valid legislative purpose."[146] Further, the recipients of subpoenas retain "common law and constitutional privileges" against the disclosure of certain materials.[147]

The Court rejected the notion that Congress has an expansive and independent investigatory power apart from what is necessary to enact and review legislation. Simultaneously, the Court rejected Trump's efforts to erect an additional barrier to obtaining presidential documents. Although Chief Justice Roberts stressed that courts need to remain conscious of the real separation-of-powers concerns raised by congressional attempts to investigate the president (as apart from efforts to investigate executive branch agencies created and funded by Congress), his opinion also rejected the claims made by President Trump and the solicitor general that all requests for presidential records require the sort of "demonstrated, specific need" necessary to overcome assertions of executive privilege. If the position advanced by the House, and embraced by the lower courts, was insufficiently solicitous of the president's interests, the president's approach paid too little regard to those of Congress.

As in *Vance*, the Court was not persuaded that serving a subpoena on third-party custodians, instead of the president himself, eliminated any burden on the executive. Intrusions on the president's

---

[142] *Id.* (quoting McGrain, 273 U.S. at 174).

[143] *Id.* at 2032 ("Congress has no 'general power to inquire into private affairs and compel disclosures.'") (cleaned up).

[144] *Id.* (quoting McGrain, 273 U.S. at 179).

[145] Watkins, 354 U.S. at 187.

[146] Quinn v. United States, 349 U.S. 155, 161 (1955).

[147] Mazars, 140 S. Ct. at 2032.

ability to perform his duties is not merely a matter of not having to produce documents himself. "Congressional demands for the President's information present an interbranch conflict no matter where the information is held—it is, after all, the President's information," Roberts wrote.[148] Because of the rivalrous relationship between the legislative and executive branches, any effort by one to investigate the other necessarily raises separation-of-powers concerns.[149] Thus "congressional subpoenas for the President's information unavoidably pit the political branches against one another."[150] (Though Chief Justice Roberts wrote as if this point were obvious, it was rejected not only by majorities on each circuit court that considered the question, but also seems not to have been recognized, at first, by the Department of Justice, as it only filed briefs in the congressional subpoena cases when invited to by the appellate courts.)

Rejecting the arguments advanced by the parties, Chief Justice Roberts laid out a "balanced approach" that would require courts to "perform a careful analysis that takes adequate account of the separation of powers principles at stake" for both the president and Congress alike.[151] Such an analysis requires consideration of at least four questions when evaluating a congressional subpoena for presidential papers, including private financial documents held by third parties:

1) Whether the asserted legislative purpose requires obtaining papers from the president, or whether the legislative purpose be served by obtaining other information or materials from other sources. In other words, if Congress can achieve its legitimate goals without intruding upon the president, it should be required to do so.

2) Whether the subpoena is "broader than reasonably necessary to support Congress's legislative objective."[152] In other words, Congress cannot engage in fishing expeditions or broad drift-net strategies to sweep up evidence of presidential wrongdoing.

---

[148] *Id.* at 2035.

[149] *Id.* at 2033 (noting the legislature and executive are "'opposite and rival' political branches").

[150] *Id.* at 2034.

[151] *Id.* at 2035.

[152] *Id.* at 2036.

3) Whether Congress has offered evidence "to establish that a subpoena advances a valid legislative purpose."[153] In other words, courts need not just take Congress's word for it but can demand evidence to support the subpoena.

4) Whether the subpoena imposes undue or unreasonable burdens on the president. In other words, courts should not help Congress use subpoenas to harass or debilitate a rival political branch.

The lower courts in these cases failed to consider such factors and, more broadly, did not account adequately for the separation-of-powers principles at stake, but would be required to on remand. In many respects, the Court embraced an analysis quite similar to that of Judge Livingston below.

This approach drew from the history of interbranch accommodation more than from the Court's own precedents but seems designed to replicate the outcome that would have been achieved had Congress and the executive been forced to negotiate a resolution. It was an approach that left neither side particularly happy. Perhaps an implicit message of the Court's test is that forcing the judiciary to intercede in such interbranch disputes is a sure way to ensure neither side gets much of what it wants.[154]

Justice Thomas offered a narrower view of Congress's oversight power in his separate dissent. Echoing the opinion below of Judge Rao (a former Thomas clerk), Justice Thomas concluded that Congress may not use its legislative power to investigate potential wrongdoing by impeachable officers. Rather, it must use the impeachment power. Further, Justice Thomas would have held "Congress has no power to issue a legislative subpoena for private, nonofficial documents— whether they belong to the President or not."[155] At the time of the Founding, Justice Thomas notes, such a power "was not included by necessary implication in any of Congress' legislative powers."[156]

---

[153] *Id.*

[154] See Jonathan L. Entin, Congress, the President, and the Separation of Powers: Rethinking the Value of Litigation, 43 Admin. L. Rev. 31, 33 (1991) ("Excessive reliance upon the Court deceives us into thinking that these disputes are purely constitutional in nature and that only the Justices can resolve them.").

[155] Mazars, 140 S. Ct. at 2037 (Thomas, J., dissenting).

[156] *Id.* at 2038.

Broader conceptions of Congress's investigatory powers, such as that embraced by the Court in *McGrain v. Daugherty* and expounded upon by the majority in *Mazars*, "are without support as applied to private, nonofficial documents."[157]

Dissenting separately, Justice Alito echoed many of the concerns he expressed in *Vance*. In his view "legislative subpoenas for a President's personal documents are inherently suspicious," and are thus deserving of careful scrutiny.[158] In this case, Justice Alito perceived an excessively broad demand for information and "disturbing evidence of an improper law enforcement purpose."[159] To overcome these concerns, he suggested the House should have to make the sort of detailed showing he would have imposed on the NYCDA in *Vance*. While agreeing with the majority's decision to remand, he found its terms "inadequate," prompting his separate dissent.[160]

A. The Question of Limits

As it was ultimately decided, *Mazars* can be seen as a case about limits on legislative power. The president and Congress framed the case in separation-of-powers terms, emphasizing the need to protect or oversee the executive, respectively. Yet for many on the Court, it presented an unresolved question about the constitutional limits on Congress, and the resulting opinion expressed disquiet with the lower courts' failure to impose any meaningful constraint on the legislature's investigative appetite.

The need to identify judicially enforceable limits on legislative power is a hallmark of the Court's modern federalism jurisprudence. A theory of legislative power typically needs to have some limiting principle if it is going to convince a majority of the current Court. A pivotal moment during oral argument in *United States v. Lopez* occurred when the solicitor general was asked whether, on the government's theory defending the constitutionality of the Gun-Free School Zones Act, there was any activity beyond the scope of Congress's power "to regulate Commerce . . . among the several States,"

---

[157] *Id.*

[158] *Id.* at 2048 (Alito, J., dissenting).

[159] *Id.*

[160] *Id.* at 2049.

and he had no reply.[161] Several years later, in *Morrison v. United States*, the solicitor general again failed to satisfy those justices interested in a clear limiting principle.[162] After both arguments, the Court rejected Congress's assertions of authority, concluding the laws in question exceeded the legislature's enumerated powers.[163]

Since *Lopez* and *Morrison*, government advocates in federalism cases are prepared for the limits question, as they were in *NFIB v. Sebelius*.[164] It does not appear the House of Representatives was prepared for this line of inquiry in *Mazars*, however. During oral argument, multiple justices pressed the House's attorney to identify documents or information that would lie beyond Congress's grasp. Each time, the attorney came up empty[165]—a point Chief Justice Roberts highlighted in his opinion.[166] At one point the attorney suggested Congress might not be able to subpoena the president's private medical records, but then he recognized that such information might well be relevant, under the House's theory, to inform legislation concerning presidential succession or the operation of the Twenty-fifth Amendment.[167] In the House's vision, it would be open-season on a president from another political party.

This question was predictable, and the inability to provide an answer seems like an unforced error. The principle that all legislative

---

[161] Tr. of Oral Argument at 5–9, United States v. Lopez, 514 U.S. 549 (1995) (No. 93-1260).

[162] Tr. of Oral Argument at 22–23, 26, United States v. Morrison, 529 U.S. 598 (2000) (No. 99-5).

[163] Lopez, 514 U.S. at 567–68; Morrison, 529 U.S. at 621.

[164] See Josh Blackman, Unprecedented 159–60 (2013) (discussing how solicitor general's office was aware the lack of a limiting principle could be a vulnerability at oral argument).

[165] Mazars Oral Argument, *supra* note 31, at 62 (Justice Alito asked the House's attorney, "But you were not able to give the Chief Justice even one example of a subpoena that would be—that would not be pertinent to some conceivable legislative purpose, were you?," to which the attorney responded, "As—as I said, Your Honor, the—that— that's correct, because this Court itself has said Congress's power is—to legislate is extremely broad, especially when you take into account appropriations.").

[166] Mazars, 140 S. Ct. at 2034 ("Indeed, at argument the House was unable to identify *any* type of information that lacks some relation to potential legislation.").

[167] Mazars Oral Argument, *supra* note 31, at 77 (the House's attorney said, "medical records of the President would, I think, almost always be not pertinent to valid legislative purpose," but then 10 seconds later, flipped and said that under "the Twenty-Fifth amendment, they would—they certainly would be pertinent").

powers must be limited matters to the Court's conservative justices, but, in this context, it appears to have mattered to the liberals as well. Justice Breyer, for example, noted his concerns at argument about the scope of the power asserted and its potential for abuse in the future. Whatever the Court rules in this case, he noted, would apply to future presidents and would empower future Congresses.[168] This was not a case about Trump. To the Court, it was a case about Congress and the executive.

Given the breadth of Congress's powers under existing doctrine, there is little information that could not be sought in pursuit of a "legitimate legislative purpose," particularly if, as the House and Second Circuit maintained, it was appropriate to single out the president as a "case study" to inform legislative action. If investigations into alleged wrongdoing may always be excused as legitimate efforts to inform remedial legislation, then there is no alleged misfeasance or malfeasance that is not up for grabs. And even if one were to identify a limit on Congress's enumerated powers that left some subject matter beyond the reach of Article I, Section 8, Congress could always claim the need to obtain information to inform a potential constitutional amendment to expand legislative power.

This is why, if a limit is necessary, it is not enough to rest on the constraints imposed by Congress's enumerated powers. Limits born of the Constitution's structure, grounded in the separation of powers, must also be identified. This is a trickier enterprise, due to the lack of relevant constitutional text, which may explain why the majority embraced a functional, history bound understanding of Congress's investigatory power. It may have been the best the Court could do the first time it was presented with this question. As the chief justice noted, "one case every two centuries does not afford enough experience" for a more definitive test.[169]

---

[168] *Id.* at 84 (Justice Breyer said, "the fact that what I hold today will also apply to a future Senator McCarthy asking a future Franklin Roosevelt or Harry Truman exactly the same questions, that bothers me.").

[169] Mazars, 140 S. Ct. at 2036.

B. The Impotent Congress and the Impeachment Alternative

Chief Justice Roberts's *Mazars* opinion stressed the unprecedented nature of the case. What was unprecedented was not that Congress sought to investigate a president, however, or that a president did not want to release information or materials that Congress desired. What was unprecedented was that the matter made its way to the Supreme Court.

The House subpoenaed third-party custodians for the president's financial records because it had every reason to believe the president would not cooperate. Indeed, the Trump administration made clear after the 2018 election that it would resist congressional oversight across the board.[170] While Mazars and the banks said they would not turn over Trump-related records voluntarily, they also indicated to Congress that they would comply if subpoenaed.[171] Yet, as noted above, by pursuing this course, Congress prevented any possibility of interbranch accommodation, and gave President Trump the opportunity to push these cases to federal court.

The House likely sought an alternative to direct demands for production by the president because it knew how that would end. The president would refuse, and Congress would not obtain the desired documents for an extended period of time, if at all. Congress's relative impotence at obtaining documents from the White House is not solely a function of executive intransigence. Some of the blame lies with Congress itself. The legislature's failure to engage in more frequent legislation and a more regular appropriations process has lessened its leverage against the executive branch.[172] By allowing its powers to atrophy, Congress is less able to bargain or coerce executive branch cooperation. If Congress wants information, whether for a legitimate legislative purpose or otherwise, it needs to be in a position to withhold things the executive branch needs and

[170] See *supra* note 3.

[171] See *supra* note 31.

[172] On Congress's general failure to utilize its legislative authority to control the executive branch, and agencies in particular, see Jonathan H. Adler & Christopher J. Walker, Delegation and Time, 105 Iowa L. Rev. 1931 (2020).

exact concessions. A Congress that is unable to legislate is not a Congress that has such leverage.[173]

Is there an alternative to relying upon legislative power? The House relied exclusively upon its legislative powers to justify the subpoenas under consideration. Even though there was palpable interest in alleged presidential wrongdoing, the House nonetheless eschewed any reliance upon the impeachment power. This was a political choice that likely made it more difficult for the House to prevail. Insofar as the committees sought information about ongoing financial relationships and activities, the documents sought would have been relevant for an impeachment inquiry. As demonstrated by historical practice dating all the way back to the Washington administration, Congress is entitled to documents sought pursuant to a valid impeachment inquiry that it could not otherwise obtain.[174] Though the matter was not before the Court, there is every reason to believe the justices would have been more receptive to an effort to obtain the president's personal financial documents for impeachment purposes than as an aid to legislation.[175]

The power to investigate wrongdoing for purposes of impeachment is more penetrating than the investigatory power to support legislation. Yet it is also more politically fraught. Invoking the specter of impeachment entails political costs—costs many in Congress

---

[173] It is fair to note that congressional leverage is also dependent upon the executive branch valuing what Congress can withhold. So, for instance, if an administration is willing to operate without Senate-confirmed individuals in key administrative positions, this dramatically lessens the Senate's ability to use its advice-and-consent power to induce executive branch cooperation.

[174] See 940 F.3d at 758 (Rao, J., dissenting) ("[I]n 1796 the House requested from President George Washington documents and diplomatic correspondence related to the Jay Treaty and its ratification in order to determine whether to appropriate the funds necessary to implement the Treaty. President Washington argued that because the House could not compel him to disclose the documents through an exercise of its legislative powers, it could demand the documents only through an exercise of its impeachment power.").

[175] See Michael Stern, "How Impeachment Proceedings Would Strengthen Congress's Investigatory Powers," Just Security, May 28, 2019. See also Amandeep S. Grewal, The President's Tax Returns, 27 Geo. Mason L. Rev. 439, 477 (2020) (noting "historical practice suggests" that many "separation of powers limitations" of concern in oversight investigations "must yield").

were not yet ready to bear.[176] And that is precisely the point. If Congress wants to be able to wield the more powerful investigative tool against a political rival, such as the president, it has to be willing to bear the political costs. Legislative reluctance to even consider invoking its impeachment power leaves it bereft of one of its most significant constitutional authorities.

An unresolved question is whether invoking the impeachment power requires some form of official act by the House, or whether a committee statement is enough. While the lower courts considered the intricacies of congressional committee authorizations,[177] the Supreme Court did not, so it remains an open question whether procedural formalities are necessary for the exercise of the legislature's investigatory power. Would it have been enough for the House Oversight Committee's memo to include a statement that it needed the financial materials from Mazars USA to help determine whether to open a formal impeachment inquiry? Would this be any different than a congressional inquiry into the nature of a problem for which proposed legislation has yet to be outlined, let alone drafted? There is little in *Mazars* to answer those questions. It is nonetheless possible to conclude that the House's unwillingness to acknowledge the need to investigate potential high crimes and misdemeanors weakened its hand in the Supreme Court.

V. Conclusion

Mazars and *Vance* reaffirmed the important principle that the president is not above the law. Article II did not create a king. Yet they also embrace the proposition that the president is special, and when the president is under investigation, the fact that it is the president is something that matters, whether that president is Donald Trump or someone else.

[176] Although the Founding generation may have seen impeachment as an "indispensable remedy" to executive malfeasance, in contemporary political discourse invoking the "I-word" conjures up "specters of wounded democracy and constitutional collapse." See Gene Healy, Indispensable Remedy: The Broad Scope of the Constitution's Impeachment Power 81–82 (2018).

[177] Mazars, 940 F.3d at 742–47 (discussing in detail House Rules X and XI, as well as various subclauses, which the court held authorizes the Oversight Committee to subpoena Trump's financial records); Deutsche Bank AG, 943 F.3d at 669 (discussing the "Committee's authorized investigative authority" and rejecting the United States's amicus curiae argument that such authority would upset the separations of power).

In rejecting claims of immunity from state criminal subpoenas and congressional oversight, the Supreme Court has not opened a Pandora's box of presidential harassment. *Clinton v. Jones* did not lead to a deluge of suits against Presidents George W. Bush and Barack Obama, and presidents will only be subject to potential criminal investigation when they engaged in potentially illegal activities before they were president. We need not worry about 2,300 local prosecutors running amok.[178]

Congressional investigations will continue, though Congress will have to be more careful and less political in its efforts. Demands for presidential materials will have to be more circumscribed, and perhaps Congress will realize that some legislative purposes do not require so much information.[179] Indeed, if Congress wants greater financial disclosure by presidents, it could amend the Ethics in Government Act to add such requirements, producing disclosure by statutory requirement rather than by oversight subpoena. That might not produce any revelations about Donald Trump, but it would advance the asserted legislative interest going forward.

As a practical matter, the *Mazars* and *Vance* decisions mean that the legal proceedings in all of the financial records cases will continue, and any documents produced are unlikely to see the light of day before the November election. *Vance* is a more decisive loss for the president, but that case involves grand jury subpoenas, so any documents eventually turned over will be covered by grand jury secrecy rules. *Mazars* is more of a split decision that leaves Congress with options—though it may not leave Congress the time to pursue those options before the existing subpoenas expire at the end of the legislative session. Going forward, if Congress wants information from a president, even about his personal finances on private financial dealings, it will have to avoid the overly partisan, blunderbuss approach that has characterized much legislative oversight in recent years.

As already noted, it is significant that not a single justice expressed support for the lower court opinions in *Mazars*. Nor was a single

---

178 Vance, 140 S. Ct. at 2452 (Alito, J., dissenting).

179 For example, Congress has had no difficulty enacting legislation governing the receipt of foreign emoluments by executive branch officials without subpoenaing extensive financial records from covered officials. See Grewal, *supra* note 175, at 461.

justice willing to write in support of an unbounded legislative oversight power. The perspective presented as self-evident by many legal commentaries was wholly absent from the opinions issued by the Court. Congress's unenumerated power to investigate has limits.

Do the financial records cases matter politically? Probably not. It is unlikely there is anything in the relevant records that would influence a significant portion of the electorate. Those who oppose President Trump need no more convincing, and given all of the revelations and allegations to date, it is not clear that additional reports alleging financial improprieties of some sort would move much of the electorate.[180] Yet information about the president's financial entanglements might encourage a future Congress to enact additional disclosure requirements for future officeholders.

Mazars and *Vance* may still matter in a different way. By rendering 7-2 rulings in these two cases, and eschewing the partisan divisions that we see throughout our other institutions, the Court has demonstrated an ability to reach careful, balanced judgments on important separation-of-powers questions with deep political significance. That is not something to be overlooked, even if it has the potential to seduce the other branches into thinking they do not have to learn to resolve their disputes among themselves.[181]

---

[180] President Trump himself has bragged that there is almost nothing he could do to lose support. See, e.g., Jeremy Diamond, "Trump: I could 'shoot somebody and I wouldn't lose voters,'" CNN, Jan. 24, 2016, https://cnn.it/2DGfQ0f.

[181] See Entin, *supra* note 154.

The Vexing Problem of Faithless Electors

*Keith E. Whittington**

The Electoral College is an unloved and mostly ignored institution. It generally operates in the background of American electoral politics and is poorly understood by most voters. It rises into our collective consciousness only when something goes wrong or when one of the two political parties decides that it is systematically working against the party's immediate interests.

We are currently living through such a moment when the Electoral College stands in the political spotlight. The contested presidential election of 2000 thrust the mechanisms of our presidential selection system to center stage, and few liked what they saw. The extended legal battle in Florida seemed to highlight not only the dirty reality of how votes are cast and counted in the United States, but also the surprising uncertainty about how contested outcomes were to be resolved. Once the dust settled, Democrats began to focus their attention on the seeming unfairness of a presidential candidate winning the election despite losing the national popular vote. That concern faded a bit in subsequent election cycles and Democrats even began to celebrate the reliable "blue wall" constructed by the Electoral College that would cement their control of the White House into the foreseeable future.

Disgust with the Electoral College returned with a vengeance in 2016. Republican Donald Trump broke down the blue wall and cobbled together an Electoral College victory despite winning nearly three million fewer votes than Hillary Clinton, his Democratic rival who ran up the score with big-state blowouts in California, New York, and Illinois. The constitutional allocation of electoral votes was once again cast as an illegitimate remnant of corrupt compromises, increasingly framed as yet another legacy of white supremacy (on the

---

* Keith E. Whittington is the William Nelson Cromwell Professor of Politics at Princeton University.

grounds that the original Electoral College gave a boost to slave-holding states relative to some alternative electoral formulas).

The aftermath of Trump's shocking victory on election night brought to the fore another, generally ignored, aspect of the Electoral College—the presidential electors themselves. Some grasped hold of this aspect of the Electoral College as a potential lifeline. An unprecedented public lobbying campaign was organized by Democratic activists to persuade some of the presidential electors pledged to vote for the Republican Party nominee to instead cast their ballot for someone—anyone—else, in the hopes of denying Donald Trump the White House. Americans were suddenly informed that the president was not in fact chosen by the general electorate in November but was instead chosen by a relative handful of unknown presidential electors meeting in December. Armed with the writings of the newly popular Alexander Hamilton, the "Hamilton Electors" urged their colleagues to ignore their pledges and instead cast their ballots for whomever they thought most qualified to be president. The movement fizzled when it turned out that electors pledged to vote for Clinton were the most easily persuaded that exercising a free choice for the most qualified individual required breaking their pledge to support the Democratic Party's nominee, but it exposed an extraordinary risk inherent in the design of the Electoral College. Americans suddenly realized that a few dozen individuals could overturn the results of a presidential election.

Despite 2016's seemingly close call, the problem of "faithless electors" soon faded into the background as politicians, activists, and the media turned their attention to new and more immediate outrages. Just as the 2000 presidential election seemed to expose an election system in desperate need of reform only to be forgotten as election season passed, so the 2016 presidential election seemed to expose the disturbing problem of faithless electors as something more than an occasional idiosyncratic quirk that could be ignored after the Hamilton Electors had failed in their mission to stop a Trump presidency.

The U.S. Supreme Court has not often been asked to weigh in on the workings of the Electoral College. The controversies surrounding the system have generally been too short-lived and too inextricably political to draw in the Court, though there have been exceptions in which judges have been asked to consider the meaning and implications of the constitutional rules guiding the selection of presidents. This is a part of the Constitution that is not encrusted with judicial precedents or surrounded by elaborate academic theories. The justices are not dug in to hardened positions on how best to think about the Electoral College and there are no great ideological battles fought over its meaning.

Justices pondering a question about the Electoral College are in the rare position of working on a nearly blank canvas. If such a proper legal case involving the Electoral College arises during a heated struggle over the possession of the White House, as in the Florida fracas of 2000, it seems inevitable that the immediate partisan contest will overshadow everything else. But the Court in the faithless elector cases of 2020 were differently situated.[1] Although the cases arose out of the 2016 election, they did not arrive at the Court until long after those particular passions had cooled. The justices were not being asked to determine who would occupy the White House on Inauguration Day. They were asked to settle a question that was more uncertain in its implications for any partisan team. In such fortuitous circumstances, it is perhaps unsurprising that the Court was able to reach a unanimous conclusion on how the cases should be resolved, though the justices could not entirely agree on how to reach that conclusion.

The greatest risk raised by the faithless elector cases was the possibility that the justices might throw a monkey wrench into the electoral machinery. They could have made it somewhat more likely that Hamilton Elector–style lobbying campaigns would become regular features of our electoral process, and as a result made it marginally more likely that the country could eventually face the constitutional crisis of the Electoral College denying victory to the declared winner of Election Day. The justices in 2020 instead took care not to further unsettle the political system. In doing so, they did not—and could not have—put an end to the possibility that a faithless elector might

---

[1] The Court consolidated two cases that were heard together, which together involved a total of six presidential electors from the 2016 cycle in two states. The Court produced a substantive opinion for only one case, but formally separated them in order to take account of the recusal of Justice Sonia Sotomayor from the case that came out of Colorado. Sotomayor is personal friends with Polly Baca, a named party in the suit, a pledged elector who cast a ballot for Hillary Clinton in 2016, and the first Latina to be elected to the Colorado state senate. The Court issued a brief *per curiam* in Colo. Dep't of State v. Baca, 140 S. Ct. 2316 (2020), which reversed the Tenth Circuit. The Court issued lengthy majority and concurring opinions in Chiafalo v. Washington, 140 S. Ct. 2316 (2020), which affirmed the Washington state supreme court.

someday swing an election result, but they did what they could to ensure that such an event was not made *more* likely to occur. They endorsed the status quo ante, and left it to politicians to take measures that would minimize the prospect and impact of faithless electors.

This essay reviews the faithless elector problem and how the Court tried to resolve it. Part I reviews the design of the Electoral College, the problem of faithless electors, and the ways we have tried to contain that problem. Part II notes how this problem of faithless electors reached the Supreme Court. Part III examines the strategy Justice Elena Kagan adopted in the majority opinion for empowering states to discipline presidential electors. Part IV examines the alternative strategy offered by Justice Clarence Thomas in his concurring opinion. Part V considers some implications of the Court's action in these cases for related controversies.

I. The Electoral College and Faithless Electors

The Electoral College was not one of the constitutional Framers' most inspired ideas. It was an ad hoc creation that built on compromises already made while attempting to address problems that never emerged. It was the first component of the 1787 Constitution to be specifically altered through constitutional amendment, when the Twelfth Amendment was ratified in 1804. It has never operated as it was originally expected to do, and politicians throughout American history have maneuvered to minimize its effects. The drafters of American state constitutions declined to emulate its design by creating their own versions of the Electoral College, and other countries that experimented with similar systems for choosing a chief executive soon abandoned them.

The constitutional process for filling the office of the president of the United States is a bit of a Rube Goldberg device, and across our historical practice we have tried to simplify it and avoid its more troubling features. Those efforts have not always been successful.

At the heart of the Electoral College are the presidential electors themselves.[2] The Constitution does not enshrine a right to vote for

---

[2] I have also described the constitutional presidential election system in Keith E. Whittington, The Electoral College: A Modest Contribution, in The Longest Night 371–72 (A.J. Jacobson & M. Rosenfeld eds., 2002) and Keith E. Whittington, Originalism, Constitutional Construction, and the Problem of Faithless Electors, 59 Ariz. L. Rev. 903 (2017).

the president or recognize a role for the general citizenry at all in filling the office of the president.[3] Formally, the president is elected when the presidential electors cast their ballots in December. The Constitution empowers Congress to specify the day on which the presidential electors of each state shall meet in their respective states, and federal law currently dictates that they "meet and give their votes on the first Monday after the second Wednesday in December next following their appointment at such place in each State as the legislature of such State shall direct."[4] The electors "vote by ballot for President and Vice President," the results in each state are recorded, and a certificate listing the results is sent to Congress to be counted.[5]

The Constitution says that electors shall be appointed "in such Manner as the Legislature thereof may direct." The only limitation is that "no Senator or Representative, or Person holding an Office of Trust or Profit under the United States, shall be appointed an Elector."[6] The Founders might have expected the state legislatures to simply appoint the presidential electors themselves, just as they would choose U.S. senators. In the beginning, a majority of the states did in fact use that method. The practice gradually declined as Jeffersonian and Jacksonian democratizing sensibilities swept the nation and new states entered the union with less inclination to follow the old tradition. The aristocratic South Carolina, which kept a property qualification on suffrage even after most states had abandoned it, stuck with legislature-appointed presidential electors until the Civil War. Some states immediately turned the matter over to the voters, however, and that manner of appointing presidential electors soon became predominant. Most preferred a single statewide vote for selecting a slate of electors. States likewise moved to adopt the "unit rule," whereby all the presidential electors would be awarded

---

[3] But see U.S. Const. amend. XIV, § 2, which would reduce a state's congressional representation based on the proportion of white male citizens, age 21 or over, who are denied the right to vote for presidential electors and certain other offices. See also Bush v. Gore, 531 U.S. 98, 104 (2000) ("When the state legislature vests the right to vote for President in its people, the right to vote as the legislature has prescribed is fundamental.").

[4] U.S. Const. art. II, § 1; 3 U.S.C. § 7.

[5] U.S. Const. amend. XII.

[6] U.S. Const. art. II, § 1.

to a single presidential candidate.[7] This approach was seen to provide states with more heft in national politics than if electors were split among multiple candidates. The unit rule was particularly consequential in large states, where winning a large cache of electors by a small margin could generate a far bigger impact on the electoral vote than on the popular vote.

The Constitution allocates to each state "a Number of Electors, equal to the whole Number of Senators and Representatives to which the State may be entitled in the Congress."[8] This has generally been the more controversial feature of the Electoral College since it is the feature that more routinely has consequences to the electoral fortunes of the political parties. The apportionment rule necessarily creates a gap between the national popular vote and the electoral vote, and that gap is exacerbated by the unit rule that the states have generally adopted in allocating their electoral votes to candidates. When Hillary Clinton narrowly lost Florida in 2016, she walked away with no electoral votes but a substantial addition to her popular vote total. When she won in a landslide in California later that night, she further inflated her popular vote total but gained no more electoral votes than if she had won the state by a bare majority. If states individually abandoned the winner-takes-all system in favor of some kind of proportional allocation of electors to the competing candidates (and there are several variations on the proportional method), the gap between the national popular vote and the electoral vote would shrink and the size of presidential margins of victory would generally shrink as well.

The Electoral College formula of awarding each state its number of representatives in Congress creates a small bias. For very small states, even getting an elector based on seats in the House of Representatives can inflate their significance relative to their share of the national population. Of course, the two electors that each state receives to mirror its equal representation in the Senate likewise gives small states extra weight in the Electoral College. By contrast, the largest states are slightly underrepresented in the Electoral College. The effect is

[7] Only Maine and Nebraska have adopted a different rule. They allocate two electoral votes to the state's popular vote winner and one electoral vote to the popular vote winner in each congressional district.

[8] U.S. Const. art. II, § 1.

not large, but depending on how partisan preferences are distributed across the country those small effects can be consequential. Donald Trump's landslide victories in such small states as Wyoming, North Dakota, and South Dakota were far more beneficial in the Electoral College than they would have been under a national popular vote (though Hillary Clinton got her own bonus when blowing out Trump in Vermont, Delaware, and the District of Columbia). Clinton's massive advantage in large states like California, New York, and Illinois was somewhat diluted by the Electoral College formula (Trump's margin of victory was smaller in Republican-leaning big states like Texas, North Carolina, and Georgia). Swing states like Ohio, Florida, and Pennsylvania become particularly pivotal not only because they are competitive, but also because they are big and use the unit rule to allocate presidential electors. Narrow victories in Ohio, Florida, and Pennsylvania go a long way in the Electoral College, just as California and New York were once critical presidential battlegrounds.

Finally, the Constitution requires that a winning candidate must receive the votes of a "majority of the whole number of Electors appointed."[9] The official counting of the votes is done by the president of the U.S. Senate in a joint meeting of the Congress. Potentially, this gives Congress an important role to play in resolving disagreements over the outcome of elections and the validity of particular ballots, though no one seems very inclined to let Congress decide such questions as who won Florida in 2000 or whether the ballots of faithless electors should be counted. If no candidate wins a majority of the electoral votes, the House, voting by state (meaning all the members from the state cast ballots and the winning candidate gets the single vote from that state), chooses the president from the top three candidates, and the Senate chooses the vice president from the top two candidates.[10]

There are consequences to the requirement that the winning candidate assemble an actual majority in the Electoral College rather than simply winning the most votes of any candidate in the race. Any close election raises the specter that a candidate might fail to win a majority of the electoral votes and that the whole contest might

[9] U.S. Const. amend. XII.

[10] *Id.* In implicit recognition of the formation of political parties, the Twelfth Amendment altered the initial rule and separated the votes for presidential and vice-presidential candidates, rather than filling the vice presidency with the runner-up in the presidential race.

be thrown into the House for resolution. In 1824, the one instance of the House having to determine the winner of a four-candidate race fed Andrew Jackson's populist candidacy in 1828.[11] His supporters nursed the view that only a "corrupt bargain" in the House had elevated John Quincy Adams to the White House, despite Adams coming in second in both the popular and electoral votes. Jackson had won 38 percent of the presidential electors, far short of the required majority but distinctly ahead of Adams, who could claim only 32 percent of the electors.

No one is eager for the legitimacy crisis that would likely follow from the House being forced to choose the president in the modern era, but it is not hard to imagine potential scenarios. A close presidential election could conceivably lead to a tie vote in the Electoral College, throwing the contest to the House. Such an outcome on Election Day would undoubtedly put inordinate pressure on the electors to break the tie themselves, by a faithless elector switching his or her vote to avoid the fight in the House. An election dispute in one or more states similar to what happened in Florida in 2000 could force Congress to decide which, if any, electors to count in order to reach a majority.

A third-party candidate with a substantial base of support who drew strength from both parties could steal enough electoral votes to deny any candidate a majority. Former president Theodore Roosevelt won an astonishing 16 percent of the presidential electors in 1912, but he did so largely by stealing votes from his Republican successor, the incumbent William Howard Taft, allowing Democrat Woodrow Wilson to sail to an Electoral College victory despite winning just over 40 percent of the popular vote. In 1860, John C. Breckenridge, John Bell, and Stephen A. Douglas divided the South amongst themselves, but Abraham Lincoln's solid hold on the North allowed him to win a comfortable Electoral College victory with less than 40 percent

---

[11] The House also had to resolve the presidential election of 1800, when the Electoral College produced a tie between Democratic-Republican candidates Thomas Jefferson and Aaron Burr at a time when the electors did not cast separate ballots for the president and vice president. Federalist shenanigans in the House nearly derailed the first peaceful transfer of power between political parties, and the Twelfth Amendment was hastily adopted to avoid a recurrence of that scenario. In 1876, rather than directly resolving the contested election, Congress created a Federal Electoral Commission to reach some solution. The result was the Compromise of 1876 that elevated Republican Rutherford B. Hayes to the White House and ended Reconstruction by removing federal troops from the soon-to-be Democratic-dominated South.

of the popular vote. A third-party candidate with a geographically concentrated base of support could play the spoiler and deny any candidate a straight majority in the Electoral College. That was the worry the Dixiecrat revolts produced in the mid-20th century when Strom Thurmond in 1948 and George Wallace in 1968 both won a nontrivial number of electoral votes, though in neither case was it enough to drag the leading candidate below the majority threshold. The more recent candidacies of Ross Perot in 1992 and 1996 might have affected the outcome of the race, but he had neither the size of support nor the geographic concentration that would have been needed to translate his popular votes into electoral votes. Third-party candidates like Ralph Nader, Pat Buchanan, Gary Johnson, or Jill Stein might tilt the electoral map to favor one or the other of the two major parties, but they did not threaten the nightmare scenario of actually siphoning off enough electoral votes to deny a candidate a clean victory in the Electoral College.

One risk of dropping the unit rule and adopting more proportional allocation of electoral votes is that third-party candidates could have a much greater chance of claiming some electoral votes—potentially enough to throw the contest to the House. Faithless electors could not only change the outcome themselves, but could toss the contest to the House with enough defections from the majority candidate. This was the Hamilton Electors' most plausible goal in 2016. By encouraging Republican presidential electors to break their pledges to vote for Donald Trump and instead cast a ballot for a different Republican like then-Ohio governor John Kasich or former secretary of state Colin Powell, the Clinton supporters hoped to at least move the fight to the House of Representatives. (Republicans enjoyed a majority there too under the one-vote-per-state-delegation rule, and it seems unlikely that Republican legislators would have been willing to do what the Republican National Convention had not and deny Trump his apparent victory).

Though this be madness, there was a method to it—at least at the beginning. The delegates in Philadelphia had a difficult political problem to solve, and this was the best they could come up with at the time. The Articles of Confederation did not create a separate executive branch at all. The Revolutionary era state constitutions generally set up exceedingly weak governors, who were often selected by and dependent on the legislature and hemmed in by a constitutionally entrenched executive council. The Federalists seeking constitutional reform in 1787 wanted something different. The Virginia Plan that set the agenda for the convention proposed the creation of a federal executive, and James Wilson soon added that the executive should be "a single person." The Framers were prepared to create a single, powerful, and independent chief magistrate, and that raised the stakes on how that magistrate was to be selected, confounding most of the existing models.

Both the Virginia Plan and the rival New Jersey Plan proposed that the national executive be chosen by the national legislature. This was the dominant model in the states at the time. Even Massachusetts, which allowed for a popular vote for the governor, had the legislature serve as a fallback if no candidate won a clean majority after the popular balloting—and in the absence of political parties to winnow down the choices, or charismatic leaders to dominate the balloting, the legislature was likely to be the effective means for choosing the governor most of the time. Only New York allowed the individual who won the greatest number of votes from the general electorate to assume the governor's office, and the dominant presence of George Clinton assured early on that the state did not have to confront the problem of governors assuming office on the basis of only a small plurality of the vote.

The Virginia and New Jersey plans diverged on the key question of how the national legislature would itself be constituted. The Virginia Plan envisioned a national legislature based on popular representation, which meant a legislature, and thus a president, controlled by the larger states. The New Jersey Plan envisioned a national legislature based on equal state delegations like the Confederation Congress, which meant a legislature, and thus a president, more heavily influenced by the smaller states. The convention bogged down in trying to resolve the tension between those two perspectives until finally settling on the Connecticut Compromise that created a bicameral legislature that embodied both principles.

The Connecticut Compromise that settled the question of how Congress would be constituted became the foundation stone for selecting the president as well. The same small-state/big-state power-sharing arrangement needed to be replicated in the executive branch. Once the possibility of an executive council was taken off the table, the power-sharing became even more delicate and depended entirely on how the chief executive would be selected (and potentially removed). But when the Framers turned their attention to the executive, the problem of how to give the executive sufficient independence from the legislature came to the fore. James Madison and others worried that the central problem facing the American republic was one of "elective despotism" in the form of unchecked legislatures.[12] In the same way that state governors were subsumed to their legislatures, a national executive chosen by the national legislature risked becoming servile to the will of the legislature. Even worse, there was a serious risk of cabals, factions, and corruption if the legislature was entrusted with the power of selecting the executive.

The best solution to this problem seemed to be the creation of a temporary Congress. A temporary Congress could be constituted on the exact same basis as the regular Congress, preserving the Connecticut Compromise. At the same time, a temporary Congress would not have the ongoing interaction with the executive and with governance that tended to undermine the independence of the executive and the separation of powers. Even better, a temporary Congress that was geographically dispersed across the states would be much harder to bribe or influence, reducing the threat of corruption and intrigue. And thus was born the Electoral College, an ephemeral doppelganger of Congress.

Notably, the Framers in Philadelphia seemed to think of the Electoral College functionally as equivalent to "election by the people."[13] James Wilson suggested the basic idea as a means for making the executive and legislature "as independent as possible with each other, as well as of the States." Wilson was also optimistic that "Continental Characters will multiply as we more [and] more coalesce, so as to enable the electors in every part of the Union to know [and] judge of them." But most of the delegates feared that once the nation moved past the one obvious choice of George Washington, average voters would have a hard time evaluating any candidates beyond the prominent personalities in their own states.[14] Patrick Henry,

[12] The Federalist No. 48 (James Madison).

[13] James Madison, The Journal of the Constitutional Convention, in 4 The Writings of James Madison 62 (Gaillard Hunt ed., 1903).

[14] James Madison, The Journal of the Constitutional Convention, in 3 The Writings of James Madison 64 (Gaillard Hunt ed., 1903) (quoting James Wilson); Madison, *supra* note 13, at 367 (quoting Wilson).

George Clinton, and John Hancock had been able to dominate gubernatorial elections in their home states, but they were hardly the kind
of "Continental Characters" that would rally the voters in states at
the other end of the country. Presidential electors might be expected
to be more familiar with the less-celebrated figures from distant
states and more likely to unite behind a dominant candidate who
could command a majority. Connecticut's Roger Sherman expressed
the sentiment typical among convention delegates in thinking that
the people at large "will never be sufficiently informed of characters,
and besides will never give a majority of votes to any one man."[15]

The Electoral College promised to solve the representation problem (by mirroring the Connecticut Compromise), the executive independence problem (by giving the president a popular foundation),
the corruption problem (by dispersing the choice of the president
across the states), and the voter information problem (by filtering
the will of the people through a set of selected representatives). It
might be awkward and unfamiliar, but it was a clever solution to
the problems that were uppermost on the minds of the Founders. If
worst came to worst, Congress could always pick the president, just
like several state legislatures picked their governors.

It turned out that there was another solution to the voter-
information problem: political parties. Their emergence in the 1790s
quickly obviated the need for presidential electors as such. The Electoral College could still serve all its other functions even if the presidential electors themselves were reduced to mere cyphers. Political
parties created "Continental Characters" by winnowing the pool
of potential candidates and coalescing support around a favorite.
Party organizations could vet potential candidates and serve as an
alternative to the personal renown of individuals. Ultimately, party
organizations made it possible for someone other than "great and
striking men," as the Victorian observer James Bryce characterized
the "heroes of the Revolution," to rise to "this great office."[16] Party
organization made it possible for men like Martin Van Buren, James
K. Polk, Franklin Pierce, Abraham Lincoln, and Rutherford B. Hayes
to rise to the presidency even if they lacked the national reputation

---

[15] Madison, 3 Writings, *supra* note 14, at 450 (quoting Roger Sherman).

[16] James Bryce, 1 The American Commonwealth 100 (1888).

of a George Washington, Thomas Jefferson, Andrew Jackson, or Ulysses S. Grant.

Political parties were also publicity machines, and they could make sure that voters across the country were informed—or at least, informed enough—about their favored candidates. James Polk might not have been a "Continental Character" when he started, but the Democratic Party communications operation was going to make him one by the time of the election. Fundamentally, political parties and the Electoral College are rival mechanisms for accomplishing a presidential "election by the people." The emergence of a party-based democracy required that the political parties gain mastery over the presidential electors, and they did. That mastery was accomplished through pledged electors.

Party organizations and pledged electors in presidential elections emerged as soon as the country needed to find George Washington's successor. The parties published the names of slates of electors pledged to support the party's favored presidential candidate and eventually simply printed ballots listing those pledged electors that the voter could deposit in the ballot box. The parties did not put forward as electors "those who know most of Eminent characters & qualifications" and could deliberate on the most suitable possibilities for exercising the president's duties.[17] They put forward loyal party apparatchiks who could be trusted to cast their ballots in a predictable way.

But as soon as there were pledged electors there were also faithless electors who broke their pledges. As early as 1796, one aggrieved Federalist voter took to the newspapers to complain when a Pennsylvania elector, Samuel Miles, who was expected to vote for John Adams instead voted for Thomas Jefferson.

> When I vote for a legislator, I regard the privilege that he is to exercise his own judgment—It would be absurd to prescribe the delegation. But when I voted for the Whelan ticket, I voted for John Adams . . . . What, do I chuse Samuel Miles to determine for me whether John Adams or Thomas Jefferson is to be the fittest man for President of the United States? No—I chose him to *act*, not to *think*.[18]

---

[17] Madison, *supra* note 13, at 69 (quoting George Mason).

[18] "For the Gazette of the United States," Gazette of the United States (New York City), Dec. 15, 1796, at 3.

Miles was not a political nonentity. He had risen to the rank of brigadier general during the American Revolution and had served briefly as mayor of Philadelphia during the Washington administration. He was the kind of man the Framers might have imagined filling the role of presidential elector and exercising independent judgment to identify the fittest candidate for president. But, by the time of the third presidential election, men like Miles were not expected to think, they were simply expected to act so as to faithfully transmit the will of the voters.

The practice of pledged electors solidified in the 19th century. There were some faithless electors in the early decades, but they primarily cast surprise ballots for the vice presidency, not the presidency. The major exception was in 1872, when the Democratic presidential nominee Horace Greeley died after losing the November general election to the incumbent President Grant but before the presidential electors cast their ballots. When they assembled a few weeks later, most of Greeley's pledged electors cast ballots for someone still alive (three stuck with the dead man, and Congress refused to count those votes as valid). Constitutional treatise writers like Justice Joseph Story took care to point out that the "expectations" of the constitutional Framers had been "completely frustrated" by the "practical operation" of the Electoral College, since it "is notorious, that the electors are now chosen wholly with reference to particular candidates, and are silently pledged to vote for them."[19] Democratic Sen. Thomas Benton explained in his memoirs that "electors have no practical power over the election." They were "an instrument, bound to obey a particular impulsion; and disobedience to which would be attended with infamy, and with every penalty which public indignation could inflict."[20] The British jurist Albert Dicey observed that "the power of an elector to elect is as completely abolished by constitutional understandings in America" as the British monarch's power to veto legislation passed by Parliament. "For him to exercise his legal power of choice is considered a breach of political honour too gross to be committed by the most unscrupulous of politicians."[21] Former president Benjamin Harrison

---

[19] Joseph Story, 3 Commentaries on the Constitution of the United States 321 (1833).

[20] Thomas Hart Benton, 1 Thirty Years' View 37 (1854).

[21] Albert V. Dicey, Lectures Introductory to the Study of the Law of the Constitution 30 (1885).

posited that "an elector who failed to vote for the nominee of his party would be the object of execration, and in times of very high excitement might be the subject of a lynching."[22] The imagery that commentators used to explain the role of the presidential electors is telling. They were "a registering machine," "mere passive instruments," "mere automata," "a messenger," "a mere cogwheel," and "party dummies."[23] As might be expected, faithless electors were, with the exception of the Greeley episode, practically unknown in the 19th century.

When, at the beginning of the 20th century, state governments took from political parties the responsibility for printing ballots, they soon began to dispense with the bother of actually listing the names of candidates for the office of presidential elector. The electors were not only cogs in the machine, they became anonymous as well. The ballots distributed by the parties to the voters in the 19th century only listed that party's candidates for office. Voters did not need to do anything other than stuff the piece of paper in the box. When the government began printing the "long ballot" that listed all the candidates running for office, voters had to recognize and check off which candidates they supported. Listing the names of the presidential electors was simply confusing, and so governments started listing the presidential candidates instead. When voters checked the box for Theodore Roosevelt in November of 1912, they were silently (and often unknowingly) *really* voting for a slate of presidential electors who were pledged to vote for Theodore Roosevelt a month later. In 1932, when a Brooklyn lawyer sued the state of New York because newfangled voting machines left off the name of the presidential electors, the judge thought the state legislature knew what it was doing in authorizing the design of the new machines. It knew "that voters were no longer interested in the personnel of the group of electors."[24]

If presidential electors exercised free choice then "they would be the most important and powerful officials voted for" and obviously the people should know their names. But they did not exercise free

[22] Benjamin Harrison, The Constitution and the Administration of the United States of America 77 (1897).

[23] See Whittington, Faithless Electors, *supra* note 2, at 933.

[24] In the Matter of the Application of William A. Thomas v. Cohen, 262 N.Y.S. 320 (N.Y.S. Kings Co., 1933).

choice and thus it did not matter that no one knew who they were. The parties spent "vast sums" informing the electorate about the presidential candidates, and their "names were heralded throughout the land." The voters expected to see those familiar names on the ballot, and they expected to know who had won the election "before they retire for the night." Modern presidential electors had no "right to defy the will of the people." Their vote in December "is a mere formality now," and their identity was irrelevant. The legislature could reasonably leave their names off the ballot because no one was voting for *them* in any case. The New York judge speculated that presidential electors had such a "bounden duty" to adhere faithfully to their pledge that a court might issue a mandamus to direct them if they "attempted to disregard that duty."[25]

For most of its history, the nation has relied on the threat of social sanction—and perhaps even physical violence—to keep the electors in line. Electors were carefully chosen for their loyalty, and everyone knew it would be a gross breach of honor to break their pledge to vote for their party's candidate. Those factors still play a dominant role. It is no accident, for example, that California election law empowers each Democratic candidate for the House and the Senate to "designate one presidential elector" to be advanced by the state Democratic Party chairperson, and that the individuals often chosen to fulfill that honor are close family members, friends, and associates to those Democratic congressional candidates.[26] Then–House Minority Leader Nancy Pelosi's daughter, Christine, was a prominent member of the Hamilton Electors movement in 2016, though she herself faithfully voted for Clinton when the California presidential electors assembled on December 19. Christine Pelosi's primary qualification for being an elector is that she is Nancy Pelosi's daughter and could be trusted to do what she was told. Pennsylvania cuts out the middleman and empowers the presidential nominee him or herself to name the electors.[27]

When the parties internally fractured in the 20th century, party loyalty no longer seemed to be enough. Faithless electors, once practically unknown, became more common and, in some cases, more

---

[25] *Id.*

[26] Cal. Elec. Code § 7100.

[27] 25 Pa. Cons. Stat. § 2878.

organized. States began to experiment with laws designed to legally bind presidential electors to their pledges. When former president Roosevelt announced an independent challenge to incumbent president Taft in 1912, several of the presidential electors chosen by the Nebraska Republican Party were subsequently nominated by the state Progressive Party to serve as Roosevelt electors. The state GOP demanded that those rogue Roosevelt electors be removed and replaced by Taft loyalists, and the state supreme court agreed. The court thought that the "candidates had, by their acts, vacated their places as republican presidential electors," and the party central committee had the right to fill those vacancies. A voter who marked his ballot for Taft was entitled to a presidential elector who would faithfully vote for Taft, and an elector who announced that he would do otherwise was behaving in a manner "incompatible" with the office of a Republican Party presidential elector.[28] When "Dixiecrats" refused to take the pledge to vote for the presidential nominee of the national convention, the U.S. Supreme Court held that the state could properly refuse to certify those individuals as candidates for the office of presidential elector.[29]

In that 1952 case, *Ray v. Blair*, the Court approved a state-required pledge but left open the question of what the state could do if a presidential elector agreed to take a pledge and then violated it. Many states adopted such a pledge requirement, and they soon began to add teeth to encourage fidelity to the pledge, imposing civil fines on electors who broke their pledge, or, in a couple states, making pledge-breaking a criminal offense. A few states specified that the unwillingness of an elector to vote in accord with the pledge created a vacancy to be immediately filled with a new elector willing and able to cast the appropriate vote.[30]

II. Donald Trump and the "Hamilton Electors"

Even as faithless electors became more common in the 20th century, they remained primarily curiosities. Electors on occasion broke their pledges to make an idiosyncratic symbolic gesture, as when

---

[28] State ex rel. Neb. Republican State Central Comm. v. Wait, 138 N.W. 159 (Neb. 1912).

[29] Ray v. Blair, 334 U.S. 214 (1952).

[30] Zachary J. Shapiro, Free Agency: The Constitutionality of Methods that Influence a Presidential Elector's Ability to Exercise Personal Judgment, 26 J.L. & Pol'y 395 (2018).

a Republican elector in 1972 voted for the Libertarian Party candidates, a 1976 Republican elector voted for Ronald Reagan, and a 2000 Democratic elector cast a blank ballot to protest the District of Columbia's lack of congressional representation. Those gestures were individual, disorganized, and specifically intended not to affect the outcome of the election (though if 251 of Richard Nixon's 520 pledged electors in 1972 thought they were playing with house money they could have accidentally brought him below the required majority threshold while casting their ballots for alternative candidates). A modicum of coordination is useful even when playing the free spirit.

All that changed in 2016. Real-estate developer and television celebrity Donald Trump had won his long-shot bid for the Republican nomination for president, but few thought he could win the general election against Democratic nominee Hillary Clinton. Nonetheless, Trump threaded the needle and won just enough votes in the right places to cobble together an Electoral College majority. Clinton supporters were in dismay and denial. Activists launched a "Hail Mary" attempt to give Clinton the White House anyway by lobbying Republican presidential electors to break their pledge. Some pitched the idea that the electors should cast their ballots for the national popular vote winner, regardless of their pledge to vote for the statewide popular vote winner—in other words, Republican electors should vote for Clinton. Others suggested that presidential electors should refuse to vote for someone who was uniquely unfit for the presidency and should vote for anyone but Trump. Still others argued that Russia had stolen the election and that presidential electors should refuse to vote for a candidate who had not legitimately won a free and fair election.

A small group of Democratic presidential electors—the aforementioned "Hamilton Electors"—argued that pledges were inconsistent with our constitutional design. Presidential electors were constitutionally obligated, they said, to "vote their conscience," as presidential aspirant Ted Cruz had similarly urged the delegates at the Republican National Convention to do a few months earlier. In selling the Constitution to the skeptical ratifiers of New York, Alexander Hamilton had predicted that the odd device of the Electoral College "affords a moral certainty, that the office of President will never fall to the lot of any man who is not in an eminent degree endowed with the requisite qualifications."[31] The Hamilton Electors glossed this prediction as a claim that the Electoral College should act as a "constitutional failsafe" when the voters failed to choose a person eminently endowed with the requisite qualifications.

An extraordinarily intense and public lobbying campaign produced a historic number of faithless electors in 2016. It did not, however, deny Donald Trump the presidency. Two Trump electors in Texas cast ballots for other candidates (John Kasich and former Texas House member Ron Paul). A Clinton elector in Hawaii voted for Sen. Bernie Sanders. Three Clinton electors in Washington state voted for Colin Powell and another voted for activist Faith Spotted Eagle. Other Clinton electors attempted to cast ballots for other candidates, but a vote in Maine for Bernie Sanders was declared out of order, and electors in Colorado and Minnesota were replaced when they attempted to vote for John Kasich and Bernie Sanders, respectively.

After the election was over, two lawsuits were filed challenging laws meant to bind presidential electors to their pledges. Colorado authorizes its secretary of state to replace a presidential elector in the case of a "vacancy," and "refusal to act" is one ground for declaring a vacancy. Refusing to adhere to the pledge was interpreted as a refusal to act under the state statute. Michael Baca, a leading member of the Hamilton Electors group, had his vote for Kasich discarded, and he was replaced with a new elector who agreed to keep her pledge. He was joined in a federal lawsuit by two other Clinton electors who claimed that they felt intimidated into adhering to their pledge. The lawsuit sought to have the law declared invalid as a violation of their constitutional rights as presidential electors. In 2016, Washington state authorized its secretary of state to impose a $1,000 civil fine on faithless electors (the state subsequently adopted a law allowing the removal and replacement of a faithless elector). The three electors who voted for Kasich were each fined, and they filed a challenge in state court arguing that the fine was unconstitutional. The Tenth Circuit ultimately declared the Colorado statute unconstitutional, while the Washington Supreme Court upheld the Washington statute. The cases were consolidated at the U.S. Supreme Court, which reversed the Tenth Circuit and affirmed the Washington court.

[31] The Federalist No. 68 (Alexander Hamilton).

III. The Majority and the Power of Appointment

The justices agreed that states could adopt measures to discourage faithless electors, but they disagreed on the source of that authority. Justice Elena Kagan, writing for a unanimous Court (although with concurrences), provided a rationale grounded in Article II and the Twelfth Amendment, which together lay out the Electoral College's contours. Her approach accords with how the Washington Supreme Court approached the case and builds on what the U.S. Supreme Court had said in *Ray*.

In upholding states' power to require that presidential electors take a pledge to vote for the party nominee, the *Ray* Court rejected the argument that "the Twelfth Amendment demands absolute freedom for the elector to vote his own choice."[32] The Court was influenced by the "long-continued practical interpretation of the constitutional propriety of an implied or oral pledge of his ballot by a candidate for elector," and thought that practice had implications for the validity of states requiring such a pledge. The majority in *Ray* was not very specific, however, about where states got the power to require such pledges. The question concerned how political parties organized their primary elections that would eventually lead to the designation of a slate of electors. That the case arose out of Alabama made it perhaps easier: The Court was inclined to let states bolster a party's ability to exclude candidates from office who were not committed to that party's principles and organization, unless there was a strong countervailing constitutional rule like the one against racial discrimination.

But the two dissenters in *Ray*, Robert Jackson and William O. Douglas, worried that presidential electors "performed a federal duty" and thought the state could no more dictate how they performed that duty than it could instruct a U.S. senator how to conduct his. Presidential electors might have refrained from exercising free choice for a long period of time, but the dissenters did not think the "powers and discretions granted to federal officials by the Federal Constitution can be forfeited by the Court for disuse."[33] "A political practice which has its origin in custom must rely upon custom for its sanctions."[34]

---

[32] 334 U.S. at 228.

[33] *Id.* at 233 (Jackson, J., dissenting).

[34] *Id.*

Since, in *Chiafalo*, Washington state was attempting to legally sanction presidential electors for how they performed their federal duty, the question of whether the political custom of pledged electors could be enforced by the state as mandatory required an answer that the *Ray* Court had not provided. Perhaps the *Ray* majority was implying that the "practical interpretation" of the Constitution had, through long usage, altered the nature of electors' federal duty. But the majority had not quite said that, and such a claim would raise thorny conceptual puzzles for how we should understand constitutional change.

Kagan found the state's authority to sanction faithless electors in the power to appoint those electors in the first place. When considering whether state legislatures could use a district method of voting for presidential electors rather than a statewide slate, the Supreme Court in *McPherson v. Blacker* emphasized that the Constitution empowered the state legislatures with "the broadest power of determination" for how presidential electors would be chosen.[35] Kagan added that if the state legislature can appoint an elector in any manner it chooses, then it must also have the "power to condition his appointment—that is, to say what the elector must do for the appointment to take effect."[36] Establishing conditions of appointment allowed for such now-uncontroversial practices as requiring that electors take a pledge or live within the state. Less clear is the idea that the power to subsequently impose sanctions goes along with the power to condition the appointment. If the state can require that an elector "live in the State or qualify as a regular voter during the relevant time period," does that also mean that the state can impose a civil fine or criminal penalty if an elector were to move out of the state in the days before he is to cast his ballot?[37] There seems to be a lot packed into the notion of conditions on appointment that Kagan did not bother to unpack and explain.

There was an additional issue of whether a state's sanctions of faithless electors violates some countervailing constitutional rule. Kagan echoed earlier decisions in pointing out that pledged electors are consistent with the constitutional language setting up the

---

[35] McPherson v. Blacker, 146 U.S. 1, 27 (1892).

[36] Chiafalo v. Washington, 140 S. Ct. 2316, 2324 (2020).

[37] *Id.*

Electoral College. She added that the constitutional text could have been written differently, as the Maryland and Kentucky constitutions were in setting up somewhat similar systems, to explicitly require that the electors deliberate and exercise independent judgment. Kagan was unpersuaded that terms like "elector" and "vote" necessarily require independence of action since we recognize the possibility of pledged votes in a variety of contexts. The presidential electors could be free agents, but the text of the Constitution does not require them to be. The state could not violate an independent constitutional rule by making it a condition of appointment that an elector be white or Christian, but Kagan saw no bar to an elector being required to vote in a specific way.

IV. The Concurrence and the Tenth Amendment

Justice Clarence Thomas, joined partially by Justice Neil Gorsuch, took a different approach. Thomas thinks the question of where the state gets the authority to sanction faithless electors is much simpler: he does not need to find that authority in the text of the Constitution at all. Instead, he thinks the authority should be understood as part of the powers the Tenth Amendment reserves to the states.

That logic is consistent with Thomas's dissent in the congressional-term-limits case in 1995. In *U.S. Term Limits, Inc. v. Thornton*, the majority of the Court held that a state's scheme of excluding long-serving incumbent members of Congress from the ballot was effectively adding new qualifications for congressional office to the ones listed in the text of the Constitution.[38] Thomas dissented, arguing that a state held a reserved power to add such qualifications and nothing in the Constitution barred it. The majority thought the state's authority over the election of members of Congress could arise only from the Constitution itself. Since the states had no pre-existing authority over federal officeholders prior to the ratification of the very Constitution that created those federal offices, then regulating those offices could not be among the powers "reserved" by the Tenth Amendment.

Thomas argued that Kagan's approach does not work. The Constitution provides that states may appoint presidential electors "in such Manner as the Legislature thereof may direct." Thomas would

[38] U.S. Term Limits, Inc. v. Thornton, 514 U.S. 779 (1995).

characterize this as a manner-of-appointment clause, which would not extend to other substantive aspects of appointments. State legislatures "set the approach for selecting Presidential electors," but selecting the manner by which electors are chosen does not give the states an authority to impose substantive conditions on their appointment or direct how electors conduct their duties after they have been appointed. The majority largely ignored the specification of a manner of selection. As a consequence, the majority gives the whole provision a reading that is at odds with how the power was discussed at the Founding and with the parallel provision of the Constitution empowering Congress to regulate the "Times, Places and Manner of holding Elections for Senators and Representatives." If the power to regulate the manner of holding federal elections extends only to procedural regulations, then it would seem that the power to choose the manner of selecting electors likewise extends only to procedural regulations. The legislature can specify who gets to select the presidential electors and how the selection process should occur, but that is different from controlling what the selected electors then do.

Thomas thinks it is important that some states do not purport to tie their directives of how electors vote to the conditions of their appointment. Some states claim the authority to penalize electors for violating the pledge they take as a condition of being appointed, but others simply declare that presidential electors have a legal duty to vote in a particular way. Kagan dismissed this as "small semantic differences" of no consequence, but Thomas certainly seems right that the states seem to be saying something different about why presidential electors are expected to vote for the winner of the statewide ballot. In all likelihood, the states acted under a variety of different theories about where the electors' duty to be faithful comes from. Plainly, some states rejected the rationale that the Court's majority ultimately embraced. Kagan effectively asserted that states like California and New Mexico have taken the wrong approach but that their mistake can be ignored under the legal fiction that their statutes can be read as if they were imposing conditions on appointment. That might be a conceivable solution given what the Court has done, but Thomas is right to highlight the novelty and awkwardness of the majority's approach.

Thomas, like Kagan, does not think the expectations of the Framers that the presidential electors would be free agents is embodied in the Constitution as written. The Framers might have expected the Electoral College to work that way, but they did not require it to work that way. Therefore, Thomas agrees that there is no constitutional bar to pledged electors or even to legal efforts to enforce the fidelity of pledged electors. In his reading, the states have the authority to punish electors for violating their public oaths as part of their general reserved power, just as states could punish oath-breaking in other contexts. Unfortunately, Thomas's approach is not only at odds with the term-limits precedent, but it also leaves a number of questions unanswered. If the states have a reserved authority to direct how presidential electors fulfill their duties, do they also have a reserved authority to direct how members of Congress fulfill theirs? Can the state legislature issue instructions to senators as to how they should vote on an upcoming bill and impose fines if the senators don't vote accordingly? Even if state legislatures can direct how presidential electors vote, can they discard a ballot and declare it invalid if the electors defy the wishes of the state legislature? Thomas seems right that the power to choose the manner of selection does not easily encompass the imposition of substantive constraints on how those selected must conduct their duties, but his own solution to the problem does not easily account for the states' actions in Washington and Colorado either.

V. Implications

The constitutional issues surrounding the Electoral College are sufficiently far off the beaten path that this case has fewer ramifications for general constitutional law than most Supreme Court decisions. The presidential selection system rarely generates justiciable issues, and the constitutional text and the justices' conceptual tools used to resolve this case are unlikely to play a major role in future cases. Constitutionally speaking, this case is relatively self-contained, which freed the justices from some of the considerations that weigh down the Court's average constitutional case. Even so, it's worth recognizing some broader implications for how the justices resolved the case.

First, note that no justice took the path suggested by the New York judge who resolved the voting-machine challenge in 1933. Essentially, that judge embraced the notion of a living constitution that could be interpreted to alter the terms of the Electoral College such that electors were under a judicially enforceable duty to vote for the candidate who won the statewide vote. Such argumentation would not be outlandish under some theories of constitutional adjudication, and it is not hard to imagine judges at various points in history embracing it, yet it got no traction on the current Court. Kagan took into account our evolving constitutional practices, but she did not suggest that changing times can alone create judicially enforceable duties on electors or alter the nature of their office. The Constitution, properly interpreted, gives electors discretion in how they vote. The relevant question for the Court was whether the states had adequate constitutional authority to impose limits on that discretion, not whether the Constitution had evolved such that the electors had lost discretion that they once possessed. The "living" components of the Constitution were properly cabined.

Second, the justices avoided unsettling the status quo. The binding laws that states have adopted in the attempt to enforce elector fidelity are relatively new and, but for the Court's intervention, might have been mostly symbolic. Still, the symbolism is potentially important. Such laws came into vogue precisely because faithless electors seemed to be a growing problem and the old ways were not seen as sufficient to deter them. The binding laws might not be the most reasonable, effective, or even constitutional means for discouraging faithless electors, but the goal of discouraging faithless electors is an admirable one, and the binding laws might be marginally helpful in preventing the disaster of a group of faithless electors attempting to change the result of a presidential election.

More troubling, the binding laws in themselves might not be very effective in deterring faithless electors but striking down the binding laws might itself have encouraged more faithless electors in the future. If we picture these laws as primarily symbolic and expressive, then we might think they serve the salutary purpose of bolstering the social norms surrounding electors' pledges and reinforcing the idea that faithless electors are doing something dishonorable, something worthy of social scorn and ostracism (if not necessarily imprisonment). If the Court had never entered into the arena—or if Washington had never fined the faithless electors in 2016—then the binding laws might have stood quietly by in the shadows, untested as coercive tools but operative as political messaging.

Unfortunately, once the courts had committed themselves to resolving such cases, they were in a difficult spot. If they struck down the laws, they might have inadvertently telegraphed the message to future presidential electors that faithlessness is tolerable, acceptable, or even desirable. No matter how carefully the justices attempted to couch their opinions, the bottom-line signal might have further undermined political norms against faithless electors and made a constitutional crisis ever so slightly more likely. That was a big risk to run, without a lot of countervailing benefit, and undoubtedly would have discouraged the justices from blithely striking down these laws if they had an alternative.

Notably, the justices did tend to positively reinforce the message that electors should be faithful, not faithless. The implicit message of the judgment was to affirm the message of the state legislatures that pledges matter and that presidential electors should not go rogue. Merely upholding the binding statutes tends to reinforce that message. In his concurrence, Thomas did not comment on the responsibility of electors to be faithful to their pledge. In her opinion for the Court, however, Kagan did emphasize the point and make the message more explicit. She highlighted the fact that presidential electors had long been understood to be "trusty transmitters of other people's decisions" and that a "tradition more than two centuries old" insisted that the "electors are not free agents."[39] She concluded with the fundamental point that the state binding laws are intended to convey: The states hoped to "impress on electors their role as agents to others" and instructs them "that they have no ground for reversing the vote of millions of its citizens."[40] And finally, "that direction accords with the Constitution—as well as with the trust of a Nation that here, We the People rule."[41] She might have hit that theme even harder, but the Court was clear that rogue electors are inherently anti-democratic and at odds with the spirit of American constitutional democracy. The Court gave no credence to the idea that there was something noble and heroic about the Hamilton Electors' project and neither did that project finally breathe life into the American constitutional scheme. The Hamilton Electors were

[39] Chiafalo, 140 S. Ct. at 2328.
[40] Id.
[41] Id.

seeking to overturn a democratic election by construing their duty as more grandiose and significant than anyone understands it to be or than they were appointed to exercise.

Third, it is also worth considering the fact that the justices did decide to resolve the case on the merits. None of the justices bothered to ask whether these cases even belonged before the Court, which is no real surprise given that the Court had scheduled them for argument in the first place and has generally embraced its own supremacy in resolving all variety of constitutional questions. The fact that the Tenth Circuit had struck down Colorado's binding laws did force the Court's hand to some degree, requiring it either to act or leave such laws in other states sitting under a constitutional cloud.

The Washington case presented the more obvious justiciable controversy that did not give the justices an easy out. Washington imposed a civil fine on the electors, and they have standing to challenge the constitutionality for such a fine. States have refrained from imposing such a fine in the past, but it seems doubtful that Washington's Republican secretary of state was concocting a collusive lawsuit to test the constitutionality of such binding laws. Washington seemed sincere in hoping to deter future faithless electors by making an example of these highly visible ones. The Court could have declined certiorari and let the Washington court's judgment stand. If the justices thought Washington had gotten the constitutional law wrong in that case, it would have been unfortunate for both the electors who had to pay the fine and for the Constitution, but at least the U.S. Supreme Court would not have set any precedents one way or the other. It would not have been the first time that the justices thought the enforcement of a constitutionally dubious state law was not worth their attention just yet. (Of course, if the justices thought that Washington was correct—as it appears that they do—then they might have been eager to reach out to take the case in order to put their own, even more visible stamp of approval on such laws.)

The justiciability of the Colorado case is more problematic. The justices could have vacated the Tenth Circuit's judgment without reaching the merits of the case. Such a move might have breathed some life into the political question doctrine and could have emphasized that the judiciary does not always have to jump into constitutional disputes. Colorado did not fine the faithless electors in 2016.

It removed and replaced Michael Baca as an elector and did not count his vote. Two other electors joined the suit because they felt "intimidated" into voting a particular way. Despite the election having long since passed, erstwhile elector Michael Baca wanted nominal monetary damages for his removal. As one amicus pointed out, allowing the Baca suit to proceed was an open invitation to collusive suits seeking advisory opinions that stretched the boundaries of federal jurisdictional statutes.[42] Moreover, there is a good argument that Congress is the proper venue for determining whether an elector's ballot is valid.[43] If Colorado had erred in trying to exclude a valid electoral vote, Baca could have sought to have the error corrected by Congress when the electors' votes were counted. He did not attempt to do so, and Congress accepted the vote of Baca's replacement.

The Court could have reasonably asserted that the matter of the validity of electoral votes is a political question the Constitution entrusts to Congress, and therefore the judiciary should not interfere. Such a move by the Court might have had broader ramifications. It might have helped funnel such disputes into Congress rather than the courts, and it might have nudged Congress into taking its constitutional responsibilities more seriously while reminding everyone that the courts are not the only constitutional interpreters in the American system. Alas, the modern Court is not very inclined to admit that some constitutional questions are outside its purview. The fact that the Court issued only a *per curiam* order in the Colorado case further swept under the rug the justiciability questions that could have been raised and addressed in a full opinion.

Fourth, the outcome of the faithless elector cases might ease the path a bit for the National Popular Vote Interstate Compact. Some states have pursued such a compact—valid only if signatory states control a majority of electoral votes—which would award their presidential electors to whichever presidential candidate wins the national popular vote. The goal is to effectively replace the Electoral College formula through voluntary state action rather than through constitutional amendment. One challenge to the success of such a

[42] Brief of Professor Michael T. Morley as Amicus Curiae in Support of Neither Side, Colo. Dep't of State v. Baca, 140 S. Ct. 2316 (2020) (No. 19-465).

[43] Brief of Professor Derek T. Muller as Amicus Curiae in Support of Neither Party, Colo. Dep't of State v. Baca, 140 S. Ct. 2316 (2020) (No. 19-465).

compact, however, is how to ensure that presidential electors actually cast their ballots in this way. The current system aligns the preferences of a state's electors with the preferences of its voters by delegating the appointment of electors to the political parties and elevating electors pledged to vote for the presidential candidate who won the state's popular vote. If a Democrat wins the national popular vote but a Republican wins the state popular vote, Republican electors would have little inclination to vote for the Democratic presidential candidate. States would need both to detach the slate of electors from party control and to create a binding pledge directing the electors to vote for the winner of the national popular vote. If states have no legal capacity to discourage faithless electors, that task becomes even more complicated. The political and legal road to a national popular vote is still not easy,[44] but the Court's decision removes one potential constitutional roadblock.

Fifth, the Court's endorsement of strong state laws binding electors' votes potentially opens the door to a great deal of mischief. Kagan tried to close that door by emphasizing that the state cannot require electors to do something that contradicts some other constitutional rule, but it is not clear that that principle can do all the work Kagan wants it to do. If states can direct how electors cast their ballots, then a host of possibilities might tempt state legislators. Can states require electors to vote only for presidential candidates who have released their tax returns? Can states require electors to vote only for presidential candidates who have previously held elective office? Can states require electors to vote only for Democrats, regardless of the outcome of the statewide or national balloting? Can states require electors to vote only for presidential candidates who have endorsed a specific policy platform? Can states require electors to vote only for presidential candidates who are part of a gender-balanced or racially diverse ticket? In a footnote, the Court says that states cannot adopt a condition of appointment "that effectively imposes new requirements on presidential candidates."[45] But what does that mean, and how can it be reconciled with the conditions that the Court is explicitly allowing? The pledge that electors will only vote

[44] See, e.g., U.S. Const. art. I, § 10 ("No State shall, without the Consent of Congress, . . . enter into any Agreement or Compact with another State").

[45] Chiafalo, 140 S. Ct. at 2324 n.4.

for presidential candidates who are a major party nominee and won the statewide balloting would seem to effectively impose new, extra-textual requirements on presidential candidates. The Court might soon find itself having to explain why a pledge to vote for a candidate who has been endorsed by a political party is not an unconstitutional qualification on presidential candidates but a pledge to vote for a candidate who has released his tax returns is.

Finally, the Court did not grapple with the differences among binding laws on the books, including the different approaches Washington and Colorado took. Washington levied a civil fine on its faithless electors. Colorado declared that Baca had vacated his office by crossing out a name on his printed ballot and writing in the name of John Kasich. Maine declared a ballot invalid and directed the faithless elector to vote again. Baca had announced his intention to violate his pledge weeks ahead of the meeting of the electors. It is imaginable that Colorado could have removed Baca as soon as he announced his intention to violate his pledge, on the same logic that Nebraska used to remove the Roosevelt electors in 1912. If taking and adhering to a pledge is a condition of appointment, then replacing electors who refuse to take a pledge or announce that they no longer regard themselves as bound by their pledge seems to fall squarely within the logic of the majority's reasoning. It is less clear that a state can retrospectively sanction electors for violating the conditions of their appointment or discard ballots that are inconsistent with the conditions of appointment of the electors. The Court did not bother to discuss the details of what measures states can take to deter faithless electors but sweepingly suggested that any measures are acceptable (presumably so long as they do not contradict some other constitutional rule).

If in the future a state's presidential electors cast their ballots for the winner of the statewide vote, and the secretary of state discards their ballots and replaces them all with electors who would vote for the winner of the national popular vote, the Court might be confronted with a case seeking a determination as to which set of ballots are the lawful ones. The Court seems to have committed itself to the view that the state legislature can direct the secretary of state to take such an action during the meeting of the duly appointed presidential electors. But the explanation is rather thin as to why that is constitutionally appropriate.

* * *

In an effort to overturn a presidential election, the Hamiton Electors launched a dangerous campaign that flew in the face of two centuries of constitutional practice. But just because faithless electors are wrong does not mean that states have all the legal tools that they might need to prevent such infidelity. The Court has papered over the problem, and perhaps that is good enough, but the presence of willful human beings in the Electoral College remains a constitutional difficulty that could someday provoke a crisis.

"Still [Not] Crazy after All These Years": *Kahler v. Kansas* and the Intersection of Criminal and Constitutional Law

Paul J. Larkin Jr. *

Law schools customarily offer separate courses in criminal law and procedure, perhaps because they appear to raise distinct issues regarding the justification for and the operation of the criminal justice system—like the difference between the highway rules-of-the-road and the guardrails. Occasionally, however, a case poses an issue that stands astride the two disciplines. It asks society to decide whether and how the government may treat someone who, through no fault of his own, committed a horrendous crime, perhaps one that killed several other people, without knowing that his conduct was wrongful. The decision last term by the Supreme Court of the United States in *Kahler v. Kansas* was, ostensibly at least, one such case.[1]

Kahler involved the insanity defense. A criminal defendant can raise a host of defenses to prove his innocence or reduce his responsibility for a charged crime.[2] Insanity, however, excites the most academic and popular interest.[3] One reason might be that insanity,

* John, Barbara & Victoria Rumpel Senior Legal Research Fellow, The Heritage Foundation, M.P.P. George Washington University, 2010; J.D., Stanford Law School, 1980; B.A., Washington & Lee University, 1977. The views expressed are my own and do not represent any official position of The Heritage Foundation. John G. Malcolm, Zack Smith, and GianCarlo Canaparo provided helpful comments on an earlier version of this article. Any mistakes are mine (and my apologies to Paul Simon for toying with his song title).

1 140 S. Ct. 1021 (2020).

2 See, e.g., 1 & 2 Paul H. Robinson, Criminal Law Defenses (1984).

3 See, e.g., Richard J. Bonnie, John C. Jeffries, Jr. & Peter W. Low, A Case Study in the Insanity Defense: The Trial of John W. Hinckley, Jr. (3d ed. 2008); Herbert Fingarette & Ann Fingarette Hasse, Mental Disabilities and Criminal Responsibility (1979); Abraham S. Goldstein, The Insanity Defense 19 (1967); Norval Morris, Madness and the Criminal Law (1982).

like crime, has been with us since our earliest days.[4] Another is that, while the mentally ill have always been an object of fear and fascination, they are even more so now since the deinstitutionalization movement of the 1970s shifted them from mental institutions onto public streets, parks, and subways in places like San Francisco, Los Angeles, Seattle, and New York City.[5] Finally, some of the people who asserted the insanity defense—such as Ted Bundy, Kenneth Bianchi, Ed Gein, Andrea Yates, John Wayne Gacy, and Jeffrey Dahmer—committed unspeakable crimes, including ghastly torture or serial murders, that lent themselves to professional, public, or media fascination.[6] Whatever the reason, cases involving an insanity plea touch on issues concerning who should be deemed "mad" rather than "bad," how the criminal process should distinguish the one from the other, and what we should do with people who wind up in each category. The answers come freighted with normative judgments, but also require us to consider how our legal system should implement our underlying values. This article will describe how *Kahler* answered those questions and what those answers signify for the insanity defense and the criminal law.

In *Kahler*, the Court was asked whether Kansas's statutory redefinition of the insanity defense was unconstitutional. In most states, a defendant can claim that a severe mental illness kept him from knowing either (1) what he was doing at the time of the crime

---

[4] See, e.g., 1 Samuel 21:12–15 (King James) (pretending to be insane, David pounded his head on the city gate and foamed at the mouth); Mark 5:1–20 (King James) (Jesus interacted with a man described as "possessed with the devil" but whose symptoms closely resemble ones characteristic of mental illness); Andrew Scull, Madness in Civilization: A Cultural History of Insanity from the Bible to Freud, from the Madhouse to Modern Medicine (2015); Daniel L. Robinson, Wild Beasts & Idle Humors: The Insanity Defense from Antiquity to the Present (1998).

[5] See, e.g., Rael Jean Isaac & Virginia C. Armat, Madness in the Streets: How Psychiatry and the Law Abandoned the Mentally Ill (1990); D.J. Jaffee, Insane Consequences: How the Mental Health Industry Fails the Mentally Ill (2017); E. Fuller Torrey, The Insanity Offense: How America's Failure to Treat the Seriously Mentally Ill Endangers Its Citizens (2008); Clayton E. Cramer, Madness, Deinstitutionalization, and Murder, 13 Engage 37 (2012).

[6] See, e.g., David Abrahamsen, Confessions of Son of Sam (1985); Donald T. Lunde & Jefferson Morgan, The Die Song: Journey into the Mind of a Murderer (1980); Donald Singleton, "In Chilling Letter, Son of Sam Tells Jimmy Breslin 'You Will See My Handiwork,'" N.Y. Daily News, June 4, 1977, https://www.nydailynews.com/news/crime/son-sam-not-asleep-article-1.3215974.

(a cognitive impairment defense) or (2) that his conduct was wrongful (a normative impairment defense). Kansas defines insanity differently. There, a defendant can offer evidence that a mental disease denied him the ability to form the mental state that Kansas law requires for proof of guilt (in the case of murder, premeditation on an intent to kill), but *not* that any such disease robbed him of the ability to know that his conduct was wrongful (in the case of murder, that it is immoral). A defendant can raise that claim at sentencing, just not at the guilt stage.[7] James Kraig Kahler argued that the Kansas insanity defense was unconstitutional because Anglo-American criminal law has always allowed a defendant to escape guilt by raising a normative impairment defense. The U.S. Supreme Court disagreed and rejected his argument.

Before analyzing *Kahler*, some background might be helpful—not the history of the insanity defense (that will come later), but the ongoing relationship between the U.S. Supreme Court and the state criminal justice systems and how *Kahler* fits into that model. Parts I and II will set that stage. Parts III and IV will then speculate about the significance of *Kahler* for the insanity defense and the criminal law, respectively. *Kahler* quite likely shut the door to constitutionalization of the centuries-old insanity defense but might have left the door slightly ajar for the reconsideration of some 20th-century substantive criminal law doctrines—in particular, strict liability.

I. A Different Type of Cold War

We have become accustomed to seeing the Supreme Court actively regulate the state criminal justice system through the U.S. Constitution. The Court began its superintendence in 1915 when it ruled in *Frank v. Magnum*, quite modestly enough, that a trial dominated by a lynch mob was not the "due process of law" envisioned by the Fourteenth Amendment.[8] Over time, the Court gradually expanded its management function by invoking the Due Process Clause to

---

[7] Kan. Stat. Ann. § 21-5209 (West 2020) ("It shall be a defense to a prosecution under any statute that the defendant, as a result of mental disease or defect, lacked the culpable mental state required as an element of the crime charged. Mental disease or defect is not otherwise a defense.").

[8] 237 U.S. 309, 335 (1915). *Frank* hardly stated a novel rule of law. See United States v. Shipp, 203 U.S. 563 (1906) (a criminal contempt prosecution against private parties who lynched a state prisoner protected by a federal court order).

condemn other, comparable abuses. Among them were trying the accused before a judge with a financial interest in the outcome, using perjured testimony against the defendant, coercing a confession from a suspect through torture, conducting a trial in a circus-like atmosphere, and forcing someone to trial where adverse pretrial publicity had poisoned the jury pool.[9]

The Court took its supervisory role to a new level in the 1960s, however, when it "incorporated" the Fifth, Sixth, and Eighth Amendments—the Bill of Rights provisions governing the operation of the federal criminal justice system—against the states.[10] Defendants in state cases now routinely raise Self-Incrimination, Confrontation, and Compulsory Process Clause claims regarding the admission or exclusion of evidence, along with (particularly in capital cases) Cruel and Unusual Punishment Clause challenges to their convictions or sentences.[11] Yet, that is not all. The Court has also invoked the Constitution to regulate the plea-bargaining process that results in 90-plus percent of the judgments of conviction in state

---

[9] See, e.g., Sheppard v. Maxwell, 384 U.S. 333, 335 (1966) (ruling that a defendant was denied a fair trial due to massive and prejudicial pretrial publicity); Estes v. Texas, 381 U.S. 532, 534–35 (1965) (ruling that live broadcasting of defendant's trial violated due process); Brown v. Mississippi, 297 U.S. 278 (1936) (ruling that the admission of a defendant's confession coerced from him via torture violates due process); Mooney v. Holohan, 294 U.S. 103 (1935) (ruling that the prosecution's knowing use of perjured testimony to incriminate the defendant would violate due process); Tumey v. Ohio, 273 U.S. 510, 514–15, 523 (1927) (holding unconstitutional a state law allocating a trial judge's compensation based on the number of convictions in his court).

[10] See, e.g., Duncan v. Louisiana, 391 U.S. 145, 148–49 (1968) (incorporating the Jury Trial Clause); Klopfer v. North Carolina, 386 U.S. 213, 222–23 (1967) (same, Speedy Trial Clause); Pointer v. Texas, 380 U.S. 400, 403 (1965) (same, Confrontation Clause); Gideon v. Wainwright, 372 U.S. 335, 342–45 (1963) (same, Counsel Clause); Robinson v. California, 370 U.S. 660 (1962) (same, the prohibition on cruel and unusual punishment). See generally Paul J. Larkin, Jr., The Lost Due Process Doctrines, 66 Cath. U. L. Rev. 293, 315 (2017). For a general explanation of the incorporation doctrine, see McDonald v. Chicago, 561 U.S. 742 (2010).

[11] See, e.g., Miller v. Alabama, 567 U.S. 460 (2012) (Cruel and Unusual Punishment Clause); Salinas v. Texas, 570 U.S. 178 (2017) (Self-Incrimination Clause); Williams v. Illinois, 567 U.S. 50 (2012) (Confrontation Clause); Taylor v. Illinois, 484 U.S. 400 (1988) (Compulsory Process Clause). Eighth Amendment claims in noncapital cases, by contrast, do not fare well. See, e.g., Lockyer v. Andrade, 538 U.S. 63 (2003); Ewing v. California, 538 U.S. 11 (2003); Harmelin v. Michigan, 501 U.S. 957 (1991); Hutto v. Davis, 454 U.S. 370 (1982).

criminal cases.[12] Even the state criminal appellate process has not escaped the Supreme Court's grasp. The Court has not demanded that the states establish an appellate review process (not yet at least),[13] but the Court has given the states orders how to apply the ones they have.[14] Finally, the Court has regulated the number of prisoners that a state may confine, as well as their treatment while in custody.[15] The result is that there is hardly any feature of the state criminal justice system not primarily governed by federal constitutional law.[16]

The Supreme Court constitutionalized the state criminal justice process for several reasons. One was the concern with racially motivated conduct by actors throughout the criminal justice system.[17] Another reason is that, at one time, the "third degree" was a standard practice in police interrogation.[18] The bottom line is that the Court did not trust state officials to enforce the law in anything approaching a fair, even-handed, responsible, humane manner. The Court saw

[12] See, e.g., Missouri v. Frye, 566 U.S. 134 (2012) (defense counsel has a duty to communicate a plea bargain offer to the defendant); Padilla v. Kentucky, 559 U.S. 356 (2010) (defense counsel must advise the accused that a guilty plea could result in his deportation); Santobello v. New York, 404 U.S. 257, 257–58, 262, 263 (1991) (due process requires a prosecutor to keep his end of a plea bargain resulting in a guilty plea); Brady v. United States, 397 U.S. 742 (1970) (plea-bargain-induced guilty pleas are not inherently coercive).

[13] See McKane v. Durston, 153 U.S. 684, 687–88 (1894) (a convicted defendant has no constitutional right to an appeal of his conviction and sentence).

[14] See, e.g., Roe v. Flores-Ortega, 528 U.S. 470 (2000) (defendant's attorney violated his client's rights by not filing a notice of appeal).

[15] See, e.g., Brown v. Plata, 563 U.S. 493 (2011) (prison overcrowding); Hutto v. Finney, 437 U.S. 678 (1978) (prison conditions that would have made Dante blanche, including use of a punishment device called a "Tucker telephone" that Alexander Graham Bell certainly did not invent); Estelle v. Gamble, 429 U.S. 97 (1976) (prisoners' medical treatment).

[16] See Edwin Meese III & Paul J. Larkin, Jr., Reconsidering the Mistake of Law Defense, 102 J. Crim. L. & Criminology 725, 733 (2012).

[17] See, e.g., Davis v. Mississippi, 394 U.S. 721 (1969) (holding unconstitutional the detention of a person for fingerprinting based simply on his race); Rogers v. Alabama, 192 U.S. 226 (1904) (ruling that the state may not discriminate based on race in the selection of grand jurors); Neal v. Delaware, 103 U.S. 370 (1880) (same, selection of trial jurors).

[18] See, e.g., Chambers v. Florida, 309 U.S. 227 (1940) (the defendant was subjected to days of intensive grilling before confessing); Brown v. Mississippi, 297 U.S. 278 (1936) (the defendant exhibited rope burns and scars from where he had been hung and whipped until he confessed).

the state systems, not as a mechanism for accomplishing impartial "justice," but as a Potemkin village or "pious charade."[19]

By contrast, the Supreme Court has left state substantive criminal law largely untouched. The Court has directed the local police to give a suspect the *Miranda* warnings that have become part of our popular culture, but the Court has not limited the crimes that the police can investigate. The Court has ordered state prosecutors to present their witnesses at trial, but the Court has not limited the charges that prosecutors can bring. Aside from cases involving an express provision of the Bill of Rights like the Free Speech Clause,[20] the states have been free to define the elements of crimes and the defenses that someone may raise largely without the Court's interference. The few times that the Supreme Court has addressed the relationship between the Constitution and state law have been in connection with some type of claimed mental illness, and the Court has refused to tell the states how they must define crimes and defenses.[21] The contrast is quite stark between the Court's readiness to tell the states what procedures they must follow and its willingness to accept whatever definitions of crimes states adopt.

Two factors might explain the Court's forbearance. One would be the Court's recognition that underlying a legislature's substantive decisions as to what conduct should be a crime are a community's moral judgments about what conduct should be *verboten*.[22] Communities have followed those judgments for at least a millennium[23]

---

[19] Anthony G. Amsterdam, The Supreme Court and the Rights of Suspects in Criminal Cases, 45 N.Y.U. L. Rev. 785, 806 (1970).

[20] See, e.g., Texas v. Johnson, 491 U.S. 397 (1989) (a state cannot make it a crime to burn the U.S. flag in protest).

[21] See, e.g., Clark v. Arizona, 548 U.S. 735 (2006) (rejecting the argument that due process requires a state to create a diminished capacity defense to a specific intent crime); Montana v. Egelhoff, 518 U.S. 37 (1996) (same, an intoxication defense); Powell v. Texas, 392 U.S. 514 (1968) (same, alcoholism); Leland v. Oregon, 343 U.S. 790, 798–801 (1952) (same, an "irresistible impulse" defense).

[22] See, e.g., Powell, 392 U.S. at 536 (plurality op.) (recognizing that the definitions of crimes and defenses reflect the "changing religious, moral, philosophical, and medical views of the nature of man").

[23] Paul J. Larkin, Jr. & GianCarlo Canaparo, Are Criminals Bad or Mad?— Premeditated Murder, Mental Illness, and Kahler v. Kansas, 43 Harv. J.L. & Pub. Pol'y 85, 126 (2020).

(likely more than one[24]), so there would be a crush of history for the Court to set aside were it to invent a new moral code. The other factor might be that the Court could invalidate those legislative decisions only by ruling that the community's underlying moral judgments are so alien to American society that they are not defensible on any remotely legitimate ground and can only be the product of the type of arbitrary exercise of state power that Magna Carta buried in 1215 or the Fourteenth Amendment sought to inter in 1868.[25] That judgment is a matter of *substantive*, not *procedural*, due process, however, and the Court has been reluctant to deny states the freedom to regulate their own affairs when no specific Bill of Rights provision stands in the way.[26] To be sure, the Court has trimmed the edges of state criminal law when a jurisdiction has legislated (or adjudicated) in a manner that denies the average person fair notice of what is a crime.[27] Nevertheless, the Court has (generally[28]) avoided butting heads with the states over what conduct can be labeled immoral and what immoral conduct can be punished through the criminal law rather than by administrative or civil sanctions or left entirely to private criticism, obloquy, and shunning. Perhaps the justices have been saving their gunpowder for different battles. Or maybe they have concluded that nullifying state crimes is a bridge too far.

That said, the Supreme Court has never surrendered its ability to second-guess a state legislature's judgment as to the content of its penal code. (Of course, even if the justices once had provided any such assurance, the changing membership of the Court over time would rob any such disclaimer of credibility.) After all, when the Court incorporated criminal procedure elements of the Bill of Rights against the states in the 1960s, the Court overturned its *own* earlier decisions ruling that those guarantees do *not* apply in state

---

[24] Exodus 20:1–17 (the Decalogue).

[25] Larkin & Canaparo, *supra* note 23, at 100–03.

[26] *Id.* at 110–11.

[27] See, e.g., Bouie v. City of Columbia, 378 U.S. 347 (1964) (holding unconstitutional a state court's unforeseeable retroactive expansion of an otherwise clear criminal law); Lanzetta v. New Jersey, 306 U.S. 451 (1939) (ruling that a statute making it a crime to be "a member of a gang" is unconstitutionally vague).

[28] But see *infra* note 84.

criminal prosecutions.[29] Even *Kahler* undertook a serious analysis of the constitutionality of the Kansas insanity defense rather than saying that its proper definition was entirely in the state's hands.[30] Accordingly, no one should confuse the Court's reluctance to define constitutional limits on criminal responsibility with a confession of its inability or unwillingness to do so. Put differently, "hasn't" doesn't mean "can't" or "won't." In fact, the Court's repeated interference with the states' operation of their criminal justice systems, along with the Court's episodic reliance on substantive due process principles to nullify substantive state moral judgments on contentious issues such as abortion,[31] always left open the possibility that five justices could be cobbled together to find a state criminal offense unconstitutional. A sort of Criminal Law Cold War existed between the Supreme Court and the states, and the war could presumably turn hot with the right triggering event.

II. *Kahler v. Kansas*: A "Hot" War Averted

Last term's decision in *Kahler v. Kansas* threatened to disrupt the status quo—not because the facts were sympathetic to Kahler; they clearly were not. Consider what he did.[32] Using a rifle, James Kraig Kahler intentionally, methodically, and systematically moved throughout the home where he knew that three family members and an in-law who had angered him would be present for Thanksgiving. As he found each target, he shot each one separately and at close range. There was no doubt about what had happened that night or that Kahler had pulled the trigger. The facts of the case also unquestionably established that Kahler acted intentionally and with premeditation, elements of the offense of murder under Kansas law. The case against Kahler was open and shut.

---

[29] See, e.g., Palko v. Connecticut, 302 U.S. 319 (1937) (no double jeopardy protection in state criminal cases), abrogated by Benton v. Maryland, 395 U.S. 784 (1969); Maxwell v. Dow, 176 U.S. 581 (1900) (no right to a jury trial in state criminal cases), abrogated by Duncan v. Louisiana, 391 U.S. 145 (1968).

[30] As the Court did when it rejected a defendant's claim that he had a constitutional right to an appeal of his conviction and sentence. See McKane, 153 U.S. at 687–88.

[31] See, e.g., Whole Woman's Health v. Hellerstedt, 136 S. Ct. 2292 (2016); Roe v. Wade, 410 U.S. 113 (1973).

[32] Larkin & Canaparo, *supra* note 23, at 93–94, 124–26.

That was what posed the threat to constitutional law—viz., the risk that the Court would manufacture an extraordinarily broad (and constitutionally required) insanity defense to reach Kahler's claim. To rule in Kahler's favor, the Court would have to construct a novel legal doctrine that might not only enable him to escape taking (figuratively speaking) a long drop with a short rope, but also completely muck up the law. The Court has done that before, and the results have not been pretty.[33] Making a hash out of another body of law would not improve the situation.

Kahler's only chance to avoid conviction and life imprisonment or execution was to claim that he was not mentally responsible at the time of the crimes, but he did so more by challenging the constitutionality of the Kansas insanity defense than by relying on it. Kahler argued that Kansas's test for insanity violated the Due Process Clause because it arbitrarily truncated the defense case. Kansas allows a defendant to use evidence of a mental disease in two ways.[34] At the guilt stage, a defendant can offer it to defeat the state's proof of the mental state required for a conviction.[35] If that fails, he can re-offer the same evidence at sentencing in the hope of being confined in a

---

[33] Consider the absolute mess that the Court's decision in *Furman v. Georgia* made of the law governing the imposition of capital punishment, a penalty that the Constitution expressly contemplates as permissible in four separate components of the Fifth and Fourteenth Amendments. 408 U.S. 238 (1972). The Court's jurisprudence has all the coherence and predictability of Brownian motion. Compare, e.g., Stanford v. Kentucky, 492 U.S. 361 (1989) (ruling that the Eighth Amendment does not prohibit the execution of an offender who was a minor at the time of the crime), with, e.g., Roper v. Simmons, 543 U.S. 551 (2005) (overruling *Stanford*); compare, e.g., Penry v. Lynaugh, 492 U.S. 302 (1989) (ruling that the Eighth Amendment does not prohibit the execution of a mentally retarded offender), with, e.g., Atkins v. Virginia, 536 U.S. 304 (2002) (overruling *Penry*); compare, e.g., Spaziano v. Florida, 468 U.S. 447 (1984), and Hildwin v. Florida, 490 U.S. 638 (1989) (ruling that a judge may override a jury's recommended sentence), with, e.g., Hurst v. Florida, 136 S. Ct. 616 (2016) (overruling *Spaziano* and *Hildwin*); compare, e.g., Jurek v. Texas, 428 U.S. 262 (1976) (upholding the Texas capital sentencing procedure), with, e.g., Abdul-Kabir v. Quarterman, 550 U.S. 233 (2007) (faulting the Texas capital sentencing procedure). At one time, the Supreme Court would apologize for the utter confusion that it has created in capital sentencing law. See, e.g., Lockett v. Ohio, 438 U.S. 586, 597–602 (1978) (plurality opinion). Now, perhaps to avoid sounding like a broken record or confessing that it has no serious intention of changing its ways, the Court has stopped that practice.

[34] See David W. Louisell & Geoffrey C. Hazard, Jr., Insanity as a Defense: The Bifurcated Trial, 49 Cal. L. Rev. 805 (1961) (describing the multi-stage trial in an insanity case).

[35] Kan. Stat. Ann. § 21-5209 (West 2020).

mental institution rather than prison.[36] Kansas, however, does not permit a defendant to avoid conviction on the ground that a mental disorder kept him from realizing that his conduct was immoral. Put differently, Kansas law exonerated a defendant if a severe mental disorder eroded his *cognitive* judgment, but not if only his *normative* judgment was impaired. That limitation, Kahler said, was unconstitutional because Anglo-American legal history has always entitled a defendant to show that a mental illness robbed him of the ability to know right from wrong.

Stop right there for a minute and evaluate the facts of his case. Kahler did not deny shooting his victims, and the jury rejected (how could they have done otherwise?) his claim that he did not premeditate on an intent to kill each of his four victims. That left him with only one defense, and it was a doozy. Kahler maintained that he did not know that the intentional and premeditated murder of four innocent people was immoral. He did not claim that God had ordered him to kill.[37] He also did not claim to be a soldier in combat. And he did not claim that any of his four victims posed an immediate threat to his life or anyone else's. Defendants with those claims at least would be in the ballpark of people who could reasonably believe that killing was morally justified. Kahler also did not select his victims at random, which might suggest that he was incapable of rational planning. Kahler knew who his victims were and where he could find them. They were family members, and his wife had told him they would spend Thanksgiving at her grandmother's house. Kahler also had a clear motive for murder: revenge. He disliked each victim—his wife, for her infidelity and initiating divorce proceedings; his daughters, for having taken his wife's side in those proceedings; and his grandmother-in-law, for offering them refuge at Thanksgiving.[38] Kahler also was discriminating in whom he chose to kill. He saw his son Sean at the home, but he left Sean unharmed because Kahler believed that his son was on his side. Despite all that, Kahler asserted that his personal

---

[36] *Id.* §§ 21-6815(c)(1)(C), 21-6625(a).

[37] As did the defendant in the famous case of People v. Schmidt, 110 N.E. 945 (N.Y. 1915). See *infra* text accompanying notes 71–78.

[38] Larkin & Canaparo, *supra* note 23, at 124–25.

family trauma kept him from knowing that murdering his victims was immoral.[39]

It is difficult to take that claim seriously. What Kahler did "has been immoral since Cain killed Abel and has been a crime since Moses came down from Mount Sinai with the Ten Commandments."[40] That is significant because, as Oliver Wendell Holmes wrote in *The Common Law*, "crimes are also generally sins,"[41] meaning "if you knew the Decalogue, you knew the penal code."[42] The English and American common law and the criminal codes of every state have always outlawed murder because Anglo-American society has always deemed the taking of innocent life a heinous offense.[43] There is a firm consensus still that such a crime is immoral.[44] Kahler therefore essentially asked the Court to reject as unconstitutional a rule of law

---

[39] Kahler's brief in the Supreme Court described his mental state as follows: "When [James] Kraig Kahler killed four members of his family, he was experiencing overwhelming obsessive compulsions and extreme emotional disturbance, and may have dissociated from reality. He had long suffered from a mixed obsessive-compulsive, narcissistic, and histrionic personality disorder, and had recently lapsed into a severe depression, causing him to reach the point of decompensation." Br. for Petitioner at 6, Kahler v. Kansas, 140 S. Ct. 1021 (2020) (No. 18-6135). Kahler's assertion that he "may have dissociated from reality" can't be taken seriously because he did not claim that he was holding a banana or that he believed he was shooting Satan and his minions. Plus, if a "narcissistic" personality disorder renders one insane, every elected official nationwide would qualify. (Although, that might explain a great deal of why they do what they do.)

[40] Larkin & Canaparo, *supra* note 23, at 126.

[41] Oliver Wendell Holmes, The Common Law 100 (Mark DeWolfe Howe ed., 1963) (1881).

[42] Larkin & Canaparo, *supra* note 23, at 127 (footnote omitted).

[43] *Id.* at 126–27.

[44] "In the case of common crime, a large body of research indicates that there *is* in fact a value consensus. People of all races and classes agree we should shun theft, violence, sexual assault, and aggression against children. They give very similar ratings to the seriousness of various kinds of offenses, and they agree to a surprising extent on how stiff the punishments ought to be for violations of the law. The issue of what is criminal has been settled politically in debate over the criminal code, and within law-abiding society there is broad consensus on such matters. These middle-class values are just about everyone's values." Wesley G. Skogan, Disorder and Decline: Crime and the Spiral of Decay in American Neighborhoods 5 (1990); see also Mark D. Yochum, The Death of a Maxim: Ignorance of Law Is No Excuse (Killed by Money, Guns and a Little Sex), 13 St. John's J. Legal Comment. 635, 636 (1999) ("[E]vil is fundamentally known. . . . Ignorance that murder is a crime is no excuse for the crime of murder."); Larkin & Canaparo, *supra* note 23, at 126–27.

holding everyone to knowledge of the most fundamental value judgment in the history of Western Civilization.

The Supreme Court declined Kahler's invitation in an opinion by Justice Elena Kagan for a six-justice majority.[45] Kahler was correct, Kagan said, that Anglo-American legal history has always distinguished parties who are "mad" from those who are "bad," reserving criminal punishment for only the latter.[46] To that extent, Kahler's premise was sound. Nonetheless, his argument from that premise contained two fundamental flaws that required the Court to reject his submission.

Kahler's first mistake was in claiming that Kansas law does not allow a defendant to argue that, because of a mental disease or defect, he could not tell right from wrong. It is true, Kagan noted, that Kansas law disallows that defense at the guilt stage of a criminal case. The Kansas criminal code permits a defendant to argue that, due to a mental illness, he could not form the mental state necessary to commit the charged offense. Otherwise, an alleged mental disease or defect does not excuse a crime.[47] Yet, "[t]hat partly closed-door policy changes once a verdict is in."[48] At the sentencing stage, a defendant has "wide latitude" to adduce proof of his normative impairment to argue that the judge should lessen his punishment or order him confined in a mental institution instead of a prison.[49] While Kansas law does not consider a defendant's normative impairment when determining if he is guilty of a crime, it does make that issue relevant when deciding where and for how long to confine him after conviction. That was sufficient, the majority concluded, because a defendant who successfully raises an insanity defense could also land in a mental institution.[50] In *Kahler* itself, Kahler used that evidence at the sentencing stage in an effort to persuade the jury not to impose the

---

[45] Kahler v. Kansas, 140 S. Ct. 1021 (2020). Justice Stephen Breyer dissented, joined by Justices Ruth Bader Ginsburg and Sonia Sotomayor.

[46] *Id.* at 1030.

[47] Kan. Stat. Ann. § 21-5209 (West 2020) (quoted *supra* note 7).

[48] *Kahler*, 140 S. Ct. at 1026.

[49] *Id.* (citing Kan. Stat. Ann. §§ 21-6815(c)(1)(C), 21-6625(a), 22-3430 (West 2020)).

[50] *Id.*

death penalty. He was unsuccessful, but he nonetheless had the opportunity to make his case.[51]

Kahler's second mistake lay in his claim that Anglo-American legal history has always exonerated someone whose normative judgment was impaired by mental illness. At the outset, the majority explained that Kahler had a steep hill to climb. Because the definition of crimes involves uniquely moral judgments, Kahler had to establish that the historical record was so wide and so deep, "so old and venerable—so entrenched in the central values of our legal system—as to prevent a State from ever choosing another."[52] In making that determination, "the primary guide" was "historical practice," as illuminated by "eminent common-law authorities" and "early English and American judicial decisions."[53] After canvassing those authorities, the Court found that Kahler had misread the relevant history.

The conclusion that Kahler drew from history was overbroad. In part, that was because the relevant history was not as uniform as Kahler represented. As the Court put it, the "historical record is, on any fair reading, complex—even messy."[54] States had experimented with different tests for insanity over time.[55] Prior to the mid-19th century, "the common-law cases reveal no settled consensus favoring Kahler's preferred insanity rule."[56] Moreover, the historical practice revealed that scholars drew two very different conclusions from a person's normative impairment.[57] Before 1843, some courts and treatise writers believed that a severe mental illness could exonerate a defendant because it prevented him from forming the mental state necessary for a crime. By contrast, some others wrote that mental illness could excuse criminality because it kept him from realizing that his conduct

[51] *Id.* at 1027 ("At the penalty phase, the court permitted Kahler to offer additional evidence of his mental illness and to argue in whatever way he liked that it should mitigate his sentence. The jury still decided to impose the death penalty.").

[52] *Id.* at 1029.

[53] *Id.* at 1027.

[54] *Id.* at 1032.

[55] As the Court had previously noted. See Clark, 548 U.S. at 749–50.

[56] Kahler, 140 S. Ct. at 1034.

[57] *Id.* at 1032–35.

was immoral.[58] There was no consensus on why mental illness mattered, even if there was agreement that it did. The year 1843 was an important dividing line because that was the occasion of the famous Daniel M'Naghten decision by the English House of Lords. The House of Lords adopted an insanity test containing both cognitive and normative elements.[59] Since then, however, the law has not been so monolithic as to demonstrate that only one standard is permissible. "States continued to experiment with insanity rules, reflecting what one court called 'the infinite variety of forms [of] insanity' and the 'difficult and perplexing' nature of the defense."[60] No one rule emerged as the consensus choice. Some jurisdictions modified the M'Naghten test to ask whether a defendant knew that he was committing an immoral act or a crime.[61] Others abandoned the M'Naghten test altogether in favor of a test that focused on whether mental illness had eroded a person's volitional capacity.[62] There has been as much diversity in the post-M'Naghten period as there was before it.[63]

At the end of the day, the Court decided, how to treat the intersection of criminal conduct and mental illness is "a project demanding hard choices among values, in a context replete with uncertainty, even at a single moment in time," let alone over centuries.[64] States have the responsibility to make those choices, and states may choose one way today and another way tomorrow if they weigh their

---

[58] *Id.* at 1034.

[59] See M'Naghten's Case (1843) 8 Eng. Rep. 718, 722; 10 Cl. & Fin. 200, 210 (HL) ("[T]o establish a defence on the ground of insanity, it must be clearly proved that, at the time of the committing of the act, the party accused was laboring under such a defect of reason, from disease of the mind, as not to know the nature and quality of the act he was doing; or, if he did know it, that he did not know he was doing what was wrong.").

[60] Kahler, 140 S. Ct. at 1035 (quoting Roberts v. State, 3 Ga. 310, 328, 332 (1847)).

[61] *Id.* at 1037.

[62] *Id.* at 1035; see, e.g., Commonwealth v. Cooper, 106 N.E. 545 (Mass. 1914).

[63] In fact, Kagan noted with some irony, the Supreme Court had twice previously rejected claims that were essentially "the flipside" of Kahler's—viz., claims that it is unconstitutional to *use* the normative incapacity that he said was required—on the ground that there is no one unique definition of insanity. *Id.* at 1028–29 (discussing Clark, 548 U.S. 735, and Leland, 343 U.S. 790).

[64] *Id.*

values differently.[65] "No insanity rule in this country's heritage or history was ever so settled as to tie a State's hands centuries later."[66]

The Criminal Law Cold War therefore remains cold, at least for now.

III. *Kahler* and the Future of the Insanity Defense

Over the past 70 years, the Supreme Court has ruled on three occasions that the Constitution requires no one particular insanity standard for every jurisdiction.[67] The definition of insanity is not like the speed of light, certain, fixed, and immutable for everyone, everywhere, and all time. The issue, then, is what other insanity-related issues remain open after *Kahler*. There are two possibilities, but neither one looks promising.

The first issue is whether a state must allow a defendant to offer proof of a mental illness–caused normative incapacity at sentencing. Kansas law did, and the Court relied on that factor to reject Kahler's argument that the state arbitrarily barred him from proving that he did not know right from wrong. Yet, the Court's carefully written opinion did not describe that feature of Kansas's law as being indispensable to its constitutionality, and it probably is not.

In *Kahler*, the Court approvingly highlighted the wide variety of approaches taken throughout history to identify the proper treatment of mental illness by the criminal justice system. The Court also noted that some jurisdictions had abandoned normative inquiries in favor of discerning whether a defendant knew that he was breaking the law or lacked the volitional capacity to stop himself from committing a crime even if he knew precisely what he

---

[65] *Id.* at 1037.

[66] In his dissent, Justice Breyer concluded that Kansas had exceeded the limits of its "broad leeway" to define its penal code because "it has eliminated the core of a defense that has existed for centuries: that the defendant, *due to mental illness*, lacked the mental capacity necessary for his conduct to be considered morally blameworthy." *Id.* at 1038 (Breyer, J., dissenting) (emphasis original). The "basic insight" of the famous M'Naghten test was its recognition that "mental illness may so impair a person's mental capacities as to render him no more responsible for his actions than a young child or a wild animal," who are "not properly the subject of the criminal law." *Id.* at 1039. The flaw in the Kansas insanity statute, according to Breyer, was not that it chose the wrong test to make that judgment, but that it rendered the matter entirely irrelevant by making no judgment at all. *Id.* at 1039–50.

[67] See also Clark, 548 U.S. 735; Leland, 343 U.S. 790.

was doing. That divergence, the Court said, demonstrated a willingness to experiment with different standards to find the best one. Demanding now that every state allow a defendant to adduce the same type of evidence that Kahler presented would retroactively render those approaches unconstitutional, even though the *Kahler* majority relied on them to uphold the Kansas insanity defense. Atop that, forcing every state to treat evidence like Kahler's as relevant to disposition would have the effect of imposing on ordinary sentencing proceedings in state and federal courts the same rules that apply in capital sentencing proceedings. A defendant staring at a jury entrusted with deciding whether he lives or dies can offer virtually whatever evidence he can think of to save his life.[68] That rule does not apply, however, when the choice is other than life or death. On several occasions, the Supreme Court has held that Congress and the states may impose mandatory sentences fixing a specific term of imprisonment regardless of the mitigating evidence that a defendant can muster.[69] In *Harmelin v. Michigan*, the Court also expressly rejected a defendant's effort to apply capital-sentencing rules to his own noncapital sentencing process because state law fixed a mandatory sentence of life imprisonment without the possibility of parole.[70] Requiring a state to consider reducing an offender's noncapital sentence due to mental illness would extend the law in a direction that the Court so far has been unwilling to go.

The second issue involves what some courts have labeled a "deific decree" defense. *Kahler* did not squarely pose the type of case that makes insanity the topic of exquisite intellectual debate: How should

[68] See, e.g., Lockett v. Ohio, 438 U.S. 586, 604 (1978) (plurality op.) ("[W]e conclude that the Eighth and Fourteenth Amendments require that the sentencer, in all but the rarest kind of capital case, not be precluded from considering, *as a mitigating factor*, any aspect of a defendant's character or record and any of the circumstances of the offense that the defendant proffers as a basis for a sentence less than death.") (footnote omitted; emphasis original). The Court later choked off that potential exception when it prohibited a state from imposing a mandatory death penalty on a prisoner who is convicted of murder while already serving a life sentence. See Sumner v. Schuman, 483 U.S. 66 (1987).

[69] See, e.g., Ewing v. California, 538 U.S. 11 (2003); Harmelin v. Michigan, 501 U.S. 957 (1991); Chapman v. United States, 501 U.S. 453, 467 (1991); Ex parte United States, 242 U.S. 27 (1916).

[70] Harmelin, 501 U.S. at 994–96.

society respond to someone who carries out a sincerely held but delusional belief in a divine command to commit murder? The problem has arisen in a small number of cases,[71] and it taxes the limits of our willingness to punish or excuse the mentally ill. Kansas law bans all insanity claims based on an alleged impairment of one's normative judgment, and it does not carve out an exception for any such defense. Kahler also did not raise that claim. Apparently, he did not have the chutzpah to allege that God had ordered him to murder his family. Since Kahler did not raise that issue, the Court could have passed on it, reserving it for another day when a defendant squarely made that claim. That would have left a hole in the majority's rationale, however, one that might be difficult to endorse in a later case, given the strong ecclesiastical hue to the defense. Perhaps for that reason, the majority effectively rejected the defense without expressly saying so.

The leading case discussing that defense is Justice (then-Judge) Benjamin Cardozo's 1915 opinion for the New York Court of Appeals in *People v. Schmidt.*[72] Arrested for murder, Schmidt repeatedly confessed and pleaded insanity. He told the examining psychiatrists that "he heard the voice of god calling upon him to kill [the victim] as a sacrifice and atonement."[73] The jury was unpersuaded, and the court sentenced Schmidt to death. At that time, New York law applied the M'Naghten insanity defense, which allowed a defendant to claim that mental illness eliminated his normative judgment. On appeal, Schmidt argued that the trial judge shortchanged his defense by leading the jury to believe that it could not acquit him if it found that Schmidt knew that his conduct was illegal, even if it also concluded that he was following a divine command. Cardozo upheld Schmidt's conviction in a lengthy opinion canvassing the scope of the insanity defense. In so doing, Cardozo noted the oddity of convicting someone for doing what the Almighty had ordered, concluding that, "If a man insanely believes that he has a command from the Almighty to kill, it is difficult to understand how such a man can

---

[71] The most famous case is People v. Schmidt, 110 N.E. 945 (N.Y. 1915) (Cardozo, J.), but it has arisen in other cases too. See, e.g., Lundgren v. Mitchell, 440 F.3d 754, 784–87 (6th Cir. 2006) (Merritt, J., dissenting) (collecting "deific decree" cases); People v. Serrano, 823 P.2d 128, 135–40 (Colo. 1992) (same); Larkin & Canaparo, *supra* note 23, at 129 n.228.

[72] 110 N.E. 945 (N.Y. 1915).

[73] *Id.* at 946.

know that it is wrong for him to do it."[74] Cardozo therefore agreed with Schmidt that the insanity defense must include cases involving a true deific decree.[75] Nonetheless, Cardozo ruled that Schmidt was not entitled to a new trial because he had effectively waived his claim of insanity on appeal.[76]

There is no doubt that the majority was fully aware of that defense. Kagan cited and quoted from *Schmidt* in three separate paragraphs of the majority opinion,[77] and Justice Stephen Breyer cited it in his dissent.[78] It therefore is fair to conclude that the Court knew that the *Schmidt* decision, written by a former Supreme Court justice, supported Kahler's argument. Yet, by upholding a state law that barred any such normative-based claim of insanity, *Kahler* forecloses

---

[74] *Id.* at 948 (quoting Guiteau's Case, 10 F. 161, 182 (D.C. 1882)).

[75] *Id.* at 949 ("We hold therefore that there are times and circumstances in which the word 'wrong,' as used in the statutory test of responsibility, ought not to be limited to legal wrong. . . . Knowledge that an act is forbidden by law will in most cases permit the inference of knowledge that, according to the accepted standards of mankind, it is also condemned as an offense against good morals. Obedience to the law is itself a moral duty. If, however, there is an insane delusion that God has appeared to the defendant and ordained the commission of a crime, we think it cannot be said of the offender that he knows the act to be wrong.") (citation omitted).

[76] *Id.* at 946–47 ("The defendant was condemned to death in February, 1914. In July, 1914, he made a motion for a new trial on the ground of newly discovered evidence. In his affidavit, upon that motion, he tells a most extraordinary tale. He now says that he did not murder Anna Aumuller, and that his confession of guilt was false. He says that she died from a criminal operation, and that to conceal the abortion, to which he and others were parties, he hacked the dead body to pieces, and cast the fragments in the river. His crime, he now says, was not murder, but manslaughter. He tells us why he chose to charge himself with the graver offense. He believed that he could feign insanity successfully, and that after a brief term in an asylum he would again be set at large. To confess to the abortion would implicate his confederates, and bring certain punishment to every one. To confess to murder, but at the same time feign insanity, might permit every one to go free. The compact was then made, he says, between himself and his confederates, that he would protect them from suspicion, and play the madman himself. The men and the women who are said to have been the confederates deny that such a compact was made. Whether they were parties or not the fraud upon the court is of little moment at this time; in any event, the defendant now tells us that he was sane; that the tale which he told the physicians, the tale of monstrous perversions and delusions, was false; and that he did not hear the divine voice calling him to sacrifice and to slay. He asks that he be given another opportunity to put before a jury the true narrative of the crime.").

[77] Kahler, 140 S. Ct. at 1025, 1026, 1036.

[78] *Id.* at 1046 (Breyer, J., dissenting).

challenges like Kahler's as well as ones like Schmidt's. To that extent, then, *Kahler* will limit the availability of the insanity defense in a category of cases not specifically at issue in that case.

Otherwise, *Kahler* is not likely to have a large practical effect on the future course of the insanity defense. Despite its prominence in academic literature, films, and prime time television shows, the insanity defense does not play a major role in the criminal law. Defendants do not often raise the defense,[79] largely for two reasons. One is that, unlike some other defenses, such as alibi and self-defense, insanity ordinarily does not offer complete exoneration, enabling a defendant to walk out of the courtroom scot-free. On the contrary, a successful insanity defense typically results in the defendant's automatic commitment to a mental institution until he can prove that he is no longer mentally ill and dangerous to society.[80] In fact, a defendant found not guilty by reason of insanity can wind up being confined for a longer period than if the jury had rejected his defense and found him guilty.[81] The other reason is that, given the often horrifying nature of the crimes to which a defendant pleads insanity and the fear that the accused might eventually be released if he is declared insane, juries generally find insane only those defendants "who had obviously lost touch with reality."[82] The result is that defendants rarely assert an insanity defense unless the proof of their guilt is overwhelming and they are facing either life imprisonment or execution. Both preconditions were certainly true in the case of James Kraig Kahler, so it is not a surprise that he claimed that he was mad. Given the state's proof of his guilt, he had no other defense, and he was not likely to convince a jury that he deserved mercy because most of his family was dead. His options were to prove that he was insane or wind up on death row. Defendants like Kahler will continue to assert that defense. Ones with a better prospect of being released, even if they could offer psychiatric

---

[79] Larkin & Canaparo, *supra* note 23, at 129 n.228 (noting that amici supporting Kahler made that argument).

[80] See, e.g., D.C. Code § 24-501(d) & (e) (2020); Joseph Goldstein & Jay Katz, Dangerousness and Mental Illness: Some Observations on the Decision to Release Persons Acquitted by Reason of Insanity, 70 Yale L.J. 225 (1960).

[81] See Jones v. United States, 463 U.S. 354 (1983).

[82] Goldstein, *supra* note 3, at 19.

proof of some mental disability, are more likely to opt for a different defense or a plea bargain.

That does not signal the end of all future controversies over the insanity defense. There was considerable debate over the subject before *Kahler*, and that debate will likely continue as psychiatry acquires a greater understanding of the mind. In fact, allowing the states, perhaps influenced by the psychiatric profession and the academy, to mull over the shape of the defense without the restraints imposed by a constitutional rule might well leave the defense better situated to conform to additional learning. Constitutionalizing the defense would more likely have put it in a straitjacket than make it the object of continued study. Wrapping insanity in a due process envelope would have left its development in the hands of judges, who have no particular education, skill, or training in psychiatry or criminology.[83] Their peculiar talent (I use "peculiar" in its full range of meanings) is the interpretation of legal documents, codes, and decisions, a skill that matters little when the clause at issue—"due process of law"—is so Delphic as to allow judges to invest it with virtually any moral content they personally prefer.[84] With the public and legislatures left out of the discussion of the development of criminal responsibility, we not only would have driven from the field the two bodies most qualified to make moral judgments, but also have given the Supreme Court yet another discipline to treat like Silly Putty, something shapeable into whatever form a majority of unqualified decisionmakers think fitting.

There certainly has been no lack of experimentation with different standards of criminal responsibility. As *Kahler* noted, from the 13th century onwards, the law was clear that no "lunatic" or "madman" could be guilty of a crime, but there has been anything but uniformity as to how that status should be defined. Numerous courts and scholars on each side of the Atlantic have developed different standards

---

[83] Larkin & Canaparo, *supra* note 23, at 150–51.

[84] Exhibit A is the Supreme Court's creation, in *Obergefell v. Hodges*, of a constitutional right of same-sex marriage grounded in the Due Process Clause. 135 S. Ct. 2584 (2015). That claim was (and still is) alien to the concept of marriage that civilization has embraced since the days of Adam and Eve and that, as recently as 1986, the Court had derided as being "at best, facetious." Bowers v. Hardwick, 478 U.S. 186, 194 (1986), abrogated by Lawrence v. Texas, 539 U.S. 558 (2003).

to define criminal responsibility in the face of severe mental illness. Among them are the "wild beast" test,[85] the "total defect of understanding" test,[86] the "right and wrong" test,[87] the M'Naghten test,[88] the "irresistible impulse" test,[89] the "product of mental illness" test,[90] and the American Law Institute test (which is essentially a modernized version of the M'Naghten test).[91] Some courts have still found those formulations of the insanity defense to be inadequate and have created a diminished capacity or responsibility test to supplement it.[92] A few states have chosen an entirely different approach by authorizing a jury to return a verdict of "guilty but mentally ill."[93] The international community is all over the lot.[94] There is no reason to

[85] Arnold's Case, 16 How. St. Tr. 695, 764–65 (1724).

[86] See, e.g., Kahler, 140 S. Ct. at 1032–34; 1 Matthew Hale, The History of the Pleas of the Crown 14–15 (George Wilson & Thomas Dogherty eds., 1800) (1736).

[87] Anthony Platt & Bernard L. Diamond, The Origins of the "Right and Wrong" Test of Criminal Responsibility and Its Subsequent Development in the United States: An Historical Survey, 54 Cal. L. Rev. 1227 (1966).

[88] M'Naghten's Case, 8 Eng. Rep. at 722, 10 Cl. & Fin. at 210 (ruling that a defendant pleading insanity must prove that, at the time of the act, he suffered from a mental disease or defect of reason so as not to know the nature of the act or, if he did know it, that it was wrong).

[89] E.g., Parsons v. State, 2 So. 854, 863 (Ala. 1887); State v. Thompson, Wright 617, 622 (Ohio 1834); Regina v. Burton (1863) 176 Eng. Rep. 354, 357, 3 F. & F. 772, 780; Regina v. Oxford (1840) 173 Eng. Rep. 941, 950; 9 Car. & P. 525, 546 ("If some controlling disease was, in truth, the acting power within [the defendant] which he could not resist, then he will not be responsible."); Hadfield's Case (K.B. 1800) 27 How. St. Tr. 1281, 1314–15, 1354–55.

[90] E.g., Durham v. United States, 214 F.2d 862, 874–75 (D.C. Cir. 1954); State v. Jones, 50 N.H. 369, 369–70 (1871); State v. Pike, 49 N.H. 399, 402 (1870); John Reid, Understanding the New Hampshire Doctrine of Criminal Insanity, 69 Yale L.J. 367, 369–70 (1960).

[91] Model Penal Code § 4.01 (Am. Law Inst. 1962) ("A person is not responsible for criminal conduct if at the time of such conduct as a result of mental disease or defect he lacks substantial capacity either to appreciate the criminality [wrongfulness] of his conduct or to conform his conduct to the requirements of law.").

[92] Peter Arenella, The Diminished Capacity and Diminished Responsibility Defenses: Two Children of a Doomed Marriage, 77 Colum. L. Rev. 827 (1977); cf. Fisher v. United States, 328 U.S. 463, 464–77 (1946) (rejecting the argument that a defendant should be free to use evidence of mental disease short of insanity to disprove the elements of premeditation and deliberation necessary to establish murder).

[93] See, e.g., Clark, 548 U.S. at 756–79.

[94] See Rita J. Simon & Heather Ahn-Redding, The Insanity Defense, The World Over (2006).

believe that stuffing this debate into the four words "due process of law" would improve it. *Kahler* was right to leave well enough alone.

IV. *Kahler* and the Future of Strict Criminal Liability

An equally interesting, and potentially more profitable, inquiry is whether *Kahler* holds any general significance for the criminal law. I am referring in particular to the issues of strict and *respondeat superior* liability, theories that the Supreme Court upheld over constitutional challenges in a handful of cases in the 20th century.[95] If the Court were open to reconsider the constitutionality of those doctrines in light of "historical practice," as illuminated by "eminent common-law authorities" and "early English and American judicial decisions," *Kahler* might offer far more significance for the doctrine of vicarious criminal liability than it does for the insanity defense.

Consider how the Supreme Court went about analyzing the issue in *Kahler*. The Court did not start with the text of the Constitution. If it had done so, the Court could have made short work of Kahler's argument. The Constitution defines only one crime—treason[96]—and mentions only two defenses—prohibitions on bills of attainder and ex post facto laws.[97] None of the three provisions mentions insanity, yet the Constitution quite clearly contemplates that Congress and the states will have a criminal justice system. That is important for several reasons. It shows that the Framers were aware of the use of the criminal law to order society; it recognizes the importance of limiting Congress's power to define the crime most susceptible to legislative and executive abuse; and, by express implication, it left the definition of all other offenses and defenses to Congress.[98] Yet, *Kahler* never once mentioned those provisions. The majority said that "the primary guide" for analysis of the constitutionality of Kansas's law was the common law's treatment of mental

---

[95] See, e.g., United States v. Park, 421 U.S. 658, 676 (1975); United States v. Freed, 401 U.S. 601, 607–10 (1971); United States v. Int'l Minerals & Chem. Corp., 402 U.S. 558, 565 (1971); United States v. Dotterweich, 320 U.S. 277 (1943); United States v. Balint, 258 U.S. 250, 252–53 (1922); Shevlin-Carpenter Co. v. Minnesota, 218 U.S. 57, 68–69 (1910).

[96] U.S. Const. art. III, § 3.

[97] U.S. Const. art. I, § 9, cl. 3; U.S. Const. art. I, § 10, cl. 1.

[98] Larkin & Canaparo, *supra* note 23, at 96–99.

responsibility,[99] and it turned straightaway to a dissection of the common-law doctrines. Yet history played a far more important role in *Kahler* than simply wearing the *maillot jaune*. Except for a few passing references to the "uncertainties" and "perennial gaps in knowledge" about the human mind that still characterize psychiatry today,[100] the Court's entire discussion consisted of a detailed analysis of the origins and evolution of the common law's treatment of a person's responsibility for crime when captured by mental illness.[101] The question, then, is whether that approach is significant. Does it suggest a willingness to evaluate other theories of liability in the same manner? If so, strict criminal liability might stand in the dock.

Like insanity, strict criminal liability has roots in the earliest days of the common law, when the definition of crimes was primitive. For example, the criminal law did not distinguish between a death caused intentionally or accidentally, by adults or children. A four-year-old could commit homicide by accidentally opening a door that pushed another child to her death.[102] Since the penalty for every felony was death, royal clemency was the only vehicle to mitigate the law's evident harshness.[103] Over time, just as the common-law courts crafted different tests for insanity, so too the courts fashioned gradations in the definitions of homicide and other crimes to differentiate blameless from blameworthy parties.[104] Principal among those distinguishing factors was the requirement that a person commit an unlawful act with a "guilty mind" or an "evil intent," as expressed in the maxim *"Actus non facit reum nisi mens sit rea"*[105]—a crime consists of "a vicious will" and "an unlawful act consequent upon such

---

[99] Kahler, 140 S. Ct. at 1027.

[100] *Id.* at 1028, 1037.

[101] See *id.* at 1027–37.

[102] See William F. Duker, The President's Power to Pardon: A Constitutional History, 18 Wm. & Mary L. Rev. 475, 479 (1977) (describing the need for royal clemency to address that incident).

[103] Larkin & Canaparo, *supra* note 23, at 116–17.

[104] See, e.g., Herbert Wechsler & Jerome Michael, A Rationale of the Law of Homicide I, 37 Colum. L. Rev. 701 (1937); Jerome Michael & Herbert Wechsler, A Rationale of the Law of Homicide II, 37 Colum. L. Rev. 1261 (1937).

[105] Francis Bowes Sayre, Mens Rea, 45 Harv. L. Rev. 974, 974 (1932) ("An act does not make one guilty unless the mind is guilty.").

vicious will."[106] Over time, the criminal law came to treat those elements, also known as *actus reus* and *mens rea*, as indispensable for conduct to be a crime even when capital punishment was no longer the penalty for every felony.[107] The *mens rea* element, in particular, became the critical factor in defending the government's resort to the criminal law, rather than administrative or civil penalties, to encourage compliance. The Supreme Court has consistently reiterated that point when construing potentially ambiguous acts of Congress.[108]

The mid-19th century, however, saw pushback against that longstanding doctrine. Responding to the perceived public health and safety threats from industrialization and urbanization, legislatures in England and the United States harnessed the criminal law to enforce health and safety codes without demanding proof that an offender acted with the "guilty mind" traditionally required for

---

[106] See, e.g., 4 William Blackstone, Commentaries *21; see also, e.g., Roscoe Pound, Introduction to Francis Bowes Sayre, A Selection of Cases on Criminal Law 8–9 (1927) ("Historically, our substantive criminal law is based upon a theory of punishing the vicious will. It postulates a free agent confronted with a choice between doing right and doing wrong and choosing freely to do wrong.").

[107] See, e.g., Morissette v. United States, 342 U.S. 246, 250–52 (1952); 1 Wayne R. LaFave, Substantive Criminal Law § 5.1, at 332–33 (3d ed. 2017).

[108] See Rehaif v. United States, 139 S. Ct. 2191, 2195 (2019):

> Whether a criminal statute requires the Government to prove that the defendant acted knowingly is a question of congressional intent. See Staples v. United States, 511 U.S. 600, 605 (1994). In determining Congress' intent, we start from a longstanding presumption, traceable to the common law, that Congress intends to require a defendant to possess a culpable mental state regarding "each of the statutory elements that criminalize otherwise innocent conduct." United States v. X-Citement Video, Inc., 513 U.S. 64, 72 (1994); see also Morissette v. United States, 342 U.S. 246, 256–58 (1952). We normally characterize this interpretive maxim as a presumption in favor of "scienter," by which we mean a presumption that criminal statutes require the degree of knowledge sufficient to "mak[e] a person legally responsible for the consequences of his or her act or omission." Black's Law Dictionary 1547 (10th ed. 2014).

See also, e.g., Elonis v. United States, 575 U.S. 723 (2015); McFadden v. United States, 576 U.S. 186 (2015); Carter v. United States, 530 U.S. 255, 269 (2000); Staples v. United States, 511 U.S. 600, 605–07 (1994); Posters 'N' Things, Ltd. v. United States, 511 U.S. 513, 524 (1994); Liparota v. United States, 471 U.S. 419, 425–27 (1985); United States v. U.S. Gypsum Co., 438 U.S. 422, 436–37 (1978); Morissette, 342 U.S. at 250–51.

common-law crimes.[109] Called "regulatory offenses" in England and "public-welfare offenses" in this country, violations of pure-food and alcohol regulations, health requirements, building codes, traffic laws, and other sundry low-level measures initially carried only minor penalties, such as small fines. Eventually, imprisonment also became an available punishment despite the lack of any *mens rea* element in the relevant statute. The Federal Food, Drug, and Cosmetic Act (FDCA) is the classic example of a 20th-century regulatory law that carries criminal and civil penalties for a violation of the statute or a rule adopted by the agency responsible for enforcing it, the Food and Drug Administration.[110] The Supreme Court has upheld the constitutionality of the FDCA on more than one occasion.[111] In fact, the Court has even applied the tort doctrine of *respondeat superior* liability in criminal cases without once stopping to see if the common law authorized the extraordinary practice of holding B liable for A's conduct.[112]

Strict liability crimes are wholly out of step with what *Kahler* described as our Anglo-American "historical practice." A legion of "eminent common-law authorities"—criminal-law scholars such as William Blackstone, Lon Fuller, H.L.A. Hart, Herbert Packer, Herbert Wechsler, and numerous others[113]—as well as "early English and

---

[109] See, e.g., Morissette, 342 U.S. at 25–56; Graham Hughes, Criminal Omissions, 67 Yale L.J. 590, 595 (1958); Paul J. Larkin, Jr., Strict Liability Offenses, Incarceration, and the Cruel and Unusual Punishments Clause, 37 Harv. J.L. & Pub. Pol'y 1065, 1072–76 (2014); Francis Bowes Sayre, Public Welfare Offenses, 33 Colum. L. Rev. 55, 56–67 (1933).

[110] Ch. 65, 52 Stat. 1010 (codified as amended at 21 U.S.C. § 301 et seq. (2019)).

[111] See United States v. Park, 421 U.S. 658, 676 (1975); Dotterweich, 320 U.S. 277; Balint, 258 U.S. at 252–53. The Court has not upheld a sentence of imprisonment for an FDCA conviction, however, over a challenge that incarceration for a strict liability crime is a cruel and unusual punishment. See Larkin, *supra* note 109, at 1102–03 & n.131.

[112] See Park, 421 U.S. at 660, 663–64, 667–76 (ruling that the FDCA makes the president of a nationwide business liable for the rodent droppings at one particular warehouse); Dotterweich, 320 U.S. at 279–85 (construing the word "person" in the FDCA to include the president of a pharmaceutical company that distributed mislabeled drugs even though the president took no part in the distribution).

[113] See, e.g., 4 Blackstone, *supra* note 106, at *21; Lon L. Fuller, The Morality of Law 77 (1964) ("Strict criminal liability has never achieved respectability in our law."); H.L.A. Hart, Negligence, Mens Rea, and Criminal Responsibility, in Punishment and Responsibility 136, 152 (H.L.A. Hart ed., 2d ed. 2008) ("strict liability is odious"); Herbert L. Packer, The Limits of the Criminal Sanction 13–31 (1968); Herbert Wechsler, The Challenge of a Model Penal Code, 65 Harv. L. Rev. 1097, 1109 (1952); see generally Larkin, *supra* note 109, at 1079 n.46 (collecting authorities).

American judicial decisions"[114]—reiterated by the Supreme Court in the last few decades[115]—condemn strict liability crimes. If history is to be the guide, strict criminal liability should be unconstitutional.

Moreover, a strong argument can be made that legislators do not use these offenses because they have made the moral judgment that we no longer deem an evil intent the mark of Cain. Two other factors are at work. One is that regulatory violations have become crimes because tasking local police officers with the enforcement of public-welfare offenses is simpler and less expensive than it is to create and fund an entirely new cadre of civil inspectors. Also related is the reality that the police will not aggressively enforce purely civil infractions.[116] The other factor is that "strict liability offenses make charges remarkably easy to prosecute" because they eliminate any consideration of the defendant's state of mind.[117] What does that mean? It does not mean that a state cannot legitimately use law enforcement officers to investigate public-welfare offenses. Rather, it means that a state's decision to treat regulatory violations as fundraising opportunities does not reflect the same type of normative judgment that underlies common-law crimes.

I have no doubt that some defendant will cite *Kahler* in support of a challenge to the constitutionality of a strict liability crime. I have far less confidence that he or she will prevail. To be sure, there is a strong

---

[114] See, e.g., Felton v. United States, 96 U.S. 699, 703 (1877) ("But the law at the same time is not so unreasonable as to attach culpability, and consequently to impose punishment, where there is no intention to evade its provisions, and the usual means to comply with them are adopted. All punitive legislation contemplates some relation between guilt and punishment. To inflict the latter where the former does not exist would shock the sense of justice of every one."); People v. Harris, 29 Cal. 678, 681 (Cal. 1866) ("It is laid down in the books on the subject that it is a universal doctrine that to constitute what the law deems a crime there must concur both an evil act and an evil intent. *Actus non facit reum nisi mens sit rea.* (1 Bish. on Cr. Law, Secs. 227 and 229; 3 Greenl. Ev. Sec. 13.).")); State v. King, 86 N.C. 603, 606–07 (1882); State v. Carson, 2 Ohio Dec. Reprint 81 (Ct. Common Pleas 1859): Miller v. People, 5 Barb. 203, 203–04 (N.Y. Sup. Ct. Gen'l Term 1849).

[115] See *supra* note 108 (collecting cases).

[116] See *id.* at 1111–16.

[117] *Id.* at 1068 (footnote omitted) (citing Laurie L. Levenson, Good Faith Defenses: Reshaping Strict Liability Crimes, 78 Cornell L. Rev. 401, 404 (1993) ("The strict liability doctrine affords both an efficient and nearly guaranteed way to convict defendants.").

case, grounded in a long history of common-law and contemporary authorities, that no one should be guilty of a crime without having the type of evil intent characteristic of the common-law crimes. Nevertheless, the Supreme Court has upheld strict criminal liability over such challenges on multiple occasions, and today's Court might well be reluctant to say that their numerous predecessors were fundamentally mistaken about the intersection of criminal and constitutional law. Add in the Court's reluctance to overrule its own precedents due to *stare decisis* considerations and you do not have a promising case. The Court might be willing to consider whether imprisoning a defendant guilty of an offense on only a strict liability basis would be a cruel and unusual punishment, and I have urged the Court so to rule.[118] That would only eliminate one potential punishment for such a defendant, though, not his conviction. Still, as Alexander Pope wrote, "Hope springs eternal. . . ."

Conclusion

Kahler v. Kansas had the potential to revolutionize the law of insanity. Kahler urged the Supreme Court to do something that it had actively resisted for decades despite repeated pleas: viz., constitutionalize the insanity defense and select a particular standard as being essential to the criminal law. Fortunately, the Court yet again declined that invitation. That outcome is a good result for everyone but Kahler (who deserves none of our sympathy). The states and Congress remain free to decide how best to reconcile the need to deter crime, as well as punish the people who disregard society's rules, with the need to define the rules of the road in a way that respects our fundamental beliefs about not holding parties accountable for conduct they truly believed was legal or lawful. The balance that Kansas adopted is a reasonable way to accommodate those interests. Of course, other balances also could be struck. Societies have adopted different rules from the distant to recent past, and legislatures are likely to define different rules in the future. *Kahler* allows them to make those decisions without having to wriggle out of federal constitutional restraints. We are better off for that freedom.

[118] See Larkin, *supra* note 109, at 1101–21.

The DACA Case: Agencies' "Square Corners" and Reliance Interests in Immigration Law

Peter Margulies*

Stewardship has long been a trope in U.S. law and governance. The Framers spoke of the "trust" that the people reposed in their government.[1] In immigration cases, the Supreme Court has on occasion curbed state enforcement, viewing states as too prone to "sudden irritation" to adequately steward abiding national interests.[2] Holding in *Department of Homeland Security v. Regents of the Univ. of California* that the U.S. Department of Homeland Security (DHS) under President Trump had failed to engage in "reasoned decisionmaking" when it rescinded the Deferred Action for Childhood Arrivals (DACA) program, the Court refined this stewardship paradigm.[3]

Chief Justice John Roberts, writing for the Court in *Regents*, noted that in announcing DACA, President Barack Obama's then–DHS secretary, Janet Napolitano, had provided two things of value to foreign nationals who came to the United States as children with no lawful immigration status: (1) a reprieve from deportation, called "removal" under the Immigration and Nationality Act (INA); and (2) eligibility for various benefits, including work permits.[4] According to Roberts,

---

*Professor of Law, Roger Williams University School of Law; B.A., Colgate University; J.D., Columbia Law School.

[1] See The Federalist No. 23 at 153–54 (Alexander Hamilton) (Clinton Rossiter ed., 1961); Andrew Kent, Ethan J. Leib & Jed H. Shugerman, Faithful Execution and Article II, 132 Harv. L. Rev. 2111, 2119 (2019) (discussing the Constitution's Take Care Clause as forging a system of laws as a trust that the president must protect).

[2] See Arizona v. United States, 567 U.S. 387, 395 (2012) (citing The Federalist No. 3 at 44 (John Jay) (Clinton Rossiter ed., 1961) (cited by Supreme Court in later edition)).

[3] 140 S. Ct. 1891 (2020).

[4] Memorandum from Janet Napolitano, Sec'y, Dep't of Homeland Sec., to David V. Aguilar et al., Acting Comm'r, U.S. Cust. & Border Prot., et al. (June 15, 2012), https://bit.ly/30wLkPh [hereinafter Napolitano Memorandum].

DHS had failed to consider whether DACA recipients' participation in employment, education, medical treatment, military service, or family life formed expectations—"reliance interests" in legal parlance—that the agency had to accommodate. Moreover, DHS had failed to consider alternatives to DACA's total rescission, such as allowing a longer wind-down of the program or keeping the reprieve from removal but ending eligibility for benefits.

The stewardship outlined in Roberts's opinion is deliberative, not substantive: it is about process, not outcomes. Roberts conceded that DHS had the power to end DACA, which DHS, based on the conclusion of Attorney General Jeff Sessions, had in September 2017 found to be unlawful.[5] DHS could have justified the rescission by stating in writing that enforcing the INA outweighed recipients' reliance interests. However, in ending the program, Roberts explained, an agency had to at least address the interests of stakeholders as part of "the agency's job" and its "responsibility."[6] Roberts did not mention stewardship per se in his opinion. Nevertheless, framing deliberation as a core component of "responsibility" for a "job" casts DHS's failure in stewardship terms. A sound steward may safeguard a trust by choosing any one of several paths. But stewardship cannot be random or heedless. It requires appropriate consideration of the risks and benefits of each choice.

The model of stewardship reflected in Roberts's opinion in *Regents* has two prongs. The first is consistency: a good steward will deliberate carefully before taking action and stick with the reasons that drove her initial decision rather than dangle a string of shifting justifications before befuddled stakeholders. In addition, a good steward will balance the equities of all parties and of the public.[7]

---

[5] Memorandum from Elaine C. Duke, Acting Sec'y, U.S. Dep't of Homeland Sec., to James W. McCament et al., Acting Dir., U.S. Citizenship & Immigration Servs., et al. (Sept. 5, 2017), https://bit.ly/2DJPcDy [hereinafter Duke Memorandum]; Letter from Jefferson B. Sessions III, Att'y General of the United States, to Elaine Duke, Acting Sec'y, U.S. Dep't of Homeland Sec. (Sept. 4, 2017), https://bit.ly/3kl3zz1 [hereinafter Sessions Letter].

[6] 140 S. Ct. at 1908–09.

[7] See Nken v. Holder, 556 U.S. 418, 426, 434 (2009) (noting that stay of removal pending appeal hinges not merely on merits of case, but also on hardship to the applicant, the countervailing factor of hardship to other parties, and consideration of the public interest); see also Winter v. NRDC, Inc., 555 U.S. 7, 24 (2008) (noting factors for preliminary injunction); see generally Peter Margulies, Taking Care of Immigration Law: Presidential Stewardship, Prosecutorial Discretion, and the Separation of Powers,

To promote consistency in *Regents*, Roberts invoked an administrative law standby, the *Chenery* doctrine, which holds that an agency explaining a decision gets only one bite at the apple.[8] Courts look at how the agency explained its action when the action was taken, not how the agency explains it later, once litigation about the action is underway. Reading *Chenery* broadly, Roberts was able to force DHS off its most favored turf. DHS had to stand or fall with Acting Secretary Duke's stark conclusion in 2017 that DACA was unlawful. Because of Roberts's broad reading of *Chenery* and its "one bite at the apple" rule, Roberts simply refused to consider the more comprehensive 2018 justification by Duke's successor as acting secretary, Kirstjen Nielsen, that DACA was flawed from both a legal and a policy perspective.[9] But, as Justice Brett Kavanaugh noted in his dissent, Roberts's broad reading of *Chenery* may be a stretch. The *Chenery* doctrine is most effective in stopping agency lawyers in litigation who would otherwise invent new rationales from scratch.[10] Acting Secretary Nielsen's 2018 justification came from a responsible agency official—one asked to create that filing by a district judge, no less—not a desperate lawyer in the throes of litigation.

Complementing Justice Kavanaugh's critique of the consistency prong in Roberts's opinion, Justice Clarence Thomas argued that Roberts's stress on recipients' reliance interests ignored the INA's structure. According to Justice Thomas, the INA is a "carefully crafted scheme" that specifically enumerates classes of people entitled legally to enter the country, including close relatives of citizens and current lawful permanent residents (LPRs), skilled employees, and refugees,

---

94 B.U. L. Rev. 105 (2014) (discussing stewardship and discretion in immigration law administration); Peter Margulies, Rescinding Inclusion in the Administrative State: Adjudicating DACA, the Census, and the Military's Transgender Policy, 71 Fla. L. Rev. 1429, 1467–74 (2019) (discussing DACA rescission).

8 140 S. Ct. at 1909 (citing SEC v. Chenery Corp., 318 U.S. 80, 94 (1943)).

9 Memorandum from Kirstjen M. Nielsen, Sec'y, U.S. Dep't of Homeland Sec. (June 22, 2018), https://bit.ly/33vMMDC [hereinafter Nielsen Memorandum]. After the Supreme Court's decision in *Regents*, current DHS Acting Secretary Chad Wolf rescinded both the Duke Memorandum and the Nielsen Memorandum, and informed the public that he was considering rescinding the Napolitano Memorandum that had announced DACA. Acting Secretary Wolf took a number of interim steps, including barring new DACA applications. See Chad F. Wolf, Acting Sec'y, U.S. Dep't of Homeland Sec., Reconsideration of the June 15, 2012 Memorandum Entitled "Exercising Prosecutorial Discretion with Respect to Individuals Who Came to the United States as Children" (July 28, 2020), https://bit.ly/3a3cG2P.

10 140 S. Ct. at 1934–35 (Kavanaugh, J., dissenting).

as well as nonimmigrants such as students and tourists.[11] Other foreign nationals seeking to enter or remain in the United States often lack either a visa that confers a lawful status or any reasonable path for gaining a lawful status. Taking the INA's structure seriously, immigration officials should not second-guess Congress's methodical distinction between foreign nationals who can receive a lawful status and those without a reasonable chance for that status. Nor should immigration officials grant crucial components of lawful status, such as a reprieve from removal or eligibility for a work permit, to a large group of otherwise removable foreign nationals. As a "sweeping nonenforcement program," DACA undermined the INA's structural integrity, in much the same way as the Obama administration's Deferred Action for Parents of Americans (DAPA) program, which had never gone into operation because courts had enjoined it as exceeding the power that Congress had delegated to immigration officials.[12]

While the question is a close one, ultimately Chief Justice Roberts's vision of deliberative stewardship best fits history and practice regarding prospective Americans. Roberts's emphasis on consistency echoes his rejection in *Department of Commerce v. New York* of the Commerce Department's "pretextual" justification for adding a citizenship question to the census.[13] Moreover, Roberts's analysis is compatible with Thomas's structural approach. According to Roberts, DHS could readily have reached its desired outcome of ending DACA. To do so, DHS merely had to expressly balance DACA recipients' reliance interests, the public interest, and enforcement of the INA. Given the interests at stake, that balancing is a reasonable expectation that leaves the INA's structure intact.

This article, like Gaul, is divided into three parts. Part I provides background on DACA and DAPA, including the courts' reliance on a structural argument in their rejection of DAPA, before discussing the Trump administration's effort to rescind DACA. Part II outlines the history of an alternative to the structural argument—a stewardship model that this article traces back to the Founding era. Part III examines Chief Justice Roberts's majority opinion in *Regents* in light of the stewardship model and contrasts Roberts's analysis with the insightful arguments made in dissent by Justices Thomas and Kavanaugh.

---

[11] *Id.* at 1930 (Thomas, J., dissenting).

[12] *Id.* at 1923–26, 1930.

[13] 139 S. Ct. 2551 (2019).

I. President Obama's Immigration Initiatives and President Trump's Response: DACA, DAPA, and the Structure of the INA

DACA was a presidential response to a legislative logjam. As a U.S. senator, Barack Obama wrote about meeting a third-grade student, Cristina, with an uncertain immigration status. That encounter, at which Cristina asked for then-Senator Obama's autograph, prompted Obama to reflect that the most urgent risk was not being "overrun by those who do not look like us," but failing to "recognize the humanity of Cristina and her family."[14] As president, Obama failed to persuade Congress to act on this sentiment by passing the DREAM Act, which would have provided legal immigration status to noncitizens who arrived in the United States as children.[15] Since the overwhelming majority of noncitizens in this category did not have a lawful immigration status, Congress's failure to act meant that noncitizens in this group faced removal. Pondering the human predicament that Congress had not resolved, Obama took executive action through DHS. President Obama later announced a larger immigration initiative: DAPA. Finally, in 2017, DHS under the Trump administration announced that it was rescinding DACA.

A. DACA's Criteria

Following President Obama's lead, then–DHS Secretary Janet Napolitano issued a memorandum announcing DACA on June 15, 2012. DACA did not confer a lawful immigration status on the "Dreamers" who were children when they entered the United States; only Congress can establish specific categories that lead to lawful permanent resident (LPR) status or various temporary nonimmigrant forms of status, such as students, tourists, or temporary workers. Rather, DACA granted eligible foreign nationals a renewable reprieve from deportation (called "removal" under current immigration laws) and permission to apply for a work permit.[16]

---

[14] Barack Obama, The Audacity of Hope: Thoughts on Reclaiming the American Dream 318 (2006).

[15] See Development, Relief, and Education for Alien Minors Act, S. 1291, 107th Cong. (2001) (as reintroduced 2011).

[16] See Napolitano Memorandum, *supra* note 4. Compare Robert J. Delahunty & John C. Yoo, Dream On: The Obama Administration's Nonenforcement of Immigration Laws, the DREAM Act, and the Take Care Clause, 91 Tex. L. Rev. 781, 856 (2013) (asserting that DACA went beyond the scope of delegation), with Shoba Sivaprasad Wadhia, Beyond Deportation: The Role of Prosecutorial Discretion in Immigration Cases 54–59 (2015) (arguing that the ambit of discretion under INA included large-scale programs such as DACA).

To be eligible, an applicant had to have come to the United States before reaching the age of 16. In addition, to ensure that applicants had sustained ties to this country, the applicant had to have resided continuously in the United States for at least five years before June 15, 2012, and be a resident of the United States on that date. Targeting DACA's benefits to those who had pursued an education or service, an applicant had to be currently enrolled in school, have received a high school diploma or general education development (GED) certificate, or be an honorably discharged veteran of the U.S. Armed Forces. To winnow out foreign nationals who had engaged in crime, Napolitano also ruled out any applicant who had a felony or "significant misdemeanor" conviction on her record or multiple misdemeanor convictions, or in any other way might threaten national security or public safety. Finally, to keep the program manageable and focused on young people who had not yet had a chance to build their lives, applicants could be no more than 30 years old.[17]

B. An Attempt to Build on DACA: DAPA's Introduction and Chilly Reception in the Courts

Following up on DACA and responding to continued inaction by Congress, President Obama sought additional programs to aid undocumented foreign nationals. In November 2014, DHS Secretary Jeh Johnson, Napolitano's successor, announced the Deferred Action for Parents of Americans (DAPA) program. DAPA extended DACA-style treatment—a two-year renewable reprieve from removal and eligibility for a work permit—to a much larger group: parents of U.S. citizens.[18]

---

[17] DHS also classified DACA recipients as "lawfully present" and thus eligible for driver's licenses.

[18] See Memorandum from Jeh Charles Johnson, Sec'y, U.S. Dep't of Homeland Sec., to León Rodríguez, Dir., U.S. Citizenship & Immigration Servs, Thomas S. Winkowski, Acting Dir., U.S. Immigration & Customs Enforcement, and R. Gil Kerlikowske, Comm'r, U.S. Customs & Border Prot., 3, 5 (Nov. 20, 2014); Memorandum from Karl R. Thompson, Prip'l Dep'y Asst. Att'y Gen., Off. of Legal Couns., The Department of Homeland Security's Authority to Prioritize Removal of Certain Aliens Unlawfully Present in the United States and to Defer Removal of Others (Nov. 19, 2014), https://bit.ly/3gu7F5L [hereinafter Thompson Memorandum]. The Fifth Circuit ultimately held that DAPA went beyond Congress's delegation of power to the executive branch under the INA. See Texas v. United States, 809 F.3d 134, 180 (5th Cir. 2015), aff'd by an equally divided Court, 136 S. Ct. 2271 (2016); cf. Josh Blackman, The Constitutionality of DAPA Part II: Faithfully Executing the Law, 19 Tex. Rev. L. & Pol. 213, 284 (2015)

The Justice Department's Office of Legal Counsel (OLC) estimated that over four million undocumented foreign nationals—roughly 40 percent of the United States's undocumented population—would be eligible. Although some DAPA-eligible persons had a theoretical path to acquiring LPR status because their children were U.S. citizens, in most cases that path would have been very difficult.[19]

In challenges to DAPA brought by states, including Texas, the Fifth Circuit held that deferred action of DAPA's size and scope conflicted with the INA's framework.[20] Its analysis applied most clearly to DAPA's grant of eligibility for work permits and other benefits. While the government had some discretion in merely deciding not to remove foreign nationals, its decision to grant the "benefits of lawful presence" to a large group of undocumented noncitizens clashed

---

(arguing that DAPA exceeded presidential power). The author of this article served as cocounsel for amici curiae at all phases of the *Texas* litigation, including proceedings before the Supreme Court, arguing that DAPA clashed with the structure and logic of the INA. See Brief for Former Homeland Security, Justice, and State Department Officials as Amici Curiae Supporting Respondents at 2, United States v. Texas, 136 S. Ct. 2271 (2016) (No. 15-674). In lower courts, the author served as cocounsel with Ilya Shapiro of the Cato Institute and Josh Blackman of South Texas College of Law, along with Leif Olson of the Olson Law Firm. Brief as Friends of the Court Supporting Plaintiffs of the Cato Institute and Law Professors, Texas v. United States, 86 F. Supp. 3d 591 (S.D. Tex. 2015) (No. 14-254), https://bit.ly/3a1FRmG.

[19] See 8 U.S.C. § 1151(b)(2)(A)(i) (requiring that a U.S. citizen be at least 21 years old to sponsor a parent for an immigrant visa); see also Thompson Memorandum, *supra* note 18, at 29 n.14 (conceding that many DAPA recipients would "need to leave the country to obtain a visa at a U.S. consulate abroad"; because of some period of unlawful presence in the United States, a DAPA recipient would then "in most instances" be subject to either a 3- or 10-year statutory bar on reentry into the United States, requiring her to wait outside the United States "for the duration of the bar").

[20] Texas, 809 F.3d at 180. For commentary on DAPA, compare Adam B. Cox & Cristina M. Rodríguez, The President and Immigration Law Redux, 125 Yale L.J. 104, 144–51 (2015) (discussing rationale for DAPA based on consistency with the INA, while also suggesting that a better rationale would look to Congress and the president as coprincipals in crafting immigration law), and Evan D. Bernick, Faithful Execution: Where Administrative Law Meets the Constitution, 108 Geo. L.J. 1, 57–61 (2019) (suggesting that the Take Care Clause provided authority for DAPA), with Peter Margulies, The Boundaries of Executive Discretion: Deferred Action, Unlawful Presence, and Immigration Law, 64 Am. U. L. Rev. 1183, 1244–52 (2015) (arguing that DAPA exceeded power Congress had delegated to the executive branch), and Zachary S. Price, Enforcement Discretion and Executive Duty, 67 Vand. L. Rev. 671, 674–75 (2014) (asserting that the Constitution curbs president's power to decline to enforce the law).

with the INA.[21] In an earlier decision denying a stay of the district court's preliminary injunction against DAPA's operation, the Fifth Circuit explained that the INA included precise categories of foreign nationals allowed to enter or remain in the United States.[22] According to the Fifth Circuit, Congress's enumeration of "narrow classes" of foreign nationals allowed to enter and remain and a large residual group subject to removal served an important purpose in Congress's plan: it protected the jobs of U.S. citizen and LPR workers.[23] The court reasoned that, from Congress's perspective, dramatically expanding the pool of foreign nationals eligible for employment could cloud the jobs outlook for citizens and LPRs.

To address this concern, the Fifth Circuit explained, Congress and immigration officials had limited the scale and scope of deferred action. Grants of deferred action have typically served as "bridges" to a lawful status or have entailed "country-specific" responses to war, political turmoil, or natural disasters such as hurricanes and earthquakes. Deferred action is also available in a small number of cases involving hardships, such as extreme youth, sickness, or old age. In light of the INA's detailed framework, it was unlikely that Congress, without saying so in the law, had *also* given immigration officials sweeping power to grant deferred action to millions of otherwise removable noncitizens. As Justice Antonin Scalia said, Congress does not "hide elephants in mouseholes."[24] Based on this analysis, the Fifth Circuit found that DAPA exceeded executive power under the immigration laws, and the Supreme Court affirmed that decision by an equally divided 4-4 vote after Justice Scalia's passing.

C. DACA's Rescission under the Trump Administration

Although DAPA never went into effect, DACA was in full swing through the remainder of the Obama administration and the first months of the Trump presidency. In the summer of 2017, however,

---

[21] Texas, 809 F.3d at 180 (noting tension with statutory scheme).

[22] Texas v. United States, 787 F.3d 733, 759–61 (5th Cir. 2015).

[23] Texas, 809 F.3d at 181 (remarking that "'a primary purpose in restricting immigration is to preserve jobs'" for U.S. citizens) (citation omitted). But see Ilya Somin, Free to Move: Foot Voting, Migration, and Political Freedom (2020) (arguing that immigration enhances employment prospects for citizens and lawful residents).

[24] Texas, 787 F.3d at 760 n.86 (citing Whitman v. Am. Trucking Ass'ns, 531 U.S. 457, 468 (2001)).

a number of states that had sued to stop DAPA, led by Texas, wrote a letter to the Trump administration arguing that DACA was illegal for the same structural reasons that the Fifth Circuit had cited in affirming the preliminary injunction against DAPA. The states threatened a lawsuit against DACA. In September 2017, Attorney General Jeff Sessions wrote a letter asserting that DACA also lacked "proper statutory authority" and thus was an "unconstitutional" exercise of executive power, citing the Fifth Circuit's DAPA decision.[25] Acting DHS Secretary Elaine Duke followed up with a memorandum that announced DHS's intention to rescind the program, referring to the stark legal conclusion in Sessions's letter and finding, without further explanation, that DACA was illegal.

Secretary Duke did not summarily revoke DACA's terms for recipients. In a nod to the "complexities . . . [of] winding down the program," DHS agreed to process all initial applications then in the pipeline and all renewal requests from recipients whose two-year term would expire by March 5, 2018.[26] Since Chief Justice Roberts highlighted the choices that DHS's wind-down entailed and the lack of explanation for those choices, further detail is useful.

Under Duke's rescission plan, DHS would not accept new DACA applications after the issuance of her memorandum and the group of some 700,000 DACA recipients would lose benefits on a staggered basis, starting on March 6, 2018, with *all* benefits terminating by March 6, 2020. As an illustration, consider a DACA recipient whose two-year period of participation in the program was due to terminate on March 6, 2018. The recipient hoped to renew her participation for an additional two-year period. Renewal was crucial, because the recipient had started a four-year undergraduate college program in September 2016, planning to major in computer science. If all went according to plan, the recipient would graduate from college in May 2020. Duke's wind-down would have changed those plans, because it barred renewals for periods of participation that expired after March 5, 2018. Under Duke's wind-down, the recipient would lose DACA almost two years into her undergraduate program, with slightly over two years remaining before she was due to obtain her degree.

[25] Sessions Letter, *supra* note 5. The Fifth Circuit did not discuss DAPA's constitutionality, since the court held that DAPA was invalid on statutory grounds, making resolution of the constitutional issue unnecessary.

[26] Duke Memorandum, *supra* note 5.

A number of courts enjoined the DACA rescission within months of its issuance, holding that Secretary Duke's explanation for the rescission was insufficient.[27] One court required DHS to submit a more detailed explanation.[28] In June 2018, new Acting Secretary Kirstjen Nielsen did so, including both legal and policy arguments. In her legal discussion, Nielsen affirmed Attorney General Sessions's conclusion that DACA was unlawful in light of the Fifth Circuit's DAPA ruling. Citing the logic and structure of the INA discussed earlier, Nielsen explained that the Fifth Circuit had held that granting deferred action to a large group of otherwise removable foreign nationals was "contrary to the statutory scheme" of specific forms of legal status and a residual category of foreign nationals subject to removal.

In her policy discussion, Nielsen again cited the structural account of the INA to pinpoint what she termed "serious doubts" about DACA's lawfulness. According to Nielsen, it was reasonable to rescind a policy in the face of such doubts, rather than maintain it in the face of legal challenges from states. Nielsen added a related policy concern that in her view Congress, not the executive, should authorize programs as extensive as DACA, thereby providing more certainty and predictability than the executive branch could offer. Nielsen also articulated a general preference in administrative trade-craft for case-by-case determinations about deferred action, not the sweeping criteria that DACA entailed. In addition, Nielsen contended that a program such as DACA would send confusing signals about the government's commitment to enforcing Congress's scheme, especially given what Nielsen called "unacceptably high levels" of unlawful immigration.

Finally, Nielsen discounted the expectations of DACA recipients that they would be able to stay in the United States or at least complete projects here, such as courses of study or medical treatment. She observed that DACA was always intended to be temporary. Reinforcing her denigration of recipients' reliance interests, Nielsen stressed that Obama administration officials, when implementing DACA,

---

[27] See Regents of Univ. of Cal. v. U.S. Dep't of Homeland Sec., 908 F.3d 476, 505–10 (9th Cir. 2018), aff'd, 140 S. Ct. 1891 (2020); Vidal v. Nielsen, 279 F. Supp. 3d 401 (E.D.N.Y. 2018); NAACP v. Trump, 298 F. Supp. 3d 209, 237–43 (D.D.C. 2018) (NAACP I); see also NAACP v. Trump, 315 F. Supp. 3d 457, 467–73 (D.D.C. 2018) (NAACP II) (finding new explanation by then–Acting DHS Secretary Nielsen inadequate).

[28] See NAACP I, 298 F. Supp. 3d at 245.

had expressly refused to grant recipients any enforceable legal rights in DACA's continuation. In any case, Nielsen concluded, in the absence of congressional approval for DACA, the erosion of the INA's structure caused by enabling the "continued presence" of a large group of foreign nationals without a lawful status outweighed any reliance interests that the program may have instilled.[29]

While lower courts gave the DACA rescission an unfavorable reception, their rationales were unpersuasive. In an illustrative example, the Ninth Circuit minimized both the structural concerns that had driven the Fifth Circuit to hold that DAPA was unlawful and the relevance of those concerns to DACA.[30] The Ninth Circuit analogized DACA to earlier uses of deferred action, failing to acknowledge that those earlier occasions encompassed either a bridge to a legal status or a response to hardship such as extreme youth, age, or infirmity. DACA failed to fit the "bridge" category; the program was beneficial to recipients precisely because they had no reasonably available path to a legal status. Taking the broadest possible view of the "hardship" category, DACA barely fit. DACA recipients came to the United States as children, and thus had something in common with past deferred action recipients who received benefits because of their youth. DACA recipients are a varied group, however, including some people as old as 29 who can still qualify for the program. If DACA's dimensions failed to fit either the "bridge" or "hardship" categories, the program conflicted with the INA's framework.

The Ninth Circuit and other courts failed to acknowledge the scope of this structural problem, let alone resolve it. As of June 2020, the key question was whether the Supreme Court would find a more satisfying approach to the difficult issues posed by the Trump administration's attempt to rescind DACA.

II. Stewardship and Prospective Americans

As an alternative to the structural analysis outlined above and in Justice Thomas's *Regents* dissent, consider an approach based on stewardship. As I conceive it, stewardship is not a license for the free-floating exercise of presidential power; instead it resides in the second category of Justice Robert Jackson's *Youngstown* concurrence,

---

[29] See Nielsen Memorandum, *supra* note 9, at 2–3.
[30] See Regents, 908 F.3d at 505–10.

as a gap-filler in cases of statutory silence.[31] From the Founding era, Congress and the public have expected that presidents will assume responsibility for the welfare of refugees and other prospective Americans imperiled by hostile nonfederal sovereigns. In that sense, deferred action is part of the foreign affairs toolkit. As described by the Supreme Court in previous decisions, immigration officials' "deferred action" in lieu of removal can spring from this stewardship rationale.[32] Indeed, President Obama's rationale for DACA entailed similar reasoning. Chief Justice Roberts's opinion in *Regents* suggests that once the executive branch has chosen to offer such protection, officials must deliberate soundly about the reasons for ending it.

A. The Framers, Historical Practice, and Stewardship's Central Values

The Framers were familiar with stewardship and similar concepts such as the role of the fiduciary in assuming responsibility for others. In Federalist No. 23, Alexander Hamilton analogized government to a private fiduciary, urging that "government ought to be clothed with all the powers requisite to complete execution of its trust."[33] Consistency is a watchword of the stewardship envisioned by the Framers, while volatility is its antithesis.

For Hamilton, consistency was built into the virtues of the presidency, including decisiveness. The Framers sought a Constitution with a strong federal government in part to ensure that the nation spoke with "one voice" in world affairs, instead of shifting between

---

[31] Youngstown Sheet & Tube Co. v. Sawyer, 343 U.S. 579, 637 (1952) (Jackson, J., concurring); see also *id.* at 610–11 (Frankfurter, J., concurring) (asserting that legislative acquiescence should prompt judicial deference); Dames & Moore v. Regan, 453 U.S. 654 (1981) (upholding presidential claims settlement as reflecting longstanding practice in which Congress has acquiesced); David J. Barron & Martin S. Lederman, The Commander in Chief at the Lowest Ebb–Framing the Problem, Doctrine, and Original Understanding, 121 Harv. L. Rev. 689 (2008) (analyzing *Youngstown*'s implications); Curtis A. Bradley & Trevor W. Morrison, Historical Gloss and the Separation of Powers, 126 Harv. L. Rev. 411, 415 (2012); Brett M. Kavanaugh, Congress and the President in Wartime, Lawfare (blog), Nov. 29, 2017, reviewing David Barron, Waging War: The Clash Between Presidents and Congress, 1776 to ISIS (2016), https://bit.ly/2XzFMlv.

[32] See Arizona, 567 U.S. at 408–09 (2012) (warning that overzealous immigration enforcement by the several states could undermine federal decisions to extend consideration to undocumented foreign nationals in the United States who were "college student[s]" or had some other functional tie to the country).

[33] See The Federalist No. 23, *supra* note 1, at 153–54; see also Kent et al., *supra* note 1, at 2130 (discussing the president's oath of office and the Constitution's Take Care Clause, which both commit the president to faithful execution of the laws of the United States).

the multiplicity of agendas that might drive individual states within the new republic.[34] Indeed, in *Rutgers v. Waddington*, a celebrated case prior to the Constitution's enactment, Hamilton persuaded a New York court to look to the law of nations as a guide in a property dispute in which New York law appeared to conflict with the treaty between the United States and Britain that concluded the Revolutionary War.[35] Judged from a stewardship perspective, consistency over time yields the same virtues as decisiveness in the executive branch or a single voice in a nation's foreign relations.

Equitable balancing is also central to deliberative stewardship. A fiduciary exercising sound stewardship will rarely if ever consider just one factor. Instead, the steward will discern how various factors interact. For example, in the law of remedies, courts address the "balance of hardships" among the parties, as well as the public interest. In some cases, equity will require a "fine adjustment" among competing interests, which the judge should analyze in crafting remedies.[36]

Consider Chief Justice Roberts's analysis in *Nken v. Holder*. There, Roberts outlined the test for a stay pending appeal of a removal

---

[34] Arizona, 567 U.S. at 409.

[35] N.Y. Mayor's Ct. 1784, reprinted in 1 The Law Practice of Hamilton: Documents and Commentary 393, 405 (Julius Goebel Jr. ed., 1964) (explaining that, because of logic of federal system established by Articles of Confederation, each of the several states must be bound by international law when conflicts arise between any one state's law and international law, and warning of the "confusion" that would arise "if each separate state should arrogate to itself a right of changing at pleasure" precepts of the law of nations). On the importance of the *Rutgers* decision to U.S. foreign relations law and the evolving institution of judicial review, see Daniel J. Hulsebosch, Constituting Empire: New York and the Transformation of Constitutionalism in the Atlantic World, 1664–1830, 193–99 (2005); David M. Golove & Daniel J. Hulsebosch, A Civilized Nation: The Early American Constitution, the Law of Nations, and the Pursuit of International Recognition, 85 N.Y.U. L. Rev. 932, 963–66 (2010). Along these lines, provisions in the Constitution and the Judiciary Act of 1789 stemmed from the Framers' concerns that individual states were failing to punish violations of international law, including violations of the principle of diplomatic immunity. See Sosa v. Alvarez-Machain, 542 U.S. 692, 715–18 (2004).

[36] See Hecht Co. v. Bowles, 321 U.S. 321, 329 (1944) (noting that "the qualities of mercy and practicality have made equity the instrument for nice adjustment and reconciliation between the public interest and private needs"); see also Winter v. NRDC, 555 U.S. 7, 24–26 (2008) (holding that in issuing and affirming injunction against navy training exercises, lower courts had failed to adequately take into account public interest served by the exercises); but see Jared A. Goldstein, Equitable Balancing in the Age of Statutes, 96 Va. L. Rev. 485, 513–20 (2010) (criticizing *Winter*'s reading of equitable balancing as not giving sufficient weight to Congress's plan).

order—a judicial variant of the reprieve prong of DACA.[37] Roberts wrote that a judge can consider whether removal would result in irreparable harm and whether the "balance of hardships" and the public interest favored the applicant for a stay. A court must determine whether a noncitizen's removal prior to full adjudication of her appeal would unduly impede her ability to appeal and thus relegate appellate review to an "'idle ceremony.'"[38] Impeding a court's chance to consider a colorable claim for relief on appeal injures the applicant for a stay, but also adversely affects the public interest in a properly functioning means of appellate review. Conversely, an appellate court should also determine whether a stay would injure the public interest served by efficient enforcement of immigration law.

Weighing of the public interest has also figured in executive branch decisions to provide assistance to prospective Americans. Before DACA, examples of practice in this vein started with a cautionary counter example during the John Adams administration and proceeded through President Theodore Roosevelt's intervention in the San Francisco school crisis of 1906–1907. In each case, a president either earned scorn for failing to help or acted decisively to intervene.

In the first example—a cautionary tale of stewardship's absence—President John Adams infuriated both Congress and the public by his delivery to British custody of Thomas Nash, who claimed to be a U.S. citizen named Jonathan Robbins. Britain then tried and executed Nash on charges of mutiny.[39] Americans at the time viewed mutiny as a valid response to brutal British navy discipline and impressment of foreign seamen, including those from U.S. vessels. In addition, Jefferson and others argued that mutiny was a political

---

[37] Nken, 556 U.S. 418. A stay pending appeal differs from DACA-style relief since an applicant for a stay first must receive a removal order from DHS, while a DACA recipient could participate in the program without ever being in removal proceedings. Moreover, a stay pending appeal lasts only so long as the court needs to resolve the appeal, while DACA is renewable indefinitely. But both a stay and DACA enable a reprieve from removal.

[38] *Id.* at 427 (citing Scripps-Howard Radio, Inc. v. FCC, 316 U.S. 4, 10 (1942)).

[39] See Margulies, Taking Care of Immigration Law, *supra* note 7, at 134–36; see also John T. Parry, International Extradition, the Rule of Non-Inquiry, and the Problem of Sovereignty, 90 B.U. L. Rev. 1973, 1975 n.10 (2010) (describing episode as a "cautionary tale . . . for decades to come"); Ruth Wedgwood, The Revolutionary Martyrdom of Jonathan Robbins, 100 Yale L.J. 229 (1990) (providing comprehensive analysis of this episode).

crime that targeted an oppressive system and was therefore not an appropriate subject for extradition. Indeed, Jefferson was skeptical about extradition because of the difficulty of distinguishing ordinary from political crimes.[40] The intervention on Nash's behalf that Adams rejected would have provided a clear, consistent signal of the president's dedication to rescuing prospective Americans. Meshing with the public interest, intervention would also have dovetailed with evolving U.S. conceptions of human rights and more mundane U.S. interests in a growing merchant fleet.

The response to Adams's failure to save Nash underlined the importance of stewardship to safeguarding prospective Americans. Adams was almost impeached. He lost the election of 1800, the Federalists ceased to be a significant political force, and extradition became a dead letter for decades. Adams's default in Nash's case was not the only cause of the first two events, but it was a primary factor in the third development and crystallized sentiment that led to Adams's loss and the Federalists' precipitous decline.

In the second example, President Franklin Pierce lived up to the stewardship model's expectations. Pierce intervened to rescue Hungarian dissident Martin Koszta, who had lived in New York before being kidnaped by Austrian agents while in Turkey.[41] Secretary of State William Marcy articulated a consistent test, announcing that the United States would use its power to protect individuals anywhere around the world who had established a domicile in the United States. Marcy linked the United States's intervention with the public interest in compliance with the "laws of humanity . . . [that] protect the weak from being oppressed by the strong, and . . . relieve the distressed."[42] This rationale suggests that for Marcy and President Pierce, positioning the United States in the vanguard of that humane effort would also enhance the nation's global reputation and

[40] See Thomas Jefferson, Secretary of State, to George Washington, President (Nov. 7, 1791), https://bit.ly/33qSXJ8 (advising Washington that it was often "difficult to draw the line between [ordinary crimes] . . . and acts rendered criminal by tyrannical laws only").

[41] Margulies, Taking Care of Immigration Law, *supra* note 7, at 138–41; In re Neagle, 135 U.S. 1, 64 (1890).

[42] See Hon. William M. Marcy, Secretary of State, to Baron von Hulsemann, Austrian Charge D'Affaires, Sept. 26, 1853, in Correspondence Between the Secretary of State and the Charge D'Affaires of Austria Relative to the Case of Martin Koszta 16 (1853), https://bit.ly/30u3qlc.

thus further U.S. interests. In *In re Neagle*, the Court cited the Koszta episode for the proposition that presidential stewardship includes not merely the "express terms" of treaties and statutes, but also U.S. "international relations and all the protection [of federal officials, U.S. nationals, and intending Americans like Koszta] implied by the nature of the government under the Constitution."[43]

B. *Stewardship and Federalism*

In an early 20th-century episode, President Theodore Roosevelt and his secretary of state, Elihu Root, practiced stewardship in their resolution of the San Francisco segregation dispute of 1906–1907. Acting under California law, San Francisco had sought to establish segregated schools for Japanese children domiciled in the United States with their families. A treaty between Japan and the United States gave those children rights to the same education as other foreign national children, including those from Europe. Roosevelt ordered federal troops into position to stop any violence against San Francisco's Japanese community and sued to enjoin the city's policy.[44] Elaborating on the rationale for Roosevelt's handling of the segregation dispute, Root echoed the concern with consistency and the public interest that drove Hamilton's arguments in *Rutgers v. Waddington*. Root faulted local passions, which could impede the consistency required for foreign affairs and erode "rules . . . essential to the maintenance of peace . . . between nations."[45]

In the last 40 years, stewardship has figured in federal responses to overly aggressive state immigration enforcement that could derail U.S. foreign policy. In *Plyler v. Doe*, the Supreme Court struck down a Texas law that excluded undocumented children from public school.[46] While Justice William Brennan, writing for the Court, analyzed the

---

[43] 135 U.S. 1, 64 (1890); see also John Harrison, The Story of In re Neagle: Sex, Money, Politics, Perjury, Homicide, Federalism, and Executive Power, in Presidential Power Stories 133, 153–54 (Christopher H. Schroeder & Curtis A. Bradley eds., 2009) (discussing role of Koszta episode in *Neagle*); cf. Henry Monaghan, The Protective Power of the Presidency, 93 Colum. L. Rev. 1, 70–71 (1993) (arguing against unduly broad reading of *Neagle* that might result in presidential overreaching).

[44] See Elihu Root, The Real Questions under the Japanese Treaty and the San Francisco School Board Resolution, 1 Am. J. Int'l L. 273, 276 (1907).

[45] *Id*. at 273–74.

[46] 457 U.S. 202 (1982).

case in equal–protection terms, Brennan's opinion framed undocumented children as recipients of a kind of tacit de facto deferred action in which federal officials expressly conceded that they could not deport each undocumented child. The likelihood that many undocumented children would grow up knowing only the United States as their home highlighted the need for stewardship's virtues of consistency and equitable balancing. Justice Brennan remarked on Congress's power, which the Court has repeatedly recognized, to set consistent national policy regarding immigration, contrasting that with states' patchwork of immigration measures. Moreover, he wrote, Texas's law impinged on the broader public interest in educating children. State laws impeding undocumented children's access to public education would "foreclose any realistic possibility that . . . [undocumented children] will contribute in even the smallest way to the progress of our Nation."[47]

In *Arizona v. United States*, the Supreme Court again addressed the conflict between restrictive state measures and federal stewardship.[48] Finding that Congress had preempted some of Arizona's laws on immigration enforcement, the Court cited Federalist No. 3, in which John Jay had warned of border states' habit of "sudden irritation" and resulting skirmishes with foreign states.[49] For Jay, easing the country back from the brink of war required the more "temperate and cool" perspective of the federal government, which could cultivate that longer-term outlook because it was physically further from the fraught border.[50]

Applying Jay's insights, Justice Anthony Kennedy noted that states could undermine U.S. foreign policy and the overall public interest through "harassment" of foreign nationals who were students pursuing higher education, veterans of the armed forces, or witnesses in criminal cases.[51] In a nod to consistency, Justice Kennedy warned that the Framers crafted the Constitution in part to spare a foreign country from dealing with "50 separate states," instead of a single

---

[47] *Id.* at 230.

[48] 567 U.S. 387 (2012); Margulies, Taking Care of Immigration Law, *supra* note 7, at 162–65.

[49] Arizona, 567 U.S. at 395 (citing The Federalist No. 3 (John Jay)).

[50] The Federalist No. 3 (John Jay).

[51] Arizona, 567 U.S. at 408.

central government that could efficiently address foreign concerns. For Kennedy, deferred action allowed the federal government to practice that consistency and speak with "one voice" in the volatile realm of foreign relations.[52]

President Obama's initiation of DACA fit within this stewardship model. As foreign nationals who arrived in the United States as children and had often known no other country as home, DACA recipients were a fit subject for interstitial executive protection. DACA also shielded these hardship cases from overzealous state enforcement efforts of the kind the Court had curtailed in *Plyler* and *Arizona*. Recipients aided the public interest, since they were able to contribute their time, effort, and talent to the American project, as Justice Brennan had envisioned in *Plyler*. The program's categorical approach provided consistency and certainty that a more piecemeal approach to immigration relief would have lacked.

The Trump administration had a different approach, which prompted judicial skepticism even before *Regents*. In a 2019 case encompassing the public interest and undocumented immigrants, the Court in *Department of Commerce v. New York* required consistency in the Trump administration's rationale for adding a citizenship question to the census.[53] Adding a citizenship question would have been a departure from recent practice: although the government had included a citizenship question in the past as part of its constitutional duty to conduct a census, officials for 60 years had not included this query. Pre-Trump officials had resisted reintroducing a citizenship question, explaining that this move would deter participation since undocumented individuals and their families would fear that an accurate response would prompt immigration enforcement action. Reduced participation would skew the population count and with it calculations on congressional representation, the composition of state legislatures, and federal funding.[54]

Against this backdrop of a high-stakes decision affecting the public interest that pivoted from decades-long agency practice,

---

[52] *Id.* at 409.

[53] 139 S. Ct. 2551 (2019). For commentary on the census decision, see Jennifer Chacón, The Inside-Out Constitution: Department of Commerce v. New York, 2019 Sup. Ct. Rev. 231 (2019); Margulies, Rescinding Inclusion, *supra* note 7, at 1461–67; Gillian E. Metzger, The Roberts Court and Administrative Law, 2019 Sup. Ct. Rev. 1 (2019).

[54] Dep't of Commerce, 139 S. Ct. at 2562, 2565.

the Court held that the Commerce Department's rationale for seeking to reintroduce a citizenship question was "pretextual."[55] Writing for the Court, Chief Justice Roberts agreed that the secretary of commerce had the power to decide to add a citizenship question. But he also indicated that, under accepted principles of administrative law, the government when making such "important decisions" had to offer "genuine justifications" that will survive judicial and public scrutiny.[56] In the census case, the Court found that Commerce Secretary Wilbur Ross had failed in his duty to provide such a sincere justification. Instead, Ross had "contrived" a pretextual rationale by persuading reluctant Department of Justice officials to assert that a citizenship question would provide information necessary for compliance with the Voting Rights Act.[57]

That "disconnect" in the census case between a high-stakes decision and the "contrived" official reason for the agency's choice would, if accepted by the Court, have made judicial review into an "empty ritual."[58] Here, Chief Justice Roberts's description echoed his concern in *Nken v. Holder* that a stay of removal pending appeal was necessary to avoid making appellate review an "idle ceremony."[59] Sound stewards do not have the time for either empty rituals or idle ceremonies. Moreover, they do not impose such futile exercises on others. Secretary Ross's "pretextual" rationale thus compromised the Administrative Procedure Act's requirement of "[r]easoned decisionmaking."[60] While Chief Justice Roberts did not find that Acting DHS Secretary Duke's reasons for ending DACA were similarly contrived, he did identify flaws in her justification that also violated the APA's "reasoned decisionmaking" goal.

III. The Court's DACA Decision: Stewardship Over Structure

This preliminary discussion of stewardship sets the stage for analysis of Chief Justice Roberts's discussion in *Regents*. In his opinion finding DHS's rationale for rescission inadequate, Roberts sounded

---

[55] *Id.* at 2574.

[56] *Id.* at 2575.

[57] *Id.*

[58] *Id.* at 2575–76.

[59] Nken, 556 U.S. at 427.

[60] Dep't of Commerce, 139 S. Ct. at 2576.

three themes in the key of stewardship. First, Roberts focused on the Duke Memorandum, describing the later Nielsen Memorandum as an impermissible *"post hoc* rationalization."[61] Second, Roberts described DACA recipients' expectations that the program would continue, and the Duke Memorandum's failure to acknowledge and address those expectations. Third, Roberts asserted that the Duke Memorandum should have considered other options besides outright termination of the entire program; in particular, Duke should have considered separating out the reprieve and work permit parts of the program and continuing the reprieve component.

The third point is striking because Chief Justice Roberts disagreed with lower-court rulings that viewed DACA as one unified exercise of executive discretion, instead agreeing with the Fifth Circuit's framing of the reprieve/benefits distinction in the DAPA case. But, compared with the Fifth Circuit's decision, Roberts's use of this frame had a very different practical effect. In the DAPA case, the Fifth Circuit had cited the inclusion of eligibility for benefits as a basis for invalidating the program. In contrast, Roberts found fault with DHS's insufficient consideration of the consequences of rescinding both parts of DACA and sent the agency back to the drawing board. I call his process-based mode of analysis "deliberative stewardship," to distinguish it from the stronger, substantive brand of stewardship that President Theodore Roosevelt championed.

A. Stewardship as Consistency: Reading Chenery Broadly to Limit DHS to One Bite at the Apple

After determining that courts could review the DACA rescission under the Administrative Procedure Act, Chief Justice Roberts turned to the important task of deciding whether the Supreme Court could only consider the conclusory justifications for the rescission in the 2017 Duke Memorandum, or whether it could also consider the more detailed explanation in Acting Secretary Nielsen's June 2018 memorandum. In a key move, Roberts read administrative law doctrine as limiting DHS to reliance on Duke's perfunctory explanation. The following subsections analyze Chief Justice Roberts's approach to this complex issue and then discuss Justice Kavanaugh's powerful dissent.

---

[61] 140 S. Ct. at 1909.

1. Chief Justice Roberts and the perils of agency post hoc rationalizations

Chief Justice Roberts stressed the need for government to "turn square corners in dealing with the American people." A sound steward deliberates systematically, without "cutting corners."[62] In contrast, an agency failing to do its job deliberates in haste and rolls out shifting rationales to suit its short-term interests.

Administrative law enforces the virtue of consistency through the *Chenery* doctrine. That doctrine takes its name from a 1943 Supreme Court decision holding that a court should only consider an agency's initial justification for a decision, not subsequent justifications that may help the agency in a lawsuit but do not candidly represent the agency's original rationale. That holding promotes "clarity in . . . [the] exercise" of administrative judgment, the responses of the agency's stakeholders, and review by courts.[63]

The *Chenery* doctrine's virtues dovetail with the uniformity that the Framers praised in the federal government's constitutional role in foreign affairs. In *Arizona v. United States*, the virtue of consistency inhered in the straightforward negotiating position of a single central government, as compared with the patchwork quilt of 50 different sets of state law enforcement officials. In the DACA case, the issue was consistency *over time*; an agency should deliberate about a position clearly and carefully when it first announces that decision, instead of issuing "'post hoc' [after-the-fact] rationalizations" that confuse the agency's audience.[64] As Roberts put it, this relentless procession of "belated justifications" forces litigants and courts to "chase a moving target."[65] The confusion that results clashes with the agency's stewardship role.

Having established the virtue of consistency over time in agency explanations, Chief Justice Roberts then applied it to limit DHS to

---

[62] *Id.* (citing St. Regis Paper Co. v. United States, 368 U.S. 208, 229 (1961) (Black, J., dissenting)).

[63] SEC v. Chenery Corp., 318 U.S. 80, 94 (1943). Justice Felix Frankfurter, who prized methodical decisionmaking by agencies, wrote the opinion of the Court in *Chenery* and an earlier decision that he cited in his *Chenery* opinion, Phelps Dodge Corp. v. NLRB 313 U.S. 177, 197 (1941). Cf. Ronald M. Levin, "Vacation" at Sea: Judicial Remedies and Equitable Discretion in Administrative Law, 53 Duke L.J. 291, 367 (2003) (explaining *Chenery* doctrine).

[64] 140 S. Ct. at 1909 (citing Citizens to Preserve Overton Park, Inc. v. Volpe, 401 U.S. 402, 419 (1971)).

[65] *Id.*

the Duke Memorandum's reasons for the DACA rescission. Roberts described the Duke Memorandum as the "natural starting point" for the Court's consideration of DHS's reasons.[66] Duke had merely cited, "without elaboration," Attorney General Sessions's legal conclusion that DACA exceeded the power Congress had delegated to immigration officials under the INA.[67] Focusing on the Duke Memorandum's stark statement of reasons put DHS at a marked disadvantage in the case, since Duke had not offered a detailed consideration of DACA recipients' expectations that the program would continue. In contrast, the Nielsen Memorandum's explanation offered a more thorough response. However, Roberts's devotion to consistency cast the Nielsen Memorandum's additional detail as a flaw, not a virtue. Citing the importance of consistency, Roberts determined that this more elaborate reasoning was "nowhere to be found" in the Duke Memorandum, and that therefore the Nielsen Memorandum relied on "impermissible *post hoc* rationalizations" that the Court would not address.[68]

2. Justice Kavanaugh's narrower reading of the *Chenery* doctrine

If the *Chenery* doctrine is about agency consistency, it is important that courts apply the doctrine in the same consistent vein. Chief Justice Roberts's expansive view of *Chenery* is not the only way to read administrative law. For Justice Kavanaugh, Roberts's approach misread the doctrine's teaching.

In his dissent, Justice Kavanaugh viewed the Nielsen Memorandum's fuller account of reasons behind the rescission as an entirely permissible "amplified articulation" of points the government had made previously.[69] For Kavanaugh, *Chenery* excluded a different subset of after-the-fact explanations: the arguments of lawyers in litigation, who have an incentive to cobble together remotely plausible rationales to satisfy reviewing courts. The Nielsen Memorandum was not a lawyer's tactic. As a mere amplification of earlier reasoning by a responsible official, the Nielsen Memorandum had all the consistency administrative law could reasonably require.

---

[66] *Id.* at 1907.

[67] *Id.* at 1910.

[68] *Id.* at 1908–09.

[69] 140 S. Ct. at 1934 (Kavanaugh, J., dissenting) (citing Alpharma v. Leavitt, 460 F.3d 1, 6 (D.C. Cir. 2006)).

But Justice Kavanaugh's more constrained view of the *Chenery* doctrine does not fully answer Chief Justice Roberts's concerns.[70] Consistency in this case would have cost DHS little. DHS could have deliberated with greater depth in 2017, instead of issuing a more comprehensive explanation only after judicial prompting. Especially given the high stakes of the decision, it was reasonable for Chief Justice Roberts to expect a more detailed explanation of DHS's reasons up front.

B. Regents and Reliance Interests

The equitable balancing dimension of stewardship took center stage for Chief Justice Roberts's analysis of DACA recipients' reliance interests. As noted above, stewardship considers both the "balance of hardships" and the public interest. In finding that the Duke Memorandum had failed to assess the weight of recipients' reliance, Roberts observed that maintaining stability for recipients also benefited the public.

As a matter of administrative law doctrine, Roberts's analysis of the Duke Memorandum's deliberative flaws invoked that staple of robust judicial review, the "hard look" doctrine.[71] Under the "hard look" doctrine, there must be a "satisfactory explanation" of the agency's decision. Moreover, the agency must engage in "consideration of the relevant factors" and address each "important aspect of the problem" at hand.[72] That commitment to "consideration" is a core tenet of equitable balancing and the duties of stewardship. Because her memorandum did not assess the weight that DHS should accord recipients' reliance interests, Acting Secretary Duke failed this threshold test.

Roberts noted that the Duke Memorandum would have terminated DACA recipients' participation starting with current terms that ended on March 6, 2018, a mere six months after the rescission's announcement, with all participation ending two years after that, on March 6, 2020. While at first blush this wind-down period might

---

[70] In the interest of full disclosure, I should explain that my own view has shifted on this point. In an earlier piece, I also took a narrow view of *Chenery* and the DACA rescission, although my discussion was limited to two sentences in a footnote. See Margulies, Rescinding Inclusion, *supra* note 7, at 1473 n.240.

[71] 140 S. Ct. 1912–13 (citing Motor Vehicle Mfrs. Ass'n v. State Farm Mut. Auto. Ins. Co., 463 U.S. 29, 43 (1983)).

[72] *Id.* at 1905 (citing Overton Park, 401 U.S. at 416); *id.* at 1913 (citing State Farm, 463 U.S. at 43).

seem reasonable, a closer look revealed that Duke had failed to either accommodate the expectations of recipients or explain why such accommodation was inappropriate. Consider again the hypothetical posed earlier of a DACA recipient who enrolled in a four-year college in September 2016 and whose two-year DACA period of participation was due to end on March 6, 2018. In Chief Justice Roberts's apt phrase, this recipient would be "caught in the middle of a time-bounded commitment," without either sufficient notice of the rescission to avoid embarking on an undergraduate degree or sufficient time to complete her college education.[73] Chief Justice Roberts described a similar predicament for persons serving in the armed forces or receiving an extended course of needed medical treatment. According to Roberts, Duke could have considered allowing our hypothetical college student and similar "caught in the middle" recipients to complete their respective periods of study, treatment, or service.[74] A good steward would have at least deliberated about a wind-down that reflected these concerns.

The dashed expectations that Chief Justice Roberts flagged also affected a large number of U.S. nationals. In our college student hypothetical, consider the interests of the U.S. school that had counted on the recipient's continued enrollment and devoted substantial resources to her education. Chief Justice Roberts suggested that those interests were also an aspect of the case that DHS should have considered.[75] Roberts did not cite the Supreme Court's decision almost 40 years earlier in *Plyler v. Doe*. Nevertheless, his argument echoed the anxiety in *Plyler* and *Arizona* about negative externalities— impacts on persons and entities beyond the parties. Echoing these risks, Roberts reminded readers that the adverse effects of the rescission would "radiate outward" from recipients to U.S. persons and institutions involved in recipients' lives, including U.S. citizen children, schools where recipients "study and teach," and employers who invested money and effort in preparing recipients to work in their companies and were now facing a loss of their investment.[76]

---

[73] *Id.* at 1914.

[74] *Id.*

[75] *Id.* (quoting the rescission's challengers and their amici as asserting that there was "much for DHS to consider," including the expectations of third parties with ties to DACA recipients).

[76] *Id.* (citing Brief for Respondent Regents of Univ. of Cal. et al. at 41–42, Dep't of Homeland Security v. Regents of the Univ. of Cal., 140 S. Ct. 1891 (2020) (No. 18-587)).

As a sound steward, DHS had to deliberate about the relative merits of rescission versus the synergy that rescission would extinguish between DACA and the public interest. Beyond deliberation, Robert disclaimed any duty by DHS to continue the program. Upon deliberation, DHS might have concluded that recipients' reliance interests were not weighty in the scheme of things or did not outweigh legal questions about the program. But the Duke Memorandum suffered from a deliberative deficit. Invoking the responsibilities of stewardship, Roberts asserted that deliberation about reliance interests was a central part of "the agency's job" and "responsibility" that the agency had neglected.[77]

C. Stewardship's Puzzle: The Practical Problems with Separation of Forbearance and Benefits

In the course of discussing DHS's failure to consider recipients' reliance interests, Chief Justice Roberts also separated out two aspects of DACA: its reprieve from deportation, which Roberts called "forbearance," and its provision of eligibility for a work permit, which Roberts referred to as DACA's "benefits" prong.[78] Roberts asserted that Acting Secretary Duke erred by failing to consider the legality of continuing forbearance under DACA, while terminating benefits. Roberts's separation of these two parts of DACA reinforced his point that DHS failed to consider reliance interests. But Roberts's separation of DACA into forbearance and benefits was artificial, since in practice the two parts are often integrally related.

Roberts clearly viewed as "important" Acting Secretary Duke's failure to separately consider the legality of benefits and forbearance, respectively.[79] For Roberts, forbearance—detached from benefits— was DACA's "centerpiece."[80] According to Roberts, the bulk of the DHS memorandum announcing DACA was "devoted entirely" to

[77] *Id.*

[78] *Id.* at 1911–13.

[79] *Id.* at 1913 (citation omitted). Harvard Law professor Benjamin Eidelson was one of the architects of advocates' strategy on this point. See Benjamin Eidelson, "Unbundling DACA and Unpacking Regents: What Chief Justice Roberts Got Right," Balkinization (blog), June 25, 2020, https://bit.ly/3gwIQpX; see also Josh Blackman, "Where Did CJ Roberts's Anti-Saving Construction in the DACA Case Come From?," Reason: Volokh Conspiracy, June 20, 2020, https://bit.ly/2Pp4jVQ (discussing origins and development of separation idea in the course of litigation over the DACA rescission).

[80] Regents, 140 S. Ct. at 1913.

forbearance, with a single isolated sentence instructing DHS to consider recipient requests for work permits.[81] However, this view of DACA as centering on forbearance and conferring eligibility for benefits as an afterthought failed to recognize benefits' crucial role.

From the start, the ability to leverage recipients' skills by providing work permits was integral to DACA's plan. In announcing DACA, DHS Secretary Napolitano cited the "productive young people" that the program would help, further noting that "many" prospective recipients had "already contributed to our country in significant ways."[82] These observations were hardly throwaway lines. Building on her description of prospective recipients' valuable contributions to U.S. society, Napolitano directed DHS to accept applications for work permits from DACA recipients. Picking up on this signal, contemporary media accounts and immigration advocates touted DACA's benefits.[83] A policy of forbearance without benefits would not have earned that level of enthusiasm.[84]

That said, separating forbearance from benefits is not entirely artificial. Consider recipients that Roberts mentioned who are enrolled in college or receiving medical treatment. A state such as California allows noncitizens to enroll in higher education programs and pay in-state tuition even if they are not lawfully present.[85] Some hospitals will provide medical treatment under similar circumstances. For at least the California cohort of recipients, forbearance alone will serve

[81] *Id.* at 1912 n.6.

[82] See Napolitano Memorandum, *supra* note 4, at 2.

[83] See Julia Preston & John H. Cushman, Jr., "Obama to Permit Young Migrants to Remain in U.S.," N.Y. Times, June 16, 2012, at A1 (citing eligibility for work permits in lead paragraph, mentioning eligibility throughout story, and quoting "[i]mmigrant student leaders as expecting that the 'majority of [immigrant] students would seize the opportunity to work and come out of the shadows'").

[84] On the practical problems with separating benefits and forbearance, the proof is in the pudding. DHS's practice under President Obama's second Senate-confirmed Homeland Security Secretary, Jeh Johnson, virtually always resulted in work authorization for successful DACA applicants. See Jie Zong et al., Migration Pol'y Inst., A Profile of DACA Recipients by Education, Industry, and Occupation 3–8 (Nov. 2017), https://bit.ly/30yWhjD (describing details of DACA recipients' work permit status based on DHS statistics, and implying that virtually all recipients who sought a work permit received one).

[85] Martinez v. Regents of Univ. of Cal., 241 P.3d 855, 861 (Cal. 2010) (citing Cal. Educ. Code § 68130.5(a)(4)); see also Ming Hsu Chen, Beyond Legality: The Legitimacy of Executive Action in Immigration Law, 66 Syracuse L. Rev. 87, 129–30 (2016) (describing state laws and policies).

reliance interests. To that extent, Roberts's point that DHS should have considered splitting up benefits and forbearance fits the model of deliberative stewardship.[86]

Viewing DHS's duty as deliberative stewardship connects *Regents* with earlier precedents such as *Plyler v. Doe* and *Arizona v. United States* and historical examples such as President Pierce's intervention in the Martin Koszta episode. *Regents* also echoes the 2019 census decision, *Department of Commerce v. New York*. In *Department of Commerce*, as noted above, Chief Justice Roberts noted the high stakes of adding a citizenship question on the census and required a clear and consistent justification. The Commerce Department's "contrived" justification on needing data for Voting Rights Act compliance failed to pass muster.[87] Admittedly, Roberts did not refer to Acting Secretary Duke's explanation for the DACA rescission as pretextual, in the way that he had characterized Commerce Secretary Wilbur Ross's reasons in the census case. Nevertheless, each decision focused on flawed and shifting explanations for momentous actions that departed from established practice. In both decisions, Roberts seems to be reminding agencies that stewardship requires sounder deliberation than the agencies saw fit to provide.

D. Justice Thomas's Dissent

On the substance of the DACA rescission, Justice Thomas's dissent stressed the structural concerns raised by the Fifth Circuit about the DAPA program. In interpreting statutes, courts generally hold that Congress does its work mindfully, drafting language to cover issues it considers crucial and specifically describing areas where it has delegated discretion to an agency such as DHS. When courts read Congress's silence as giving vast power to an agency, the courts risk making the text of the law "wholly superfluous."[88] Treating the

---

[86]Chief Justice Roberts rejected the claim of the rescission's challengers that the rescission violated the Equal Protection Clause. 140 S. Ct. at 1915–16. Justice Sonia Sotomayor dissented from this part of Chief Justice Roberts's opinion. *Id.* at 1916–18 (Sotomayor, J., dissenting in part).

[87]139 S. Ct. 2551, 2575–76 (2019).

[88]*Id.* at 1925 (Thomas, J., dissenting). Justice Thomas also stated that if the statute permitted a vast program like DACA to be created under executive fiat, the INA would be an unconstitutional delegation of legislative power. *Id.* at 1929 n.13. Cf. Gary Lawson, "I'm Leavin' It (All) Up to You": Gundy and the (Sort-of) Resurrection of the Subdelegation Doctrine, 2018–2019 Cato Sup. Ct. Rev. 31 (2019) (discussing recent indications that the Supreme Court is ready to revive the nondelegation doctrine).

actual words of the statute as a useless ornament that the executive branch can sweep aside would make Congress a supporting player in the legislative arena, when Congress should have the lead role.

Applying these principles, Justice Thomas asserted that DACA, like DAPA, was far too large a program to fit within the INA's specific framework. Congress's careful drafting would have been a waste of time if DHS could establish a program of DACA's size "at the stroke of a Cabinet secretary's pen."[89] By invalidating an effort by a subsequent administration to end this clash with the INA's framework, the Court's majority had disregarded a crucial tenet of statutory interpretation.

Furthermore, Thomas reminded the majority that regard for the reliance interests of DACA recipients did not fit past practice on deferred action, which Justice Scalia in an earlier decision had described as rooted in administrative "convenience."[90] Indeed, when it announced DACA during the Obama administration, DHS had stated that it could "terminate . . . deferred action at any time at the agency's discretion."[91] Thomas warned that while deferred action's ease of implementation had been a virtue, the majority's decision would henceforth make future officials hesitate to grant it, since rescinding such grants will in the future entail "years of litigation."[92]

While Thomas's critique of the majority's position is cogent, ultimately Roberts's focus on DACA recipients' reliance interest is more convincing from a stewardship perspective. Thomas's dissent insightfully outlined the structural argument against DACA. But Roberts's focus on DHS's deliberative deficit sidestepped this point. Stewardship's equitable balancing strand helps support Roberts's analysis. As mentioned above, under longstanding equitable principles that govern how a court devises a remedy for a particular illegal act, the court must consider a range of factors, including the balance of hardships and the public interest.[93] That may mean that a court will not order an immediate end to a practice, but will instead

---

[89] 140 S. Ct. at 1925–26 (Thomas, J., dissenting).

[90] *Id.* at 1931 n.16 (citing Reno v. American-Arab Anti-Discrimination Comm., 525 U.S. 471, 484 (1999)).

[91] *Id.* (citation omitted).

[92] *Id.*; cf. Ilya Shapiro, "DACA Ruling: Bad Judging on Top of Bad Lawyering, Good for Dreamers but Makes Immigration Reform Harder," Cato at Liberty (blog), June 18, 2020, https://bit.ly/2XwReho.

[93] See Hecht Co., 321 U.S. at 329.

order a gradual termination. While a court has discretion to craft a remedy that includes a wind-down or opt for immediate termination of the challenged practice, the court will have to show that it balanced all the necessary factors in reaching its result.[94] This is exactly what DHS failed to do in rescinding DACA. That failure of due deliberation about remedy was problematic, regardless of DACA's legal merits. In this sense, Roberts's approach fit the stewardship model and deflected much of Thomas's critique.

Conclusion

Like the Court's 2019 census decision, *Department of Commerce*, in which Chief Justice Roberts also authored the majority opinion, *Regents* imposes a higher than usual burden of justification on executive branch officials. In the census case, the Court found the Department of Commerce's "voting rights enforcement" rationale for a census citizenship question to be pretextual. It did so even though that finding involved looking behind the Commerce Department's stated justifications, into its "contrived" interactions with a Justice Department that—truth to tell—seemed largely uninterested in the Commerce Department's ostensible voting rights rationale. *Regents* did not find that DHS's reasons for rescinding DACA were pretextual. But Chief Justice Roberts still looked beyond the structural issue of DACA's fit with the INA and found the agency's deliberative process flawed, especially in its failure to consider DACA recipients' reliance interests and alternatives to the outright termination by March 2020 that DHS had announced.

Although Chief Justice Roberts did not mention stewardship per se in his opinion, his analysis of DHS's "job" and "responsibility" in deliberating about reliance interests and alternatives to outright rescission sounded in that key. Starting with the cautionary tale of stewardship's absence in the Jonathan Robbins episode during the John Adams administration, executive practice has contemplated a gap-filling role in protecting prospective Americans against nonfederal sovereigns. The stewardship suggested by this interstitial role has highlighted the virtues of consistency and equitable balancing,

---

[94] See N.Y. State Ass'n for Retarded Citizens v. Carey, 706 F.2d 956, 969–72 (2d Cir. 1983). In this decision, Judge Henry Friendly discussed the role of factors such as the public interest and effects on persons or entities not before the court in modification of an equitable decree reforming a government institution.

especially synergies between the welfare of prospective Americans and the public interest. Cases like *Plyler v. Doe* and *Arizona v. United States* illustrate these virtues in restraining individual states' efforts at immigration enforcement when that enforcement might affect the national interest and U.S. foreign relations. *Department of Commerce* touched on similar virtues, particularly in its skeptical look at the Commerce Department's stated rationale for departing from decades of practice omitting a citizenship question from the census.

In *Regents*, the dissenters made cogent arguments that the majority's review lacked a clear basis in either administrative law doctrine or the statutory scheme. Justice Kavanaugh's dissent pointed out that Chief Justice Roberts's opinion, which limited DHS to reliance on the stark Duke Memorandum and barred any consideration of the later, more detailed Nielsen Memorandum, rested on an expansive reading of the *Chenery* doctrine. Excluding the Nielsen Memorandum may not serve *Chenery*'s premises, which center on the need to limit agency *lawyers'* litigation-driven rationales.

Justice Thomas's dissent argued to great effect that Chief Justice Roberts failed to fully address the large DACA program's poor fit with the INA's carefully crafted framework of enumerated categories of foreign nationals who can enter or legally remain in the United States and its residual category of persons subject to removal. That structural concern drove the courts' halt of the Obama administration's even larger DAPA program. The role of similar structural concerns on DACA raises difficult questions that Roberts did not try to definitively answer.

Nevertheless, the stewardship model supports Chief Justice Roberts's focus on the deliberative virtues of consistency, consideration of synergies between DACA recipients' expectations and the public interest, and assessment of alternatives. Acting Secretary Duke would have lost little by a fuller explanation of reasons in September 2017, when DHS first announced the DACA rescission. Moreover, analogy to the law of equitable remedies shows that DHS could have deliberated with greater care about resolving tensions between DACA and the statutory scheme.

Taking care of the laws of the United States is a key part of the executive branch's constitutional responsibility. The DACA rescission affected the implementation of the INA and the interests of millions of U.S. citizens, LPRs, domiciliaries, and organizations. A duty of deliberative stewardship in a matter with such high stakes is a reasonable requirement to impose on a responsible agency.

The Removal Power: A Critical Guide

*Ilan Wurman**

Introduction

In *Seila Law v. Consumer Financial Protection Bureau* (CFPB), the Supreme Court held that the creation of an independent agency headed by a single director with for-cause removal protections violated the executive-power provisions of the Constitution. This essay summarizes the scholarly and judicial debates over the removal power, specifically over the meaning of "the executive power," the historical practice, and the Court's crucial precedents. Although it seeks to provide a reasonable survey of the competing positions, it stakes out and tentatively defends particular answers. It then critically assesses the Court's decision in *Seila Law*. In summary, the Court took a minimalist approach by refusing to extend earlier precedents upholding for-cause removal provisions to the "new" situation of single-director agencies. Nevertheless, it is unclear what is left of the reasoning of the earlier, functionalist precedents after *Seila Law*. The decision thus represents the Court's continued return to formalist constitutional interpretation in separation-of-powers cases. The essay then also assesses the dissent, which is littered with citations to the academic literature and other historical materials. Interrogating those sources shows that most do not actually support the dissent's position.

* Associate Professor, Sandra Day O'Connor College of Law, Arizona State University. Author, A Debt Against the Living: An Introduction to Originalism (2017), and The Second Founding: An Introduction to the Fourteenth Amendment (forthcoming 2021). Significant portions of this article are based on a forthcoming article in the *Duke Law Journal*, see Ilan Wurman, In Search of Prerogative, 70 Duke L.J. (forthcoming Oct. 2020), and an amicus brief that I filed on behalf of myself and other law professors in the *Seila Law* case. Brief for Separation of Powers Scholars, Seila Law LLC v. Consumer Fin. Prot. Bureau, 140 S. Ct. 2183 (2019) (No. 19-7). The same thanks are owed here and any mistakes remain my own.

Part I canvasses four plausible readings of Article II's Executive Vesting Clause:[1] the cross-reference theory, the residual theory, and two versions of the law-execution theory. Which theory is correct has implications for the removal power. The prevailing formalist theory is the residual theory, which maintains that all "executive" power is vested in the president except as otherwise limited in the Constitution, and that removal is an "executive" power that is therefore vested in the president. I shall suggest (and I have elsewhere argued) that the residual theory is likely wrong. But that should not affect the removal question: "Removal" is part of "the executive power" to execute law. In fact, Chief Justice William Howard Taft, the author of *Myers v. United States*,[2] rejected the residual theory.

Part II briefly canvasses the historical record and responds to related recent scholarship. Without retreading too much old ground, it argues that removal was likely understood to be part of "the executive power" to execute law under the British Constitution and that recent scholarship maintaining the contrary is not persuasive. This part then turns to American practice. It argues that the proponents of a presidential removal power in the 1789 removal debates are best understood as arguing that the removal power was part of "the executive power" to execute law. Although the ultimate conclusion of the First Congress in the "Decision of 1789" is open to conflicting interpretations, what matters is the force of the arguments. This part then argues that there is no distinction between agencies enforcing financial legislation and agencies enforcing other types of legislation.

Part III (briefly) explains the Court's most important precedents. It argues that Chief Justice Taft did not embrace a residual theory of executive power in *Myers v. United States*, but rather the position that the removal power is part of "the executive power" to execute law. It then maintains that *Humphrey's Executor v. United States*,[3] decided only nine years after *Myers*, was wrongly decided. Although there is most assuredly government power that can be exercised

---

[1] "The executive Power shall be vested in a President of the United States of America." U.S. Const. art. II, § 1. To avoid confusion with the Constitution's other vesting clauses, I interchangeably refer to this clause as the Executive Power Clause, the Executive Vesting Clause, or Article II's vesting clause.

[2] 272 U.S. 52 (1926).

[3] 295 U.S. 602 (1935).

by more than one branch, *Humphrey's* stands for the mistaken and unconstitutional proposition—at least if the Executive Vesting Clause is a grant of power—that there is some government power that need not be exercised by *any* of the named constitutional actors. As I shall explain, however, *Humphrey's* is possible to defend on originalist grounds if the only power the president has to execute law is that which can be derived from the duty of faithful execution. Finally, this part examines the two most recent of the important removal decisions, *Morrison v. Olson*[4] and *Free Enterprise Fund v. PCAOB*,[5] one of which was thoroughly functionalist, the other of which was semiformalist.

Part IV then critically assesses *Seila Law v. CFPB* in light of these debates over meaning, historical practice, and precedent. It concludes that not much is left of the functionalist precedents after *Seila Law*, notwithstanding the plurality's attempt to issue a limited decision. It then critically assesses the dissent's arguments, particularly its use of academic literature and historical materials.

I. Four Textual Possibilities

Article II provides that "[t]he executive Power shall be vested in a President of the United States of America."[6] This formulation is distinct from the Vesting Clause of Article I, which provides that "[a]ll legislative Powers herein granted" are vested in Congress.[7] There is, however, a subsequent enumeration of presidential powers. The president is commander-in-chief, may grant pardons, and may demand the opinions in writing of the principal officers of the executive departments.[8] The president also has the power, shared with the Senate, to make treaties and appointments (although Congress may delegate the appointment of inferior officers to the president alone, to the heads of departments, or to the courts).[9] The president then has a series of duties, mostly to Congress: from time to time to give Congress information about the state of the union; to convene

---

[4] 487 U.S. 654 (1988).

[5] 561 U.S. 477 (2010).

[6] U.S. Const. art. II, § 1.

[7] U.S. Const. art. I, § 1.

[8] U.S. Const. art. II, § 2, cl. 1.

[9] U.S. Const. art. II, § 2, cl. 2.

Congress on extraordinary occasions and adjourn it in the event the House and Senate disagree about adjournment; to "take Care that the Laws be faithfully executed"; to "Commission all the Officers of the United States"; and to "receive Ambassadors and other public Ministers."[10]

What to make of the apparent general grant of "the executive power" along with the subsequent enumeration? Does the enumeration suggest that the executive power merely identifies who is to exercise the subsequently granted powers? If the Vesting Clause is a grant of substantive power, is the subsequent enumeration superfluous? There are four possible ways to read the text and its implication for the removal power.

A. The Cross-Reference Theory

The "cross-reference" theory maintains that the Executive Vesting Clause simply establishes *who* is to exercise the executive power. Justice Robert Jackson advanced this view in his *Youngstown* concurrence: "I cannot accept the view that [the executive power] clause is a grant in bulk of all conceivable executive power but regard it as an allocation to the presidential office of the generic powers thereafter stated."[11] The cross-reference theory may still be the most prominent view in the academy.

There are two reasons, however, to be skeptical of the cross-reference theory. First, if the clause merely identifies who is to exercise the subsequently granted powers, then the Take Care Clause must be a grant of power to execute the laws. That clause, however, is framed as a duty and not a power, although, to be sure, it is not implausible to think that a duty implies the necessary power. Perhaps more convincingly, the Vesting Clause in Article III, which is formulated in the same manner as the parallel clause in Article II,

---

[10] U.S. Const. art. II, § 3. Michael McConnell thinks the clause respecting commissioning officers was left over from an earlier draft of the Constitution when the Senate had most of the appointment power. See Michael W. McConnell, The President Who Would Not Be King (forthcoming 2020). In any event, that clause, and the receptions clause, serves to clarify a presidential duty where power is otherwise shared with the Senate.

[11] Youngstown Sheet & Tube Co. v. Sawyer, 343 U.S. 579, 641 (1952) (Jackson, J., concurring).

must be a grant of substantive power to judges; otherwise, nothing in Article III allows judges to exercise any power.[12]

If the cross-reference theory is correct, then there is no basis for an unlimited presidential removal power on originalist grounds. The removal power would have to derive solely from the duty (and whatever power that implies) to take care that the laws be faithfully executed. The extent to which the president must (or should) have control over subordinates would seem to require an entirely functional analysis. It could be inferred that the president must have the power to remove at-will any principal executive officer to be able properly to supervise the faithful execution of the laws, but that the president need not have such control over inferior officers. It is also plausible, however, to infer that Congress may limit the ability of the president to remove even principal officers to specified causes. The standard grounds for removal in such provisions—malfeasance, neglect, and inefficiency—although not necessarily coterminous with faithless execution, could all be understood as faithless execution.

To sharpen the difference between the implications of the cross-reference theory and the implications of the other possible readings of the Executive Vesting Clause, consider what the president would not be able to do if the removal power derived solely from the Take Care Clause. If the law granted discretion but the president was not tasked with personally executing the law, then the president would have no grounds to remove an officer who exercised discretion contrary to the president's wishes. So long as the subordinate officer's exercise of discretion was within the bounds of the law, there would be no faithless execution. This means the president could not insist on the policy priorities of the administration. The president could not direct an administrative officer as to how to interpret an ambiguous statute, nor direct prosecutors as to how they should exercise their prosecutorial discretion. Each officer tasked by Congress with discretionary duties would be able to decide how to exercise that discretion.

[12] U.S. Const. art. III, § 1 ("The judicial Power of the United States, shall be vested in one supreme Court, and in such inferior Courts as the Congress may from time to time ordain and establish."); Steven G. Calabresi & Kevin H. Rhodes, The Structural Constitution: Unitary Executive, Plural Judiciary, 105 Harv. L. Rev. 1155, 1176 (1992) (arguing that Article III's vesting clause is the "only explicit constitutional source of the federal judiciary's authority to act").

B. The Residual Theory

The prevailing view among formalists may be termed the "residual theory." According to this view, Article II's Vesting Clause vests all executive-type powers in the president, including those traditionally exercised by the British monarch. The subsequent enumeration in Article II—and elsewhere in the Constitution—is then largely a limitation on the president's ability to exercise specific executive powers, or perhaps a confirmation of them.[13] Michael W. McConnell explains this view: the Vesting Clause "vests all national powers of an executive nature in the President, except for that portion of the executive power that is vested elsewhere (mostly in Congress in Article I, Section 8), and except for the limitations and qualifications on the particular executive powers that are set forth in the text."[14] Article I, for example, assigns a number of traditionally executive or prerogative powers to Congress, such as the powers to declare war, issue letters of marque, coin money, and regulate fleets and armies.[15] Article II assigns some of this "executive" power (over treaties and appointments) to the president and the Senate together. Historically the king could prorogue Parliament,[16] but the American president may only adjourn Congress in the event of a disagreement between the two houses. Further, the president has a duty to execute Congress's laws *faithfully.*

---

[13] Curtis A. Bradley & Martin S. Flaherty, Executive Power Essentialism & Foreign Affairs, 102 Mich. L. Rev. 545, 549 (2004) (the residual theory "reconciles the text of the Constitution with the breadth of presidential power by stipulating that the Article II Vesting Clause grants the President all powers that are in their nature 'executive,' subject only to the specific exceptions and qualifications set forth in the rest of the Constitution"); Saikrishna B. Prakash & Michael D. Ramsey, The Executive Power over Foreign Affairs, 111 Yale L.J. 231, 253 (2001) ("[T]he President's executive foreign affairs power is residual, encompassing only those executive foreign affairs powers not allocated elsewhere by the Constitution's text. The Constitution's allocation of specific foreign affairs powers or roles to Congress or the Senate are properly read as assignments away from the President. Absent these specific allocations, by Article II, Section 1, all traditionally executive foreign affairs powers would be presidential.").

[14] McConnell, *supra* note 10, at 185.

[15] See Ilan Wurman, In Search of Prerogative, 70 Duke L.J. (forthcoming 2020) (discussing the historically prerogative powers).

[16] 1 William Blackstone, Commentaries on the Laws of England *180 ("[A]s the king has the sole right of convening the parliament, so also it is a branch of the royal prerogative, that he may (whenever he pleases) prorogue the parliament for a time, or put a final period to its existence.").

As I have argued at length elsewhere, the residual theory is probably mistaken.[17] First, the preponderance of the textual evidence from the 17th and 18th centuries is that "the executive power," in the singular, referred to the power to execute law.[18] John Locke, for example, distinguished "the executive power" from a "federative" power over war, treaties, ambassadors, and the like—powers that the residual theorists typically associate with "executive" power.[19] And Blackstone, in a chapter on the king's suite of prerogative powers, includes as a subset of those prerogatives "the executive power of the laws," which he seems to equate to law-execution.[20] There is some countervailing evidence, but at a minimum the textual evidence does not prove the residual theory.[21]

There are other reasons to doubt the residual theory. First, the Constitutional Convention voted to grant the national executive authority only to execute law and to appoint officers not otherwise provided for. If the Executive Vesting Clause were a plenary grant of all prerogative powers, then the Committee of Detail would have blatantly ignored this instruction.[22] To be sure, the Constitution does assign some additional powers to the president—the commander-in-chief power, the pardon power—but otherwise it assigns most of the traditionally prerogative powers to Congress. Reading the grant of executive power to be a grant of law-execution power would be more consistent with the committee's instruction as well as with the textual evidence. And, as I have previously argued, a residual grant is inconsistent with the apparent desire of the delegates to deny the

---

[17] Wurman, *supra* note 15.

[18] *Id.*; see also Julian Davis Mortenson, Article II Vests Executive Power, Not the Royal Prerogative, 119 Colum. L. Rev. 1169 (2019).

[19] John Locke, The Second Treatise, Two Treatises on Government 364–65 (Peter Laslett ed., 2004) (1689).

[20] Under the same heading, Blackstone explains that the king is the chief prosecutor and may issue proclamations as to the "manner, time, and circumstances of putting [the] laws in execution." Blackstone, *supra* note 16, at *259–61. He also says that the king may create judicial tribunals "for, though the constitution of the kingdom hath entrusted him with the whole executive power of the laws, it is impossible, as well as improper, that he should personally carry into execution this great and extensive trust," and so "courts should be erected, to assist him in executing this power." *Id.* at *257.

[21] See Wurman, *supra* note 15.

[22] *Id.*

national government any power to erect corporations, which was a prerogative power. When making that determination, the delegates did not conceive of the possibility that the Vesting Clause might nevertheless vest such a power in the president alone.[23] More still, not a single opponent of ratification so much as mentioned the possibility of a residual grant, even among those who feared the scope of powers conferred upon the national executive.[24]

If the residual reading is correct, the implications for the removal power are different from the implications of the cross-reference reading. If it can be shown that removal was an executive or prerogative power, then that power, whatever its scope, must belong to the president by virtue of the Executive Vesting Clause. The Take Care Clause would not limit the extent to which the president must have this power. The scope of the removal power under the residual theory would likely be historically contingent. It is possible, for example, that the historical removal power was only understood to encompass principal or high officers of state, and not inferior officers. In any event, as Part II explains, at a minimum such a removal power seems to have included the high officers, and therefore at least for-cause removal provisions relating to such officers would probably be unconstitutional.

C. The Law-Execution Theories

There is a third possible reading of the Executive Vesting Clause: the clause is indeed a substantive grant of power, but only the power to execute law. Scholars who have advanced this reading in recent years include Julian Mortenson,[25] John Harrison,[26] Matthew Steilen,[27] Seth Barrett Tillman,[28] and, most recently, myself.[29] There are two accounts

---

[23] Id.

[24] McConnell, supra note 10, at 71.

[25] Julian Davis Mortenson, The Executive Power Clause, 167 U. Pa. L. Rev. (forthcoming 2020); Mortenson, Royal Prerogative, supra note 18.

[26] John C. Harrison, Executive Power (June 3, 2019) (unpublished manuscript), https://papers.ssrn.com/sol3/papers.cfm?abstract_id=3398427.

[27] Matthew J. Steilen, How to Think Constitutionally about Prerogative: A Study of Early American Usage, 66 Buff. L. Rev. 557 (2018).

[28] Seth Barrett Tillman, The Old Whig Theory of the Executive Power, New Reform Club (blog), Jan. 18, 2019, https://reformclub.blogspot.com/2019/01/the-old-whig-theory-of-executive-power.html.

[29] Wurman, supra note 15.

of this theory, a "thin" account and a "thick" account. The thin account does not appear to allow for a constitutionally mandated presidential removal power; the thick account does.

1. Thin account

What I call the thin account of the law-execution reading of the Executive Power Clause appears to be Mortenson's account, and possibly the account of some of the other scholars who have taken the law-execution view of the executive power. Reading "the executive power" to refer to the single power of law-execution is persuasive for the reasons the residual theory is unpersuasive. The law-execution reading is more consistent with the textual uses of the term "the executive power" in the 17th and 18th centuries, more consistent with the proceedings at the Constitutional Convention, and more consistent with the silence of the Ratification debates.

The thin account of the law-execution reading maintains that the president can only execute law with the precise tools, and with the precise limitations, imposed by Congress. Justice James McReynolds, in dissent in *Myers v. United States*, argued:

> Concerning the insistence that power to remove is a necessary incident of the President's duty to enforce the laws, it is enough now to say: The general duty to enforce all laws cannot justify infraction of some of them. Moreover, Congress, in the exercise of its unquestioned power, may deprive the President of the right either to appoint or to remove any inferior officer, by vesting the authority to appoint in another. Yet in that event his duty touching enforcement of the laws would remain. He must utilize the force which Congress gives. He cannot, without permission, appoint the humblest clerk or expend a dollar of the public funds.[30]

Or, as Justice Louis Brandeis wrote in response to something like the residual theory, the power to remove at least inferior officers "is not a power inherent in a chief executive"; rather, "[t]he President's power of removal from statutory civil inferior offices, like the power of appointment to them, comes immediately from Congress."[31] "The end to which the President's efforts are to be

---

[30] 272 U.S. at 187 (McReynolds, J., dissenting).

[31] *Id.* at 245 (Brandeis, J., dissenting).

directed is not the most efficient civil service conceivable, but the faithful execution of the laws consistent with the provisions therefor made by Congress."[32]

It is not entirely clear whether Justices McReynolds and Brandeis believed the Executive Power Clause was a grant of substantive power at all, but to the extent it was, they argued that the power to execute law cannot include the power to ignore congressional laws on removal.[33] The bottom line is that one can believe "the executive power" is the power to execute law and that such a power does not entail a power of removal.

2. Thick account

I have argued that the grant of "the executive power" in the Constitution was indeed likely only a grant of the power to execute law and did not include a residuum of royal powers.[34] But, I argued, the Founders seem to have understood that this "executive power" to execute law included a variety of incidental, derivative, or component powers. For example, the power of appointment was part and parcel of "the executive power" because the chief executive could not possibly hope to execute the law alone. As Mortenson has explained, many at the Founding considered "the appointment of publick officers" as "closely linked to the executive power—sometimes as a strict conceptual element of the thing itself, other times more loosely as an indispensable buttress for its meaningful exercise."[35] Blackstone explained that the king also had a power, incident to the executive power, to issue proclamations (or executive orders) as to the "manner, time, and circumstances of putting [the] laws in execution."[36]

Based on the history that I summarize in Part II, I concluded that the power to appoint, direct, and remove subordinate officers was understood to be part of "the executive power" of law-execution.[37] Put another way, the residuum theory is not necessary to find a

[32] *Id.* at 247.

[33] Justice Brandeis was at least willing to concede to precedent that perhaps Congress could not limit the removal of principal officers.

[34] Wurman, *supra* note 15.

[35] Mortenson, *supra* note 25, at 54.

[36] Blackstone, *supra* note 16, at *261.

[37] Wurman, *supra* note 15.

constitutionally mandated presidential removal power. Indeed, both James Madison in the famous removal debates of 1789, and Chief Justice Taft in *Myers*, seem to have adhered to a law-execution view of the executive power, but nevertheless found that this power entailed the power to remove.

D. *Summary*

The implications of the various textual theories for the removal power may be represented as follows:

	Residual	Thin-Law Execution	Thick-Law Execution	Cross Reference
Removal	Presidential	Congressional discretion	Presidential	Congressional discretion/ only for faithless execution/ functional analysis

II. The Historical Debate

At least under the residual and law-execution theories, the extent to which the removal power is "executive" or part of "the executive power" will be based partly on history. Historical practice might also inform the extent to which removal is essential "to take care that the laws be faithfully executed." Although the history can certainly be read in more ways than one, it appears that the best reading of the history is that the president must at least have the ability to remove principal officers at will.

A. *British Practice*

As my coauthors and I explained in our amicus brief to the Court, the delegates to the Constitutional Convention were attentive to the powers of the monarch as set forth in William Blackstone's *Commentaries*, allocating almost every single power discussed in Blackstone to Congress, to the president, or to the president with a senatorial check, or eliminating some from the reach of federal power altogether.[38] The power to remove principal executive officers, however,

[38] Brief for Separation of Powers Scholars at 6–11, Seila Law LLC v. Consumer Fin. Prot. Bureau, 140 S. Ct. 2183 (2019) (No. 19-17); Blackstone, *supra* note 16, at *245–69; McConnell, *supra* note 10; Wurman, *supra* note 15.

was one of the few royal powers not explicitly discussed by the Framers nor discussed very much by Blackstone. But the weight of the evidence is that removal was part of the executive power, necessary to law execution.

In the 18th-century British Constitution, like in the U.S. Constitution, the "supreme executive power" of the nation was vested in a single person.[39] Matthew Hale wrote in his 17th-century work *Prerogatives of the King* that "the supreme administration of this monarchy is lodged in the king, and that not only titularly, but really."[40] The king, according to Blackstone, was understood to be the "fountain of justice and general conservator of the peace of the kingdom."[41] Accordingly, the king was the "proper person to prosecute for all public offenses and breaches of the peace"; he could grant pardons; and he could nominate judges.[42] Writing in 1774, James Wilson described the king as "intrusted" with "the direction and management of the great machine of government."[43]

To discharge these responsibilities, however, the king required ministers and officers, who, according to Blackstone, therefore "act[ed] by commission from, and in due subordination to him."[44] The king thus created offices and appointed and supervised officers. Additionally, the power to remove principal executive officers unquestionably belonged to the executive magistrate as a necessary component of the executive power to carry law into execution. Blackstone wrote that the king is "the fountain of honour, of office, and of privilege."[45] As to "officers," Blackstone wrote, this meant that "the law supposes, that no one can be so good a judge of their several merits and services, as the king himself who employs them," from which principle "arises the prerogative of erecting and disposing of offices."[46]

[39] Blackstone, *supra* note 16, at *183.

[40] Sir Matthew Hale's The Prerogatives of the King 11 (D.E.C. Yale ed., Selden Society 1976).

[41] Blackstone, *supra* note 16, at *257.

[42] *Id.* at *259.

[43] James Wilson, On the Legislative Authority of the British Parliament, 2 Works of James Wilson 505, 520 (J. Andrews ed., 1896) (1774).

[44] Blackstone, *supra* note 16, at *243.

[45] *Id.* at *261.

[46] *Id.* at *262.

In a section of his *Commentaries* entitled "Of Subordinate Magistrates," Blackstone described the principal officers—namely, "the lord treasurer, lord chamberlain, the principal secretaries, [and] the like"—as "his majesty's great officers of state" and explained that these offices are not "in any considerable degree the objects of our laws."[47] In other words, the principal officers of state were executive, not legislative, creatures. In a famous incident just four years before the Constitutional Convention, King George III cashiered Prime Minister Charles James Fox, notwithstanding Fox's majority support in the House of Commons, and replaced him with William Pitt the Younger, who continued in office despite a no-confidence vote in the Commons.[48]

Other officers involved in the execution of the laws, such as sheriffs and justices of the peace, also served at the pleasure of the Crown.[49] Removal restrictions appear to have existed only for officers exercising judicial or ministerial functions,[50] and possibly for certain local or municipal officials who related to "mere private and strictly municipal rights, depending entirely upon the domestic constitution of their respective franchise."[51]

Other parts of Blackstone likewise indicate that the power to appoint, control, and remove officers was part of "the executive power." Blackstone wrote that the king had a right to erect a particular kind of office—courts—because it was "impossible" for the king to exercise "the whole executive power of the laws" on his own.[52] (At the Constitutional Convention, Madison similarly argued that the executive authority would need assistants to help execute the laws, and he thus stated that the power to carry into execution the laws and to

---

[47] *Id.* at *327.

[48] Michael Duffy, The Younger Pitt 18–27 (2013); Murray Scott Downs, George III and the Royal Coup of 1783, 27 The Historian 56, 72–73 (1964) (noting that it was "manifestly [the king's] constitutional prerogative of dismissing his ministers and dissolving the parliament").

[49] Blackstone, *supra* note 16, at *331 (sheriffs); *id.* at *341 (justices of the peace).

[50] Act of Settlement, 12 & 13 Wm. 3. c. 2 (judges in Britain); Blackstone, *supra* note 16, at *336–37 (coroners).

[51] Blackstone, *supra* note 16, at *328.

[52] *Id.* at *257.

appoint officers not already provided for were in their nature "executive" powers.)[53]

Finally, as noted earlier, Blackstone described a power to issue proclamations as to "the manner, time, and circumstances of putting [Parliament's] laws in execution."[54] These proclamations were "binding upon the subject" when they "only enforce[d] the execution of such laws as are already in being."[55] And if they were binding on subjects, presumably these executive directives would have been binding on executive officers, too.

In sum, Blackstone's discussion indicates that the power to appoint and direct assistants was part of "the executive power of the laws." The power to create offices, dispose of (appoint to and remove from) those offices, and direct those officers was part of the king's power to carry law into execution.

Daniel Birk has recently suggested, however, that the king did not in fact have an inherent removal power in the 18th century, citing a number of statutes in which this power was limited.[56] As I have suggested elsewhere, Birk's evidence does not quite prove the proposition that removal is not part of the executive power.[57]

First, many of Birk's examples of nonremovable principal officers are lifelong, hereditary officeholders from as early as the 14th century up to the 17th century, when offices were considered to be personal property and where such tenures were entirely up to the king.[58] It is not at all clear, however, that much of this survived into the late 18th century, and there is some reason to doubt that such examples provide insight into the meaning of a constitution rooted in popular sovereignty. It is of little weight that James I appointed Francis Bacon as his attorney general for life, or that in those early

---

[53] 1 The Records of the Federal Convention of 1787, 66–67 (Max Farrand ed., 1966) (1911).

[54] Blackstone, *supra* note 16, at *261.

[55] *Id.*

[56] Daniel D. Birk, Interrogating the Historical Basis for a Unitary Executive, 73 Stan. L. Rev. (forthcoming 2021).

[57] Wurman, *supra* note 15.

[58] *Id.* at Part III.A.1.

centuries Parliament tried to regulate tenure to restrict hereditary and lifetime tenures.[59]

Second, many of Birk's examples involve officers exercising judicial, ministerial, or municipal functions.[60] Even Blackstone recognized the monarch could not remove such officers at will, but arguably none of these functions are, strictly speaking, part of "the executive power" to execute law.[61]

Finally, a handful of statutes do create "commissioners" of various sorts, some of which contain for-cause removal provisions.[62] These independent commissions appear to be exercising not executive power, but rather Parliament's historical inquisitorial power.[63] The statutes Birk cites seem to fall within this power. They were enacted "for better examining and auditing the publick accounts of this kingdom";[64] "to examine, take, and state the publick accounts of the kingdom," "to report what balances are in the hands of accountants," and "what defects there are in the present mode of receiving, collecting, issuing, and accounting for publick money";[65] "to enquire

---

[59] Birk, *supra* note 56. Blackstone, of course, argued that principal officers were entirely under the control of the king. Blackstone, *supra* note 16, at *327 ("the lord treasurer, lord chamberlain, the principal secretaries, [and] the like," namely "his majesty's great officers of state," are not "in any considerable degree the objects of our laws").

[60] Birk, *supra* note 56, at Part III.A.1, III.A.3.

[61] See Act of Settlement, *supra* note 50 (granting lifetime tenure to judges in Britain); Blackstone, *supra* note 16, at *336–37 (coroners not removable at pleasure of the king); *id.* at *328 (local and municipal officials relate to "mere private and strictly municipal rights, depending entirely upon the domestic constitution of their respective franchise").

[62] Birk, *supra* note 56; see Audit of Public Accounts Act 1780, 20 Geo. 3 c. 54 (Eng.); Inquiry into Fees, Public Offices Act 1785, 25 Geo. 3 c. 19 (Eng.); Audit of Public Accounts Act 1785, 25 Geo. 3 c. 52 (Eng.); American Loyalists Act 1786, 26 Geo. 3 c. 68 (Eng.); Losses from Cession of East Florida Act 1786, 26 Geo. 3 c. 75 (Eng.); Crown Land Revenues, etc. Act 1786 26 Geo. 3 c. 87 (Eng.).

[63] See, e.g., 2 Cobbett's Parliamentary History of England 69 (1806) (House of Commons asserting in 1626 that it was "the antient, constant, and undoubted right and usage of parliaments, to question and complain of all persons, of what degree soever, found grievous to the common-wealth, in abusing the power and trust committed to them by their sovereign."); 21 Cobbett's Parliamentary History of England 436 (1814) (the Lord Chancellor stating in a 1780 debate that the matter of members of parliament receiving public contracts is subject to the "inquisitorial" power of Parliament).

[64] 25 Geo. 3 c. 52.

[65] 20 Geo. 3 c. 54.

into the fees, gratuities, perquisites, and emoluments, which are, or have been lately, received in the several publick offices therein mentioned; to examine into any abuses which may exist in the same"; and also "to report such observations as shall occur to them, for the better conducting and managing the business transacted in the said offices";[66] to "enquire into the losses and services of all such persons who have suffered in their right properties, and possessions, during the late unhappy dissentions in America";[67] "to enquire into the losses of all such persons who have suffered in their properties, in consequence of the cession of the province of East Florida to the king of Spain";[68] and "to enquire into the state and condition of the woods, forests, and land revenues, belonging to the crown."[69] It is not clear that these legislative commissions did anything but make recommendations, although the last of these commissioners were permitted to sell public lands.[70]

In short, the evidence from British practice tends to support the proposition that the chief magistrate had the authority to remove at will at least principal officers involved in the execution of the law.

B. American Practice

In the *Seila Law* case, the evidence of American practice was particularly contested. The significance of the "Decision of 1789" was questioned, and some scholars argued that financial agencies and departments were historically treated differently than other executive departments. Both points were championed by the dissenters.

1. The Decision of 1789

The Constitution, of course, assigns some of the traditionally royal law-execution powers to Congress. It assigns the power to create offices to Congress,[71] and the power to appoint to office to the president and Senate together (for principal officers).[72] Yet it does not assign

---

[66] 25 Geo. 3 c. 19.

[67] 26 Geo. 3 c. 68.

[68] 26 Geo. 3 c. 75.

[69] 26 Geo. 3 c. 87.

[70] *Id.*

[71] U.S. Const. art. I, § 8, cl. 18.

[72] U.S. Const. art II, § 2, cl. 2.

the removal power in this manner. The question thus arose in the First Congress, when it sought to establish the first departments of the national government, whether their principal officers had to be removed by the president with the advice and consent of the Senate; whether the Constitution vested that power in the president alone; or whether Congress in its discretion could delegate that power to the president alone.[73] Madison first argued that "the executive power" was vested in the president, but that the Constitution had assigned some of that power to the Senate:

> The Constitution affirms, that the Executive power shall be vested in the President. Are there exceptions to this proposition? Yes, there are. The Constitution says, that in appointing to office, the Senate shall be associated with the President, unless in the case of inferior officers. Have we a right to extend this exception? I believe not.[74]

Madison thus argued that all "the executive power" not assigned away from the president belonged to the president. The question according to Madison, then, was: "Is the power of displacing, an Executive power?" Madison conceived "that if any power whatsoever is in its nature Executive, it is the power of appointing, overseeing, and controlling those who execute the laws."[75] "[I]f any thing in its nature is executive," Madison added later on, "it must be that power which is employed in superintending and seeing that the laws are faithfully executed."[76]

Representative Fisher Ames agreed with Madison. "The Constitution places all Executive power in the hands of the President," exhorted Ames, "and could he personally execute all the laws, there

---

[73] 1 Annals of Cong. 381, 484 (1789) (Joseph Gales ed., 1834). Also, some representatives argued that impeachment was the only mode of removing officers—an argument that was not seriously advanced because, as Madison pointed out, impeachment is a method by which Congress can remove officers; that says nothing of the president's power. *Id.* at 375. Much of this discussion on the Decision of 1789 borrows from Wurman, *supra* note 15, and Brief for Separation of Powers Scholars, *supra* note 38.

[74] 1 Annals of Cong. 463. As Madison said subsequently, "[T]he Executive power shall be vested in a President of the United States. The association of the Senate with the President in exercising that particular function, is an exception to this general rule; and exceptions to general rules, I conceive, are ever to be taken strictly." *Id.* at 496.

[75] *Id.* at 463.

[76] *Id.* at 500.

would be no occasion for establishing auxiliaries; but the circum-scribed powers of human nature in one man, demand the aid of others."[77] Because the president cannot possibly handle all the mi-nutiae of administration, he "must therefore have assistants."[78] But "in order that he may be responsible to his country, he must have a choice in selecting his assistants, a control over them, with power to remove them when he finds the qualifications which induced their appointment cease to exist."[79] The executive power thus includes, Ames concluded, a "choice in selecting [] assistants, a control over them, with power to remove them."[80]

Madison's argument is often taken as evidence of the residual theory. But note that Madison's and Ames's arguments are consistent with the law-execution reading of the "the executive power." There is no indication in the debates that anyone in Congress understood them to be referring to the entire suite of royal authorities when they said "the executive power." The discussion was entirely in the con-text of "appointing, overseeing, and controlling those who execute the laws." When Madison discussed "exceptions" to the proposition that the executive power is vested in the president, he referred only to the appointment power—historically part of the law-execution power.

Whether or not Madison or Ames articulated the residual theory or merely a law-execution theory of the executive power, it is clear that they believed that the removal power, at least over principal of-ficers, was constitutionally vested in the president.

The predominant alternative theory on the table in 1789, ad-vanced by several representatives in the debate, was that the Neces-sary and Proper Clause[81] is an assignment away from the president because Congress's power to establish (or abolish) offices might in-clude the power to set conditions on the removal of officers. As we explained in our amicus brief, however, the Necessary and Proper

[77] *Id.* at 474.

[78] *Id.*

[79] *Id.*

[80] *Id.*

[81] U.S. Const. art. I, § 8, cl. 18 ("Congress shall have Power . . . To make all Laws which shall be necessary and proper for carrying into Execution the foregoing Pow-ers, and all other Powers vested by this Constitution in the Government of the United States, or in any Department or Officer thereof.").

Clause does not give Congress power to derogate from the president's executive power; it only gives power to help carry the executive power into execution. A restriction on the power to remove would not be in furtherance of the president's power but arguably a hindrance to it.

James Madison addressed this argument as follows:

> [W]hen I consider, that, if the Legislature has a power, such as is contended for, they may subject and transfer at discretion powers from one department of our government to another; they may, on that principle, exclude the President altogether from exercising any authority in the removal of officers; they may give to the Senate alone, or the President and Senate combined; they may vest it in the whole Congress, or they may reserve it to be exercised by this House. When I consider the consequences of this doctrine, and compare them with the true principles of the Constitution, I own that I cannot subscribe to it.[82]

In other words, if the power to establish and abolish offices included the power to restrict removal, then it is unclear what limits on the power to restrict there might be. Madison thus argued that such a doctrine would be entirely incompatible with the "true principles of the Constitution."

Even under a cross-reference theory, the Take Care Clause may support the view that the president must have the ability to remove at least principal executive officers; as explained, such an analysis would be a functionalist one. Madison argued that "[i]f the duty to see the laws faithfully executed be required at the hands of the Executive Magistrate, it would seem that it was generally intended he should have that species of power which is necessary to accomplish that end."[83] Similarly, Ames argued:

> In the Constitution the President is required to see the laws faithfully executed. He cannot do this [unless] he has a control over officers appointed to aid him in the performance of his duty. Take this power out of his hands, and you virtually strip him of his authority; you virtually destroy his responsibility.[84]

[82] 1 Annals of Cong. 495–96.

[83] *Id.* at 496.

[84] *Id.* at 539–40.

Some modern scholars have argued that the Take Care Clause supports limiting the president's ability to remove executive officers. In particular, these scholars argue that the president can only remove officers in good faith.[85] As previously explained, it is certainly plausible to make such an argument under the cross-reference reading of the Executive Power Clause, because any such analysis would be a functionalist one.

In any event, with the various arguments on the table, the House in 1789 devoted over five full days of debate to the question of the president's removal power. After the first day, a majority agreed to retain the clause that the principal officer would be "removable by the President,"[86] and further rejected a proposal to include the modifying phrase "by and with the advice and consent of the senate."[87]

After the fifth day, the House altered the bill to ensure that its language would not be construed as a *conferral* of the removal power. The amended provision stated that "whenever the said principal officer shall be removed from office by the President," the departmental papers would then be under the control of the department's clerk.[88] As Representative Egbert Benson, the sponsor of this amendment, explained, the alteration was intended "so that the law may be nothing more than a declaration of our sentiments upon the meaning of a Constitutional grant of power to the President."[89] The amendment passed by a vote of 30-18,[90] and the Senate agreed by a vote of 10-10, with Vice President John Adams breaking the tie.[91]

Despite the close nature of the vote in the Senate, Madison thought that Congress's decision on this question, which has come to be

---

[85] See, e.g., Andrew Kent et al., Faithful Execution and Article II, 132 Harv. L. Rev. 2111, 2112 (2019) ("Our history supports readings of Article II . . . that limit Presidents to exercise their power in good faith. . . . So understood, Article II may thus place some limits on the pardon and removal authority.").

[86] 1 Annals of Cong. 371, 383.

[87] *Id.* at 382.

[88] *Id.* at 578.

[89] *Id.* at 505.

[90] *Id.* at 580.

[91] William Maclay, Journal of William Maclay, United States Senator from Pennsylvania, 1789–1791, 116 (Edgar S. Maclay ed., 1890), https://memory.loc.gov/ammem/amlaw/lwmj.html.

known as the "Decision of 1789,"[92] would become the "permanent exposition of the Constitution."[93] And with a few highly controversial exceptions—such as the Tenure of Office Act, enacted by radical Republicans to prevent Andrew Johnson from removing certain members of Abraham Lincoln's cabinet—so it remained. Alexander Hamilton and Chief Justice John Marshall wrote that Congress's decision reflected its constitutional interpretation that the removal power was constitutionally vested in the president.[94]

Some of the most prominent scholars of the 20th century suggested, however, that the Decision of 1789 was no decision at all because, they argued, the majority in favor of Benson's amendment was actually cobbled together by representatives who believed the removal power was *constitutionally* vested in the president and those who believed Congress could *confer* such power.[95] It is certainly possible to read the vote in this manner. But any reader of the debates would be cognizant of the fact that the representatives were overwhelmingly arguing in constitutional terms. As Madison reminded the representatives toward the end of the debate, "Gentlemen have all along proceeded on the idea that the Constitution vests the power in the President."[96]

Even if the Decision of 1789 is ambiguous—as the dissent in *Seila Law* argued and as recent scholarship once again argues[97]—few scholars or judges suggest that the Decision of 1789 governs by its own force. And those who do should probably walk back such claims. "Liquidating" ambiguous constitutional meaning requires a series of discussions and adjudications.[98] The better lessons from the

[92] See, e.g., Humphrey's Ex'r, 295 U.S. 602, 630 (1935).

[93] 1 Annals of Cong. 495.

[94] See 15 Alexander Hamilton, The Papers of Alexander Hamilton 40 (Harold C. Syrett ed., 1969); 5 John Marshall, The Life of George Washington 200 (1807).

[95] Myers, 272 U.S. at 285 n.75 (Brandeis, J., dissenting); Edward S. Corwin, Tenure of Office and the Removal Power Under the Constitution, 27 Colum. L. Rev. 353, 362–63 (1927); David P. Currie, The Constitution in Congress: The Federalist Period, 1789–1801, 40–41 (1997).

[96] 1 Annals of Cong. 578.

[97] Jed H. Shugerman, The Indecision of 1789: Strategic Ambiguity and the Imaginary Unitary Executive (Part I) (May 5, 2020) (unpublished manuscript), https://papers.ssrn.com/sol3/papers.cfm?abstract_id=3596566.

[98] William Baude, Constitutional Liquidation, 71 Stan. L. Rev. 1 (2019).

debate are the various arguments that were put on the table. It is not unreasonable to think that Madison and Ames simply got it right: their arguments are compelling interpretations of the Constitution.

2. Financial institutions

In recent decades, some scholars have claimed that financial and other "Article I" agencies are distinct from "Article II" agencies tasked with assisting the president in exercising inherent constitutional power. A number of scholars made this precise argument in their briefs to the Supreme Court in the *Seila Law* case and to the D.C. Circuit in the related *PHH Corp.* litigation.[99] For example, in their brief to the D.C. Circuit in *PHH Corp.*, a number of scholars made the claim that the CFPB's

> independence is consistent with governmental structures dating back to the earliest days of the Republic. At that time, the first Congress distanced the Department of the Treasury from the President's direct control, in stark contrast to its choices for the Departments of State and War. Around the same time, Congress created the relatively independent Office of the Comptroller and the National Bank. Thus began a long national history of granting independence to financial institutions and regulators, which has continued through the present day.[100]

More generally, Professors Lawrence Lessig and Cass Sunstein have argued for "another conception of the original understanding" inspired by the distinction made by 19th-century theorists between "politics" and "administration."[101] Applying this distinction, Lessig and Sunstein argue that executive power "derive[s] from Article II," but administrative power "stem[s] from Article I."[102] "Applying the nineteenth century vision as mechanically as possible to some

---

[99] See Brief of Harold H. Bruff et al. as Amici Curiae in Support of Court-Appointed Amicus Curiae, in Support of the Judgment Below, Seila Law v. Consumer Fin. Prot. Bureau, 140 S. Ct. 2183 (2020) (No. 19-7); Brief of Separation of Powers Scholars as Amici Curiae in Support of CFPB, PHH Corp. v. Consumer Fin. Prot. Bureau, 881 F.3d 75 (D.C. Cir. 2018) (No. 15-1177).

[100] Brief of Separation of Powers Scholars, *supra* note 99, at 2.

[101] Lawrence Lessig & Cass R. Sunstein, The President and the Administration, 94 Colum. L. Rev. 1, 35 (1994).

[102] *Id.* at 71.

modern developments," they argue, "we think that Congress could not constitutionally make the Department of Defense into an independent agency; but it could allow at least a degree of independence for such modern institutions as the National Labor Relations Board and the Federal Communications Commission"[103]—and, presumably, the CFPB.

As argued in our amicus brief, however, the Founding generation recognized no such distinction, which appears to be an anachronistic imposition of late 19th-century views. For example, the treasury department was designated an executive department under the Articles of Confederation, in the Convention, during the ratifying debates, and during the First Congress's debates.[104] Treasury officials were also designated "executive" officers in the First Congress's act providing salaries to executive branch officials.[105] And the president received written opinions from Treasury Secretary Alexander Hamilton—relying upon the Opinions Clause that speaks of "principal Officer[s] in each of the executive Departments."

In their Supreme Court brief, the scholars writing in support of the CFPB argued that the treasury statute was silent on the removability of the comptroller, and that the comptroller was given "significant authority and independence"; for example, Congress even gave the comptroller the power to institute proceedings to recover money owed to the treasury.[106] It is hard to conclude from these general observations, however, that the comptroller exercised discretion in any way "independently" of the secretary of the treasury.

These scholars also pointed to the early Sinking Fund Commission and to the Bank of the United States as examples of federal financial institutions over which the president did not have direct control.[107] The Sinking Fund Commission could make open-market debt purchases at the direction of the vice president, the chief justice, the secretary of state, the secretary of treasury, and the attorney general. Two of these officers (the vice president and the chief justice)

---

[103] *Id.*

[104] Saikrishna Prakash, The Essential Meaning of Executive Power, 2003 U. Ill. L. Rev. 701, 804.

[105] Act of Sept. 11, 1789, ch. 13, § 1, 1 Stat. 67, 67.

[106] Brief of Harold H. Bruff, *supra* note 99, at 14–15.

[107] *Id.* at 16–17.

were not removable by the president at all. I am not confident that
the statutory appointment of the vice president or the chief justice
was constitutional, but in any event it does not undermine the central point: the president could clearly direct and remove a majority
of the officers who constituted the commission. As for the Bank of
the United States, it was not considered an arm of the federal government at all. It was a private, profit-making corporation, of which the
United States was a minority shareholder.[108]

Professors Lessig and Sunstein further assert that constitutional
text supports their view that there is a distinction between "executive departments" headed by "principal officers," and Article I "administrative" departments headed by "heads of department" but not
"principal officers."[109] It is of course true that the Constitution uses
various terms to denominate principal officers. The Opinions Clause
refers to "principal officer[s]" of the "executive [d]epartments."[110] The
Appointments Clause distinguishes between "inferior officers" and
"Heads of Departments."[111] Moreover, Lessig and Sunstein point
out, the First Congress denominated the secretaries of foreign affairs and war as "principal officers" but the secretary of treasury as a
"head of department."[112] They suggest that these textual differences
make sense for the 19th-century understanding that certain departments are inherently executive, derived from Article II, and that the
Opinions Clause ensures the president has authority to control the
principal officers of these departments, but not the heads of all the
departments of government.[113]

The evidence most likely does not bear out this view, however.
The reference to "executive" departments in the Opinions Clause
was probably in response to proposals that would have given the

[108] Bank of United States v. Planters' Bank of Ga., 22 U.S. (9 Wheat.) 904, 908 (1824)
(noting that the government is not a party in cases against the bank); see also Lebron
v. Nat'l R.R. Passenger Corp., 513 U.S. 374, 399 (1995) ("[A] corporation is an agency
of the Government . . . when the State has specifically created that corporation for the
furtherance of governmental objectives, and not merely holds some shares but controls the operation of the corporation through its appointees.").

[109] Lessig & Sunstein, *supra* note 101, at 34–38.

[110] U.S. Const. art. II, § 2, cl. 1.

[111] U.S. Const. art. II, § 2, cl. 2.

[112] Lessig & Sunstein, *supra* note 101, at 35.

[113] *Id.* at 37–38.

president power to demand opinions from the chief justice and officers of the House and the Senate.[114] As for the distinction between "principal officers" and other "heads of departments," the Framers used these terms interchangeably—I have seen no evidence that they thought of them differently, and indeed the members of the First Congress used both terms routinely in the removal debate. Moreover, as noted, treasury was referred to as an executive department under the Articles of Confederation, at the Constitutional Convention, in the ratification debates, and throughout the First Congress; the secretary was denominated an "executive officer" in the act providing for his salary; and the president received written opinions from Alexander Hamilton—relying upon the Opinions Clause that speaks of "principal Officer[s] in each of the executive Departments."

III. Formalism, Functionalism, and Precedent

Besides text and history, the Court in *Seila Law* was not writing on a clean slate. Several precedents bear on the question of the president's removal power. This part briefly canvasses the four most important—*Myers*, *Humphrey's*, *Morrison*, and *Free Enterprise Fund*—and highlights only the points important for understanding the *Seila Law* decision.

A. Myers v. United States

In *Myers v. United States*, Chief Justice Taft, a former president, held that the power to remove any officer appointed by and with the advice and consent of the Senate—including inferior officers so appointed—constitutionally belonged to the president by virtue of the Executive Vesting Clause. At issue was the removal of a first-class postmaster, whom President Woodrow Wilson removed despite the requirement in the statute that any such removal also be with the "advice and consent" of the Senate.

In some respects, Taft's decision was an expansion of the Decision of 1789, which merely stood (arguably) for the proposition that principal officers must be removable by the president. Taft extended this proposition to all officers appointed by and with the advice and consent of the Senate, including inferior ones such as the postmaster.

---

[114] 2 The Records of the Federal Convention of 1787, 342, 367; Steven G. Calabresi & Saikrishna B. Prakash, The President's Power to Execute the Laws, 104 Yale L.J. 541, 628–29 (1994).

The idea was that Congress can choose to vest the appointment of inferior officers in the heads of departments, and, if it does so, it can then restrict how those principal officers can remove the inferior ones, as the Court held in *United States v. Perkins*.[115] But unless Congress actually vests the appointment of the inferior officer in a head of department and as a condition restricts the removal of the inferior officer at the hands of the superior one, Congress could not restrict the ability of the president to remove any officer.

Note that even if Congress were to vest the appointment of an inferior officer in a head of department and restrict the ability of that head to remove the inferior officer, that does not mean the president could not remove such an officer. Neither the Court in *Perkins* nor the Court in *Myers* said that the president could not remove such officers at will—only that *if* the principal officer removes the inferior officer, that principal officer must follow Congress's instructions in doing so. Whether the president can remove such inferior officers is still an unanswered question.[116] Chief Justice Taft also noted that the Court has never said Congress could restrict the president's power to remove an inferior officer if Congress vested the appointment of that officer in the president alone. Indeed, Taft argued there was reason to doubt Congress could do so.[117]

The upshot of *Myers* was that any officer, principal or inferior, appointed by and with advice and consent, could be freely removed by the president. Congress could restrict the removal of inferior officers when their appointments were vested in a head of department; but even here the Court had never held that the president could not order the removal of such officers.

The basis of the Court's reasoning, importantly, was not the view that the Executive Vesting Clause was a residual grant of all executive

---

[115] 116 U.S. 483 (1886).

[116] To which we might soon get an answer if the erstwhile U.S. Attorney for the Southern District of New York files a lawsuit against the Trump.

[117] Myers, 272 U.S. at 161–62 ("Whether the action of Congress in removing the necessity for the advice and consent of the Senate, and putting the power of appointment in the President alone, would make his power of removal in such case any more subject to Congressional legislation than before is a question this Court did not decide in the *Perkins* case. Under the reasoning upon which the legislative decision of 1789 was put, it might be difficult to avoid a negative answer, but it is not before us and we do not decide it.").

or prerogative powers. In 1916, 10 years before Taft published the opinion in *Myers*, he had published a book on the powers and duties of the president. He argued that Presidents James Garfield and Theodore Roosevelt's "ascribing an undefined residuum of power to the president is an unsafe doctrine and that it might lead under emergencies to results of an arbitrary character."[118] He elaborated on his own view:

> The true view of the Executive function is, as I conceive it, that the President can exercise no power which cannot be fairly and reasonably traced to some specific grant of power or justly implied and included within such express grant as proper and necessary to its exercise. Such specific grant must be either in the Federal Constitution or in an act of Congress passed in pursuance thereof. There is no undefined residuum of power which he can exercise because it seems to him to be in the public interest. . . . The grants of Executive power are necessarily in general terms in order not to embarrass the Executive within the field of action plainly marked for him, but his jurisdiction must be justified and vindicated by affirmative constitutional or statutory provisions, or it does not exist.[119]

Nothing in *Myers* suggests that Taft's views had evolved. Quite the opposite. Taft wrote:

> The vesting of the executive power in the President was essentially a grant of the power to execute the laws. But the President alone and unaided could not execute the laws. He must execute them by the assistance of subordinates. This view has since been repeatedly affirmed by this court.[120]

Further, the Court's "conclusion on the merits," Taft summarized, "is that Article 2 grants to the President the executive power of the Government—i.e., the general administrative control of those executing the laws, including the power of appointment and removal of executive officers—a conclusion confirmed by his obligation to take care that the laws be faithfully executed."[121]

[118] William Howard Taft, Our Chief Magistrate and His Power 144 (1916).

[119] *Id.* at 139–40.

[120] Myers, 272 U.S. at 117.

[121] *Id.* at 163–64.

B. *Humphrey's Executor v. United States*

Myers thus stood, and still stands, for the proposition that the removal power in such instances is the president's. The Senate cannot retain a role for itself. But can Congress, while not retaining any role for itself, place some restrictions on the president's exercise of the removal power? This was the issue in *Humphrey's Executor.*

When Congress created the Federal Trade Commission (FTC), it provided that "any commissioner may be removed by the President for inefficiency, neglect of duty, or malfeasance in office."[122] Importantly, the removal power still belonged to the president, but Congress purported merely to restrict the president's use of that power to "cause." President Franklin Roosevelt nevertheless sought to remove a commissioner whom President Herbert Hoover had appointed because, as Roosevelt wrote the commissioner, "You will, I know, realize that I do not feel that your mind and my mind go along together on either the policies or the administering of the Federal Trade Commission, and, frankly, I think it is best for the people of this country that I should have a full confidence."[123]

In *Humphrey's*, the Supreme Court first held that the statute by its terms precluded the president from removing a commissioner for reasons other than those specified in the statute. The Court reasoned,

> The commission is to be nonpartisan; and it must, from the very nature of its duties, act with entire impartiality. It is charged with the enforcement of no policy except the policy of the law. Its duties are neither political nor executive, but predominantly quasi-judicial and quasi-legislative.[124]

The Court concluded that the "general purposes of the legislation . . . demonstrate the Congressional intent to create a body of experts who shall gain experience by length of service—a body which shall be independent of executive authority, except in its selection, and free to exercise its judgment without the leave or hindrance of any

[122] Humphrey's Ex'r, 295 U.S. at 619.
[123] *Id.*
[124] *Id.* at 624.

other official or any department of the government."[125] Indeed, the statute created a five-member commission on which "[n]ot more than three of the commissioners shall be members of the same political party."[126]

The Court held this arrangement constitutional. The Court concluded that the reach of *Myers* affirming the Decision of 1789 "goes far enough to include all purely executive officers," but "goes no farther;—much less does it include an officer who occupies no place in the executive department and who exercises no part of the executive power vested by the Constitution in the President."[127] The presidential removal power was inapplicable to the FTC, which was "an administrative body created by Congress to carry into effect legislative policies embodied in the statute in accordance with the legislative standard therein prescribed, and to perform other specified duties as a legislative or as a judicial aid."[128] Thus the FTC "acts in part quasi-legislatively and in part quasi-judicially."[129] In sum, the Court concluded, an unfettered presidential removal power "threatens the independence of a commission, which is not only wholly disconnected from the executive department, but which, as already fully appears, was created by Congress as a means of carrying into operation legislative and judicial powers, and as an agency of the legislative and judicial departments."[130]

In our brief, we argued that the Court's holding in *Humphrey's* cannot be reconciled with the Constitution's text or structure. The opinion relies on the fallacy that there is a category of legislative-like or judicial-like power that need not be exercised by Congress or the judiciary, but which is also not part of "[t]he executive Power." As the Court has said before, however, exercises of executive power often take legislative or judicial *form*, but they are

---

[125] *Id.* at 625–26 (emphasis omitted).

[126] *Id.* at 620 (quoting Federal Trade Commission Act, Pub. L. No. 63-203, ch. 311, § 1, 38 Stat. 717, 718 (1914)).

[127] *Id.* at 627–28.

[128] *Id.* at 628.

[129] *Id.*

[130] *Id.* at 630.

still ultimately exercises of executive power.[131] Or to put the point another way, and as I have argued elsewhere,[132] there is certainly government power that can be exercised by more than one branch. Some adjudications (over public rights cases, for example) could be conducted entirely within the executive branch, or Congress could assign their adjudication to the courts. Many regulations could certainly be passed as legislation by Congress, but Congress can also leave such matters to the executive. The problem with *Humphrey's Executor* is that it stands for the proposition that there is some government power that need not be exercised by *any* of the named constitutional actors.

Of course, *Humphrey's Executor* could be consistent with the constitutional text if one adopts the cross-reference theory. Under that theory, there is no actual grant of law-execution power to the president. The only power that the president has in this regard is what can be implied from the duty to take care that the laws be faithfully executed. Merely disagreeing with how other executive officers are executing the law does not mean they are faithlessly executing the law. Often the law allows discretion, and so long as the subordinate officer is staying within the bounds of legal discretion, the officer is faithfully executing the law.

The parties in *Seila Law* argued that *Humphrey's* was in any event distinguishable from the CFPB. Even if the Supreme Court were not inclined to revisit *Humphrey's*, it at least could hold that for-cause removal provisions are unconstitutional when the agency is headed by a single director. As we explained in our brief, what made the FTC a "judicial" and "legislative" aid in *Humphrey's* was the nature of the commission as much as its duties. The commission was to be "nonpartisan" and "act with entire impartiality." It was "a body of experts who shall gain experience by length of service."

---

[131] See City of Arlington v. FCC, 569 U.S. 290, 305, n.4 (2013) ("Agencies make rules . . . and conduct adjudications. . . and have done so since the beginning of the Republic. These activities take 'legislative' and 'judicial' forms, but they are exercises of—indeed, under our constitutional structure they *must be* exercises of—the 'executive Power.'") (citation omitted); cf. Mistretta v. United States, 488 U.S. 361, 417 (1989) (Scalia, J., dissenting) (noting that "a certain degree of discretion, and thus of lawmaking, *inheres* in most executive or judicial action.").

[132] Ilan Wurman, The Specification Power, 168 U. Pa. L. Rev. 689 (2020); Ilan Wurman, Nondelegation at the Founding, 130 Yale L.J. (forthcoming 2021).

We suggested that in *Humphrey's* the Court perhaps was embracing the distinction of early 19th-century theorists between "politics" and "administration." But a key component of this distinction is that administrative officials worthy of insulation from politics must be impartial. As Woodrow Wilson wrote, "The field of administration is a field of business. . . . [A]dministration lies outside the proper sphere of *politics*."[133] Frank Goodnow wrote that "there is a large part of administration which is unconnected with politics, which should therefore be relieved very largely, if not altogether, from the control of political bodies," because it embraces "semi-scientific" fields.[134] Administrative officials "should be free from the influence of politics because . . . their mission is the exercise of foresight and discretion, the pursuit of truth, the gathering of information," "efficient" organization, and "the maintenance of a strictly impartial attitude toward the individuals with whom they have dealings."[135]

Simply put, if the exception to the presidential removal power is to apply, we argued that it should apply only when the prerequisites identified by the Court in *Humphrey's* are present. A single principal officer, who is a partisan of one political party and who enjoys a sweeping portfolio over all the nation's consumer protection laws, is far removed from the FTC. The CFPB director, who has no need to convince, reason, or debate fellow commissioners, can hardly be counted on to be nonpartisan, impartial, or to act as an "expert."

In his amicus brief defending the CFPB, Paul Clement turned this argument around: if the problem is that for-cause removal provisions create too much insulation between the president and actual law-execution, then the problem is compounded by multimember commissions. This is undoubtedly true *if the Court wants to be originalist*. On any understanding of the text or the history, the answer does not depend on whether there is a multimember agency or a single officer. But the point is that *Humphrey's Executor* was a functionalist decision untethered to the text. Or, to the extent it is consistent with the cross-reference theory, it is still an entirely functionalist matter how much control the president must have to ensure faithful execution. And if we are arguing on functionalist grounds, then

---

[133] Woodrow Wilson, The Study of Administration, 2 Pol. Sci. Q. 197, 209–10 (1887).

[134] Frank J. Goodnow, Politics and Administration: A Study in Government 85 (1900).

[135] *Id.*

Humphrey's is justified on the "functional" basis of administrative expertise and deliberation—arguments that simply do not apply to single directors.

C. Morrison v. Olson

In *Morrison v. Olson*, the Supreme Court established an entirely new functionalist analysis for analyzing removal power questions. It is not clear how much of this approach survives (more anon), but *Morrison* remains an important precedent.

In 1978, Congress enacted the Ethics in Government Act, giving a special court the power to appoint, at the recommendation of the attorney general, an "independent counsel" to investigate high-level government misconduct.[136] This independent counsel had the "full power and independent authority to exercise all investigative and prosecutorial functions and powers of the Department of Justice, the Attorney General, and any other officer or employee of the Department of Justice."[137] In other words, the counsel was a prosecutor, and was to be "independent" of the president—the president could not remove the counsel, and the attorney general could only remove her for good cause.[138]

The Supreme Court upheld the constitutionality of the independent counsel in a 7-1 decision. The lone dissent was Justice Antonin Scalia, who famously wrote: "Article II, § 1, cl. 1, of the Constitution provides: 'The executive Power shall be vested in a President of the United States.' As I described at the outset of this opinion, this does not mean some of the executive power, but *all of* the executive power."[139] And prosecution was clearly part of "the executive power." Indeed, Blackstone argues that the king is the chief prosecutor because the public has delegated to him all powers and rights "with regard to the execution of the laws."[140] There have been several attempts in the literature to claim that "prosecution" was never an executive function, at least not one that had to be done by the president, and so Congress can limit the president's control over

---

[136] 28 U.S.C. § 49.

[137] 28 U.S.C. § 594(a); see generally *id.* § 591 et seq. (full statute).

[138] Morrison v. Olson, 487 U.S. 654, 660–63 (1988).

[139] *Id.* at 705 (Scalia, J., dissenting) (emphasis original).

[140] Blackstone, *supra* note 16, at *258–59.

prosecution. Elsewhere I have sought to demonstrate that these arguments are probably mistaken.[141]

The Court in *Morrison* agreed that prosecution was a "purely executive" function, thus distinguishing it from the functions in *Humphrey's*, but argued that that did not resolve the case. "[O]ur present considered view," the Court explained,

> is that the determination of whether the Constitution allows Congress to impose a "good cause"-type restriction on the President's power to remove an official cannot be made to turn on whether or not that official is classified as "purely executive." The analysis contained in our removal cases is designed not to define rigid categories of those officials who may or may not be removed at will by the President, but to ensure that Congress does not interfere with the President's exercise of the "executive power" and his constitutionally appointed duty to "take care that the laws be faithfully executed" under Article II.[142]

The inquiry thus boiled down to a purely functionalist one: whether the restrictions "interfere impermissibly with [the president's] constitutional obligation to ensure the faithful execution of the laws."[143] The Court held that the independence of the independent counsel, who the Court also held was an inferior officer, did not "interfere impermissibly."

D. Free Enterprise Fund v. PCAOB

The Court's most recent foray (aside from *Seila Law*) into the removal question was *Free Enterprise Fund v. PCAOB*. Unlike in *Morrison*, the agency there (the Public Company Accounting and Oversight Board, which was under the umbrella of the Securities and Exchange Commission [SEC]) was part of a traditional "independent" agency.[144] Unlike *Humphrey's*, however, it involved an inferior officer. The novelty was two layers of for-cause removal provisions: the president could only remove SEC commissioners for cause, and

---

[141] Wurman, *supra* note 15.

[142] Morrison, 487 U.S. at 689–90.

[143] *Id.* at 693.

[144] Although the organic statute does not restrict the removal of SEC commissioners, it has long been assumed that the president can only remove them for cause.

those commissioners in turn could only remove PCAOB members for cause. Recall that in *Perkins*, the Court held that Congress could restrict the ability of a principal officer to remove an inferior, and in *Humphrey's* the Court held that Congress could restrict the ability of the president to remove a principal officer (at least of an independent agency). Could these two restrictions be combined?

The Court said no: "[S]uch multilevel protection from removal is contrary to Article II's vesting of the executive power in the President. The President cannot 'take Care that the Laws be faithfully executed' if he cannot oversee the faithfulness of the officers who execute them."[145] It is unclear how much of this opinion depends on the Court's reading of the Vesting Clause. The Court seems to presume that the grant of executive power is at least a grant of the power to execute law; but its analysis turns largely on its view of how much power is necessary to ensure the faithful execution of the laws. Importantly, however, the Court did not cite or rely on *Morrison's* functionalist "impermissibly interferes" test. It cited *Morrison* for the same proposition that it cited *Perkins*—that Congress could restrict the ability of a principal officer to remove an inferior officer.[146]

IV. The *Seila Law* Decision

That brings us to *Seila Law*. In a nutshell, five justices held that the for-cause removal provision insulating the director of the CFPB was unconstitutional. Two of these justices (Clarence Thomas and Neil Gorsuch) would have overruled *Humphrey's Executor*. Those two also would have found that the removal provision was not severable from the remainder of the statute. The three other justices (John Roberts, Samuel Alito, and Brett Kavanaugh), along with the four dissenters, held that the removal provision was severable and therefore remanded to the lower courts to determine whether the enforcement action against petitioner Seila Law LLC had been ratified by a director (an acting director more specifically) who was removable at will. This part will not address the severability or remedial questions, only the removal power question.

---

[145] Free Enter. Fund, 561 U.S. at 484.

[146] *Id.* at 483 ("[I]n *United States v. Perkins* and *Morrison v. Olson*, the Court sustained similar restrictions on the power of principal executive officers—themselves responsible to the President—to remove their own inferiors.") (internal citations omitted).

A. Majority Opinion

Chief Justice Roberts's majority opinion[147] did not examine in-depth much of the debate discussed above. After all, the Court had already done so in *Free Enterprise Fund*, and so the majority largely fell back on that decision. It is not entirely clear which reading of the Executive Power Clause the majority adopts, but it does appear to believe it is a grant of some kind of substantive power (at a minimum the power to execute law):

> Article II provides that "[t]he executive Power shall be vested in a President," who must "take Care that the Laws be faithfully executed." The entire "executive Power" belongs to the President alone. But because it would be "impossib[le]" for "one man" to "perform all the great business of the State," the Constitution assumes that lesser executive officers will "assist the supreme Magistrate in discharging the duties of his trust."[148]

The president's removal power, moreover, "has long been confirmed by history and precedent."[149] It was "discussed extensively" in the First Congress.[150] Relying on *Free Enterprise Fund* and a letter from James Madison to Thomas Jefferson, the Court again noted that the view that "prevailed" as "most consonant" with the Constitution was that the power of removal was constitutionally vested in the president.[151]

The majority held that there were only two "exceptions" to this general rule: the exception of *Humphrey's Executor* and *Morrison v. Olson*. The Court agreed with the petitioner (and a variety of amici) that the *Humphrey's* exception was limited to bipartisan, multimember commissions whose commissioners could check and balance each other and decide things impartially on the basis of expertise. The Court then did with *Morrison* what it did with that decision

---

[147] I do not refer to this opinion as the plurality opinion because of the agreement of five justices on the merits of the removal question.

[148] Seila Law LLC v. Consumer Fin. Prot. Bureau, 140 S. Ct. 2183, 2197 (2020) (majority opinion) (citations omitted).

[149] *Id.*

[150] *Id.*

[151] *Id.*

in *Free Enterprise Fund*: it argued that *Morrison* stood for the same proposition as *Perkins*, namely that Congress could insulate inferior officers from removal. Gone entirely was the actual functionalist test of that opinion.

The Court then reached its main holding: that these two exceptions did not apply to, and should not be extended to, the case of a single-director agency. Importantly, the Court first noted that single-director independent agencies were a novelty. The only other examples of such an arrangement were the comptroller of the currency during the Civil War, and there the removal protection was repealed by Congress the following year; the Office of Special Counsel, which "does not bind private parties" but only enforces certain rules against government officials; the Social Security Administration, which drew an objection from President Bill Clinton for the very reason that it was amended to be headed by a single director and which in any event "lacks the authority to bring enforcement actions against private parties";[152] and finally the Federal Housing Finance Agency, which regulates primarily government-sponsored entities and whose single-director structure the Fifth Circuit has held to be unconstitutional.

The majority did not find the historical anomaly to be dispositive, though surely it was suggestive. The majority's central point was that the Constitution, unlike its strategy with respect to legislative power, centralizes all executive power in a single individual. To ensure that individual is accountable for the exercise of this undivided executive power, he or she is to be elected, and by the people of the whole nation. "The resulting constitutional strategy is straightforward: divide power everywhere except for the Presidency, and render the President directly accountable to the people through regular elections."[153] The CFPB is unconstitutional because it violates this strategy:

> The CFPB's single-Director structure contravenes this carefully calibrated system by vesting significant governmental power in the hands of a single individual accountable to no one. The Director is neither elected by the people nor meaningfully controlled (through the threat of removal) by someone who

[152] *Id.* at 2202.
[153] *Id.* at 2203.

is. The Director does not even depend on Congress for annual appropriations. Yet the Director may *unilaterally*, without meaningful supervision, issue final regulations, oversee adjudications, set enforcement priorities, initiate prosecutions, and determine what penalties to impose on private parties. With no colleagues to persuade, and no boss or electorate looking over her shoulder, the Director may dictate and enforce policy for a vital segment of the economy affecting millions of Americans.[154]

The majority thus adopted the view that if there is to be an "exception" to the general rule of presidential removal, the agency must be headed by multiple commissioners. There must be "colleagues to persuade."[155] This makes it more likely that the purpose of the "exception" will be fulfilled—that is, such agencies will exercise power impartially and based on expertise. The Court held the single-director structure was enough to invalidate the CFPB, but it also noted that at least two other features heightened the constitutional problem. First, the five-year term meant that some presidents may never get to appoint a director. Second, the CFPB received its funding entirely outside the appropriation process, and so the president could not even control the agency through his role in the appropriations process.

B. Concurring Opinion

On the merits of the removal question, Justice Thomas, joined by Justice Gorsuch, concurred in the chief justice's opinion. But, Thomas noted, "with today's decision, the Court has repudiated almost every aspect of *Humphrey's Executor*," and therefore in a future case he "would repudiate what is left of this erroneous precedent."[156] Justice Thomas argued that "[t]he Constitution does not permit the creation of officers exercising 'quasi-legislative' and 'quasi-judicial' powers' in 'quasi-legislative' and 'quasi-judicial agencies.'"[157] Indeed, "[n]o such powers or agencies exist" because "Congress lacks the authority to delegate its legislative power" and "it cannot

---

[154] *Id.* at 2203–04.

[155] *Id.* at 2204.

[156] *Id.* at 2212 (Thomas, J., concurring).

[157] *Id.* at 2216.

authorize the use of judicial power by officers acting outside of the bounds of Article III."[158] Nor, Thomas added, can Congress "create agencies that straddle multiple branches of Government."[159] Simply put, "[t]he Constitution sets out three branches of Government and provides each with a different form of power—legislative, executive, and judicial."[160]

Importantly, Justices Thomas and Gorsuch reiterated that "it is hard to dispute that the powers of the FTC at the time of *Humphrey's Executor* would at the present time be considered 'executive,' at least to some degree."[161] They cited *Morrison* for the proposition but also footnote seven of Justice Elena Kagan's dissent in *Seila Law*. In that footnote, Justice Kagan wrote:

> The majority is quite right that today we view *all* the activities of administrative agencies as exercises of "the 'executive Power.'" But we well understand, just as the *Humphrey's* Court did, that those activities may "take 'legislative' and 'judicial' forms." The classic examples are agency rule-makings and adjudications, endemic in agencies like the FTC and CFPB.[162]

This concession suggests that all nine justices on the Supreme Court believe that the reasoning of *Humphrey's Executor* was erroneous. There is no such thing as quasi-legislative or quasi-judicial power that need not be exercised by at least one of the constitutionally named departments. If for-cause removal provisions can be sustained at all, it must be because the president only has whatever power to execute law that is implied by the duty to take care that the laws be faithfully executed.

C. Dissenting Opinion

Justice Kagan, with whom Justices Ruth Bader Ginsburg, Stephen Breyer, and Sonia Sotomayor joined, dissented. As is typical of Justice Kagan's opinions, this one is a masterful piece of writing with

[158] *Id.*

[159] *Id.*

[160] *Id.*

[161] *Id.* at 2217 (internal citations omitted).

[162] *Id.* at 2234 n.7 (Kagan, J., dissenting) (internal citations omitted).

some incredible "zingers." But I am not convinced that she has the better argument.

Justice Kagan begins with the text: "Nothing in [the Constitution] speaks of removal." "And it grants Congress authority [via the Necessary and Proper Clause] to organize all the institutions of American governance, provided only that those arrangements allow the President to perform his own constitutionally assigned duties."[163] Not only is the majority's "rule" regarding presidential removal therefore incorrect, but its "exception" is wrong too. Nothing in *Humphrey's Executor* or *Morrison* limits the reach of those decisions to multimember commissions or inferior officers, Kagan argues. Surely on this score the dissent is correct. The Court was, undeniably, trying to limit what it finds to be objectionable precedents without quite overruling them, which raises the usual question of whether such an approach wreaks more havoc on the law by creating untenable distinction after untenable distinction. Perhaps it does, and it would have been better for the Court to overrule *Humphrey's Executor* and *Morrison*.

Justice Kagan then begins her historical analysis with two pieces of evidence:

> First, in [the Founding] era, Parliament often restricted the King's power to remove royal officers—and the President, needless to say, wasn't supposed to be a king. See Birk, Interrogating the Historical Basis for a Unitary Executive, 73 Stan. L. Rev. (forthcoming 2021). Second, many States at the time allowed limits on gubernatorial removal power even though their constitutions had similar vesting clauses. See Shane, The Originalist Myth of the Unitary Executive, 19 U. Pa. J. Const. L. 323, 334–344 (2016). Historical understandings thus belie the majority's "general rule."[164]

Justice Kagan does not actually interrogate the cited articles, however. Part II.A explained why Birk's argument is unconvincing at least as applied to principal officers. And Justice Kagan relies on Peter Shane's article for the proposition that state constitutions with similar executive vesting clauses "allowed limits on gubernatorial removal power." Shane's article, however, is about legislative

---

[163] *Id.* at 2225.
[164] *Id.* at 2228.

appointments under the state constitutions, and not removals.[165] As Mortenson argues, appointments were understood to be part of the executive power except as otherwise provided for by law.[166] Both Madison and James Wilson defined the executive power at the Constitutional Convention as including the power "to appoint to offices *in cases not otherwise provided for.*"[167]

Indeed, the Constitution specifically assigns part of the appointment power to the Senate or to Congress as a whole. The whole premise of the Decision of 1789 is that removal is different from appointment. Appointments are more amenable to legislative input because various legislators are likely to know the potential officers in their states and districts. But it is the president who is in the best position to know whether such officers are discharging their duties appropriately once appointed.

Justice Kagan then cites Edwin Corwin's 1927 article, *Tenure of Office and the Removal Power under the Constitution,*[168] for the proposition that "New York's Constitution of 1777 had nearly the same [vesting] clause, though the State's executive had 'very little voice' in removals."[169] I was intrigued by this citation. If the language of the similar executive power clause in New York's Constitution, widely acknowledged to be a model for the U.S. Constitution, did not convey a removal power, then that would be serious evidence against a removal power. But it turns out not to be true—at least, the citation

---

[165] Indeed, Shane explains, "Not much is added to [his] analysis [of state constitutions] by an inquiry into gubernatorial removal powers. The federal Constitution, of course, makes no mention of presidential removal power. This is the pattern of most state constitutions as well, except insofar as they authorize gubernatorial removals of judicial or militia officers on address by two-thirds of a few of the state legislatures. . . . [And] the early state constitutional texts pertaining explicitly to removal powers generally do not add anything to an original public meaning argument for a unitary executive in the states, but the topic is generally left to implication, as it is in the federal Constitution." Peter M. Shane, The Originalist Myth of a Unitary Executive, 19 U. Pa. J. Const. L. 343–44 n.66 (2016). The only mention of a removal power dispute under state law, moreover, is a single example from Pennsylvania after the famous removal debate in Congress. *Id.* at 351.

[166] Mortenson, *supra* note 25, at 55.

[167] 1 The Records of the Federal Convention of 1787, *supra* note 53, at 66–67 (cleaned up) (Madison); *id.* at 70 (Wilson) ("Executive powers are designed for the execution of Laws, and appointing Officers not otherwise to be appointed.").

[168] 27 Colum. L. Rev. at 385.

[169] Seila Law, 140 S. Ct. at 2228 (Kagan, J., dissenting).

does not prove it. Corwin did indeed say that New York's constitution "gave the executive of that state very little voice in either appointments or removals."[170] For this proposition Corwin cites the "take care" clause of the New York constitution and pages 36–37 and 53 of Charles Thach's well known work *The Creation of the Presidency.*[171] None of those pages mentions anything about removal, however.

Justice Kagan next cites two famous passages from *The Federalist*:

> In Federalist No. 77, Hamilton presumed that under the new Constitution "[t]he consent of [the Senate] would be necessary to displace as well as to appoint" officers of the United States. He thought that scheme would promote "steady administration": "Where a man in any station had given satisfactory evidence of his fitness for it, a new president would be restrained" from substituting "a person more agreeable to him." By contrast, Madison thought the Constitution allowed Congress to decide how any executive official could be removed. He explained in Federalist No. 39: "The tenure of the ministerial offices generally will be a subject of legal regulation, conformably to the reason of the case, and the example of the State Constitutions."[172]

The majority does not have much to say about these statements from Hamilton and Madison except to say they later changed their views. I think there's much more to say, to wit: It is not clear that either statement suggests the president does not have a removal power. Start with Hamilton's statement.[173] Hamilton's entire paragraph is about "the business of appointments." Thus, he speaks of "displacing" an officer after a *new president* is elected. This seems most logically to be a reference to the advice and consent of the Senate to a new appointment. The president would not need the advice and consent to remove an officer, but to displace the officer (that is, replace the officer with a new one), the president certainly would

---

[170] Corwin, *supra* note 95.

[171] Charles C. Thach, The Creation of the Presidency (1922).

[172] Seila Law, 140 S. Ct. at 2229 (Kagan, J., dissenting).

[173] I am indebted to Josh Blackman for this insight. Josh Blackman, "Justice Kagan on Hamilton in Federalist No. 77," Reason: Volokh Conspiracy, July 1, 2020, https://reason.com/2020/07/01/justice-kagan-on-hamilton-in-federalist-no-77/.

need the advice and consent of the Senate.[174] As for Madison's statement, it is true that Congress regulates the "tenure" of "offices" by establishing the length of the term—the length of time before a new individual has to be nominated and appointed to the position. That is not controversial. It is not clear that Madison meant to suggest anything about presidential removal.

Justice Kagan finally arrives at the Decision of 1789. She argues that the Decision of 1789 is ambiguous, which, as explained, is certainly a plausible interpretation of the debates. Kagan then argues that, in any event, Congress always treated financial institutions differently. Justice Kagan relies on the arguments discussed in Part II.B.2 but does not address any of the counterarguments. The dissenting opinion even adds two points that the amici in support of the CFPB had advanced in the *PHH* case but abandoned in their *Seila Law* case.

First, Justice Kagan noted that the "Comptroller of the Treasury's settlements of public accounts" was "final and conclusive," thereby "preventing presidential overrides" and marking "the Comptroller

---

[174] Here is the full text:

> It has been mentioned as one of the advantages to be expected from the co-operation of the Senate, in the business of *appointments*, that it would contribute to the stability of the administration. The consent of that body would be necessary to displace as well as to appoint. *A change of the Chief Magistrate,* therefore, would not occasion so violent or so general a revolution in the officers of the government as might be expected, if he were the sole disposer of offices. Where a man in any station had given satisfactory evidence of his fitness for it, a new President would be restrained from attempting a change *in favor of a person* more agreeable to him, by the apprehension that a discountenance of the Senate might frustrate the attempt, and bring some degree of discredit upon himself. Those who can best estimate the value of a steady administration, will be most disposed to prize a provision which connects the official existence of public men with the approbation or disapprobation of that body which, from the greater permanency of its own composition, will in all probability be less subject to inconstancy than any other member of the government.
>
> To this union of the Senate with the President, *in the article of appointments,* it has in some cases been suggested that it would serve to give the President an undue influence over the Senate, and in others that it would have an opposite tendency, a strong proof that neither suggestion is true.

The Federalist No. 77 at 458 (Alexander Hamilton) (Clinton Rossiter ed., 1961) (emphases added).

as exercising independent judgment."[175] But ordinarily finality and conclusiveness has to do with the availability of judicial review in matters of public rights—not with presidential supervision.[176] Second, Justice Kagan wrote that "even James Madison, who at this point opposed most removal limits, told Congress that 'there may be strong reasons why an officer of this kind should not hold his office at the pleasure' of the Secretary or President."[177] She fails to mention that Madison's actual proposal included the proviso "unless sooner removed by the President."[178] Additionally, his observation was limited to the settling of individual claims against the government, and therefore would not have applied very broadly:

> I question very much whether [the President] can or ought to have any interference in the settling and adjusting the legal claims of individuals against the United States. The necessary examination and decision in such cases partake too much of the Judicial capacity to be blended with the Executive. I do not say the office is either Executive or Judicial; I think it rather distinct from both, though it partakes of each, and therefore some modification, accommodated to those circumstances, ought to take place.[179]

The very next day, in any event, Madison "withdrew the proposition which he yesterday laid upon the table."[180] We can't know for

---

[175] Seila Law, 140 S. Ct. at 2230–31 (Kagan, J., dissenting).

[176] Whether an executive branch agency or official could act conclusively—or whether her acts would be judicially reviewable—had to do with the rights/privileges distinction in the 19th century. As Caleb Nelson has written, "the public/private distinction had considerable resolving power; it formed the basis for a framework that was used throughout the nineteenth century to separate matters that required 'judicial' involvement from matters that the political branches could conclusively adjudicate on their own." Caleb Nelson, Adjudication in the Political Branches, 107 Colum. L. Rev. 559, 564 (2007). Courts routinely determined whether agency determinations were "conclusive" as opposed to being subject to judicial review. *Id.* at 577–82 (citing numerous cases). Attorney General William Wirt did think, however, that this provision of the treasury statute meant that the president could not personally interfere with the settling of accounts. The President & Accounting Offices, 1 U.S. Op. Atty. Gen. 624 (1823).

[177] Seila Law, 140 S. Ct. at 2231 (Kagan, J., dissenting).

[178] 1 Annals of Cong. 612.

[179] *Id.* at 614.

[180] *Id.* at 615.

sure why, but maybe he came to see an inconsistency in his position. Although this episode is rather ambiguous, it hardly proves much support for the dissenting position. One would think that the full contours of the episode should have been discussed.

Justice Kagan also relied on a letter from Thomas Jefferson and a handful of attorney general opinions for the proposition that the president could not interfere with the decisions of the comptroller.[181] This evidence suggests that the president cannot personally execute laws when their execution is tasked to subordinate officers, and perhaps it suggests the president cannot generally direct those officers, either. But none of that suggests the president could not freely remove officers.

Justice Kagan does cite one attorney general opinion for the proposition that "Congress could restrict the President's authority to remove such officials, at least so long as it 'express[ed] that intention clearly.'"[182] But this opinion only had to do with inferior officers whose appointments Congress vested in the president alone (and thus it was similar to the *Perkins* case). Attorney General Wirt's opinion said that if Congress did not further specify the tenure of such an inferior officer, then the office is of course held during the pleasure of the president. Although that is somewhat suggestive that the president might not be able to remove at-will such an officer if Congress does impose restrictions, that question was not squarely presented to the attorney general. And even if it had been, the question would again only apply to inferior officers. It is true that in a better known opinion, unfortunately not cited by the dissenting opinion, Attorney General Wirt was much more explicit that the president could only remove officers for faithless execution.[183] That is undeniably some evidence that some prominent individuals in government

---

[181] Letter from T. Jefferson to B. Latrobe (June 2, 1808), in Thomas Jefferson and the National Capital 429, 431 (S. Padover ed., 1946) ("[W]ith the settlement of the accounts at the Treasury I have no right to interfere in the least," because the Comptroller of the Treasury "is the sole & supreme judge for all claims of money against the U.S. and would no more receive a direction from me" than would "one of the judges of the supreme court."); 1 Op. Att'y Gen. 636, 637 (1824) ("the President has no right to interpose in the settling of accounts" because Congress had "separated" the comptroller from the president's authority); 1 Op. Att'y Gen. 678, 680 (1824) (same).

[182] 1 Op. Att'y Gen. 212, 213 (1818).

[183] The President & Accounting Offices, 1 U.S. Op. Att'y Gen. 624, 625–26 (1823).

in the 19th century rejected a general removal power, as indeed did many in the First Congress in the great removal debate.

Although I have criticized significant parts of Justice Kagan's historical analysis, a high point of her opinion was its response to the chief justice's argument about the novelty of the CFPB. Justice Kagan rightly noted that "novelty is not the test of constitutionality when it comes to structuring agencies," and that "Congress regulates in that sphere under the Necessary and Proper Clause, not (as the majority seems to think) a Rinse and Repeat Clause."[184] That's surely true. But nor does the Necessary and Proper Clause permit just any innovation. Congress can seek to effectuate the president's powers; it cannot try to supplant them.

Perhaps the most important takeaway from the opinions in the *Seila Law* case, in summary, is that history is contested and never clear cut. The majority would do well to accept the ambiguity of the Decision of 1789 and state clearly that its force has to do with the force of the arguments of Madison and Ames. The dissenters, for their part, would do well to recognize the existence of academic literature counter to the literature they cited. There is a growing body of scholarship suggesting that the Executive Power Clause was a substantive grant of power, even if only to execute law. The implications are potentially very different from what follows if the president's power is only what can be inferred from the Take Care Clause. The dissent would also do well to accept that nothing in principle separates financial agencies from other types of agencies, except perhaps Congress's historical interest in more carefully monitoring and constructing the duties of such agencies.

Conclusion

The *Seila Law* decision represents the same approach the Court took in *Free Enterprise Fund*: narrowly construe the functionalist exceptions of *Humphrey's* and *Morrison* and decline to extend them to new circumstances. The dissenters are surely right, however, that nothing in the Constitution really distinguishes between single-director agencies and multimember agencies, unless the analysis is entirely a functionalist one under the Take Care Clause. It may be better in the future to recognize that the reasoning of *Humphrey's* has

---

[184] Seila Law, 140 S. Ct. at 2241 (Kagan, J., dissenting).

been abandoned. If it can be justified at all, it is only on the grounds that the Executive Vesting Clause is not a grant of substantive power. In that case, the analysis of all removal cases will depend on how much power can be implied from the president's duty to take care that the laws be faithfully executed. If the Executive Vesting Clause is at least a grant of law-execution power, however, then *Humphrey's* and *Morrison* simply can no longer stand and should be overruled.

Liu v. SEC: Limiting Disgorgement, but by How Much?

*Jennifer J. Schulp**

I. Introduction

To extract what it calls "ill-gotten gains" from wrongdoers, the Securities and Exchange Commission (SEC) relies heavily on the amorphous remedy of "disgorgement." Last year, the SEC obtained $4.3 billion in monetary remedies for violations of the federal securities laws.[1] Of that total, about $3.2 billion was from disgorgement orders.[2]

Disgorgement is "[t]he act of giving something (such as profits illegally obtained) on demand or by legal compulsion."[3] And the disgorgement remedy is "[r]estitution measured by the defendant's wrongful gain."[4] Easily stated, but the remedy of disgorgement itself—particularly the way the SEC uses it—is not so clearly defined.[5]

* Jennifer J. Schulp is the director of Financial Regulation Studies at the Cato Institute's Center for Monetary and Financial Alternatives. She thanks Madison Breshears, intern with the Center for Monetary and Financial Alternatives, for her assistance with this article and Russ Ryan for his always thoughtful comments.

[1] U.S. Sec. & Exch. Comm'n, Div. of Enf't, 2019 Ann. Rep. 16 [hereinafter 2019 Annual Report].

[2] *Id.*

[3] Disgorgement, Black's Law Dictionary (11th ed. 2019).

[4] Restatement (Third) of Restitution & Unjust Enrichment § 51 cmt. a (Am. Law Inst. 2011); see also *id.* at § 51(4) ("The object of restitution in such cases is to eliminate profit from wrongdoing while avoiding, so far as possible, the imposition of a penalty. Restitution remedies that pursue this object are often called 'disgorgement' or 'accounting.'").

[5] *Id.* at § 51 cmt. e ("The object of the disgorgement remedy—to eliminate the possibility of profit from conscious wrongdoing—is one of the cornerstones of the law of restitution and unjust enrichment. . . . While its purpose is easily stated and readily understandable, the application of the remedy involves well-known, sometimes intractable difficulties.").

The SEC initially grounded disgorgement in the district court's equitable authority to order remedies separately from those the SEC was explicitly authorized to pursue. Later, Congress explicitly authorized the SEC to seek equitable relief. Nevertheless, disgorgement has strayed far from this equitable authority. As a practical matter, SEC disgorgement often penalizes by leaving the defendant worse off, and it routinely fails to return disgorged funds as restitution to those harmed by the wrongdoer.

In *Liu v. SEC*,[6] the Supreme Court considered whether the SEC is authorized to seek, and district courts are empowered to grant, disgorgement by statutory authority providing for "any equitable relief that may be appropriate or necessary for the benefit of investors."[7] The Court found that the SEC may pursue disgorgement, but only insofar as it stays within the bounds of a traditional equitable remedy: "a disgorgement award [must not] exceed a wrongdoer's net profits and [must be] awarded for victims."[8]

Neither accepting the SEC's expansive view of disgorgement nor the petitioner's request to strike the remedy altogether, the Supreme Court landed in the middle. Specifically, the Court recognized that Congress authorizes the SEC to seek equitable remedies but found that the agency's disgorgement orders often exceed the scope of its authority. While *Liu* leaves many questions unanswered, its immediate effects are welcome, and include increased scrutiny of SEC requests for disgorgement, more frequent return of disgorged funds to victims, and increased transparency and consistency in the application of SEC remedies.

II. A Brief History of SEC Remedies and Disgorgement

Before examining the *Liu* decision in detail, it is useful to understand the history of the SEC's remedial authority and about how the SEC has used the disgorgement remedy.

A. SEC Remedies

Although the SEC has been enforcing the securities laws since its inception in 1934, its regulatory toolkit has expanded over time.

---

[6] Liu v. SEC, 140 S. Ct. 1936 (2020).

[7] 15 U.S.C. § 78u(d)(5).

[8] *Liu*, 140 S. Ct. at 1940.

In the beginning, Congress limited the SEC's remedial authority to injunctions barring future violations of the securities laws and referring cases to the Department of Justice for criminal prosecution.[9] Back then, courts generally refused to provide broad injunctive relief, confining their orders to the conduct at issue. Accordingly, SEC injunctions were of limited scope, usually restricting the defendant's conduct or trading with respect to a particular stock; defendants could simply resume their unlawful activities with other securities not subject to the injunction.[10]

For the first 30 years or so of its existence, the level of SEC enforcement activity waxed and waned, but the remedies available to the commission remained constant.[11]

By the 1960s, the commission began advancing more expansive interpretations of the securities laws, including developing a substantial insider-trading doctrine.[12] The SEC also broadened its remedial power by appealing to the inherent equitable authority of courts to order ancillary relief.[13]

In 1970, the SEC for the first time obtained a monetary order for equitable relief in *Texas Gulf Sulphur*.[14] In this insider-trading case, the district court ordered corporate insiders who had traded in advance of public knowledge about a mineral strike to disgorge their trading profits.[15] The Second Circuit upheld the ruling, in relevant part, noting that "the SEC may seek other than injunctive relief in order to

---

[9] See 1 T. Hazen, Law of Securities Regulation §1:37 (7th ed., rev. 2016); see also SEC Historical Society, Oral Histories Committee, Roundtable on Enforcement, A Brief History of the SEC's Enforcement Program 1934–1981, 2 (Sept. 25, 2002).

[10] SEC Historical Society, *supra* note 9, at 5.

[11] *Id.* at 2–3 (discussing SEC's early enforcement activity); *id.* at 13 (noting that the commission obtained in civil actions permanent injunctions against 1,059 firms and individuals in its first decade of operation); *id.* at 14 (noting that only 50 enforcement actions originating out of the home office were brought during the 1950s although enforcement actions continued from the regional offices).

[12] *Id.* at 3 (describing the 1960s as a "period distinguished by the staff's creativity and innovation in using enforcement actions to facilitate the interpretive development of the securities laws").

[13] *Id.* at 20.

[14] SEC v. Tex. Gulf Sulphur, 312 F. Supp. 77, 91–92 (S.D.N.Y. 1970), aff'd in part, rev'd in part, 446 F.2d 1301 (2d. Cir. 1971); see also SEC Historical Society, *supra* note 9, at 21; Lisa M. Fairfax, From Equality to Duty: On Altering the Reach, Impact, and Meaning of the Texas Gulf Legacy, 71 S.M.U. L. Rev. 729, 748 (2018).

[15] Tex. Gulf Sulphur, 312 F. Supp. at 91–92.

effectuate the purposes of the Act, so long as such relief is remedial relief and is not a penalty assessment."[16] This case laid the foundation for the disgorgement remedy the Supreme Court considered in *Liu*.

In the years that followed, Congress further expanded the SEC's available remedies. Fulfilling a request from the SEC, the Insider Trading Sanctions Act of 1984 gave the SEC authority to exact monetary penalties in insider-trading cases.[17] A few years later, the Securities Enforcement Remedies and Penny Stock Reform Act of 1990 (Remedies Act) ushered in the modern era of SEC enforcement remedies.[18] The Remedies Act granted the SEC broad civil penalty authority, calculated through a three-tier framework based on the nature of the violations. Within each tier, "the fine may not exceed the higher of the gross pecuniary gain or maximum statutory amount."[19] The Remedies Act also explicitly granted the SEC the authority to "enter an order requiring accounting and disgorgement" in administrative proceedings.[20]

The Sarbanes-Oxley Act of 2002 again altered the SEC's remedial authority, explicitly authorizing the commission to "seek, and any Federal court may grant, any equitable relief that may be appropriate or necessary for the benefit of investors."[21] Unlike the Remedies Act

---

[16] SEC v. Tex. Gulf Sulphur, 446 F.2d at 1308.

[17] See Paul S. Atkins & Bradley J. Bondi, Evaluating the Mission: A Critical Review of the History and Evolution of the SEC Enforcement Program, 13 Fordham J. Corp. & Fin. L. 367, 385 (2008); The Insider Trading and Securities Fraud Enforcement Act of 1988, Pub. L. No. 100-704, § 3, 102 Stat. 4677 (permitting the SEC to seek three times the profits realized [or losses evaded] as a civil penalty).

[18] Atkins & Bondi, *supra* note 17, at 391–92; see also, Securities Enforcement Remedies and Penny Stock Reform Act of 1990, Pub. L. No. 101-429, 104 Stat. 931 (1990); Richard A. Spehr & Michelle J. Annunziata, The Remedies Act Turns Fifteen: What Is Its Relevance Today?, 1 N.Y.U. J.L. & Bus., 587, 588 (2005).

[19] 15 U.S.C. §§ 77t(d)(2)(A)-(C), 78u(d)(3)(A)-(B); see also Spehr & Annunziata, *supra* note 18, at 589, 591–92; Atkins & Bondi, *supra* note 17, at 392.

[20] 15 U.S.C. § 77h-1(e); see also Spehr & Annunziata, *supra* note 18, at 593. The Remedies Act gave the SEC two additional remedies: administrative authority to seek temporary and permanent cease and desist orders, permitting the SEC to bypass the onerous process of getting an emergency restraining order which required injunction proceedings (15 U.S.C. § 77h-1; Spehr & Annunziata, *supra* note 18, at 589–90); and officer and director bars in federal court (15 U.S.C. § 78u(d)(2); Spehr & Annunziata, *supra* note 18, at 594).

[21] 15 U.S.C. § 78u(d)(5). The Sarbanes-Oxley Act also allowed the SEC to seek a forfeiture of bonuses received by executives who headed noncompliant companies and lowered the burden to obtain administrative director and officer bars. See Spehr & Annunziata, *supra* note 18, at 598–99.

grant of disgorgement authority in administrative proceedings, the Sarbanes-Oxley Act amendments do not delineate any specific type of equitable relief the SEC may seek in judicial proceedings.

Today, the SEC wields a wide range of remedial authorities. In federal court proceedings, the SEC can seek "a permanent or temporary injunction" punishable by contempt, including an injunction preventing a defendant from serving on boards of directors.[22] The SEC also may seek civil monetary penalties and equitable relief.[23]

In administrative proceedings, the SEC can issue orders requiring a person "to cease and desist from committing or causing a violation" of the securities laws, requiring affirmative "steps to effect compliance" with the law, prohibiting a person "from acting as an officer or director" of a publicly traded company, and requiring accounting and disgorgement.[24] The SEC also may impose civil penalties.

B. Disgorgement in Practice

While the SEC's ability to obtain disgorgement has become relatively well-accepted by the courts, there has been little clarity as to what exactly the SEC is entitled to under a "disgorgement" order.[25]

Because disgorgement has long been considered an equitable remedy, the SEC has enjoyed substantial procedural and evidentiary advantages when pursuing it.[26] Courts generally require the SEC to distinguish between legally and illegally obtained profits and identify the causal link between the unlawful activity and the profit to be disgorged. But because these calculations are logistically difficult to verify, courts have said that the SEC needs to proffer only a "'reasonable approximation of profits causally connected to the violation,'"[27]

---

[22] 15 U.S.C. § 77t(b); see also *id.* § 78u(d).

[23] 15 U.S.C. § 77t(d)(2)(A)-(C); *id.* §§ 78u(d)(3)(B), (d)(5).

[24] 15 U.S.C. §§ 77h-1(a), (f), (e).

[25] See, e.g., SEC v. Cavanaugh, 445 F.3d 105, 118–20 (2d Cir. 2006); SEC v. Huffman, 996 F.2d 800, 802–03 (5th Cir. 1993).

[26] See Russell G. Ryan, The Equity Façade of SEC Disgorgement, 4 Harv. Bus. L. Rev. Online 1, 4–5 (2013).

[27] SEC v. Whittemore, 659 F.3d 1, 7 (D.C. Cir. 2011) (quoting SEC v. First City Fin. Corp., Ltd., 890 F.2d 1215, 1231 (D.C. 1989)); see also, e.g., SEC v. Calvo, 378 F.3d 1211, 1217–18 (11th Cir. 2004) ("Exactitude is not a requirement; '[s]o long as the measure of disgorgement is reasonable, any risk of uncertainty should fall on the wrongdoer whose illegal conduct created that uncertainty.'") (quoting SEC v. Warde, 151 F.3d 42, 50 (2d Cir. 1998)).

and then the burden shifts to the defendant to disprove the SEC's calculation.[28]

As a result, the SEC's disgorgement awards are often difficult to square with traditional equitable remedies that do not punish the offender.[29] In practice, they are often untethered from the violation in question and exceed the value of illegally obtained profits, leaving a defendant worse off.[30]

In some circumstances, disgorgement has little causal connection to the underlying offense. For example, the SEC often pursues disgorgement as a remedy for violating the accounting provisions of the Foreign Corrupt Practices Act (FCPA).[31] But it is difficult to see how incorrectly accounting for payments—rather than bribes themselves—result in ill-gotten gains. The SEC nevertheless has received sizable disgorgement orders in cases where the only offense charged was recordkeeping.[32]

---

[28] See, e.g., SEC v. Benson, 657 F. Supp. 1122, 1133–34 (S.D.N.Y. 1987) (holding that, for the purposes of disgorgement, once the SEC has demonstrated the "existence of a fraudulent scheme to misappropriate corporate funds, defendant bears the burden of demonstrating that he received less than the full amount allegedly misappropriated and sought to be disgorged"). In addition, the equitable nature of the remedy means that defendants facing SEC disgorgement do not have the right to a jury trial. Courts have also accepted the SEC's position that a disgorgement order is enforceable through contempt sanctions and is not a debt that triggers the protections normally afforded to judgment debtors under the Federal Debt Collection Procedures Act. See Ryan, *supra* note 26, at 4–5.

[29] See Brief for Law Professors as Amici Curiae Supporting Petitioners at 8, Liu v. SEC, 140 S. Ct. 1936 (2020) (No. 18-1501); see also *id.* at 15 ("Equity's broad powers are tolerable—as a matter of political morality and as a matter of constitutional principle—only because there are limits. There is much that equity can do, but only because there are things it cannot do. Because there is no right to a civil jury trial for an equitable claim, one of those things that equity cannot do is inflict punishment.").

[30] See Brief for Cato Institute as Amicus Curiae Supporting Petitioners at 11, Liu v. SEC, 140 S. Ct. 1936 (2020) (18-1501) [hereinafter Cato Amicus].

[31] See 15 U.S.C. § 78m(b)(2)(A)-(B) (requiring public companies to make and keep accurate books, records, and accounts and to devise and maintain internal accounting controls).

[32] See, e.g., SEC v. Chevron Corp., No. 07 CV. 10299 (SHS), 2007 WL 9612123, at *1 (S.D.N.Y. Nov. 20, 2007) (imposing $25 million in disgorgement); SEC v. Textron, Litig. Release No. 20251, 91 SEC Docket 1197 (Aug. 23, 2007) (imposing $2.3 million in disgorgement); see also Cato Amicus, *supra* note 31, at 12–13; Mike Koehler, "The SEC Has Collected Approximately $4.6 Billion in Disgorgement in FCPA Enforcement Actions," FCPAProfessor.com Apr. 20, 2020, http://fcpaprofessor.com/sec-collected-approximately-4-6-billion-disgorgement-fcpa-enforcement-actions/ (stating that "the SEC has secured approximately $775 million in approximately 60 corporate no-charged bribery disgorgement actions").

In other circumstances, defendants are required to disgorge benefits that they do not possess. For example, in insider-trading cases, disgorgement can include the profits that others have made on trading linked to the defendant.[33] These profits, however, never belonged to the defendant. Disgorgement awards also are routinely entered without regard for whether the defendant still possesses the funds to be disgorged.[34]

Under still other circumstances, courts have accepted the SEC's broad view of what constitutes illegally obtained profits and ordered disgorgement without subtracting legitimate expenses incurred by the defendant.[35]

Given this wide latitude, disgorgement awards are an increasingly important part of the SEC's enforcement efforts. Approximately 75 percent of the $4.3 billion the SEC obtained in 2019 was disgorgement.[36] This is not a new trend; disgorgement has outpaced monetary penalties for years.[37]

Yet money returned to those harmed by securities law violations is consistently well below the amount of disgorgement ordered. In 2019, the SEC returned approximately $1.2 billion to investors.[38] In 2016, that number was just $140 million.[39]

---

[33] See, e.g., Warde, 151 F.3d at 49 ("A tippee's gains are attributable to the tipper, regardless whether benefit accrues to the tipper"); SEC v. Clark, 915 F.2d 439, 441, 454 (9th Cir. 1990) (requiring defendants to disgorge the profits that his stockbroker made from unlawful trades); see also SEC v. Contorinis, 743 F.3d 296, 302 (2d Cir. 2014) (requiring defendant to disgorge both his gains and the benefit that accrued to third parties); *id.* at 310 (Chin, J., dissenting) (noting that the disgorgement order was for more than the criminal forfeiture order).

[34] See, e.g., SEC v. Banner Fund Int'l, 211 F. 3d 602, 617 (D.C. Cir. 2000) (ordering disgorgement where defendant no longer possessed the ill-gotten gains); see also Ryan, *supra* note 26, at 10 (disgorging gains akin to "a doctor advising an emaciated patient to disgorge last year's Thanksgiving dinner").

[35] See, e.g., SEC v. Brown, 658 F.3d 858, 860–61 (8th Cir. 2011) (per curiam) (ordering joint-and-several disgorgement of funds collected from investors and concluding that "the overwhelming weight of authority hold[s] that securities law violators may not offset their disgorgement liability with business expenses").

[36] 2019 Annual Report, *supra* note 1, at 16.

[37] *Id.* (showing penalties and disgorgement from 2015 to 2019). Prior to 2015, the SEC does not appear to have systematically reported civil penalties and disgorgement separately, but disgorgement was a substantial portion of the total penalties ordered.

[38] *Id.* at 17. Because the amount of disgorgement distributed is tied to when it is collected, the amount of money returned to those harmed may not be closely tied to the disgorgement ordered in any particular fiscal year.

[39] *Id.*

Thus, despite the wide range of remedies available, the SEC, perhaps not surprisingly, has grown increasingly reliant on disgorgement, a remedy that it has enjoyed wide and largely unchecked discretion in fashioning.

III. The SEC and the Supreme Court before *Liu*

The SEC is no stranger to Supreme Court review of its enforcement authority. In the last seven years, the Supreme Court has reviewed five SEC enforcement actions, including *Liu*. The SEC prevailed in only one of those cases,[40] and two of the agency's losses laid the groundwork for *Liu*.[41]

Those two cases—*Gabelli* and *Kokesh*—both addressed the statute of limitations in 28 U.S.C. § 2462, which requires enforcement suits for "any civil fine, penalty, or forfeiture" to be brought within "five years from the date when the claim is first accrued." In *Gabelli*, the Supreme Court unanimously rejected the SEC's argument that the statute of limitations for fraud claims begins running when the fraud is discovered, not when it occurred.[42] The Court ruled that the SEC, which "as enforcer is a far cry from the defrauded victim the discovery rule evolved to protect[,]" is limited to five years from the date the fraud began because its cases "involve[] penalties, which go beyond compensation, are intended to punish, and label defendants wrongdoers."[43]

Gabelli opened the door to the litigation in *Kokesh*, which specifically addressed whether SEC disgorgement is a "penalty" subject to the five-year time limit of § 2462.[44] The Supreme Court, again unanimously, rejected the SEC's argument that disgorgement orders are not subject to the limitations period, holding that "[d]isgorgement in the securities-enforcement context is a 'penalty' within the meaning of § 2462."[45]

The Court described three characteristics that make SEC disgorgement a penalty. First, "SEC disgorgement is imposed by the courts as

---

[40] Lorenzo v. SEC, 139 S. Ct. 1094 (2019).

[41] Kokesh v. SEC, 137 S. Ct. 1635 (2017); Gabelli v. SEC, 568 U.S. 442 (2013).

[42] Gabelli, 568 U.S. at 445.

[43] *Id.* at 451–52; see also *id.* at 454 (finding a "lack of textual, historical, or equitable reasons to graft a discovery rule onto the statute of limitations of § 2462").

[44] Kokesh, 137 S. Ct. 1635.

[45] *Id.* at 1639.

a consequence for violating . . . public laws," meaning that the violation is against the United States as opposed to an individual victim.[46] Second, "SEC disgorgement is imposed for punitive purposes."[47] Deterrence is "inherently punitive," and the Court explained that in the years since *Texas Gulf Sulphur*, "it has become clear that deterrence is not simply an incidental effect of disgorgement."[48] Third, disgorged funds are not necessarily paid to victims, rendering SEC disgorgement often "not compensatory."[49] By exceeding the profits gained by the violation and failing to account for a defendant's expenses, the Court recognized that SEC disgorgement "does not simply restore the status quo; it leaves the defendant worse off."[50]

Although the Court explicitly reserved the question of "whether courts possess the authority to order disgorgement in SEC enforcement proceedings,"[51] its blunt language casting disgorgement as a penalty invited *Liu*.

IV. *Liu* Litigation

A. Background and Lower-Court Litigation

The SEC filed suit in district court against Charles Liu, Xin Wang (his wife), and several corporate defendants alleging violations of Rule 10b-5 and Section 17(a) of the Securities Act.[52] Liu and Wang solicited nearly $27 million from foreign investors under the EB-5 Program, which provides U.S. visas in return for investment in certain job-creating projects. The funds were supposed to be used to build a cancer treatment center, but although some steps were taken to advance the project (such as bulldozing the chosen site), no center was completed. Only a fraction of the funds raised were used for the purposes described in the program's offering memorandum.

---

[46] *Id.* at 1643.

[47] *Id.*

[48] *Id.* (noting that the *Texas Gulf Sulphur* court emphasized the need "to deprive the defendants of their profits in order to . . . protect the investing public by providing an effective deterrent to future violations") (quoting Tex. Gulf Sulphur, 312 F. Supp. at 92).

[49] *Id.* at 1644 (explaining that "[w]hen an individual is made to pay a noncompensatory sanction to the Government as a consequence of a legal violation, the payment operates as a penalty").

[50] *Id.* at 1645.

[51] *Id.* at 1642 n.3.

[52] SEC v. Liu, 262 F. Supp. 3d 957 (C.D. Cal. 2017).

The district court granted summary judgment to the SEC, finding that Liu and Wang misappropriated most of the money raised, paying $12.9 million to marketing firms (arguably controlled by Liu and Wang) to solicit new investors and paying themselves approximately $8.2 million in salaries, none of which was authorized by the private offering memorandum for the securities. The district court ordered Liu and Wang to pay civil penalties equal to the $8.2 million they had personally received from the project, permanently enjoined them from future solicitation of EB-5 Program investors, and ordered them to disgorge the entire amount they had raised from investors (minus a small amount that was left in the corporate accounts).

The district court rejected the defendants' argument that disgorgement should be offset by their legitimate expenses, stating that "the Ninth Circuit has indicated that the proper amount of disgorgement is the entire proceeds from a scheme minus amounts paid to investors."[53]

The Supreme Court issued its opinion in *Kokesh* shortly after the district court's decision. On appeal to the Ninth Circuit, Liu argued that because *Kokesh* found disgorgement to be a penalty, the SEC lacked authority to seek (and the district court to order) disgorgement. The Ninth Circuit found that "*Kokesh* expressly refused to reach" the authority to order disgorgement and therefore relied on its own "longstanding precedent" to uphold the district court's order.[54] The Ninth Circuit also rejected Liu's argument seeking credit for legitimate business expenses, maintaining that "the proper amount of disgorgement in a scheme such as this one is the entire amount raised less the money paid back to the investors."[55]

B. Supreme Court Litigation

1. Liu's arguments

Liu reasoned that because *Kokesh* found disgorgement to be a penalty and held that penalties are "outside 'the well-established rules of equity jurisprudence,'" disgorgement is not available as equitable relief.[56] Liu distinguished Congress's express authorization

---

[53] *Id.* at 975 (citation omitted).

[54] SEC v. Liu, 754 Fed. Appx. 505, 509 (9th Cir. 2018).

[55] *Id.*

[56] Brief for Petitioners at 1, Liu v. SEC, 140 S. Ct. 1936 (2020) (No. 18-1501) (quoting Livingston v. Woodworth, 56 U.S. 546, 559 (1854)).

for "disgorgement" in administrative proceedings, arguing that Congress did not authorize the SEC to obtain "limitless monetary penalties under the label 'disgorgement'" when authorizing "equitable" relief in federal court actions.[57]

Pointing out that disgorgement leaves defendants worse off by failing to offset legitimate expenses and requiring repayment of benefits accrued by third parties, Liu argued that disgorgement "bears all the hallmarks" of a penalty.[58] Additionally, because disgorgement seeks payment without considering whether the defendant retained a particular asset or fund, and because disgorgement typically does not return funds to the victims, disgorgement "is the type of 'merely . . . personal claim'" that is "a quintessential action at law."[59] As Liu saw it, disgorgement "was invented by creative agency lawyers in the 1960s and 1970s" and is not historically an equitable remedy.[60]

Liu argued that where Congress has provided a comprehensive remedial scheme for the SEC to use in federal court actions, conspicuously leaving out any reference to disgorgement, "the explicit authorization of certain remedies is 'strong evidence that Congress did not intend to authorize other remedies that it simply forgot to incorporate.'"[61] Liu stressed that "Congress has given the SEC ample enforcement tools to protect investors from wrongdoers," including the power to seek monetary penalties that force a defendant to surrender his ill-gotten gains.[62] "If the SEC needs still more tools," Liu concluded, "it must appeal to Congress, not the courts."[63]

---

[57] *Id.*

[58] *Id.* (quoting Kokesh, 137 S. Ct. at 1644).

[59] *Id.* at 32 (citing Montanile v. Bd. of Trs. of the Nat'l Elevator Indus. Health Ben. Plan, 136 S. Ct. 659 (2016)). Using his own case as an example, Liu asserted that the district court found that Liu and Wang gained $6,714,580 and $1,538,000 respectively from their scheme; the rest of the funds were no longer in their possession. Yet the court ordered them to disgorge—jointly and severally—nearly $27 million.

[60] *Id.* at 2.

[61] *Id.* at 15 (quoting Mass. Mut. Life Ins. Co. v. Russell, 473 U.S. 134, 147 (1985)); see also *id.* at 33 ("Where law authorizes a complete enforcement scheme, the agency may pursue the relief included in that scheme. But where law withholds or limits a remedy, equity may not invent another to fill the gap, no matter how appealing the invention may seem.") (citation omitted).

[62] *Id.* at 14. Such monetary penalties measured by "the gross amount of pecuniary gain" to the defendant were also imposed on Liu and Wang.

[63] *Id.*

2. The SEC's arguments

The SEC, on the other hand, argued that "'disgorgement of improper profits' has 'traditionally [been] considered an equitable remedy,'" comparing the SEC disgorgement remedy to an "accounting of profits," which "required wrongdoers to surrender profits from their wrongs."[64]

Limiting *Kokesh* to its effect on the statute of limitations, the SEC argued that the three *Kokesh* hallmarks of a penalty are not inconsistent with equitable relief; indeed, equitable remedies are routinely premised on violations of federal statutes, often have a deterrent effect, and are usually noncompensatory.[65] The SEC admitted that disgorgement calculations can leave a wrongdoer worse off, but that even if some courts have awarded excessive amounts of disgorgement, these decisions do "not cast doubt on the established understanding that disgorgement, if properly calculated, is an available form of 'equitable relief.'"[66]

Even if SEC disgorgement is not traditionally equitable, the SEC asserted that the Supreme Court is tasked with interpreting the words "any equitable relief."[67] In enacting the statute, Congress "was aware of, relied on, and ratified the preexisting view that disgorgement was

[64] Brief for Respondent at 5, Liu v. SEC, 140 S. Ct. 1936 (2020) (No. 18-1501) (quoting Tull v. United States, 481 U.S. 412, 424 (1987)); *id.* at 9 (citing Root v. Railway Co., 105 U.S. 189, 207 (1882)); see also *id.* ("'Disgorgement' is simply the modern name for 'accounting.'") (citing Restatement (Third) of Restitution and Unjust Enrichment § 51 cmt. a).

[65] *Id.* at 33–34; see also *id.* at 34 ("To give an example that combines all three factors: The constructive trust remedy that prevents murderers from inheriting their victims' estates is imposed upon violation of the law against murder, serves in part to deter murder, and does not compensate—yet it has always been considered equitable.") (citation omitted).

[66] *Id.* at 42; see also *id.* at 40 ("Courts have understood that those rules would sometimes leave the wrongdoer worse off than if he had followed the law, but they have reasoned that '[t]he conduct of the [wrongdoers] has not been such as to commend them to the favor of a court of equity,' that '[a] more favorable rule would offer a premium to dishonesty,' and that a wrongdoer who finds himself in a worse position 'has only himself to blame.'") (citations omitted).

[67] *Id.* at 45 ("One could view the award of disgorgement in this setting as a substantial departure from traditional norms (since disgorgement was historically awarded to private plaintiffs whose own legal rights had been violated), or instead as a natural means of achieving the traditional objective of disgorgement (ensuring that a wrongdoer does not profit from his wrong).").

a permissible remedy in civil actions."[68] Because there is no basis to conclude that Congress "intended to withhold an equitable remedy that lower courts had uniformly concluded was already available,"[69] the SEC concluded, the statute must include disgorgement.

C. The Supreme Court Opinion

Justice Sonia Sotomayor, writing for an 8-1 majority of the Supreme Court, vacated the judgment against Liu and remanded the case to ensure that the disgorgement award is consistent with the Court's opinion.[70] Accepting neither Liu's nor the SEC's arguments, the Court took a middle approach by upholding the SEC's remedial authority, but placing limitations on the scope of its disgorgement remedy. The Court held that a disgorgement award that "does not exceed a wrongdoer's net profits and is awarded for victims is equitable relief permissible under 15 U.S.C. § 78u(d)(5)."[71]

The majority opinion focused its analysis on the statutory language of § 78u(d)(5). Describing its "task [as] a familiar one," the Court analyzed "whether a particular remedy falls into 'those categories of relief that were *typically* available in equity.'"[72] The Court acknowledged that "equity practice long authorized courts to strip wrong-doers of their ill-gotten gains, with scholars and courts using various labels for the remedy," but "to avoid transforming an equitable remedy into a punitive sanction, courts restricted the remedy to an individual wrong-doer's net profits to be awarded for victims."[73]

The Court outlined three limits on equitable remedies. First, "the profits remedy often imposed a constructive trust on wrongful gains for wronged victims," turning the wrongdoer into a trustee of the profits.[74] Second, "equity courts also generally awarded profits-based

---

[68] *Id.* at 13–14.

[69] *Id.* at 7–8.

[70] Liu, 140 S. Ct. at 1940. The majority remanded the decision "[b]ecause the parties focused on the broad question whether any form of disgorgement may be ordered and did not fully brief these narrower questions" of what an appropriate disgorgement order in this matter would be. *Id.* at 1947.

[71] *Id.* at 1940.

[72] *Id.* at 1942 (emphasis in original) (quoting Mertens v. Hewitt Assocs., 508 U.S. 248, 256 (1993)) (other citations omitted).

[73] *Id.*

[74] *Id.* at 1944.

remedies against individuals or partners engaged in concerted wrongdoing, not against multiple wrongdoers under a joint-and-several liability theory."[75] Third, "courts limited awards to the net profits from wrongdoing, that is 'the gain made upon any business or investment, when both the receipts and payments are taken into account.'"[76] Unless the entire profit resulted from wrongful activity, "courts consistently restricted awards to net profits from wrongdoing after deducting legitimate expenses."[77] The Court found that Congress incorporated these "longstanding equitable principles" into § 78u(d)(5).[78]

Recognizing the SEC's disgorgement authority, the Court nonetheless concluded that the SEC's remedy has come into "considerable tension with equity practices."[79] The Court proceeded to identify three examples of this "tension": (1) where courts have "order[ed] the proceeds of fraud to be deposited in Treasury funds instead of disbursing them to victims"; (2) where courts have "impos[ed] joint-and-several disgorgement liability"; and (3) where courts have "declin[ed] to deduct even legitimate expenses from the receipts of fraud."[80] The Court addressed these instances in turn.

First, the relevant statute expressly limits equitable relief to what is "appropriate or necessary for the benefit of investors." Noting that the statute provides limited guidance, the Court stated that "[t]he equitable nature of the profits remedy generally requires the SEC to return a defendant's gains to wronged investors for their benefit."[81]

---

[75] *Id.* at 1945.

[76] *Id.* at 1949–50 (quoting Rubber Co. v. Goodyear, 76 U.S. 788, 804 (1870)) (other citations omitted).

[77] *Id.* at 1946.

[78] *Id.* The Court found that Congress's use of the term "disgorgement" in other statutes does not counsel otherwise. The Court reasoned that explicitly using the term disgorgement when granting the SEC administrative remedies makes sense because administrative bodies have no inherent equitable authority. *Id.* at 1946–47. And "Congress does not enlarge the breadth of an equitable, profits-based remedy simply by using the term 'disgorgement' in various statutes." *Id.* at 1947. Congress cannot be presumed to have ratified a lower court understanding of the term when passing 15 U.S.C. § 78u(d)(5) because, "among other things, the scope of disgorgement was 'far from settled.'" *Id.* (quoting Armstrong v. Exceptional Child Care Center, Inc., 575 U.S. 320, 330 (2015)).

[79] *Id.* at 1946.

[80] *Id.*; see also *id.* at 1946 n.3 (citing several circuit court decisions upholding orders that violated these principles).

[81] *Id.* at 1948.

The Court rejected the SEC's long-held view that the primary function of disgorgement is to deny wrongdoers the "fruits of their ill-gotten gains, not to return the funds to victims as a kind of restitution," concluding that disgorgement "must do more than simply benefit the public at large by virtue of depriving a wrongdoer of ill-gotten gains."[82]

Second, "impos[ing] disgorgement liability on a wrongdoer for benefits that accrue to his affiliates, sometimes through joint-and-several liability" could transform disgorgement into a penalty.[83] Declining to "wade into all the circumstances" where a judgment against multiple individuals might withstand scrutiny, the Court made clear that such a determination is fact-intensive.[84]

Finally, "courts must deduct legitimate expenses before ordering disgorgement."[85] Recognizing that expenses "incurred for the purposes of furthering an entirely fraudulent scheme" are not legitimate, the Court again established a fact-intensive inquiry to "ascertain[] whether expenses are legitimate or whether they are merely wrongful gains 'under another name.'"[86] The Court provided little guidance for this inquiry, but suggested that "some expenses from petitioners' scheme went toward lease payments and cancer-treatment equipment . . . [which] arguably have value independent of fueling a fraudulent scheme."[87]

Justice Clarence Thomas dissented, concluding that disgorgement "is not a traditional equitable remedy," and he cautioned that the majority's ruling "threatens great mischief."[88] Distinguishing disgorgement from an accounting of profits, which required a defendant to account for and repay to a plaintiff the profits that belong to the plaintiff, Justice Thomas characterized the majority's definition of

---

[82] *Id.* The Court explicitly left open the question whether depositing funds with the Treasury is appropriate where it is "infeasible to distribute the collected funds to investors." *Id.*

[83] *Id.* at 1949.

[84] *Id.* The Court suggested some factual circumstances that may be relevant, including whether Liu and Wang commingled their finances and whether they both enjoyed the fruits of the scheme, among other things. *Id.*

[85] *Id.* at 1950.

[86] *Id.* (quoting Goodyear, 76 U.S. at 803).

[87] *Id.*

[88] *Id.* at 1950, 1953 (Thomas, J., dissenting).

disgorgement as "compel[ling] each defendant to pay his profits (and sometimes, though it is not clear when, all of his codefendant's profits) to a third-party Government agency (which sometimes, though it is not clear when, passes the money on to victims)."[89] Justice Thomas noted the lack of tracing required with a constructive trust or equitable lien, and warned that "[a]s long as courts continue to award 'disgorgement,' both courts and the SEC will continue to have license to expand their own power."[90]

V. *Liu's* Open Questions

On first read, the Supreme Court's decision is deceptively simple: disgorgement is allowable, but only so long as it is limited to the wrongdoer's profits and the money collected is returned to investors. But *Liu* leaves open several questions about how such a remedy will work.

A. *What Does It Mean to Be for "the Benefit of Investors"?*

The *Liu* decision gives great weight to § 78u(d)(5)'s language restricting equitable relief to that which "may be appropriate or necessary for the benefit of investors." The Supreme Court counseled that the equitable nature of disgorgement "generally requires the SEC to return a defendant's gains to the wronged investors for their benefit."[91] This restriction is a seismic shift for the SEC, which, despite touting the return of some disgorgement funds to investors,[92]

---

[89] *Id.* at 1951.

[90] *Id.* at 1954. Justice Thomas also noted that the majority's decision will cause confusion in administrative practice because it is "unclear whether the majority's new restrictions on disgorgement will apply to these proceedings as well. If they do not, the result will be that disgorgement has one meaning when the SEC goes to district court and another when it proceeds in-house." *Id.* Acknowledging the majority's acceptance of disgorgement, Justice Thomas would have implemented bright-line rules to limit disgorgement orders "to be consistent with the traditional rules of equity": (1) "the order should be limited to each petitioner's profits"; (2) "the order should not be imposed jointly and severally"; and (3) "the money paid by petitioners should be used to compensate petitioner's victims." *Id.* at 1954–55.

[91] *Id.* at 1948.

[92] See, e.g., 2019 Annual Report, *supra* note 1, at 17 ("The Commission returned a substantial amount of money to harmed investors."); *id.* at 21 ("The Supreme Court's June 2017 decision in *Kokesh v. SEC* continues to impact adversely the Commission's ability to disgorge and return funds to investors injured by long-running frauds,

does not view disgorgement as primarily compensatory.[93] Post-*Liu*, the SEC must do more than merely deposit disgorgement proceeds in the U.S. Treasury.

But what more must it do? This question touches not only on what should be done with disgorgement proceeds, but also on the circumstances under which disgorgement is permissible at all.

It seems obvious that where victims are easily identified and easily compensated, disgorged funds should be returned to them. Yet it is easy to underestimate the complexity of this endeavor. Not only must the total amount to be disgorged be calculated, but also the amount to be returned to each eligible investor. If the SEC must establish these facts prior to entry of a disgorgement order, this will delay resolution and could drag the court into detailed factual determinations about individual investors who are not parties to the SEC's civil action. The SEC may seek to avoid this complication by expanding its use of Fair Funds, which were created by the Sarbanes-Oxley Act to collect and distribute disgorgement proceeds and civil monetary penalties "for the benefit of investors who were harmed by the violation."[94] With a Fair Fund, the SEC could determine who the victims are and how much they should receive after the disgorgement order has been entered.[95] But using this mechanism is no

---

such as Ponzi schemes, that often directly impact retail investors."); Steven Peikin, Co-Director, Division of Enforcement, Remedies and Relief in SEC Enforcement Actions, PLI White Collar Crime 2018: Prosecutors and Regulators Speak (Oct. 3, 2018) (transcript available at SEC.gov) [hereinafter Peikin Speech] ("Even where a defendant or respondent cooperates and agrees to meaningful undertakings, it should not be entitled to keep its ill-gotten gains, which we are often in a position to restore to harmed investors.").

[93] Securities and Exchange Commission, Report Pursuant to Section 308(c) of the Sarbanes-Oxley Act of 2002, 20 (2003) ("While the Commission may seek to return disgorged funds to injured investors, the main objective of disgorgement is to take the profits away from wrongdoers and thereby make violations unprofitable."); see also, e.g., SEC v. Commonwealth Chem. Sec., Inc., 574 F.2d 90, 102 (2d Cir. 1978) ("the primary purpose of disgorgement is not to compensate investors"); see also SEC v. Huffman, 996 F.2d 800, 802 (5th Cir. 1993) ("Disgorgement does not aim to compensate the victims.").

[94] 17 C.F.R. § 201.1100, et seq. (allowing funds collected under 15 U.S.C. § 7246(a) to be included in the Fair Fund).

[95] *Id.* (describing requirements for, among other things, a plan to administer the fund including specifying who is potentially eligible to receive fund proceeds, how individuals will be notified of the fund's existence, and procedures for approving claims).

panacea; it will be subject to challenges over the SEC's distribution plans, including questions about who qualifies as a harmed investor and what payment an eligible investor is due. In other words, even under the simplest circumstances, disgorgement just got a whole lot more complicated.

Circumstances in which victims that can be identified but not easily compensated raise other issues. The SEC suggests that in these cases, depositing disgorgement funds with the Treasury is appropriate.[96] But the Supreme Court specifically left open the "question whether, and to what extent, [depositing disgorgement funds with the Treasury] nevertheless" is consistent with § 78u(d)(5).[97] Indeed, the Supreme Court even declined to weigh in on whether "feasibility" of distribution is "relevant at all to equitable principles."[98] Thus, it is unclear whether the SEC can collect disgorgement at all if it cannot distributed the funds to harmed investors.[99] Assuming that it can, the SEC's Investor Protection Fund already collects undistributed disgorgement awards, which are used to pay whistleblower awards and fund the SEC's inspector general.[100] While this fund arguably benefits investors by supporting the SEC's enforcement activities, it is not clear whether it satisfies the limitations of § 78u(d)(5), which might require a closer relationship between the violation and the investors benefited.[101] If no such relationship is required, the SEC could be empowered to use disgorgement funds for more general purposes, like whistleblower awards or investor education, perhaps regardless of whether funds could be returned to harmed investors.

Where victims cannot be easily identified, *Liu* will likely make it more difficult for the SEC to obtain disgorgement. The SEC brings suit

[96] Liu, 140 S. Ct. at 1948.

[97] *Id.*

[98] *Id.* at 1948 n.5.

[99] A similar question may arise where investors have already been compensated, for example, by insurance. Disgorging the profits under those circumstances may restore the status quo for the wrongdoer but would result in a windfall to the harmed investors.

[100] Liu, 140 S. Ct. at 1948 n.5.

[101] The *Liu* decision does not address the relationship between § 78u(d)(5)'s requirement that the relief "be appropriate or necessary for the benefit of investors," and the Court's own finding that equity requires that the remedy be "awarded for the victims." See Liu, 140 S. Ct. at 1940. The equitable principle appears to require a relationship between the misconduct and the recipient of the disgorgement award, which one may argue should inform the statutory language in § 78u(d)(5).

for a host of violations where an ill-gotten gain may be identifiable, but where it is hard, if not impossible, to identify any particular victims of the violation. For example, the SEC routinely seeks disgorgement of profits in insider-trading cases. But in "classical" insider-trading cases, it is difficult to identify the victims of an unlawful trade. And in "misappropriation" insider-trading cases, the victim from whom the information was appropriated is almost never an investor and the injury rarely matches up with a defendant's benefit.

Violations under the FCPA present a similar situation. Even where the SEC charges a violation that results in identifiable ill-gotten gains to the defendant, the victims of that violation may not be easily identified. Victims of FCPA violations, where one can even be identified, may be a foreign government or the defendant's competitors.[102] In the past, these FCPA and insider-trading cases have resulted in substantial disgorgement orders (sometimes hundreds of millions of dollars).[103] But such disgorgement awards have traditionally been returned to the Treasury, which is unlikely to be permissible under *Liu*.

At bottom, *Liu*'s limitation that disgorgement must be for "the benefit of investors" will likely limit the SEC's authority to obtain disgorgement awards, although the bounds of its authority remain murky in light of these unanswered questions.[104]

B. What Are "Net Profits"?

Under *Liu*, a disgorgement award must "not exceed a wrongdoer's net profits."[105] Deducting "legitimate expenses" before ordering disgorgement would seem to be a familiar task, but liability for net profits is not so simple.[106]

---

[102] It is also unclear if these types of victims would satisfy § 78u(d)(5)'s requirement that equitable remedies are for the benefit of *investors*, as opposed to some other type of victim.

[103] Peikin Speech, *supra* note 92 ("The Commission has obtained disgorgement in a wide variety of matters, including offering frauds, and most all FCPA resolutions."); see Koehler, *supra* note 32 (identifying FCPA cases); see also, e.g., In re Microsoft Corp., Admin. Proc. No. 3-19260 (July 22, 2019) (ordering $13.8 million in disgorgement in connection with FCPA books and records violations).

[104] All of this added complexity further highlights a question, beyond the scope of this article, of whether the SEC should be involved in the business of seeking compensation for private losses.

[105] Liu, 140 S. Ct. at 1940.

[106] See *id.* at 1950.

Perhaps the easier question is the mechanical one of calculating net profits. Except where "the 'entire profits of a business or undertaking' result from the wrongdoing," disgorgement must account for a defendant's legitimate expenses.[107] This fact-intensive inquiry will raise a host of interpretive questions about deductibility of expenses. Some of these questions may be answered by analogy to precedent, but many will be questions of first impression.

Another loose end is whether the SEC will continue to enjoy the same evidentiary and procedural advantages. *Liu* requires more precision in the accounting for disgorgement; requiring the defendant to provide that precision by rebutting the SEC's "reasonable approximation" of disgorgement seems counterintuitive. These questions likely will be grappled with for years to come.

A more difficult question is whether the defendant must possess the net profits subject to disgorgement. The Court's analysis focused on whether disgorgement was available at equity, drawing parallels to remedies in equity that "imposed a constructive trust on wrongful gains for wronged victims."[108] But in providing guidance on the disgorgement remedy itself, the Court focused only on the end of that statement—"wrongful gains for wronged victims"—while providing little discussion as to applicability of the limitations of the "constructive trust."

As the Supreme Court explained in *Great-West Life & Annuity Insurance Co. v. Knudson*, a constructive trust requires that the "money or property identified as belonging in good conscience to the plaintiff . . . clearly be traced to particular funds or property in the defendant's possession."[109] An equitable remedy is tied specifically to those funds: "for restitution to lie in equity, the action generally must seek not to impose personal liability on the defendant, but to restore to the plaintiff particular funds or property in the defendant's possession."[110] Many of the SEC's disgorgement orders would not meet this test, either because the defendant was ordered to disgorge benefits that never accrued to him in the first place or because

---

[107] *Id.* (quoting Root, 105 U.S. at 203).
[108] *Id.* at 1944.
[109] 534 U.S. 204, 213 (2002).
[110] *Id.* at 214.

the defendant was ordered to disgorge benefits that she no longer possessed.[111]

But it is not clear whether *Liu* intended to impose a tracing requirement on the funds to be disgorged. Justice Thomas, in his dissent, said that the majority imposed "no tracing requirement," and, accordingly, that the remedy cannot be equitable.[112] But the majority's opinion is not as clear as Justice Thomas's characterization. While the majority never explicitly addressed tracing, the Court specifically identified cases where the defendants were ordered to disgorge profits earned by associates as "test[ing] the bounds of equity practice."[113] And the Court's discussion about collective liability suggests other limits on the SEC's ability to reach profits that are not in a wrongdoer's possession. Noting that the "common law [permitted] liability for partners engaged in concerted wrongdoing," the Court suggested that joint-and-several liability for codefendants may be unjust where one "was a mere passive recipient of profits."[114] This could support the notion that liability attaches only to funds that remain in a wrongdoer's possession, but it is far from a clear statement.

Given that a tracing requirement would incentivize wrongdoers to quickly dissipate profits, the SEC is unlikely to concede a tracing requirement where the Court did not explicitly require one, setting up the likelihood of future litigation to resolve this question.

C. Is Disgorgement Still Subject to a Five-Year Statute of Limitations?

Liu did not explicitly overrule *Kokesh*, but it calls into question the applicability of the earlier decision's reasoning. The Court's holding in *Kokesh* that disgorgement was a penalty and thus subject to the statute of limitations in § 2462 rested on three characteristics of disgorgement: (1) that disgorgement is imposed as a consequence of

---

[111] See Ryan, *supra* note 26, at 7–8 ("Common examples include insider-trading cases in which tippers are ordered to disgorge not only their own profits but also those of their tippees. Other cases involve defendants who have spent, squandered, or transferred their ill-gotten gains before being caught by the SEC, yet are still ordered to disgorge what they no longer possess.").

[112] Liu, 140 S. Ct. at 1954–55 (Thomas, J., dissenting).

[113] *Id.* at 1946, 1946 n.3 (citing Clark, 915 F.2d 439 and Contorinis, 743 F.3d at 304–06).

[114] *Id.* at 1949. This language also calls into question the SEC's ability to obtain disgorgement from relief defendants, who did not engage in wrongdoing, but who have received illicit gains resulting from violations committed by others.

violating public law; (2) that disgorgement is imposed for punitive purposes; and (3) that disgorgement is, in many cases, not compensatory. *Liu*'s reformation of disgorgement, however, undermines the second and third characteristics by suggesting that disgorgement should restore the status quo and compensate victims. Even assuming that a "penalty" for the purposes of § 2462 may not be a "penalty" in equity (or under the securities laws), the reasoning the Court laid out in *Kokesh* now seems to rest on the weak thread of the remedy being employed for a violation of public law.[115] While there may be other good arguments for holding disgorgement to the five-year limitation period—for instance, that disgorgement is a "forfeiture" within the meaning of § 2462—*Kokesh* did not address them.

The SEC has recognized the significant headwinds that *Kokesh* created for collecting disgorgement, particularly for long-running frauds.[116] As a response, the SEC may choose to argue that disgorgement is not subject to the statute of limitations to recapture some disgorgement authority. But the other limitations *Liu* imposed may make seeking it, particularly for aged misconduct, even more difficult to obtain and administer.

D. Can the SEC Order Broader "Disgorgement" in Administrative Proceedings?

The *Liu* decision specifically addressed disgorgement ordered in civil actions, where the relevant statute provides the SEC with the authority to seek "equitable relief."[117] The Court's analysis focused on the characteristics of equitable remedies, and assumed that the statutory language did not intend to override the traditional meaning of equity. But the SEC's remedial authority for administrative proceedings is provided by a different statutory provision that specifically grants the authority to order "disgorgement."[118] That statute

---

[115] Indeed, the SEC seems willing to assume that the term "penalty" is subject to different meanings. See, e.g., In re John M.E. Saad, Admin. Proc. No. 3-13678, 11 (Aug. 23, 2019) ("courts have repeatedly recognized that the inquiry under Section 2462 is distinct from the inquiry into whether a remedy is appropriate as a substantive matter").

[116] 2019 Annual Report, *supra* note 1, at 21.

[117] 15 U.S.C. § 78u(d)(5).

[118] 15 U.S.C. § 77h-1(e).

arguably would entail to a different analysis—one that considers what Congress meant by the term "disgorgement," a term that resists a standard meaning (let alone the one that the Supreme Court assigned it in *Liu*). Justice Thomas cautioned that the result may be that "disgorgement has one meaning when the SEC goes to district court and another when it proceeds in-house."[119]

Whether this confusion will become anything more than theoretical remains to be seen. Different versions of disgorgement would only add to the different remedies available in administrative proceedings and civil court actions. The SEC's decision about which forum to pursue rarely turns on a binary choice between the ability to recover more money in one forum versus another.[120] But competing definitions of disgorgement may result in a greater shift to administrative cases for certain types of misconduct, including cases where victims are less easily identifiable and receiving disgorgement in a judicial forum is now limited by *Liu*. On the other hand, the SEC could just choose to apply the same definition of disgorgement regardless of the proceeding to facilitate decision-making and settlement of matters, the vast majority of which do not proceed to litigation.[121]

---

[119] Liu, 140 S. Ct. at 1954 (Thomas, J., dissenting).

[120] For example, certain types of cases are difficult to bring in administrative proceedings as a practical matter, such as asset freezes.

[121] The *Liu* decision also raises ancillary questions about how disgorgement orders will be treated for insurance and tax purposes. For example, the SEC's standard settlement papers have prohibited defendants from seeking indemnification or reimbursement for penalties, but it is unclear if disgorgement should be considered a penalty under this provision. The tax treatment of disgorgement, which turns on whether disgorgement is a penalty under I.R.C. § 162(f), is also called into question by *Liu*.

Liu may also open questions for the remedial authority of other agencies. The Federal Trade Commission (FTC), for example, has a similar statutory framework wherein the FTC Act does not expressly mention monetary relief, but the courts have nonetheless allowed disgorgement as a remedy. The Supreme Court has granted certiorari in AMG Cap Mgmt v. FTC, 910 F.3d 417 (9th Cir. 2018), cert. granted, No. 19-508 (July 9, 2020) on the question of whether Section 13(b) of the Federal Trade Commission Act, by authorizing "injunctions," also authorizes the Federal Trade Commission to demand monetary relief such as restitution. *Liu* and the litigation of its open questions may also affect the understanding of "disgorgement" pursued by the Commodity Futures Trading Commission and Consumer Financial Protection Bureau, both of which have explicit statutory "disgorgement" authority. See 7 U.S.C. § 13a-1(d)(3)(B) (CFTC); 12 U.S.C. §§ 5565(a)(1), (a)(2)(D) (CFPB).

VI. Conclusion: *Liu*'s Impact

The SEC continues to enjoy access to a full panoply of remedies in civil actions and administrative proceedings to enforce the federal securities laws. Disgorgement is one tool, among many, but it is a tool that the SEC seems to have favored in recent years. The *Liu* decision is likely to change that reliance.

Even with all its open questions, *Liu* will produce observable and immediate effects. First, disgorgement awards will be more difficult to obtain. The *Liu* decision has wiped away the ease with which the SEC was permitted to estimate a reasonable approximation of a defendant's unlawful gains. Post-*Liu*, disgorgement will be subject to a more fact-intensive inquiry into what gains were truly unearned, what expenses were truly legitimate, and who is responsible for returning unlawful profits. This inquiry—even once all the open questions above are settled—will result in more scrutiny by courts of SEC disgorgement requests.

Second, and relatedly, disgorgement awards will be for more limited sums. The *Liu* decision should limit the SEC to disgorgement that restores the status quo—that is, the decision should eliminate punitive disgorgement awards that exceed the value of illegally obtained profits. In addition, net profits often will be less than the profits disgorged under the SEC's pre-*Liu* understanding of disgorgement, as courts must consider whether expenses incurred have a value independent of fueling a fraudulent scheme.

Third, a higher percentage of disgorgement, awarded and collected, will be returned to investors. The Supreme Court's decision forces the SEC to view disgorgement as restitution—not deterrence—and the rule, rather than the exception, likely will be to return disgorged funds to those who were harmed by the misconduct. Whether or not the SEC is ultimately required to return every dollar collected to a harmed investor, the SEC will return a higher percentage of disgorgement ordered to injured parties.

From a bigger-picture perspective, *Liu* should result in more transparency and predictability in remedies imposed for violations of the federal securities laws. In *Gabelli* and *Kokesh*, the Supreme Court reined in an SEC that had strayed beyond its statutory authority. The Court has done the same in *Liu*, limiting the SEC's discretion. Some lamented the decision as letting wrongdoers get off easy,[122]

---

[122] See, e.g., Jack Rodgers, "Investment Fraudsters Get a High Court Break on Legitimate Expenses," Courthouse News Service, June 22, 2020, https://bit.ly/3a6ezvx.

but this viewpoint ignores the SEC's flexible powers to seek other penalties, including significant civil penalties calculated based on the ill-gotten pecuniary gain to the defendant.[123] *Liu* ultimately may not result in lighter monetary punishment for wrongdoers, as the SEC may shift what it would have requested in disgorgement to a request for civil penalty instead. *Liu*'s limitations on the SEC's discretion, however, will force the SEC to make clearer distinctions between remedies meant to punish and remedies meant to restore the status quo. Drawing more distinct boundaries between the two will increase transparency and consistency in the SEC's enforcement efforts and will make it easier to assess the effectiveness of the SEC's remedial tools. Then, if Congress concludes that the SEC needs additional tools, Congress can provide them.[124]

---

[123] See Ryan, *supra* note 26, at 12–13 ("In short, securities law violators do not get off scot-free simply because the SEC cannot seek disgorgement in a particular case.").

[124] Congress has been responsive to the SEC's requests for additional remedies in the past, including granting the SEC the authority to seek civil penalties in insider-trading cases. See Atkins & Bondi, *supra* note 17, at 385. After *Kokesh*, Congress also considered a bill extending the statute of limitations for disgorgement to 14 years. The Investor Protection and Capital Markets Fairness Act, H.R. 4344 116th Cong. (2019), passed the House on November 19, 2019. A similar bill was introduced in the Senate in March 2019, extending the statute of limitations for disgorgement and authorizing a separate restitution remedy. Securities Fraud and Investor Compensation Act 2019, S. 799 116th Cong. (2019).

The Administrative State as a New Front in the Culture War: *Little Sisters of the Poor v. Pennsylvania*

Tanner J. Bean* & Robin Fretwell Wilson**

Culture-war clashes are now routinely decided by the United States Supreme Court. In the past decade, the Court has considered access of same-sex couples to civil marriage,[1] government funding of religious organizations,[2] the intersection of religious freedom with laws protecting LGBTQ persons from discrimination,[3] the propriety of religious symbols in the public square,[4] and religious organizations' autonomy to employ only those who share and inculcate their faith notwithstanding civil-rights protections,[5] to name a few. Despite the clear need for lawmaking that puts these predictable culture-war fights to rest,[6]

---

* Attorney, Fabian VanCott.

** Mildred Van Voorhis Jones Chair in Law, University of Illinois College of Law, and Director, Institute of Government and Public Affairs, University of Illinois System. We thank Professors Aaron Nielsen and Sean Anderson for their thoughtful advice and visiting scholar Marie-Joe Noon for careful review and assistance.

[1] Obergefell v. Hodges, 135 S. Ct. 2584 (2015).

[2] Fulton v. City of Philadelphia, 922 F.3d 140 (3d Cir. 2019), cert. granted, 140 S. Ct. 1104 (2020); Espinoza v. Mont. Dep't of Revenue, 140 S. Ct. 2246 (2020); Trinity Lutheran Church of Columbia, Inc. v. Comer, 137 S. Ct. 2012 (2017).

[3] Bostock v. Clayton County, 140 S. Ct. 1731 (2020); Masterpiece Cakeshop, Ltd. v. Colo. Civil Rights Comm'n, 138 S. Ct. 1719 (2018); Arlene's Flowers, Inc. v. Washington, 138 S. Ct. 2671 (2018); State v. Arlene's Flowers, Inc., 193 Wn.2d 469 (Wash. 2019), pet. for cert. filed (No. 19-333).

[4] Am. Legion v. Am. Humanist Ass'n, 139 S. Ct. 2067 (2019).

[5] Our Lady of Guadalupe Sch. v. Morrissey-Berru, 140 S. Ct. 2049 (2020); Hosanna-Tabor Evangelical Lutheran Church & Sch. v. EEOC, 565 U.S. 171 (2012).

[6] See Tanner Bean & Robin Fretwell Wilson, Common Sense Case for Common Ground Lawmaking: Three Cheers for Why Conservative Religious Organizations and Believers Should Support the Fairness for All Act, J. Legis. Online Supp. (July 23, 2020), https://bit.ly/3ksjYlj; Robin Fretwell Wilson, Common Ground Lawmaking: Lessons of Peaceful Coexistence from Masterpiece Cakeshop and the Utah Compromise, 51 Conn. L. Rev. 3 (2019); Tanner Bean, "Fairness for All Act Seeks to Balance LGBTQ, Religious Rights," Idaho Statesman, Dec. 17, 2019, https://bit.ly/3gImd1N.

"Congress has proven useless in reaching any kind of resolution," punting "the most contentious questions."[7] Americans are fed up.

Into the legislative vacuum left by Congress comes the administrative state. As government increases its footprint, agencies are asked to grapple with values questions—over the meaning of nondiscrimination, access to services, the importance of gender equity, protection of vulnerable minorities, the needs of religious and other communities, and how these different values are in tension. Nowhere is this more apparent than in the series of decisions made by agencies and subagencies over what drugs women are entitled to under the terms of the Patient Protection and Affordable Care Act (ACA). The ACA guaranteed all covered employees that they would receive "essential health benefits," including "preventive and wellness services," under their employer's plan.[8]

Through regulations, the Obama administration directed covered (nongrandfathered) employers to pay for all FDA-approved contraceptives (coverage mandate), citing "compelling health and gender equity goals."[9] The required drugs included four that objectors see as cutting off a life,[10] as if no thought was given to the deep divisions around abortion that have riven Americans since *Roe v. Wade*. Churches were exempted at this early step because regulators believed that any church employee would share the church's values, so nobody would be denied something they desire.[11] Whether this supposition holds is questionable—a 2016 study found that of "Catholics who attend Mass weekly, just 13% say contraception is

---

[7] David French, "The Supreme Court Tries to Settle the Religious Liberty Culture War," Time, July 14, 2020, https://bit.ly/2F8zm6o. Michael McConnell observes that the Court "seems to reach results that very likely would carry the day in Congress on many of these issues, if Republicans and Democrats were inclined to talk to one another and compromise." Michael W. McConnell, "On Religion, the Supreme Court Protects the Right to Be Different," N.Y. Times, July 9, 2020, https://nyti.ms/2DEktbB.

[8] ACA §§ 1302, 2713; 42 U.S.C. § 18022; 42 U.S.C. § 300gg-13.

[9] Coverage of Preventive Services under the ACA, 77 Fed. Reg. 8725, 8729 (Feb. 15, 2012) (citing Institute of Medicine, Clinical Preventive Services for Women 16 (2011)).

[10] Burwell v. Hobby Lobby, 573 U.S. 682, 701 (2014); Robin Fretwell Wilson, The Calculus of Accommodation: Contraception, Abortion, Same-Sex Marriage, and Other Clashes between Religion and the State, B.C. L. Rev. 1417, 1454–60 (2012).

[11] 76 Fed. Reg. 46621 (Aug. 3, 2011) ("Specifically, the Departments seek to provide for a religious accommodation that respects the unique relationship between a house of worship and its employees in ministerial positions.").

morally wrong, while 45% say it is morally acceptable and 42% say it is not a moral issue."[12]

The coverage mandate ran headlong into the religious conscience of faith groups that operate outside the four walls of the church, as well as countless other objectors.[13] Some objected to paying for drugs that act before conception, removing the potential for life; others to four drugs that have the potential to disrupt a life in being, a fact stipulated to in litigation. Providing coverage for the latter, objectors contended, was tantamount to being complicit in "murder because it is the killing of an innocent person."[14] Just as Americans believe that Congress has walked away from charting common ground, it seemed that agency personnel had, too.

Religious objectors vehemently opposed the coverage mandate. To his credit, President Barack Obama took the pushback seriously. He directed his administration to fashion an accommodation for nonprofit religious groups that did not sacrifice coverage for women, but took some religious objectors (although not all) out of the position of providing those drugs.

Extended litigation followed over whether the set of objectors who could be accommodated should extend to closely held corporations. In *Burwell v. Hobby Lobby Stores, Inc.*, the Supreme Court decided that the Religious Freedom Restoration Act (RFRA) required the administration to respond to the substantial burden it was imposing on religious practice.[15] The Obama administration's accommodation for some objectors showed that there was a less restrictive means of accomplishing the administration's goals.[16]

Less visible than who qualified for the accommodation was the claim made in *Little Sisters of the Poor Saints Peter and Paul Home v.*

---

[12] "Very Few Americans See Contraception as Morally Wrong," Pew Research Center, Sept. 28, 2016, https://pewrsr.ch/2XJMtl3.

[13] See Helen Alvare, "The Endless War on the Little Sisters of the Poor," Wall St. J., May 5, 2020, https://on.wsj.com/3abmLef; HHS Case Database, Becket, https://bit.ly/3kqu06x.

[14] See Complaint, The QC Group, Inc. v. Sebelius, No. 13-1726, (D. Minn. July 2, 2013), https://bit.ly/2PHf1Hm.

[15] Hobby Lobby, 573 U.S. at 701.

[16] Robin Fretwell Wilson, Demystifying Hobby Lobby, 2015 Int'l Surv. of Fam. L. 343, 361–68 (2015).

Pennsylvania.[17] The Little Sisters of the Poor Saints Peter and Paul Home (Little Sisters) are Roman Catholic nuns who have cared for the elderly poor since 1869 and employ roughly 2,719 workers. They qualified for the accommodation but rejected its mechanics. For them, filing the needed forms would initiate a causal chain ultimately resulting in the provision of drugs used to both end life and prevent life.[18] Many, including administration officials, saw the Little Sisters' objection as premised on too little. How could merely executing a form that requires others to pay for an objected-to drug be objectionable?[19]

This culture-war claim, too, got a hearing in the Supreme Court in *Zubik v. Burwell*.[20] Sensing room to remove objectors from the equation without sacrificing needed access, the Court issued an overarching instruction to the parties: agree on how religious organizations can "do nothing more than contract for a plan that does not include coverage for some or all forms of contraception," while women still receive seamless "cost-free contraceptive coverage" from the same insurer.[21] Until *Zubik's* per curiam opinion, the protracted litigation over whether the government had accommodated religious objectors *enough* had taken on a winner-takes-all quality.[22] As we have

---

[17] Little Sisters of the Poor Saints Peter & Paul Home v. Pennsylvania, 140 S. Ct. 2367 (2020).

[18] Little Sisters of the Poor Home for the Aged v. Burwell, 794 F.3d 1151, 1167 (10th Cir. 2015) ("The Little Sisters have always excluded coverage of sterilization, contraception, and abortifacients from their health care plan in accordance with their religious belief that deliberately avoiding reproduction through medical means is immoral."). In *Hobby Lobby*, Justice Ruth Bader Ginsburg in dissent stressed that decisions "whether to claim benefits under the plans are made not by Hobby Lobby or Conestoga, but the covered employees and dependents, in consultation with their health care providers," implying that the employers' objections were too attenuated to be cognizable. Hobby Lobby, 573 U.S. at 760–61.

[19] "Obama to Little Sisters: It's Just a Piece of Paper," Denver Catholic, Jan. 3, 2014, https://bit.ly/2DRrNQF.

[20] Zubik v. Burwell, 136 S. Ct. 1557 (2016).

[21] *Id.* at 1560.

[22] The Court envisioned one possible compromise: whether "contraceptive coverage may be obtained by petitioners' employees through petitioners' insurance companies, [without] involvement of petitioners beyond their own decision to provide health insurance without contraceptive coverage to their employees." Order Requesting Supplemental Briefing in Zubik v. Burwell. Burwell (14-1418), Sup. Ct. Order List (Mar. 29, 2016).

said elsewhere,[23] in a pluralistic society, we should embrace creative fixes that preserve as much religious freedom as possible while enabling government to do its important work. But in the Obama administration's waning hours, the Court's challenge to the parties to solve this morass proved too much.

Enter the Trump administration. Just four months after taking office, President Donald Trump, speaking in the Rose Garden, congratulated the Little Sisters for having "just won a lawsuit" and that their "long ordeal w[ould] soon be over."[24] In one of its first actions, his administration issued interim final rules, later finalized, that kept the coverage mandate, but exempted not only all religious objectors but also moral objectors (exempted employers). Unlike the accommodation, this approach allows employers to step aside with no provision for women's access to the objected-to drugs (wholesale exemption). In effect, every objector can now elect to be treated like churches, with no duty to anyone.

The Trump administration's fix precipitated its own legal challenge, resolved, *for now*, in the Court's decision in *Little Sisters of the Poor*. Two states, Pennsylvania and New Jersey, balked at shouldering the financial burden of providing contraceptives to women working for exempted employers.[25] The Court upheld the wholesale exemption. In just three words out of the ACA's more than 400,000 words—"as provided for"—Congress had delegated ample discretion to agencies to not only decide what should be covered under the coverage mandate, but who was required to abide by its terms, the majority concluded. Those three little words allowed both presidential administrations to inflame Americans' perennial culture war over abortion.

The Court's decision upholding the authority of agencies under both administrations to shape the contours of the law ensures that agencies will remain a locus of culture-war fights. From administration to

[23] Robin Fretwell Wilson & Tanner Bean, "Why Jack Phillips Still Cannot Make Wedding Cakes: Deciding Competing Claims under Old Laws," Berkeley Center for Religion, Peace & World Affairs, June 29, 2018, https://bit.ly/2CdG5e5.

[24] Michael J. O'Loughlin, "White House Signing Ceremonies Showcase Two Styles of U.S. Catholicism," America: The Jesuit Review, May 9, 2017, https://bit.ly/2PAFRRv.

[25] Pennsylvania v. President of the U.S., 930 F.3d 543, 560–61 (3d Cir. 2019). The states argued that if employers did not provide needed drugs through the coverage mandate, they would incur additional costs under their state-funded family planning and contraceptives services programs. *Id.*

administration, political appointments are reaching farther into the apparatus of agencies that interpret and administer our laws. This means that political appointees are supplying more of the substance of the law when Congress delegates its decisionmaking. Agencies, which have been lauded for bringing technical, apolitical expertise, also may be agents in the culture wars.[26] Unless Congress changes its practice of broad delegation of authority, or regulations are no longer seen as up for grabs by each changing administration, Americans should expect to see more decade-long disputes over the questions that divide us.

In Part I, we place *Little Sisters of the Poor* in a longer arc of laws about abortion and legislative accommodations that have walled objectors off from being compelled to violate their faith or conscience. Part I details why the initial coverage mandate—by exempting only churches while covering drugs that implicate life—was destined to be seen as a fundamental breach of trust by the Obama administration regarding abortion. In one sense, the wholesale exemption returned America to the *status quo ante* before the coverage mandate.

Part II reviews the Court's decision in *Little Sisters of the Poor*, including why the Court rejected the states' procedural attack on the wholesale exemption. It recaps the reading of the ACA that seven members of the Court found justified the actions of both administrations. Part II also flags Justice Elena Kagan's prediction that the wholesale exemption may be attacked as arbitrary and capricious— one state has already said it will file suit again. It also discusses opinions from both wings of the Court urging the justices to finally weigh in on whether RFRA demands a concession that walls off religious objectors from the coverage mandate.

Part III observes that Congress could call an armistice in this specific culture-war clash, just as Congress set it in motion in the ACA. Congress could finally give the Little Sisters the certainty that they seek—that they will not be made to be complicit in the provision to their employees of drugs they see as ending a life or preventing one. Congress could amend the Employee Retirement Income Security Act (ERISA) to mirror the accommodation: codifying an *organizational* exemption for all religious employers while providing *individual* employees of all objecting employers, including churches, coverage under a stand-alone contraceptive plan. Like

[26] Clyde Wayne Crews, The Administrative State Lacks Its Own Justification: Expertise, Cato Unbound, June 2, 2016, https://bit.ly/2Ds8hL6.

the accommodation, the cost of this stand-alone coverage would be funded by the insurers who run ACA exchanges. Carrying forward the Obama administration's clever financing of the accommodation is crucial because, as explained in Part I, the Hyde amendment prevents federal dollars from being used to fund abortion, including the four drugs stipulated to work on the implantation site. This congressional enactment would provide contraceptive coverage to the employees of more employers than either the Trump-era rule or the Obama-era rule. It also disconnects entirely religious and moral objectors from the provision of drugs that implicate their most deeply held commitments.

Part IV looks forward from *Little Sisters of the Poor*. We argue that culture-war battles will continue to be waged inside agencies whose workings are opaque to most Americans. Part IV highlights the costs of seesawing regulation. Administrative whiplash is bad for the nation. Momentous decisions should command respect from more than just the plurality or bare majority of Americans who voted for the last administration.

I. The Makings of a Culture-War Battle over Abortion

The Court's opinion in *Little Sisters of the Poor* picks up the controversy over the coverage mandate late in a still-unfolding story.

As we chronicle below, a core commitment about the handling of abortion was made to Americans to secure the ACA's passage in 2010.[27] Long before then, Americans reached an uneasy détente over, on the one hand, access to abortion and, on the other, whether Americans would be asked to support abortion by their actions or their tax dollars.

Shortly after the Supreme Court's 1973 decision in *Roe v. Wade*,[28] Congress clarified that receiving federal hospital construction funds did not compel objecting institutions to provide abortions, in what has become known as the "Church amendment."[29] Three years later,

---

[27] Patient Protection and Affordable Care Act, Pub. L. No. 111-148, 124 Stat. 119 (2010).

[28] 410 U.S. 113 (1973).

[29] 42 U.S.C. § 300a-7(c)(1); see also Robin Fretwell Wilson, Unpacking the Relationship between Conscience and Access, in Law, Religion, and Health in the United States (2017). Congress also protected individual physicians from losing staff privileges or suffering other "discrimination" for doing abortions or refusing to do them. Jody Feder, Cong. Res. Serv., The History and Effect of Abortion Conscience Clause Laws, 5 (2005). This equal opportunity conscience protection reveals that conscience protections need not imperil access.

Congress passed the Hyde amendment. First included as a rider to the Departments of Labor and Health, Education, and Welfare Appropriations Act, the effect of the Hyde amendment is to, generally, prohibit federal funds from being used to perform abortions except in cases of incest or rape, or where the failure to perform an abortion would "place the woman in danger of death," "as certified by a physician."[30] The amendment has endured because, decades after *Roe v. Wade*, many Americans still believe that abortion is wrong, both within faith communities and outside them.

These guarantees, made in the Church amendment and the Hyde amendment, long appeared unassailable. Indeed, far from being under constant retreat, Congress expanded conscience guarantees in successive pieces of legislation since 1973—acts that received bipartisan support and were signed into law by presidents from both parties.[31]

In 2009–2010, as Congress debated whether to enact the ACA, the question of what the bill meant for our decades long détente over abortion played a central role. Pro-life Democrats, whose linchpin votes were vital to passage, tied their support for the ACA to leaving these guarantees untouched.[32] A half-dozen members of Congress withheld support until President Obama "agreed to issue [an executive] order to placate [the] group."[33] This executive order, issued the

---

[30] Consolidated Appropriations Act, 2012, Pub. L. No. 112-74, 125 Stat. 786 (2011). The Hyde amendment allows states to choose to fund abortions through Medicaid, a federal- and state-supported program, that do not meet its restrictions. States must fund Hyde-ineligible abortions exclusively with state funds. To comply with the Hyde amendment, the ACA does not require coverage for any abortion. ACA, § 1303(b)(1). Although health plans may elect to provide coverage for abortions in cases of incest, rape, or to preserve the mother's life. ACA, § 1303(b)(2)(B).

[31] Congress has attached these funding restrictions to appropriations every year since 1976, with strong bipartisan support, until 2019. See Pub. L. No. 94–439 (H.R. 14232), Pub. L. No. 94-439, 90 Stat. 1418 (1976). The Hyde amendment enjoyed overwhelming support. For example, when the Hyde amendment was renewed in 2007, it passed 76-17 in the Senate and 272-142 in the House. Consolidated Appropriations Act, 2008, Pub. L. No. 110-161, 131 Stat. 1844 (2007). But in the lead up to the 2020 election, Democrats are increasingly calling for the end of the Hyde amendment. Emma Green, "Why Democrats Ditched the Hyde Amendment," The Atlantic, June 14, 2019, https://bit.ly/31xK0eA.

[32] See "Pro-Life Democrats Expect the Obama Administration to Issue Final Rule That Will Allow Religious Exemption," ChristianNewsWire, Nov. 21, 2011, https://perma.cc/K6X3-2RDW.

[33] Mimi Hall, "Both Sides of Abortion Issue Quick to Dismiss Order," USA Today, Mar. 25, 2010, https://bit.ly/2XJSpdP.

day after the ACA's passage, largely reflected provisions in the ACA itself, which bans "the use of federal funds" for certain abortions in the health exchanges.[34] After the president made these additional assurances, the bill passed the House 219-212.[35]

For groups like the Catholic Health Association, these assurances were crucial to their eventual support of the ACA. In effect, President Obama promised that the ACA would not upend years of consensus about whether the federal government will fund abortions and whether private individuals can stay out of the abortion business. Afterward, critics on both sides would label President Obama's executive order as "basically meaningless."[36]

But the members of Congress who changed their votes in reliance on the executive order believed it meant something—and that abortion restrictions in the ACA meant something, too. Rep. Joe Stupak said of the coverage mandate, "I am perplexed and disappointed that, having negotiated the Executive Order with the President, not only does the HHS mandate violate the Executive Order but it also violates statutory law."[37] He explained elsewhere that "it violates the Hyde law [amendment] that's been statutory for 40-some years."[38] Former Rep. Kathy Dahlkemper—who also voted for the ACA, only to lose her seat—echoed Stupak's sentiment: "We worked hard to prevent abortion funding in health care and to include clear conscience protections for those with moral objections to abortion and contraceptive devices that cause abortion. I trust that the President will honor the commitment he made to those of us who supported final passage."[39] Imagine the surprise or even betrayal that these

---

[34] ACA § 1303(b)(2).

[35] See Patient Protection and Affordable Care Act, H.R. 3590, 111th Cong. (2010).

[36] Hall, *supra* note 33. The National Right to Life Committee called it "[a] transparent political fig leaf," while Planned Parenthood said it was "[a] symbolic gesture." "Obama's Closed-Door Signing of Executive Order on Abortion Funding Raises Objections," Kaiser Health News, Mar. 25, 2010, https://bit.ly/3amq9mF.

[37] See, e.g., Tabitha Hale, "Stupak: HHS Mandate Violates My Obamacare Compromise," Breitbart, Sept. 4, 2012, https://bit.ly/3kvld3t.

[38] Fred Lucas, "Stupak: 'No Regrets' on Obamacare; But Contraception Mandate 'Violates Freedom of Religion,'" CNSNews, Sept. 4, 2012, https://bit.ly/2DMRBOp.

[39] John McCormack, "Kathy Dahlkemper: I Wouldn't Have Voted for Obamacare If I'd Known about HHS Rule," Wash. Exam'r, Feb. 7, 2012, https://washex.am/2E31S8L.

measured supporters of the ACA felt when the Obama administration issued its guidelines.

The ACA, in a late-added portion of text known as the Women's Health Amendment, fleshed out what preventive health services that covered health plans and insurers must provide:

> A group health plan and a health insurance issuer offering group or individual health insurance coverage shall, at a minimum, provide coverage for and shall not impose any cost sharing requirements for . . . with respect to women, such additional preventative care and screenings . . . as provided for in comprehensive guidelines supported by the Health Resources and Services Administration.[40]

Importantly, Congress nowhere mentioned abortion, abortion-inducing drugs, or drugs that would act after conception. Congress nowhere defined "preventative care and screenings." It nowhere provided the Health Resources and Services Administration (HRSA), a subagency of the Department of Health and Human Services (HHS), guidance on how to arrive at these "comprehensive guidelines." Instead, Congress left that responsibility and vast discretion to HRSA with three little words commonly used in statutes: "as provided for."

To fulfill this responsibility, HRSA turned to the National Academy of Medicine, a nonprofit group of medical advisers, to make recommendations. The departments' first statement on developing guidelines failed to mention contraceptives or religious exemptions or accommodations.[41] The resulting guidelines, to the great consternation of religious organizations,[42] grafted onto the requirement for preventive care and screenings that employers cover "[a]ll Food and Drug Administration approved contraceptive methods, sterilization procedures, and patient education and counseling for all women with reproductive capacity."[43]

---

[40] ACA § 2713(a)(4); 42 U.S.C. § 300gg-13(a)(4).

[41] 75 Fed. Reg. at 41728 (July 19, 2010).

[42] Matthew Larotonda, "Catholic Churches Distribute Letter Opposing Obama Healthcare Rule," ABC News, Jan. 30, 2012, https://abcn.ws/3fHIIYR; Thomas Cloud, "Cardinal George: Catholic Hospitals Will Be Gone in 'Two Lents' under Obamacare Regulation," CNSNews, Feb. 28, 2012, https://bit.ly/2DEro4z.

[43] 77 Fed. Reg. 8725 (Feb. 15, 2012); Women's Preventive Services Guidelines: Affordable Care Act Expands Prevention Coverage for Women's Health and Well-Being, HRSA, https://bit.ly/2PGYW4k.

Relying on the HRSA guidelines, the Obama administration finalized rules requiring coverage of "preventive care . . . provided for in the comprehensive guidelines supported" by HRSA.[44] The same day, the Obama administration finalized an exemption for churches from the coverage mandate (church exemption),[45] flagging that the administration understood the religious commitments implicated by the set of drugs being mandated. Unlike churches, other employers that might object to subsidizing the full complement of drugs faced massive fines.[46]

This tone-deaf agency action shattered the uneasy peace around abortion animating the ACA. Religious organizations expressed sharp dissent. The Catholic Health Association said, "[t]he impact of being told we do not fit the new definition of a religious employer and therefore cannot operate our ministries following our consciences has jolted us. . . . From President Thomas Jefferson to President Barack Obama, we have been promised a respect for appropriate religious freedom."[47] Religious leaders said the coverage mandate treated them as "second-class citizens."[48] At the same time, women's rights groups like the National Women's Law Center praised the Obama administration

---

[44] Notice of Guidelines Development: July 19, 2010, 75 Fed. Reg. 41726 (July 19, 2010); Amendment to the interim final rule: August 3, 2011, by the Departments of HHS, Labor and Treasury, 76 Fed. Reg. 46621 (Aug. 3, 2011); Final rule: February 15, 2012, by the Departments of HHS, Labor, and Treasury, 77 Fed. Reg. 8725 (Feb. 15, 2012).

[45] 76 Fed. Reg. 46621 (Aug. 3, 2011) ("[T]he Departments are amending the interim final rules to provide HRSA additional discretion to exempt certain religious employers from the Guidelines where contraceptive services are concerned."); *id.* ("[A] religious employer is one that: (1) has the inculcation of religious values as its purpose; (2) primarily employs persons who share its religious tenets; (3) primarily serves persons who share its religious tenets; and (4) is a non-profit organization under section 6033(a)(1) and section 6033(a)(3)(A)(i) or (iii) of the Code. Section 6033(a)(3)(A)(i) and (iii) refer to churches, their integrated auxiliaries, and conventions or associations of churches, as well as to the exclusively religious activities of any religious order."); 77 Fed. Reg. 8725 (Feb. 15, 2012) (maintaining definition). This definition was later simplified to require only the fourth prong. See 78 Fed. Reg. 8456 (Feb. 6, 2013) (proposed rule); 78 Fed. Reg. 39870 (July 2, 2013) (final rule).

[46] In *Hobby Lobby*, by the Court's calculation, if Hobby Lobby refused to provide mandated coverage, it would be taxed $100 per day per individual, amounting to $1.3 million a day or $475 million per year. 573 U.S. at 691.

[47] Carol Keehan, "Something Has to Be Fixed," Catholic Health Ass'n of the United States, Feb. 15, 2012, https://bit.ly/2Z3APSp.

[48] Letter from Thomas J. Olmsted, Catholic Bishop of Phx., to Brothers and Sisters in Christ (Jan. 25, 2012).

for establishing "a major milestone in protecting women's health [be-cause] . . . [c]ontraception is critical preventive health care."[49]

President Obama attempted to mitigate the fallout. He directed the departments entrusted with administering the ACA to fashion an accommodation that would allow women to receive "contraceptive care free of charge without co-pays, without hassle" but also not compel religious nonprofits to pay for that coverage.[50]

The Obama administration signaled its intent to effect the president's directive in a notice of proposed rulemaking published on March 21, 2012.[51] Importantly, the administration asked for comments on which organizations should be eligible for the accommodation.[52] At that point, "not even Jesus and the apostles would qualify for" the church exemption, as one commentator quipped.[53]

The resulting accommodation extended to faith-based organizations recognized by the IRS and attempted to separate them from payment of contraceptives by shifting the financial burden elsewhere. For objecting employers that purchase insurance through the marketplace, the accommodation directed the employer's insurer to provide add-on contraceptive coverage to women and "assume sole responsibility" for its cost.[54] The insurer is made whole for providing the add-on coverage by the savings it reaps from "lower costs from improvements in women's health, healthier timing and spacing of pregnancies, and fewer unplanned pregnancies."[55] In theory, the add-on coverage comes at no cost to the employer.

[49] National Women's Law Center, "HHS Decision on Contraceptive Coverage a Major Milestone," Jan. 20, 2012, https://bit.ly/2XWFK79.

[50] Richard Wolf, "Obama Tweaks Birth Control Rule," USA Today, Feb. 10, 2012, https://bit.ly/2EgDtwJ.

[51] 77 Fed. Reg. 16501 (Mar. 21, 2012).

[52] Id.

[53] Robin Fretwell Wilson, The Erupting Clash between Religion and the State over Contraception, Sterilization, and Abortion, in Religious Freedom in America: Constitutional Traditions and New Horizons 135, 138 (Allen Hertzke ed., 2014).

[54] 78 Fed. Reg. 39870 (July 2, 2013); 78 Fed. Reg. 8456 (Feb. 6, 2013). For objecting employers who self-insure, there is no insurer providing coverage. As a result, the third-party administrator for the objecting employer's plan would arrange for coverage through the FFE insurer or provide that coverage directly itself.

[55] 80 Fed. Reg. 41318, 41335 (July 14, 2015).

For objecting employers who self-fund, the accommodation directs the entity administering the ACA's federally facilitated exchange (FFE insurer) to provide add-on contraceptive coverage for employees at no cost to the objecting employer or the employees. The FFE insurer is reimbursed for these costs through a convoluted mechanism: what the insurer owes the U.S. government for running the exchanges is reduced dollar for dollar by what it shelled out for the add-on contraceptive coverage for employees.[56]

When crafting the accommodation, President Obama faced a hard limit in trying to honor all his commitments. He promised in his executive order that no federal funds "will be used to pay for abortions in health insurance exchanges to be set up by the government."[57] The Hyde amendment itself gets tripped when dollars hit the federal fisc, specifically HHS,[58] and are used for ineligible abortions.[59] The contractual discount, although convoluted, technically skirts the Hyde amendment and became the Obama administration's workaround. Federal taxpayer dollars would not pay for what some viewed as abortifacients.

In order to avail themselves of the accommodation, religious nonprofits were required to provide written notice to their insurer or, if self-funded as nearly all plans are, the third-party administrator (TPA) for their health-insurance plan.[60] That notice not only triggers someone else to provide the objected-to coverage,[61] it effected any needed plan changes. For example, the TPA became an ERISA plan administrator solely for the purpose of contraceptive coverage by operation of law, and the objecting nonprofit was "considered to comply with" the coverage mandate.[62]

---

[56] 80 Fed. Reg. 41318.

[57] Hall, *supra* note 33.

[58] The Hyde amendment actually is a restriction on specific streams of money—namely those funds being appropriated to the departments funded by the appropriations bill and any trust funds those monies go into.

[59] Four drugs were stipulated to be abortifacient, that is acting on the implantation site. We recognize that not all people would see the objected-to drugs as abortion-inducing. See Wilson, Calculus, *supra* note 10, at 1454–60.

[60] ERISA-exempt "church plans" also had to file notice. 45 C.F.R. § 147.131(c)(1); 26 C.F.R. § 54.9815-2713A(b)(1).

[61] 45 C.F.R. § 147.131(d).

[62] 78 Fed. Reg. at 39879 (July 2, 2013); 29 C.F.R. § 2510.3-16(b); 29 U.S.C. § 1002(16) (defining plan administrator); 45 C.F.R. § 147.131(c)(1); 26 C.F.R. § 54.9815-2713A(b)(1); 29 C.F.R. § 2590.715-2713A(b)(1).

Even as the accommodation hijacks insurers and TPAs to do the work, the add-on contraceptive coverage nonetheless was appended to the religious employer's health plan.[63] Thus, religious employers believed they maintained some connection to objected-to coverage, making them complicit. Put differently, although they did not have to pay for it, include it in their plans, or administer coverage, the existence of their health plan infrastructure made the provision of objected-to drugs possible.

This accommodation provided much needed relief for many objectors, but not all were interested. Catholic Cardinal Timothy Dolan, Archbishop of New York and president of the U.S. Council of Bishops, together with more than 500 scholars, university presidents, and religious leaders, wrote a letter labeling the accommodation "unacceptable" and as hiding a "grave violation" of religious liberty behind a "cheap accounting trick."[64]

The Little Sisters challenged the accommodation. As a religious nonprofit ineligible for the church exemption, they faced an impossible choice: provide objected-to coverage and be complicit in a sin; accept the accommodation's terms and be complicit in a sin; or face heavy fines under the ACA. As Yuval Levin cleverly noted, "somehow these religious employers are supposed to imagine that they're not giving their workers access to abortive and contraceptive coverage. If religious people thought about their religious obligations the way HHS lawyers think about the law, this might just work. But they don't."[65]

According to the Little Sisters' most recent tax filings as a nonprofit, the Little Sisters employ at least 2,719 people across their 31 locations nationwide.[66] As with the hefty fines facing Hobby Lobby,[67]

---

[63] 78 Fed. Reg. at 39876 (July 13, 2013) ("[P]lan participants and beneficiaries (and their health care providers) do not have to have two separate health insurance policies (that is, the group health insurance policy and the individual contraceptive coverage policy).").

[64] Letter from Timothy Dolan et al., Unacceptable (Feb. 27, 2012), https://perma.cc/CS57-ZXVT ("It is no answer to respond that the religious employers are not 'paying' for this aspect of the insurance coverage.").

[65] Yuval Levin, "A New Round of Intolerance," Nat'l Rev. Online, Feb. 1, 2013, https://bit.ly/33H4lAz.

[66] U.S. Homes, Little Sisters of the Poor, https://bit.ly/2PC5zEW; *infra* note 117.

[67] Hobby Lobby, 573 U.S. at 686.

the Little Sisters would pay $99,243,500 a year if ultimately made to pay the ACA's $100-a-day penalty for each employee covered by a noncompliant plan.[68]

Numerous religious organizations shared the Little Sisters' concerns and filed similar lawsuits, eventually resulting in *Zubik v. Burwell*.[69] The key issue in *Zubik* was whether the accommodation violated RFRA. RFRA tests government-imposed burdens on religion against the necessity of imposing those burdens.[70]

The *Zubik* Court never reached the merits. Rather, after supplemental briefing, the departments confirmed that they could separate the Little Sisters' plan entirely from the causal chain of contraceptive coverage for the Little Sisters' employees. "[C]ontraceptive coverage could be provided to [Little Sisters'] employees, through [their] insurance companies, without any . . . notice from [them]."[71] And the Little Sisters agreed that their complicity concern would be met by an accommodation where they "need to do nothing more than contract for a plan that does not include coverage for some or all forms of contraception, even if their employees receive cost-free contraceptive coverage from the same insurance company."[72] The Court remanded, directing the departments to accommodate the Little Sisters' "religious exercise while at the same time ensuring that women covered by [their] health plans receive full and equal health coverage, including contraceptive coverage."[73] It seemed that the litigation had finally yielded a way to resolve the conflict without giving up on religious liberty or the access needs of women.

In parallel, religious objectors eligible for neither the church exemption nor the accommodation challenged the coverage mandate as encroaching on their religious practice without sufficient reason, in violation of RFRA. In *Burwell v. Hobby Lobby Stores, Inc.*, the Court consolidated the appeals of three for-profit, closely held corporations.

---

[68] 26 U.S.C. §§ 4980D(a)–(b).

[69] Zubik, 136 S. Ct. 1557.

[70] Robin Fretwell Wilson, When Governments Insulate Dissenters from Social Change: What Hobby Lobby and Abortion Conscience Clauses Teach about Specific Exemptions, U.C. Davis L. Rev. 704, 710 (2014).

[71] Zubik, 136 S. Ct. at 1559.

[72] *Id.* at 1560.

[73] *Id.*

The owners "have religious objections to abortion, and according to their religious beliefs the four contraceptive methods at issue are abortifacients."[74] By complying with the coverage mandate, they believed they would be facilitating abortions.[75] During the litigation, the departments stipulated that the drugs acted after conception.[76]

The *Hobby Lobby* Court held that the coverage mandate did violate RFRA as to these closely held corporations, pointing to the accommodation as one less restrictive means to accomplish the departments' goals of gender equity through contraceptive coverage.[77] The holding in *Hobby Lobby*, combined with the Court's direction in *Zubik*, challenged the departments to extend and revise the accommodation.

Ultimately, the departments under President Obama concluded there was "no feasible approach" to solve the problem.[78] In the last days of the Obama administration, on January 9, 2017, the departments instead insisted that the accommodation was consistent with RFRA, reassuming their initial position in *Zubik*. Before any further litigation ensued, President Trump took office.

Under President Trump, the departments did a 180-degree shift. Less than a year into the Trump administration, the departments issued the wholesale exemption carving out religious organizations from the coverage mandate entirely—and nobody stepped into the void to pay for the missing coverage.[79] This wholesale exemption could be triggered by religious beliefs of nonprofit and for-profit religious employers alike.

---

[74] Hobby Lobby, 573 U.S. at 691.

[75] *Id.*

[76] "HHS acknowledge[d] that the objected-to drugs and devices may result in the destruction of an embryo." Hobby Lobby, 573 U.S. at 720. This was done despite the departments' statements that no covered drug or device under the ACA is an "abortifacient[]" within the meaning of federal law." See 62 Fed. Reg. 8610, 8611 (Feb. 25, 1997); 45 C.F.R. § 46.202(f).

[77] Hobby Lobby, 573 U.S. at 730.

[78] Dept. of Labor, FAQs about Affordable Care Act Implementation, Part 36 at 4 (Jan. 9, 2017).

[79] 82 Fed. Reg. 47792, 47812 (Oct. 13, 2017) ("[E]xemptions for objecting entities will apply to the extent that an entity described in § 147.132(a)(1) objects to its establishing, maintaining, providing, offering, or arranging (as applicable) coverage, payments, or a plan that provides coverage or payments for some or all contraceptive services, based on its sincerely held religious beliefs.").

In a parallel rule, the Trump administration also exempted any employer that could not provide coverage for moral reasons (moral exemption).[80] The departments left in place the accommodation for those organizations that wanted to step aside from providing coverage under their plan but *also* wanted their employees to have the mandated coverage.[81] In other words, employers that wanted to say "not me, but glad for others to pay" could avail themselves of the accommodation.

It is stunning that, after all the culture-war machinations over *Hobby Lobby*, the Trump administration's 180-degree turn garnered far less public attention. Media mentions of *Hobby Lobby* dwarf that of *Little Sisters of the Poor*.[82] Surely, a change this big—carving out of the coverage mandate a whole category of additional employers—should have prompted outrage and debate on the same scale as *Hobby Lobby*. But no. Apparently inundated with other dramas of the Trump administration, the media and the nation simply blanked on the size of the culture-war move being made by the departments.

The departments justified the wholesale and moral exemptions, pointing to multiple sources of authority. First, they stated that the ACA itself, through its broad delegation of power to HRSA, granted them authority to exempt entities from the coverage mandate—the Supreme Court would ultimately agree. Second, they explained that the wholesale exemption was directly responsive to the Court's holdings in *Zubik* and *Hobby Lobby*. Third, they reasoned that RFRA compelled the wholesale exemption or, at the very least, authorized

---

[80] *Id.* at 47838.

[81] *Id.* at 47812 ("The Departments now believe it is appropriate to modify the scope of the discretion afforded to HRSA in the July 2015 final regulations to direct HRSA to provide the expanded exemptions and change the accommodation to an optional process if HRSA continues to otherwise provide for contraceptive coverage in the Guidelines.").

[82] As one gauge, we examined media coverage of Hobby Lobby and Little Sisters of the Poor during their litigation timelines. Between April 1, 2012, and December 30, 2014, Hobby Lobby was mentioned over 10,000 times. In contrast, from March 1, 2013 to July 20, 2020, Little Sisters of the Poor garnered 6,000 mentions. A Lexis search for ("Little Sisters" or "Zubik") and contracept! and ("case" or "Supreme Court" or "SCOTUS") between the dates Mar. 1, 2013 and July 20, 2020, yielded 6,336 results. A Lexis search for ("Hobby Lobby" or "Mardel") and contracept! and ("case" or "Supreme Court" or "SCOTUS") between the dates Apr. 1, 2012, and Dec. 30, 2014, yielded over 10,000 results.

the departments to create it. And, fourth, the moral exemption was directly supported by the Church amendment because four of the mandated drugs "prevent implantation," meaning "many persons believe [they] are abortifacient."[83]

Litigation followed within days.[84] Pennsylvania filed suit, later joined by New Jersey, arguing that the wholesale and moral exemptions were both substantively and procedurally invalid and would cause the states to shoulder the cost of contraceptives for employees working for exempted employers.[85] The district court granted a nationwide preliminary injunction against the wholesale and moral exemptions. When the Little Sisters moved to intervene to defend the wholesale exemption, they were rebuffed by the district court. But on appeal, the Third Circuit permitted their intervention. Otherwise, at the Third Circuit, the states prevailed against the wholesale and moral exemptions. The Supreme Court granted certiorari.

II. The Court's Decision

At the Supreme Court, the Little Sisters and the Trump administration together defended the concessions for religious and moral objectors. The *Little Sisters* decision ultimately rested on a close reading of three words in the ACA, "as provided for." A 7-2 majority ruled for the Little Sisters and the departments, upholding the wholesale and moral exemptions. The ACA authorized the agencies both to fill in the details of preventive care and screenings and to leave aside large swaths of covered employers. Technical shortcomings of the Trump administration rulemaking did not violate the substantive requirements of the Administrative Procedure Act (APA) or cause prejudicial error. The Court avoided the meta question of whether the Obama administration's accommodation was insufficient and had to do more for religious objectors under RFRA.

---

[83] 82 Fed. Reg. at 47838.

[84] Complaint, Pennsylvania v. Trump, 281 F. Supp. 3d 553, 564 (E.D. Pa. 2017) (17-4540) (filed October 11, 2017, just five days after the wholesale exemption and moral exemption interim final rules' effective date, and two days before the interim final rules themselves were published in the Federal Register).

[85] Pennsylvania, 930 F.3d at 560–61 ("The States expect that when women lose contraceptive insurance coverage from their employers, they will seek out these state-funded programs and services.").

A. Finding Broad Delegation under the ACA

Writing for the Court, Justice Clarence Thomas hinged his analysis on Congress's decision to define the contours of preventive care and screenings "as provided for in comprehensive guidelines by [HRSA]." This handoff to HRSA allowed HRSA both to "identify what preventative care and screenings must be covered [under the ACA] and to exempt or accommodate certain employers' religious objections."[86] In other words, this phrase authorized HRSA not only to specify *what* was required but *who* had to provide coverage. Employing a textualist interpretation of the phrase, the Court held that on its face "the provision grants sweeping authority to HRSA to craft a set of standards defining the preventive care that applicable health plans must cover," so that "HRSA has virtually unbridled discretion."[87] This unchecked discretion to define coverage requirements, the Court found, also permitted HRSA to "identify and create exemptions from its own Guidelines."[88]

Although the Court recognized that this discretion could result in contraceptives not being provided to numerous women working for exempted employers, it put the blame on Congress: "it was Congress, not the Departments, that declined to expressly require contraceptive coverage in the ACA itself."[89] If tens of thousands of employees were left without coverage that other employees receive under the ACA,[90] that, too, was on Congress, which had made a "deliberate choice to issue an extraordinarily 'broad general directiv[e]' to HRSA to craft the Guidelines, without any qualifications as to the substance of the Guidelines or whether exemptions were permissible. Thus, it is Congress, not the Departments, that has failed to provide the protection for contraceptive coverage."[91]

---

[86] Little Sisters of the Poor, 140 S. Ct. at 2380.

[87] *Id.*

[88] *Id.*

[89] *Id.* at 2382.

[90] 83 Fed. Reg. at 57578–80 (Nov. 15, 2018) (estimating tens of thousands of women would lose coverage under religious rule).

[91] Little Sisters of the Poor, 140 S. Ct. at 2382. There is an obvious reason for Congress's failure. It barely had enough votes to pass the ACA, much less an ACA that mandated the provision of contraceptive care. Similarly, Republicans wanting to undo the ACA since then have also not carried enough votes. Hence, both fights are being waged in the agencies. See Summary of Administration Actions Undermining the Affordable Care Act, Center on Budget and Policy Priorities, https://bit.ly/2XHCJra.

In dissent, Justice Ruth Bader Ginsburg castigated the Trump administration for crafting an exemption that "casts totally aside" and "tossed entirely to the wind" the interest of providing contraceptives to women.[92] She argued that the departments should have taken a "balanced approach . . . that does not allow the religious beliefs of some to overwhelm the rights and interests of others who do not share those beliefs."[93] For Justice Ginsburg, the words "as provided for" permitted HRSA only to determine *what* services the guidelines cover, but not *who* is required to provide them.[94] In other words, HRSA could decide to include the full complement of drugs in the guidelines, but it could not exempt religious or other organizations from providing them. Because of this, Justice Ginsburg concluded the departments had no authority under the ACA to craft the wholesale or moral exemptions.

Justice Elena Kagan took issue with premising broad authority on the ACA's words "as provided for." Instead, because of the ACA's ambiguity, she would defer to an agency's reasonable interpretation under *Chevron, U.S.A., Inc. v. Natural Resources Defense Council.*[95] Examining the coverage mandate's history, Justice Kagan noted that there has been no change in interpretation across the Obama and Trump administrations of the ACA as giving HRSA the ability to "create exemptions to the contraceptive-coverage mandate."[96] Because of this, Justice Kagan would defer to the departments' understanding of the phrase "as provided for."

B. Rejecting Procedural Defects under the APA

The states also challenged whether the departments had complied with the APA when issuing the wholesale and moral exemptions. Under the APA, executive agencies are required to hold a notice-and-comment period to receive public comments on a proposed rule.[97] But there are exceptions. For instance, agencies may bypass notice

---

[92] Little Sisters of the Poor, 140 S. Ct. at 2400 (Ginsburg, J., dissenting); Oral Argument, *infra* note 120, at 10:18–20.

[93] Little Sisters of the Poor, 140 S. Ct. at 2400.

[94] *Id.* at 2404–05.

[95] *Id.* at 2397 (Kagan, J., concurring).

[96] *Id.*

[97] 5 U.S.C. § 553.

and comment for "good cause" and proceed by way of an interim final rule (IFR).[98] Both administrations used IFRs in this context.[99]

The states had argued that the Trump administration's October 2017 IFRs set forth the wholesale and moral exemptions almost exactly as they were finalized. The states contended that the Trump administration lacked good cause to avoid notice and comment, that this procedural defect invalidated the November 2018 final rules, and that the departments had failed to evidence "open-mindedness" in response to public comments. The Little Sisters and the Trump administration countered that the IFRs complied with the APA. They pointed to similar practices under the Obama administration and, in any event, argued that the November 2018 final rules rendered the IFRs harmless.

The Court upheld the procedural validity of the November 2018 final rules. Instead of relying on the names traditionally given to specific agency actions—such as "Interim Final Rule," "Request for Comments," or "General Notice of Proposed Rulemaking"—the Court asked if the departments' actions met the APA's substantive requirements. The Court held that they did. The departments' request for comments in the October 2017 IFRs contained a reference to the departments' legal authority and an explanation of the proposed rules. That gave the public a fair opportunity to comment on the proposals, meeting these important APA requirements.[100]

On the question of "open-mindedness" to public comments when promulgating final rules, the Court rejected open-mindedness as a test for validity; no such test is found in the APA. All that is required under the APA is that the public be given notice and time to make

---

[98] 5 U.S.C. § 553(b)(3)(B) ("[W]hen the agency for good cause finds (and incorporates the finding and a brief statement of reasons therefor in the rules issued) that notice and public procedure thereon are impracticable, unnecessary, or contrary to the public interest.").

[99] As one example, HRSA announced it would develop guidelines in an IFR. 75 Fed. Reg. 41726 (July 19, 2010). After a change in administration, the departments issued two new IFRs which created the wholesale exemption and the moral exemption. 82 Fed. Reg. at 47812 (Oct. 13, 2017); 82 Fed. Reg. 47838 (Oct. 13, 2017). After Pennsylvania launched its action, the departments formalized the October 2017 IFRs into final rules in November 2018. 83 Fed. Reg. 57536 (Nov. 15, 2018); 83 Fed. Reg. 57592 (Nov. 15, 2018). The November 2018 final rules contained explanations of the departments' decision regarding the accommodation.

[100] Little Sisters of the Poor, 140 S. Ct. at 2384–85.

comments on agency proposed rules, that the final rule include a statement of the rule's basis and purpose, and that the rule is published 30 days before it becomes effective. The Court found that each requirement was followed as to the November 2018 final rules, even though nearly identical to the October 2017 IFRs. Given compliance with the APA, the question of good cause for bypassing notice and comment was mooted.[101]

Justice Kagan in her concurrence sketched the next line of attack in the Little Sisters' saga: whether the wholesale and moral exemptions reflect arbitrary and capricious action forbidden by the APA.[102] Justice Kagan pointed to a "mismatch between the scope of the [wholesale exemption] and the problem the agencies set out to address"[103]—namely, the wholesale exemption is cast so broadly that it encompasses religious employers who gladly would accept the accommodation. She believes this overbreadth fails to make good on the departments' obligation to minimize the impact on access of any concessions made for religious objectors. For Justice Kagan, the moral exemption is more problematic; it lacks even the justification that the departments sought to prevent violations of RFRA by failing to narrowly tailor encroachments on religious practice.

C. Leaving RFRA for Another Day, Again

Even as Justice Thomas anchored the majority decision to a textualist interpretation of the ACA, he weighed in on the meta question of whether RFRA demanded such a robust response to claims of religious burden. The majority noted that it was "appropriate for the Departments to consider RFRA."[104] The Court pointed to its holding in *Hobby Lobby* "that the mandate violated RFRA as applied to entities with complicity-based objections," that the "conflict between the [coverage] mandate and RFRA is well settled," and that the Court's decisions in *Zubik* and *Hobby Lobby* "all but instructed the Departments to consider RFRA going forward."[105] "Against this backdrop,"

---

[101] *Id.* at 2385–86.

[102] *Id.* at 2397–2400 (Kagan, J., concurring).

[103] *Id.* at 2398.

[104] *Id.* at 2383 (Thomas, J., majority op.).

[105] *Id.*

the Court said, "it is unsurprising that RFRA would feature prominently in the Departments' discussion[s]."[106] Justice Thomas went further: "The Departments had authority under RFRA to 'cure' any RFRA violations caused by its regulations."[107] All of these observations are, of course, *dicta* since the majority rested its decision on a reading of the ACA. On the fundamental question—what would constitute a RFRA violation in the context of the accommodation—the Court did not say.

Justice Samuel Alito's concurrence lamented this omission. By not dealing with the RFRA question head on, Justice Alito feared that the "Little Sisters' legal odyssey [would not come] to an end."[108] Justice Alito, the author of the majority opinion in *Hobby Lobby*,[109] would have held that the accommodation violated RFRA. Justice Alito helpfully walks through each step of RFRA's multistaged analysis.[110] As to the Little Sisters' religious belief regarding complicity as a result of using the accommodation, he saw a substantial burden—failing to comply with the accommodation hastens severe financial penalties for noncompliance. The government lacked a compelling interest in providing contraceptive coverage to working women, as shown by Congress's failure to nail down a duty to provide contraceptive coverage in the text of the ACA. Any compelling interest in the coverage mandate is further undermined by the crazy quilt of exemptions in the ACA itself:[111] (1) "The ACA does not provide contraceptive coverage for women who do not work outside the home," (2) the ACA's exemption of employers with fewer than 50 employees, and (3) the ACA's expansive grandfathering of pre-existing plans. Practically, these exemptions mean that "tens of millions of people" do not receive the benefits of the ACA aside from concessions for religious practice.[112]

---

[106] *Id.*

[107] *Id.* at 2382.

[108] *Id.* at 2389 (Alito, J., concurring).

[109] Hobby Lobby, 573 U.S. 682.

[110] Little Sisters of the Poor, 140 S. Ct. at 2387–96. See also Tanner Bean, "To the Person": RFRA's Blueprint for a Sustainable Exemption Regime, 2019 BYU L. Rev. 1, 14 (2019), https://perma.cc/G44S-EC53.

[111] Little Sisters of the Poor, 140 S. Ct. at 2392 (Alito, J., concurring).

[112] *Id.* at 2393.

Last, the accommodation was not the least restrictive means of accomplishing what valid interest the government did have. Other alternatives exist for providing contraceptives: "the Government . . . [could] assume the cost of providing the . . . contraceptives . . . to any women who are unable to obtain them under their health-insurance policies"—assuming the Hyde amendment did not restrict such payment, as we explain above.[113] In sharp distinction to Justice Kagan's mismatch analysis, Justice Alito concluded that "it is not clear that the [wholesale exemption's] provisions concerning entities that object to the mandate on religious grounds go any further than necessary to bring the mandate into compliance with RFRA."[114] Overbreadth, in fact, is permissible as RFRA does not require corrective measures to be "the narrowest permissible corrective."[115]

Justice Ginsburg appears to agree that the departments may take RFRA into account to prevent RFRA violations, but urges a limit to proactive measures: they may not "benefit religious adherents at the expense of the rights of third parties."[116] She believes female employees of employers carved out of the coverage mandate by the wholesale and moral exemptions suffer a third-party harm. Indeed, there is now no way for these employees to obtain cost-free coverage for contraceptives if their employer refuses to accept the accommodation.[117] Below, we describe action Congress may take now to end this saga while ensuring employees the promised access.

---

[113] *Id.* at 2394 (Alito, J., concurring).

[114] *Id.* at 2396.

[115] *Id.*

[116] *Id.* at 2408 (Ginsburg J., dissenting).

[117] We do not discount the impact the Church exemption, accommodation, and wholesale exemption have on women working for religious employers that seek contraceptive coverage. Of the Little Sisters' 2,719 employees (reported on the Little Sisters' publicly available Form 990s for 2018), some who do not share the Little Sisters' religious belief regarding contraception may desire free contraception. See Results for Tax Exempt Organization Search, Internal Revenue Service (last visited July 25, 2020), https://bit.ly/3akWVo8 (searched IRS databases by organization name for "Little Sisters of the Poor"). This should be no surprise. Because of the litigation surrounding the coverage mandate, the Little Sisters' employees, third parties to the litigation, have never had the benefit of a system like the accommodation which would provide coverage while attempting to meet their employer's religious objection.

For Justice Ginsburg, the wholesale exemption is "neither required nor permitted by RFRA."[118] Justice Ginsburg believes that requiring an objecting employer to file the necessary paperwork to avail themselves of the accommodation does not substantially burden religious organizations' free exercise of religion. Under the accommodation, an "employer is absolved of any obligation to provide the contraceptive coverage to which it objects; that obligation is transferred to the insurer."[119] Ultimately, Justice Ginsburg would strike the wholesale and moral exemptions and leave the accommodation in place.

III. Congress Can Bring These Clashes to an End

The Supreme Court need not be the body that resolves this particular saga in the broader culture war over abortion, as the justices themselves have noted.[120] Congress set in motion the process of defining preventative care and screenings, and it can step in to fashion a remedy that respects both the needs of women and of religious objectors.

After supplemental briefing in the *Zubik* litigation, the departments conceded that "contraceptive coverage could be provided to [the Little Sisters'] employees, through [their] insurance companies, without any . . . notice from [them]."[121] The departments later backtracked, saying such a fix was not feasible. But what the departments once thought feasible could be done by Congress by writing such a procedure into ERISA, which governs employer-sponsored health insurance coverage, including self-funded health plans.

---

[118] Little Sisters of the Poor, 140 S. Ct. at 2409 (Ginsburg, J., dissenting).

[119] *Id.* at 2410.

[120] Justices expressed their dismay that the parties could not resolve this conflict on their own. At oral argument, some justices were noticeably frustrated with the parties' failure to come to a negotiated solution that both accounted for religious liberty and assured the availability of contraception. Justice Breyer said plainly, "I don't understand why this can't be worked out." Tr. Oral Argument at 35:23–24, Little Sisters of the Poor Saints Peter and Paul Home v. Pennsylvania, 140 S. Ct. 2367 (2020) (No. 19-431). Chief Justice Roberts asked, "Is it really the case that there is no way to resolve th[e] differences?" *Id.* at 30:15–16. He lamented that "the problem is that neither side in this debate wants the accommodation to work. The one side doesn't want it to work because they want to say the mandate is required, and the other side doesn't want it to work because they want to impose the mandate." *Id.* at 30:8–14.

[121] Zubik, 136 S. Ct. at 1559.

The Obama administration's coverage mandate, its church exemption, its accommodation, and the Trump administration's wholesale and moral exemptions are all creatures of regulation, not statute. Only one of these, the accommodation, strived to have it both ways: respecting women's access as well as religious conscience. By contrast, the wholesale and moral exemptions that the Trump administration opened broadly to employers, and the church exemption that the Obama administration offered narrowly to churches, all gave short shrift to women. Under each of these, female employees lost, whether they shared their employer's convictions or not.

Making workable the Obama administration's accommodation should be the goal: it gives up neither on women's access nor on religious liberty. To be workable, it must take seriously the complicity claims that have complicated and raised barriers to its use.

Congress has had the ability all along to short circuit this saga. Consider one simple approach: Amend ERISA so that *individual employees* of exempt religious employers have the benefit of the accommodation.[122] This approach would place the ability to trigger the accommodation in the hands of individual employees. An employee working for an exempt employer would simply provide a Form 700 (modified for individuals seeking contraceptives who work for exempt employers) to the TPA administering her employer's self-insured or ERISA-exempt church health plan. Alternatively, the employee could notify HHS that she seeks contraceptives and is working for an exempt employer, and then HHS could turn around and contact the applicable TPA. This individual notification would have the same effect as the accommodation: It would require the TPA to reach out to the FFE insurer, which would then assume the financial and administrative burden of contraceptive coverage for that individual employee. It would also cause TPAs to be considered ERISA plan administrators for contraceptive coverage. To completely sever objecting employers from the causal chain of contraceptive coverage,

---

[122] Of course, given the politicization of the coverage mandate and exemptions to it, Congress may also want to amend the ACA to specify a duty to provide contraceptive coverage while making explicit the carve-outs from that duty for specified objectors. Carveouts might be limited to religious objectors as the Obama administration did in regulation or extended to religious and moral objectors as the Trump administration and the archetypal conscience clause, the Church amendment, did.

this approach utilizes separate contraceptive coverage plans rather than co-opting the plan infrastructure of the objecting employer. [123]

This proposal has two advantages. It better solves for the objection at issue (any complicity in ending a life or, for some, preventing it), and it gives access to more women than even the Obama administration's rules. Specifically, employees working for churches could receive coverage. This itself is important since not all employees share their employer's convictions. Under the church exemption, neither women employees nor eligible family members could access cost-free care under the accommodation—no provision was made for them. Under Trump's wholesale and moral exemptions, a woman's employer decides whether someone will step into the access void left by the employer's decision. If Congress amended ERISA, these employees, too, would receive coverage.

This approach would leverage President Obama's innovation in the accommodation, giving a contractual discount to the provider of the stand-alone coverage, thereby honoring the Hyde amendment. But unlike the accommodation, objecting employers would be removed from the causal chain. Importantly, the Little Sisters have said that their complicity concerns are resolved if they "need to do nothing more than contract for a plan that does not include coverage for some or all forms of contraception."[124]

Of course, this congressional fix would be limited to this specific controversy. It would do little for other culture-war conflicts waged in the administrative state. To avoid whiplashing Americans back and forth across culture-war divides every four or eight years, and to provide much-needed stability in the law, some additional principle of permanence needs to be developed.[125] Without a stabilizing device, regulations are nothing more than temporary orders reflecting moral positions of the day. They provide no guarantee of closure, nor do they allow businesses to accurately plan for the future.

---

[123] Amending ERISA to effect standalone coverage without action by an objecting employer would require technical changes to ERISA, which space does not allow to be explored in full here but are eminently feasible.

[124] Zubik, 136 S. Ct. at 1560.

[125] See, e.g., Aaron L. Nielson, Sticky Regulations and ~~Net Neutrality~~ Restoring Internet Freedom, Hastings L.J. (forthcoming), https://bit.ly/2XN6I0V (advancing a theory of "sticky regulations" and suggestions for creating regulatory stability).

Indeed, something like *stare decisis* in the administrative world would go a long way to calm culture-war battles.

How to impose such a principle on a branch of government that is used to being handed extraordinary discretion by Congress is a big question. But the states offer food for thought. Some states permit the legislature to review proposed regulations within a prescribed period of time or the regulations become effective. The agencies could be required to demonstrate that their work is premised on technical expertise, not culture-war positions. And in order for a subsequent administration to rescind or remake a rule, the administration could be required to provide an interest more compelling than simply gratifying a political base.

Certainly, many will oppose the development of such a *stare decisis*–like principle, especially those seeking a change in the current occupant of the White House. But for those Americans interested in coming together as a nation rather than perpetual moral divides, study of such regulatory reform would be worthwhile.

IV. Looking Forward: Agencies Will Remain a Prime Locus for Culture-War Conflict

Despite its reception, *Little Sisters of the Poor* is not a solid win for religious liberty. What victory the Little Sisters now enjoy is likely to last only as long as the Trump administration. Democratic presidential contender Joe Biden has said he would "restore the Obama-Biden policy that existed before the *Hobby Lobby* ruling: providing an exemption for houses of worship and an accommodation for nonprofit organizations with religious missions."[126]

Just as *Little Sisters of the Poor* will not lay to rest conflicting claims over the coverage mandate, the holding that broad delegation by Congress supports virtually any agency action (that is not arbitrary or capricious) almost certainly means that administrative whiplash will become commonplace for culture-war clashes.

The traditional theory justifying the existence, enormity, and power of the administrative state is that administrative agencies are technical, scientific bodies whose particular expertise lends itself

---

[126] Nicholas Rowan, "Biden Says He Would Undo Contraception Exemptions for Little Sisters of the Poor," Wash. Exam'r, July 9, 2020, https://washex.am/33M1VAI.

to speedy, yet thoughtful policymaking. In this account, agencies make up for Congress and its characteristic slow pace, lack of expertise on technical matters, and lack of time to address the minutiae of a policy's implementation. This justification for the administrative state is challenged when it comes to culture-war conflicts where moral convictions, not scientific conclusions, often matter most. Further, as culture-war conflicts increasingly dominate presidential politics, the decisionmakers ensconced in agencies by each new administration will carry into their positions pre-existing commitments more and more.[127]

There is a growing appreciation that, like judicial nominations and senior administration appointments, the staffing of agencies has increasingly become a matter of political award or loyalty. Administrative agencies are being staffed more deeply not with subject-matter experts, but with those that share the president's values or come out of the president's base.

New databases examining links to policy groups and groups that supported presidential campaigns find significant permeation into the mechanics of government.[128] Many government actors rotate out of these government positions back to think tanks and lobbying firms, just to return in future administrations. This practice has placed political operatives in key agency positions to influence the outcome of culture-war battles. It would be surprising if such appointees arrived in their roles without significant priors—that is, increasing numbers of agency actors will have worked out positions about the substance of the law appointees are now charged to implement.

Consider one of the key regulators with authority over the coverage mandate, Roger Severino, head of HHS's Office for Civil Rights (OCR). Under Severino, OCR has launched a "new Conscience and Religious Freedom Division," the first federal office for civil rights with a separate division dedicated to ensuring compliance with and enforcement of laws that protect conscience and free exercise

---

[127] See, e.g., Emma Green, "The Man Behind Trump's Religious-Freedom Agenda for Health Care," The Atlantic, June 7, 2017, https://bit.ly/3fKtnBl.

[128] As one example, the Trump Town database contains a list of roughly 263 staffers who formerly worked for Trump campaign groups. Trump Town, ProPublica & Columbia Journalism Investigations (last updated Oct. 15, 2019), https://bit.ly/3gQ9QRi.

of religion.[129] Severino explained the new division was needed because for "too long, governments big and small have treated conscience claims with hostility instead of protection, but change is coming and it begins here and now."[130] During the same news conference, speakers pointed to the federal government "trying to strongarm nuns."[131] Later that year, the departments promulgated the wholesale and moral exemptions.[132]

To his credit, Severino early on disavowed his priors, saying he would "give everything, to the extent humanly possible, a fresh look" and that his "views before coming into this role cannot dictate what [he does] in this role now."[133] Before entering the administration, Severino took positions that rankled civil-rights organizations. "The Human Rights Campaign, for example, called him a 'radical anti-LGBTQ-rights activist' who 'has made it clear that his number-one priority is to vilify and degrade' people who are lesbian, gay, bisexual, and transgender."[134]

This deep suspicion is anchored in Severino's extensive substantive writings, including about the Little Sisters.[135] In a January 2016 report that Severino coauthored with Heritage Foundation colleague Ryan Anderson, who led Heritage's campaign against legalization of same-sex marriage, the pair argued that "'gender identity and sexual orientation . . . are changeable, self-reported, and entirely self-defined characteristics' that do not deserve the protected-class status given to sex, race, and several other categories under federal civil-rights statutes."[136] Upon entering the administration, Severino quickly proposed rescinding the Obama administration rule that defined sex discrimination under the ACA as including

---

[129] Trump Administration Actions to Protect Life and Conscience, Dep't of Health & Human Serv. (Jan. 24, 2020), https://bit.ly/33NWKjY.

[130] Susan Morse, "HHS Announces Conscience and Religious Freedom Division," Healthcare Finance, Jan. 18, 2018, https://bit.ly/3iyEkb7.

[131] *Id.*

[132] Green, *supra* note 127.

[133] *Id.*

[134] *Id.*

[135] Roger Severino & Elizabeth Slattery, "Little Sisters of the Poor Win Big in Obamacare Case," The Daily Signal, May 16, 2016, https://dailysign.al/3gL7CTp.

[136] Green, *supra* note 127.

gender identity; the rule rescinding the Obama approach was finalized on June 12, 2020.[137] Three days later, the Supreme Court disagreed in *Bostock v. Clayton County.* The Court found the bans on
discrimination based on sex necessarily encompass not only sexual
orientation but also gender identity.[138]

But the Office of Civil Rights is charged with enforcing the laws
that together protect Americans' fundamental rights of nondiscrimination, conscience, religious freedom, and health-information privacy, not with making them over wholesale. Whether the Obama
or Trump administration, no one can reasonably doubt that OCR
has impressed a political, nontechnical vision of abortion, contraception, LGBT rights, and other matters in federal law.[139]

OCR is not alone in impressing a political agenda on an agency's
technical work. Just weeks into the Trump administration, Department of Education Acting Assistant Secretary for Civil and Attorney
General for Civil Rights Sandra Battle, together with Acting Assistant Attorney General for Civil Rights T.E. Wheeler, II, rescinded
an Obama-era guidance letter that interpreted Title IX to require
schools to provide transgender students access to bathrooms and
locker rooms according to their gender identity.[140] The Department
of Education has yet to respond to *Bostock*.[141]

The impact of reaching further into administrative agencies with
political appointees is predictable. Loosely speaking, if Democrats
see government as a force for good in people's lives, one can expect that agencies under those administrations will work to extend

---

[137] HHS Finalizes Rule on Section 1557 Protecting Civil Rights in Healthcare, Restoring the Rule of Law, and Relieving Americans of Billions in Excessive Costs, HHS.gov
(June 12, 2020), https://bit.ly/3ipXdNa.

[138] Bostock v. Clayton County, 140 S. Ct. 1731, 1744 (2020) ("When an employer fires
an employee for being homosexual or transgender, it necessarily and intentionally
discriminates against that individual in part because of sex.").

[139] Green, *supra* note 127. For a recent appraisal of OCR's role, see "Majority Staff
Report: Children at Risk: The Trump Administration's Waiver of Foster Care Non-
discrimination Requirements," House Committee on Ways & Means, U.S. House of
Representatives (Aug. 19, 2020).

[140] Dear Colleague Letter, U.S. Department of Justice Civil Rights Division and U.S.
Department of Education Office for Civil Rights (Feb. 22, 2017), https://bit.ly/31KC75E.

[141] Rina Grassotti & Sheila Willis, "What the Supreme Court's LGBTQ Decision May
Mean for Bathroom and Locker Room Access in Title IX Schools: A 4-Step Best Practices Guide," JDSupra, July 15, 2020, https://bit.ly/3h5xVE1.

their influence over more Americans. The Obama administration, for example, produced 7 out of the 10 largest volumes of the *Federal Register*.[142] If Republicans favor more limited government or prize individual freedom from government, one can expect that agencies under those administrations will pull back the net of regulatory coverage, freeing individuals and organizations from government's reach. Indeed, the Trump administration has rescinded scores of regulations touching on topics like environmental policy, drug testing, affirmative action, endangered species, farming, firearms, internet privacy, health care, television, nondiscrimination, fracking, education, abortion, transgender rights, overtime pay, and, of course, the ACA itself.[143]

As administrative agencies flex their authority over culture-war issues, the raison d'être for deference to them as efficient expert bodies is undermined. Assuming agencies take the APA's required procedural steps (and sometimes even when they do not), few practical limits are placed on an administration's shaping or remolding of regulatory schemes. The APA does require evidence-based, reasoned decisionmaking.[144] But by sustaining, under the guise of broad delegation to agencies, approaches that take diametrically opposed moral views of the same question, *Little Sisters of the Poor* undermines the very idea of scientifically arrived-at and evidence-based judgments guiding our agencies.

Parties are increasingly turning to litigation to stall, or stop altogether, the effect of new, rescinded, or reshaped regulations. Some presidential administrations may never see their administrative restyling take effect. The Trump administration is a prime example. Consider the sheer number of major administrative decisions under President Trump that have been met with a lawsuit.[145] The

---

[142] Clyde Wayne Crews, "Obama's Legacy: 2016 Ends with a Record-Shattering Regulatory Rulebook," Forbes, Dec. 30, 2016, https://bit.ly/2XNBuHa.

[143] Interactive: Tracking Deregulation in the Trump Era, The Brookings Inst., https://brook.gs/3fKzHJc.

[144] Little Sisters of the Poor, 140 S. Ct. at 2385–86.

[145] Roundup: Trump-Era Agency Policy in the Courts, Inst. for Pol'y Integrity (July 27, 2020), https://bit.ly/3aaXvom; see, e.g., Trump Lawsuit Tracker, Center for Biological Diversity (July 2020), https://bit.ly/2XPXX6i (noting that a single environmental group has filed 214 lawsuits against Trump and has "won 9 out of every 10 resolved cases").

administrative state, far from being seen as efficient and expert, is marked by delay and contempt.

Conclusion

The coverage mandate held the promise of having it both ways: providing meaningful access for women to contraceptives that give control over their lives and ability to work while respecting America's durable détente over abortion and respect for religious belief and conscience. These values could have been, and still may be, reconciled.

Yet deciding what the ACA demanded in terms of preventive care and screenings became an occasion for agencies to stamp very different visions of what matters into the law: that women's reproductive access should be prized above all else, or that religious autonomy should be prized over women's interests. As agencies become the locus for a constant push and pull over culture-war questions, the justification for deferring to them as nonpartisan technocrats recedes.

Ultimately, *Little Sisters of the Poor* is a case about statutory interpretation. Just as the Obama administration was authorized by Congress to create the coverage mandate, the Trump administration is authorized by Congress to gut it, the Court held. The net effect of the *Little Sisters of the Poor* will be to permanently ensconce the administrative state in the culture war. Despite their "long ordeal," the Little Sisters of the Poor almost certainly will be back before the Court.[146]

---

[146] Christensen Smith, "Pennsylvania AG Says 'Fight Not Over' after SCOTUS Upholds Affordable Care Act Birth Control Exemptions," The Center Square, July 8, 2020, https://bit.ly/3kqZKsp.

The Disingenuous Demise and Death of *Bivens*

Stephen I. Vladeck*

If you read only Justice Samuel Alito's majority opinion or Justice Clarence Thomas's concurrence in the Supreme Court's February 2020 ruling in *Hernández v. Mesa* ("*Hernández II*"), you might think that the Court's 1971 decision in *Bivens v. Six Unknown Named Agents of the Federal Bureau of Narcotics* was, among other things, a bolt from the blue; an indefensible judicial "usurpation of the legislative power"; and "a relic of the heady days in which [the Supreme] Court assumed common-law powers to create causes of action."[1]

In *Bivens*, of course, the Supreme Court recognized at least some circumstances in which federal courts can and should fashion a judge-made damages remedy for constitutional violations by federal officers.[2] And even though a claim under *Bivens* is often the *only* possible remedy today for those whose constitutional rights are violated by federal officers, it has become an article of faith among conservative jurists and commentators that *Bivens* was wrongly decided.[3] Against that backdrop, *Hernández II*—in which the Court refused to recognize a *Bivens* remedy for the parents of a 15-year-old Mexican national who was shot and killed (allegedly without provocation) while standing in Mexico by a U.S. Border Patrol agent standing

---

* A. Dalton Cross Professor in Law, University of Texas School of Law. I was counsel of record in the Supreme Court for—and argued on behalf of—the Petitioners in Hernández v. Mesa, 140 S. Ct. 735 (2020) ("Hernández II"). The views expressed in this essay are mine alone and do not necessarily represent those of either the Petitioners or their (other) counsel.

[1] Hernández v. Mesa, 140 S. Ct. 735, 750 (2020) (Thomas, J., concurring) (internal quotations and citations omitted). I use "*Hernández II*" throughout this essay to distinguish the 2020 ruling from the Court's earlier decision in the same case with the same caption, Hernández v. Mesa, 137 S. Ct. 2003 (2017) (per curiam) ("Hernández I").

[2] 403 U.S. 388 (1971).

[3] See, e.g., Corr. Servs. Corp. v. Malesko, 534 U.S. 61, 74 (2001) (Scalia, J., concurring).

on U.S. soil—appears to be an easy case. Even though the Court assumed, as it had to, that the shooting was unconstitutional, it nevertheless held that the parents were not entitled to any remedy under U.S. law.

The problem with *Hernández II* is that, like the conservative case against *Bivens* more generally, it rests on two distinct analytical moves that simply don't withstand meaningful scrutiny. First, for the proposition that *Bivens* is an arrogation of legislative power, both the majority and concurring opinions rest on a stunningly superficial reading of the Supreme Court's landmark 1938 ruling in *Erie R.R. Co. v. Tompkins*—which disclaimed the power of the federal courts to fashion *general* common law, but which in no way repudiated the federal courts' lawmaking authority (and responsibility) in *specific* classes of cases.[4] Indeed, the Supreme Court today often fashions and applies federal common law to satisfy unique and uniquely important federal interests, *including* in damages suits against federal officers; the question in *Hernández II* should have been whether judicial recognition of *Bivens* remedies is similarly justified.

Second, even if *Bivens* remedies can't be justified solely under what Judge Henry Friendly famously called the "new federal common law,"[5] the *Hernández II* opinions—and conservative attacks on *Bivens*—almost entirely fail to grapple with the availability and relevance of constitutional remedies against federal officers under *state* tort law. After all, in *Bivens* itself, the federal government's position was not that the plaintiff should have no remedy; it was that he had an adequate remedy for the Fourth Amendment violation under New York trespass law—a remedy that traced all the way back to the Founding.[6] But state tort law, which routinely provided a means of redress against federal officers well into the 20th century, is no longer an option in most cases today because of the Westfall Act—a 1988 statute that has been interpreted to preempt *all* state tort claims against federal officers acting within the scope of their employment.[7]

---

[4] 304 U.S. 64 (1938).

[5] Henry J. Friendly, In Praise of Erie—and of the New Federal Common Law, 39 N.Y.U. L. Rev. 383 (1964).

[6] See Brief for the Respondents at 34–40, Bivens v. Six Unknown Named Agents of the Fed. Bureau of Narcotics, 403 U.S. 388 (1971) (No. 301), 1970 WL 116900.

[7] 28 U.S.C. § 2679(b); see Carlos M. Vázquez & Stephen I. Vladeck, State Law, the Westfall Act, and the Nature of the Bivens Question, 161 U. Pa. L. Rev. 509 (2013).

In a case like *Hernández II*, then, it's *Bivens* or nothing. By taking away state remedies in cases arising out of federal constitutional violations in which no alternatives are available, the Westfall Act raises an undeniably serious Fifth Amendment due process question. But even though that precise question was presented to the justices in *Hernández II*, they ignored it twice—first by refusing to grant certiorari on the issue and then by refusing to grapple with the implications for the Westfall Act of their *Bivens* analysis. Reasonable minds may still conclude that, these omissions notwithstanding, the Court reached the right result in *Hernández II*. The purpose of this essay is to explain that, if nothing else, it certainly shouldn't have been that easy.

I. *Hernández II*: The Factual Background

Hernández II arose out of an allegedly unprovoked cross-border shooting[8]—in which, while on duty along the Texas-Mexico border, U.S. Border Patrol Agent Jesus Mesa Jr. shot and killed Sergio Adrián Hernández Güereca while Hernández was standing on Mexican soil. Hernández's parents brought a damages action against Mesa in federal district court, alleging that Mesa's conduct violated both the Fourth Amendment and the Due Process Clause of the Fifth Amendment.

In *Hernández I*, a three-judge panel of the Fifth Circuit held that, as a noncitizen standing on foreign soil, Hernández was not protected by the Fourth Amendment. But it held that the shooting *did* violate the Due Process Clause of the Fifth Amendment, that a *Bivens* remedy was available for the parents' Fifth Amendment claim, and that Agent Mesa was not entitled to qualified immunity.[9] On rehearing en banc, the Fifth Circuit held—unanimously—that Mesa *was* entitled to qualified immunity because it was not "clearly established" that Hernández was protected by the Constitution at all, sidestepping the more contested *Bivens* and merits questions.[10]

In June 2017, the Supreme Court vacated the Fifth Circuit's ruling. Among other things, the per curiam opinion held that Mesa was not

---

[8] Even though the case reached the Supreme Court on appeal of the grant of a motion to dismiss (in a posture in which the well-pleaded allegations in the complaint are supposed to be taken as true), Justice Alito's majority opinion instead treated the facts as disputed. See Hernández II, 140 S. Ct. at 740 & n.1.

[9] Hernández v. United States, 757 F.3d 249 (5th Cir. 2014).

[10] Hernández v. United States, 785 F.3d 117 (5th Cir. 2015) (en banc).

entitled to qualified immunity on the theory adopted by the Fifth Circuit because Mesa did not know, at the time he pulled the trigger, that Hernández was a noncitizen with no connections to the United States.[11] The justices returned the case to the Fifth Circuit for reconsideration in light of its intervening decision in *Ziglar v. Abbasi*—which had further refined (and narrowed) the proper framework in *Bivens* cases.[12]

On remand in *Hernández II*, the en banc Fifth Circuit held, by a 12-2 vote, that no remedy was available under *Bivens*. Writing for the majority, Judge Edith Jones first emphasized that the parents' claims arose in a "new context," in which recognition of *Bivens* remedies is "disfavored." She then identified three "special factors"—"national security," "foreign relations," and "extraterritoriality"—that all militated against recognition of a judge-made damages remedy.[13]

Given the terms of the remand in *Hernández I*, matters might have ended there. But while the petition for certiorari in *Hernández II* was pending, the Ninth Circuit, in an eerily similar cross-border shooting case, reached the opposite conclusion—holding that a *Bivens* remedy *was* available for an allegedly unconstitutional cross-border shooting by a Customs and Border Protection officer.[14] After calling for the views of the solicitor general (who recommended granting certiorari in *Hernández II*), the Court granted certiorari in May 2019, and heard argument on November 12.

On February 25, 2020, the Court sided with the Fifth Circuit. Writing for a 5-4 majority, Justice Alito agreed that the claims in *Hernández II* arose in a "new context," and largely echoed the Fifth Circuit's special-factors analysis—holding that recognition of a *Bivens* remedy in such a case might impinge on foreign relations and undermine border security.[15] Concurring, Justice Thomas, joined by Justice Neil Gorsuch, would have "abandoned [*Bivens*] altogether."[16] Justice Ruth Bader Ginsburg, joined by Justices Stephen Breyer,

---

[11] Hernández I, 137 S. Ct. 2003. Three justices dissented. Justices Breyer and Ginsburg would have resolved the case by holding that the Fourth Amendment applies—and remanding for further proceedings. Justice Thomas would have held that no *Bivens* remedy was available.

[12] 137 S. Ct. 1843 (2017).

[13] Hernández v. Mesa, 885 F.3d 811 (5th Cir. 2018) (en banc).

[14] Rodriguez v. Swartz, 899 F.3d 719 (9th Cir. 2018).

[15] Hernández II, 140 S. Ct. at 743–50.

[16] *Id.* at 750–53 (Thomas, J., concurring).

Sonia Sotomayor, and Elena Kagan, dissented, explaining that, even if the parents' claims arose in a "new context,"

> plaintiffs lack recourse to alternative remedies, and no "special factors" counsel against a *Bivens* remedy. Neither U.S. foreign policy nor national security is in fact endangered by the litigation. Moreover, concerns attending the application of our law to conduct occurring abroad are not involved, for plaintiffs seek the application of U.S. law to conduct occurring inside our borders.[17]

On the surface, then, *Hernández II* comes across as a fairly routine dispute among the justices about how to apply their existing precedents to a new set of facts. In fact, the backstory is far more complicated—and the potential implications of the Court's ruling are far more significant.

II. The Road to *Bivens*

At the Founding, and for much of American history, there was no question as to whether federal courts had the power to provide judge-made damages remedies against individual federal officers. Not only did federal courts routinely provide such relief, but the Supreme Court repeatedly blessed the practice.

In *Little v. Barreme*, for example, the Court, in an opinion by Chief Justice John Marshall, held a U.S. Navy officer liable for trespass after he seized a neutral ship pursuant to an invalid presidential order. As Marshall explained: "If [an officer's] instructions [from the executive branch] afford him no protection, then the law must take its course, and he must pay such damages as are legally awarded against him. . . ."[18] To similar effect was *Wise v. Withers*. There, the Court considered an action for trespass in which the defendant federal officer had entered the plaintiff's home to collect a fine that had been (improperly) imposed by a court-martial. Because the court-martial had no jurisdiction, "[t]he court and the officer [were] all trespassers" and were subject to a judge-made damages remedy.[19] Likewise, *Slocum v. Mayberry* held that a customs officer who had no authority to seize cargo was properly subject to suit in Rhode Island

---

[17] *Id.* at 753 (Ginsburg, J., dissenting).
[18] 6 U.S. (2 Cranch) 170, 178 (1804).
[19] 7 U.S. (3 Cranch) 331, 337 (1806).

state court. As Chief Justice Marshall wrote for a unanimous Court, "the act of congress neither expressly, nor by implication, forbids the state courts to take cognizance of suits instituted for property in possession of an officer of the United States not detained under some law of the United States; consequently, their jurisdiction remains."[20]

And in considering a tort action brought by the master of a French ship that had been seized by a U.S. official while in Spanish waters, Justice Joseph Story's opinion for the Court in *The Apollon* dismissed the diplomatic ramifications, explaining that "this Court can only look to the questions, whether the laws have been violated; and if they were, justice demands, that the injured party should receive a suitable redress." Because the seizure in question was "wholly without justification under our laws," the U.S. official could not avoid plaintiff's common-law damages claim—even though the seizure took place outside the territorial United States.[21]

In *Elliott v. Swartwout*, the justices reviewed an assumpsit claim against a customs official who had collected duties from the plaintiff, despite the plaintiff's challenge to the collection. Because the relevant statute did not authorize the collection, the Court held that the defendant was personally liable.[22] And *Mitchell v. Harmony* affirmed a jury verdict awarding damages in a diversity case against a U.S. Army lieutenant colonel who, pursuant to direction from his commanding officer, unlawfully seized the plaintiff's goods. There, the Court observed that "the law did not confide to [the defendant's commanding officer] a discretionary power over private property"; as such, the order was "to do an illegal act; to commit a trespass upon the property of another."[23]

There was no suggestion in any of these early, seminal cases that federal courts lacked the authority or ability to fashion such judge-made tort remedies against rogue federal officers—including, in the years after *Swift v. Tyson*,[24] remedies arising under the general common law rather than state law. The only recurring issue in these cases was whether the claims properly belonged in state or federal court, a statutory jurisdictional issue that evolved as Congress initially enacted—and later expanded—the federal officer removal statute.

---

[20] 15 U.S. (2 Wheat.) 1, 12 (1817).

[21] 22 U.S. (9 Wheat.) 362, 367, 372 (1824).

[22] 35 U.S. (10 Pet.) 137, 158 (1836).

[23] 54 U.S. (13 How.) 115, 137 (1852).

[24] 41 U.S. (16 Pet.) 1 (1842).

Actions against federal officials for common-law torts remained routine throughout the 19th century. For example, in *Buck v. Colbath*, the Supreme Court affirmed the plaintiff's ability to bring a trespass action against a federal marshal, "[seeing] nothing . . . to prevent the marshal from being sued in the State court, in trespass for his own tort, in levying [the writ] upon the property of a man against whom the writ did not run, and on property which was not liable to it."[25] And in *Bates v. Clark*, the justices affirmed a judgment finding U.S. Army officers liable for trespass when they seized the plaintiff's goods without lawful authority.[26]

Twenty years later, the Court again reiterated that federal officials could be held personally liable for actions exceeding their authority through common-law tort suits. In *Belknap v. Schild*, the plaintiff sued U.S. naval officers for patent infringement. As Justice Horace Gray wrote in sustaining the plaintiff's claims,

> the exemption of the United States from judicial process does not protect their officers and agents . . . from being personally liable to an action of tort by a private person whose rights of property they have wrongfully invaded or injured, even by authority of the United States. Such officers or agents . . . are therefore personally liable to be sued for their own infringement of a patent.[27]

And so it continued—even after the Supreme Court's 1938 decision in *Erie*. As late as 1963, the Supreme Court would explain that, "[w]hen it comes to suits for damages for abuse of power, federal officials are usually governed by local law," even when the case was brought in or removed to federal court.[28] And none of these cases—from 1804 onwards, and to either side of *Erie*—voiced the slightest objection to the constitutional or normative propriety of federal courts fashioning such judge-made remedies.

If anything, "the Court [also] appears to have treated trespass remedies against the wrongdoing governmental actor—with their deep roots in the common law—as existing independent of the will of the legislature and as resistant to state legislative and

25 70 U.S. (3 Wall.) 334, 347 (1866).

26 95 U.S. 204, 209 (1877).

27 161 U.S. 10, 18 (1896) (citation omitted).

28 Wheeldin v. Wheeler, 373 U.S. 647, 652 (1963).

judicial uprooting."[29] Remedies against federal officers were therefore not viewed as being committed to the states' grace, and the Court suggested that in some cases "the existence of the common law tort action for certain types of official invasions of liberty or property may itself be a constitutional requirement."[30]

This pattern of judge-made tort remedies against rogue federal officers included cases in which the plaintiff's underlying claim was that the defendant had violated the Constitution. As the justices explained in 1949, "if [wrongful actions by federal officers] are such as to create a personal liability, whether sounding in tort or in contract, the fact that the officer is an instrumentality of the sovereign does not . . . forbid a court from taking jurisdiction over a suit against him."[31] Indeed, "the principle that an agent is liable for his own torts is an ancient one and applies even to certain acts of public officers or public instrumentalities."[32] Federal officers might have had defenses to such actions arising under the Constitution, statutes, or the common law, but the power of the courts to provide a common-law damages remedy in the abstract was taken as a given.[33]

III. *Bivens* and Its Aftermath

With that in mind, consider how Justice Anthony Kennedy, writing for a 4-2 majority (with three justices not participating) in *Ziglar v. Abbasi*, described the origins of *Bivens* in 2017:

> In 1871, Congress passed a statute that was later codified at 42 U.S.C. § 1983. It entitles an injured person to money damages if a state official violates his or her constitutional rights.

[29] Ann Woolhandler, The Common-Law Origins of Constitutionally Compelled Remedies, 107 Yale L.J. 77, 123 (1997) (footnote omitted).

[30] *Id.* at 121 (citing Poindexter v. Greenhow, 114 U.S. 270, 303 (1885)); cf. Harper v. Va. Dep't of Taxation, 509 U.S. 86, 101 (1993) (holding that the Due Process Clause of the Fourteenth Amendment requires states without adequate pre-deprivation tax-refund remedies "to provide meaningful backward-looking relief to rectify any unconstitutional deprivation") (internal quotation marks omitted).

[31] Larson v. Domestic & Foreign Com. Corp., 337 U.S. 682, 686 (1949) (citations omitted).

[32] *Id.* at 687 (citations omitted).

[33] See, e.g., Barr v. Matteo, 360 U.S. 564 (1959); cf. Armstrong v. Exceptional Child Ctr., Inc., 575 U.S. 320, 327 (2015) (noting the "long history of judicial review of illegal executive action, tracing back to England").

> Congress did not create an analogous statute for federal officials. Indeed, in the 100 years leading up to *Bivens*, Congress did not provide a specific damages remedy for plaintiffs whose constitutional rights were violated by agents of the Federal Government.

> In 1971, *and against this background*, this Court decided *Bivens*.[34]

In fact, *Bivens* was decided against a rich doctrinal background in which state tort law provided the principal mechanism for holding federal officers accountable, even for constitutional violations. In *Bivens*, the Supreme Court granted certiorari to decide whether, even after *Erie*, there were circumstances in which an allegation that a rogue federal officer had violated the Constitution stated a federal cause of action for damages—not just a claim under state law.[35] In arguing that the answer was no, the solicitor general repeatedly pointed to the tradition of holding federal officers to account under state law— and why that tradition rendered a federal remedy unnecessary.[36]

In contrast, where a federal remedy was necessary to vindicate a plaintiff's constitutional rights, including where a plaintiff had no state tort remedy against the offending federal officer, the solicitor general agreed that federal courts had the power—and obligation— to fashion such relief on their own, and, indeed, that they had been doing so for decades.[37] The question in *Bivens* was therefore whether a federal damages remedy truly was "indispensable" for vindicating constitutional rights. In the government's view, the availability of New York tort law proved that the answer was "no."

Justice William Brennan's majority opinion disagreed that the availability of a state claim precluded a judge-made federal damages remedy. But as Justice John Marshall Harlan II pointed out in

---

[34] 137 S. Ct. at 1854 (emphasis added).

[35] See Bell v. Hood, 327 U.S. 678, 684 (1946) (reserving this question).

[36] Brief for the Respondents, *supra* note 6, at 33–38.

[37] See, e.g., *id*. at 19 ("[T]he judicially created federal remedy under the Constitution was essential to protect against infringement of secured rights."); *id*. at 24 ("[C]auses of action under the Constitution in the absence of a statutory basis have been created only in the rare case where such a remedy was indispensable for vindicating constitutional rights."); *id*. at 40 ("In the absence of implementing legislation, judicial creation of a new, affirmative remedy to enforce a constitutional right should not be undertaken unless such a remedy is absolutely necessary.").

his opinion concurring in the judgment, the dispute the Court was resolving was therefore one grounded in federalism more than the separation of powers—whether the liability of federal officers for violations of the Constitution should depend upon 50 different state tort regimes or one uniform body of federal judge-made law. Framed in those terms, the case for a federal remedy was, in Harlan's view, compelling:

> It seems to me entirely proper that these injuries be compensable according to uniform rules of federal law, especially in light of the very large element of federal law which must in any event control the scope of official defenses to liability. Certainly, there is very little to be gained from the standpoint of federalism by preserving different rules of liability for federal officers dependent on the State where the injury occurs.[38]

Whoever had the better of the argument concerning whether a judge-made federal remedy was preferable to a judge-made state remedy, the relevant point for present purposes is that no one in *Bivens* thought that the choice the Court was making was between a *Bivens* remedy and nothing. So framed—in terms of federalism as much as the separation of powers—*Bivens* looks quite a bit different.[39]

As is by now familiar, the Court expanded *Bivens* twice over the next decade. In *Davis v. Passman*, the Court sustained a *Bivens* claim by a former congressional staffer who claimed unconstitutional discrimination on the basis of sex in violation of the Due Process Clause of the Fifth Amendment.[40] And one year later, in *Carlson v. Green*, the Court allowed a federal prisoner's estate to bring an Eighth Amendment claim against his jailers for inadequate medical treatment that contributed to his untimely death. Even though the plaintiff could also have brought a claim under the Federal Tort Claims Act, the Court held that the act did not displace *Bivens*.[41] As Justice

---

[38] Bivens, 403 U.S. at 409 (Harlan, J., concurring in the judgment) (citations omitted); see also *id.* (questioning "the desirability of leaving the problem of federal official liability to the vagaries of common-law actions").

[39] See generally Stephen I. Vladeck, Constitutional Remedies in Federalism's Forgotten Shadow, 107 Cal. L. Rev. 1043 (2019).

[40] 442 U.S. 228 (1979).

[41] 446 U.S. 14 (1980).

Brennan explained, no special factors counseled hesitation because federal officials "do not enjoy such independent status in our constitutional scheme as to suggest that judicially created remedies against them might be inappropriate." And "we have here no explicit congressional declaration that persons injured by federal officers' violations of the Eighth Amendment may not recover money damages from the agents but must be remitted to another remedy, equally effective in the view of Congress."[42] In other words, *Bivens* was to be the rule and cases in which *Bivens* was unavailable were to be the exception.

In retrospect, *Carlson* was the doctrinal high-water mark. In 10 subsequent decisions over the next 37 years, the Court gradually—but consistently—scaled back *Bivens* until almost nothing was left. And the first lever the Court used to narrow *Bivens* was the putative availability of alternative remedies.

In *Bush v. Lucas,* for instance, the Court declined to recognize a *Bivens* claim by a government employee claiming that he was subject to retaliatory employment action in violation of the First Amendment, holding that the modest relief provided by the Civil Service Reform Act of 1978 displaced *Bivens*—even though Congress had not said as much and the remedies available under the statute were hardly commensurate with the relief available under *Bivens*.[43]

To similar effect was the Court's decision five years later in *Schweiker v. Chilicky,* which refused to recognize a *Bivens* claim for wrongful denial of social security benefits in violation of the Due Process Clause of the Fifth Amendment. Even though Congress had not expressly displaced *Bivens* through the Social Security Act, and even though the only "remedy" available under that statute was the restoration of wrongly terminated benefits, the Court held that the alternative was sufficient to displace *Bivens*.[44]

More recently, the Court has held that the alternative remedy can even come from *state* law. Thus, in *Minneci v. Pollard,* the Court refused to recognize an Eighth Amendment *Bivens* claim against *private* corrections officers largely because, as nonfederal employees, they could be sued under California tort law. Even though *Bivens*

---

[42] *Id.* at 19.

[43] 462 U.S. 367 (1983).

[44] 487 U.S. 412 (1988).

itself had rejected the government's claim that the availability of state tort remedies mooted the need for a federal cause of action, by 2012, the availability of such state remedies was enough for every justice except Justice Ginsburg to eschew a federal judge-made cause of action.[45]

But perhaps the real shift in the Court's *Bivens* jurisprudence came in its "special factors" cases—as the justices found more and more reasons to decline to recognize *Bivens* remedies even in the absence of alternatives. At first, the only special factors the Court identified was interference with the military—which led the Court to decline to recognize *Bivens* claims by servicemembers in *Chappell v. Wallace*[46] and *United States v. Stanley.*[47] That logic expanded to encompass claims against federal *agencies* (as opposed to federal officers) in *FDIC v. Meyer,*[48] and claims against private corporations in *Correctional Services Corporation v. Malesko.*[49] None of these cases involved nonservicemember plaintiffs suing individual federal officers, but the Court's growing hostility to *all Bivens* claims was increasingly difficult to miss. Thus, in *Malesko,* Justices Antonin Scalia and Thomas for the first time argued that *Bivens* should be limited to its facts, pointing to the Court's contemporaneous scaling back of implied *statutory* causes of action:

> *Bivens* is a relic of the heady days in which this Court assumed common-law powers to create causes of action— decreeing them to be "implied" by the mere existence of a statutory or constitutional prohibition. As the Court points out, we have abandoned that power to invent "implications" in the statutory field. There is even greater reason to abandon it in the constitutional field, since an "implication" imagined in the Constitution can presumably not even be repudiated by Congress.[50]

---

[45] 565 U.S. 118 (2012).

[46] 462 U.S. 296 (1983).

[47] 483 U.S. 669 (1987).

[48] 510 U.S. 471 (1994).

[49] 534 U.S. 61 (2001).

[50] *Id.* at 75 (Scalia, J., concurring) (citations omitted). For why the analogy between *Bivens* and implied statutory causes of action does not hold, see Stephen I. Vladeck, Bivens Remedies and the Myth of the "Heady Days," 8 U. St. Thomas L.J. 513 (2011).

After *Malesko,* the Court extended its hostility to *Bivens* even to suits against individual federal officers. *Wilkie v. Robbins* declined to recognize a *Bivens* claim against Bureau of Land Management employees who allegedly used extortion in an attempt to force the plaintiff to grant an easement to the federal government.[51] *Ashcroft v. Iqbal* categorically foreclosed *Bivens* claims based upon a theory of supervisory liability—noting that recognition of a *Bivens* claim had become a "disfavored" judicial activity.[52] And *Hui v. Castaneda* held that a statute that did not provide an alternative remedy, but instead provided immunity from *other* federal claims, also foreclosed a *Bivens* claim.[53]

These trendlines came to a head in *Ziglar v. Abbasi,* a case arising out of the post-9/11 immigration roundup of hundreds of Muslim men and men of Arab descent in and around the New York City metropolitan area. The plaintiffs in *Abbasi* sued six senior government officials—including Attorney General John Ashcroft and FBI Director Robert Mueller—claiming that various aspects of their detention and administrative segregation while detained were unconstitutional.[54]

Ignoring the history described above, Justice Kennedy went out of his way to narrow the circumstances in which a *Bivens* remedy would be appropriate. Building on *dicta* from *Malesko, Abbasi* held that plaintiffs cannot use *Bivens* as a means of challenging government policy, and that the plaintiffs' claims also presented "special factors" counseling hesitation insofar as (1) they implicated "sensitive issues of national security"; (2) Congress had been silent on the specific question of remedies like those sought by the plaintiffs; and (3) the plaintiffs had an alternative remedy while they were subject to detention—even though it was likely an illusory one. *Abbasi* thereby conflated the alternative-remedy and special-factors analyses, and also opened the door to treating national security as a special factor in any case remotely touching upon the subject. More generally, *Abbasi* made clear that the special-factors inquiry "must concentrate on whether the Judiciary is well suited, absent congressional

---

51 551 U.S. 537 (2007).

52 556 U.S. 662 (2009).

53 559 U.S. 799 (2010).

54 Abbasi, 137 S. Ct. 1843.

action or instruction, to consider and weigh the costs and benefits of allowing a damages action to proceed," an analysis that will, in almost all cases, militate in favor of judicial passivity.[55]

For all of that, though, *Abbasi* also reinforced the significance of that part of *Bivens* it preserved. As Justice Kennedy explained,

> this opinion is not intended to cast doubt on the continued force, or even the necessity, of *Bivens* in the search-and-seizure context in which it arose. *Bivens* does vindicate the Constitution by allowing some redress for injuries, and it provides instruction and guidance to federal law enforcement officers going forward. The settled law of *Bivens* in this common and recurrent sphere of law enforcement, and the undoubted reliance upon it as a fixed principle in the law, are powerful reasons to retain it in that sphere.[56]

Thus, even as it took as skeptical an approach to *Bivens* as any majority opinion by the Court to date, the *Abbasi* Court went out of its way to suggest that *Bivens* would still be available to challenge "individual instances of discrimination or law enforcement overreach, which due to their very nature are difficult to address except by way of damages actions after the fact."[57]

IV. *Hernández II* and/as the Conservative Critique of *Bivens*

Enter, *Hernández II*—which, all agree, involved a challenge to an "individual instance[] of . . . law enforcement overreach." Without so much as noting the preceding language from *Abbasi*, the majority held that the plaintiffs' claims arose in a "new context," and that three separate special factors—"national security," "foreign relations," and congressional inaction—all militated against recognition of a *Bivens* remedy.[58] As noted above, Justice Thomas, joined by Justice Gorsuch, wrote separately to note that he would have just overruled *Bivens*, claiming that "[t]he analysis underlying *Bivens* cannot be defended."[59]

---

[55] *Id.* at 1857–58.

[56] *Id.* at 1856–57.

[57] *Id.* at 1862.

[58] Hernández II, 140 S. Ct. at 743–48.

[59] *Id.* at 752 (Thomas, J., concurring).

Writing for herself and Justices Breyer, Sotomayor, and Kagan, Justice Ginsburg dissented. But the thrust of her relatively mild opinion was to dispute the majority's special-factors analysis—noting how closely the claims in *Hernández II* resembled those in *Bivens*, save for "the fortuity that the bullet happened to strike Hernández on the Mexican side of the embankment," and noting the significance of the fact that the plaintiffs in *Hernández II* had no other remedy.[60]

In the process, *Hernández II* settled that *Abbasi* did not mean what it said when it refused to cast doubt on the continued availability of redress for injuries caused by garden-variety abuses of power by federal officials. And, for the first time, the Court declined to recognize a *Bivens* claim against a rogue federal law enforcement officer. But the Court also finally grappled with the doctrinal and analytical origins of its hostility to *Bivens*—albeit in a way that raises more questions than it answered.

Tellingly, none of the conservative critiques of *Bivens*, none of the Court's decisions prior to *Hernández II*, and neither Justice Alito's nor Justice Thomas's opinion in *Hernández II* disputes the history surveyed above or the conclusion that federal courts, from the Founding and well into the 20th century, routinely recognized and/or fashioned judge-made damages remedies against federal officers in appropriate cases. For those methodologically committed to originalism as a means of interpreting the Constitution, there is little doubt that the original public meaning of the Constitution was one in which state judge-made tort remedies were of central importance in holding federal officers—and, through them, the federal government—accountable. Indeed, if the lower federal courts were themselves optional under the Constitution's text, how could it have been any other way?[61]

---

[60] *Id.* at 756–59 (Ginsburg, J., dissenting).

[61] See Henry M. Hart, Jr., The Power of Congress to Limit the Jurisdiction of Federal Courts: An Exercise in Dialectic, 66 Harv. L. Rev. 1362, 1401 (1953) ("In the scheme of the Constitution, [state courts] are the primary guarantors of constitutional rights, and in many cases they may be the ultimate ones."); see also Browder v. City of Albuquerque, 787 F.3d 1076, 1084 (10th Cir. 2015) (Gorsuch, J., concurring) ("Often, after all, there's no need to turn federal courts into common law courts and imagine a whole new tort jurisprudence under the rubric of § 1983 and the Constitution in order to vindicate fundamental rights when we have state courts ready and willing to vindicate those same rights using a deep and rich common law that's been battle tested through the centuries.").

Most of the critiques simply ignore these historical precedents and originalist arguments. But in *Hernández II*, the Court for the first time at least offered one explanation for why they are irrelevant: *Erie*. As Justice Alito wrote,

> *Erie* held that "[t]here is no federal general common law," and therefore federal courts today cannot fashion new claims in the way that they could before 1938. With the demise of federal general common law, a federal court's authority to recognize a damages remedy must rest at bottom on a statute enacted by Congress, and no statute expressly creates a *Bivens* remedy.[62]

The first sentence is unquestionably correct. But the second sentence does not follow from the first, for *Erie* did not generally repudiate the federal courts' power to fashion common law; it merely repudiated the power to do so generally. On the same day as *Erie*, and in dozens of decisions since, the Supreme Court has recognized circumstances in which federal common-law-making remains appropriate—including in cases implicating "the rights and obligations of the United States," even if the United States itself is not a party.[63] As Justice Scalia wrote for the majority in one such case, "[a]nother area that we have found to be of peculiarly federal concern, warranting the [judicial] displacement of state law, is the civil liability of federal officials for actions taken in the course of their duty."[64] Although the cases Scalia cited all involved the fashioning of federal common-law immunity defenses, the same considerations govern the availability of a cause of action— for the cause of action likewise implicates "the civil liability of federal officials for actions taken in the course of their duty." And as Justice Harlan noted in his opinion concurring in the judgment in *Bivens*, in deciding between subjecting federal officers to the vagaries of 50 different state tort regimes and one uniform body of federal common law, the case for a federal common-law rule is especially compelling.[65]

---

[62] Hernández II, 140 S. Ct. at 742 (majority op.) (citations omitted); cf. Jesner v. Arab Bank, PLC, 138 S. Ct. 1386, 1413 n.1 (2018) (Gorsuch, J., concurring in part and concurring in the judgment) (tracing the modern Court's hostility to judge-made remedies back to *Erie*).

[63] Tex. Indus., Inc. v. Radcliff Materials, Inc., 451 U.S. 630, 641 (1981).

[64] Boyle v. United Techs. Corp., 487 U.S. 500, 505 (1988).

[65] Bivens, 403 U.S. at 409 (Harlan, J., concurring in the judgment).

Indeed, even as the Supreme Court has shown increasing hostility toward judge-made remedies, it has continued to identify circumstances in which they are appropriate, if not affirmatively necessary. As Justice Scalia explained five years ago with regard to prospective relief, "[t]he ability to sue to enjoin unconstitutional actions by state and federal officers is the creation of courts of equity, and reflects a long history of judicial review of illegal executive action, tracing back to England," and, presumably, uninterrupted by *Erie*.[66] Why should the ability to sue to obtain *damages* for unconstitutional actions by federal officers be any different? Neither Justice Alito's majority opinion nor Justice Thomas's concurrence in *Hernández II* answers that question.

V. The Unnoticed Shadow of the Westfall Act

It would be one thing, of course, if the evisceration of *Bivens* returned the doctrine to the status quo circa 1971—in which federal officers were routinely subjected to damages liability under state tort law. Indeed, even after *Bivens*, victims of constitutional violations by federal officers could still pursue relief under state law separate and apart from a damages claim grounded directly in the Constitution.[67] Thus, the unsatisfying reliance upon *Erie* as the hook for criticizing *Bivens* might not be so problematic if the result were simply to remit plaintiffs to claims under state tort law.

But things changed in 1988, when Congress enacted the Westfall Act, which specifies that the Federal Tort Claims Act "is exclusive of any other civil action or proceeding for money damages by reason of the same subject matter against the employee whose act or omission gave rise to the claim or against the estate of such employee."[68] To be sure, the Westfall Act expressly carved out "a civil action against an employee of the government . . . which is brought for a violation of the Constitution of the United States."[69] Nevertheless, courts and commentators have generally assumed that this language only preserves *Bivens* suits—and not *state*-law constitutional tort suits against federal officers that are consistent with the pre-*Bivens* model.[70]

---

[66] Armstrong, 575 U.S. at 327.

[67] See, e.g., Westfall v. Erwin, 484 U.S. 292, 297–98 (1988).

[68] 28 U.S.C. § 2679(b)(1).

[69] *Id.* § 2679(b)(2)(A).

[70] See, e.g., Hui, 559 U.S. at 807.

So construed, the Westfall Act has had the effect of eliminating *all* state-law constitutional tort claims against federal officers within the scope of their employment. As a result, in cases in which there is no alternative federal legal remedy for the violation, the Westfall Act does not just leave plaintiffs with a choice between "damages or nothing"; it leaves courts to choose between *Bivens* or nothing. And although the Court has heard over a dozen *Bivens* cases (including six since the Westfall Act was enacted), *Hernández II* was the first case the justices considered in which, thanks to the Westfall Act, the choice really was *Bivens* or bust.

The Westfall Act should therefore have factored into the analysis in *Hernández II* in at least two different respects. First, by preempting the Texas tort remedy that would otherwise have been available to Sergio Hernández's parents, the statute eliminated the only other remedy that would traditionally have been available for a claim of excessive force against a rogue federal law enforcement officer—giving rise at least to the possibility that Congress *intended* to endorse *Bivens* remedies. Second, if no *Bivens* remedy was available either, then the Westfall Act's preemption of Texas tort law might well be unconstitutional—if, as the Supreme Court has long hinted but never held, the Due Process Clause of the Fifth Amendment protects a right of access to *some* judicial forum for the resolution of colorable constitutional claims.

But the only discussion of the Westfall Act in Justice Alito's majority opinion is for almost the opposite point—that it militates *against* recognition of a damages remedy insofar as "the provision simply left *Bivens* where it found it" (a claim for which Justice Alito offers precisely zero support).[71] Ditto Justice Thomas's concurrence—which notes that, rather than providing a cause of action against federal officers, Congress "has pre-empted the state tort suits that traditionally served as the mechanism by which damages were recovered from federal officers."[72] The implications of that preemption remained wholly unaddressed by the *Hernández II* Court.

To be sure, the constitutional question the Westfall Act raises in a case like *Hernández II* is a difficult one. The Court has assiduously avoided deciding whether the Due Process Clause protects a right

---

[71] Hernández II, 140 S. Ct. at 748 n.9.

[72] *Id.* at 752 (Thomas, J., concurring).

of access to a judicial forum for constitutional claims—often by deploying an especially strong version of the constitutional avoidance canon to justify less-than-obvious interpretations of statutes that bypass the problem.[73] But whatever valence those constitutional concerns might otherwise have in other cases, they are arguably at their zenith in cases like *Hernández II*—in which the underlying claim is for a classical common-law tort, such as excessive force by a rogue law enforcement officer, for which, without *Bivens*, the statute at issue took away the only remedy that had historically been available. At the very least, then, the possible implications for the Westfall Act should have been an independent justification for recognizing a *Bivens* claim in *Hernández II*—to allow the Court to avoid, whether in *Hernández II* or a future case, the difficult question of whether, without *Bivens*, the Westfall Act's elimination of state claims for federal constitutional torts would violate the Due Process Clause.

It may well be that the current Court, if forced to decide the matter, would hold that the Westfall Act is constitutional because there is no such due process right. The relevant point for present purposes is that *not* addressing the question in *Hernández II* produced a decision that disingenuously limits *Bivens*—and, if Justices Thomas and Gorsuch had had their way, would have killed it outright.

Conclusion: After *Hernández II*

To be sure, three of the five justices in the majority were unwilling to formally overrule *Bivens*—whether because they believe there are some cases in which it still has utility or because they believe overruling it is unnecessary given how thoroughly it has been circumscribed. And it is at least possible to identify factors present in *Hernández II* that would not be present in other cases challenging unconstitutional conduct by rogue federal law enforcement officers. If the facts of *Bivens* were to literally repeat, for instance (and the government made no

[73] See, e.g., Webster v. Doe, 486 U.S. 592, 603 (1988) (noting "the 'serious constitutional question' that would arise if a federal statute were construed to deny any judicial forum for a colorable constitutional claim") (quoting Bowen v. Mich. Acad. of Family Physicians, 476 U.S. 667, 681 n.12 (1986)); see also Bartlett ex rel. Neuman v. Bowen, 816 F.2d 695, 699 (D.C. Cir. 1987) ("[I]t has become something of a time-honored tradition for the Supreme Court and lower federal courts to find that Congress did not intend to preclude altogether judicial review of constitutional claims in light of the serious due process concerns that such preclusion would raise.").

claim of interference with national security), nothing in *Hernández II* suggests that a damages claim would be unavailable.

It is therefore possible that, in retrospect, *Hernández II* will be seen as a relatively modest ruling—one that further narrowed the availability of *Bivens* by declining to recognize a remedy on rather specific facts, but that left the core of the remedy intact relative to how thoroughly it had already been circumscribed by prior rulings.

But there are at least two problems with such a reading. First, it is belied by how lower courts have further narrowed *Bivens*. Including the Fifth Circuit's (now-affirmed) decision in *Hernández II*, different courts of appeals have, in the last two years, effectively foreclosed all *Bivens* claims against Transportation Security Administration officers;[74] Immigration and Customs Enforcement officers;[75] and officers in Customs and Border Protection[76]—self-described as the country's largest law enforcement agency. Indeed, the average American is far more likely to cross paths with officers from one of these three agencies than from the DEA (the successor agency to the Federal Bureau of Narcotics in *Bivens*) or the FBI. A world in which no *Bivens* remedies are available against any officer working for any of those agencies—regardless of the specific factual context in which the claim arises—is one in which *Bivens* is doing very little work, indeed.

Second, and in any event, what the analysis in *Hernández II* makes clear is that, at least for a majority of the current Court, there's no remaining affirmative case *for Bivens*. At least in *Ziglar v. Abbasi*, in which the Court in 2017 further tightened the availability of *Bivens* claims, Justice Kennedy's majority opinion went out of its way to *distinguish* claims against rogue law enforcement officers, explaining that "[t]he settled law of *Bivens* in this common and recurrent sphere of law enforcement, and the undoubted reliance upon it as a fixed principle in the law, are powerful reasons to retain it in that sphere."[77] Later in the same opinion, Kennedy emphasized the "continued force, or even the necessity, of *Bivens* in the search-and-seizure context in which it arose."[78] After all, unlike other misconduct,

---

[74] See Vanderklok v. United States, 868 F.3d 189 (3d Cir. 2017).

[75] See Tun-Cos v. Perrotte, 922 F.3d 514 (4th Cir. 2019).

[76] See Hernández, 885 F.3d at 814.

[77] 137 S. Ct. 1843, 1857 (2017).

[78] *Id.* at 1856.

"individual instances of . . . law enforcement overreach . . . are difficult to address except by way of damages actions after the fact."[79]

But *Hernández II* eviscerated those distinctions, too—again, without any acknowledgment that it was doing so or any explanation for why. In one sense, no explanation was needed: The petition for a writ of certiorari in *Hernández II* was filed on June 15, 2018; Justice Kennedy announced his retirement 12 days later, and his successor, Justice Brett Kavanaugh, joined Justice Alito's majority opinion without comment.

* * *

The decline—and potential death—of *Bivens* might be dismissed as little more than an interesting, but largely academic, federal courts project. I'm biased, of course, but I think such dismissiveness is deeply myopic. It is certainly true that American courts have long since abandoned the maxim that for every right, there is a remedy. In the qualified-immunity context, for example, it has been settled (if increasingly controversial) law for decades that even many *constitutional* violations by state and federal officers will go unremedied. Against that backdrop, the evisceration of *Bivens* might seem like a drop in the bucket.

But the absence of a cause of action, although it sounds technical, is tantamount to a form of functional absolute immunity where no recourse is available no matter how far over the line federal officers tread. Even as Congress continues to debate whether to narrow or abolish the qualified-immunity defense in the aftermath of the killing of George Floyd and the resulting protests, *none* of the leading proposals would make clear that victims of such abuses by *federal* law enforcement officers are entitled to a damages remedy. Simply put, Congress may well decide to eliminate qualified immunity for state and local law enforcement officers even as the Court has effectively bestowed a form of absolute immunity on federal law enforcement officers. It shouldn't be difficult to see why that distinction is unsatisfying.

True, injunctive relief is still a possibility where the unconstitutional conduct is ongoing—even though equity is supposed to follow the law, and not the other way around. But the Supreme Court

---

[79] *Id.* at 1862.

has long made clear that this is a narrow category—and one in which the "remedy" is simply for the conduct to cease. More generally, as *Abbasi* itself recognized, in the run of cases in which individual officers act *ultra vires*, the constitutional violation is usually complete long before the victim can repair to court. Thus, those who are comfortable with the demise of *Bivens* are necessarily comfortable with the proposition that, in most cases in which federal officers violate the Constitution, they will be absolutely immune from any civil liability—not only because federal courts won't hold them accountable, but because Congress has affirmatively prevented state courts from doing so.

The easy and obvious response is to suggest that, just as Congress caused (or, at least, exacerbated) the problem with the Westfall Act, and just as Congress provided an express cause of action for constitutional violations by *state* officers, so, too, Congress should provide a federal damages remedy for constitutional violations by federal officers. As with many of the hardest questions facing the federal courts, life would certainly be easier if Congress acted more responsibly. And drafting a statute would be pretty simple; Congress would only need to add five words to 42 U.S.C. § 1983:

> Every person who, under color of any statute, ordinance, regulation, custom, or usage, of any State or Territory or the District of Columbia, *or of the United States*, subjects, or causes to be subjected, any citizen of the United States or other person within the jurisdiction thereof to the deprivation of any rights, privileges, or immunities secured by the Constitution, shall be liable to the party injured in an action at law, suit in equity, or other proper proceeding for redress, except that in any action brought against a judicial officer for an act or omission taken in such officer's judicial capacity, injunctive relief shall not be granted unless a declaratory decree was violated or declaratory relief was unavailable.

But the fact that Congress *could* solve the problem is hardly proof that *only* Congress can solve it—especially where constitutional rights are concerned. After all, as Justice Harlan observed in his separate opinion in *Bivens*, "it would be at least anomalous to conclude that the federal judiciary . . . is powerless to accord a damages remedy to vindicate social policies which, by virtue of their inclusion in the Constitution, are aimed predominantly at restraining the Government as an instrument of the popular will."[80] There wouldn't be much point to *having* constitutional rights if their enforceability depended upon the beneficence of those against whom they would be enforced.

More fundamentally, if, as *Hernández II* suggests, the current Court believes that there is no affirmative case for a meaningful federal judicial role in fashioning *damages* for constitutional violations by federal officers, what is the affirmative case for such a role in fashioning *injunctive* relief? Put another way, as bad as the demise and death of *Bivens* would be for a meaningful judicial role in holding the federal government accountable, what is to stop the Court from applying similar modes of analysis to suits for injunctive relief—and from leaving enforcement of the Constitution against the federal government entirely to Congress's whim? At least for claims against state officers, three of the current justices have already taken a sobering step in that direction.[81]

In his opinion for the Court in *Armstrong v. Exceptional Child Center, Inc.*, Justice Scalia's answer, at least, was the need for contemporary American courts to respect the "long history of judicial review of illegal executive action, tracing back to England."[82] But *Bivens*, too, rested at least indirectly on a similarly long history—and as *Hernández II* makes clear beyond peradventure, Scalia, like Kennedy, is no longer on the bench.

---

[80] Bivens, 403 U.S. at 403–04 (Harlan, J., concurring in the judgment).

[81] Douglas v. Indep. Living Ctr. of S. Cal., 565 U.S. 606, 616–24 (2012) (Roberts, C.J., dissenting).

[82] 575 U.S. at 327.

The Dimming of Blaine's Legacy

By Clint Bolick*

The world brightened for school choice advocates with the U.S. Supreme Court's decision in *Espinoza v. Montana Department of Revenue*.[1]

In that decision, the Court curtailed the remarkably enduring legacy of a largely forgotten politician, U.S. Senator James G. Blaine. Blaine ran for president in 1884 against Grover Cleveland, whose Democratic Party was castigated for ostensibly supporting "rum, Romanism, and rebellion." Though Blaine was never elected president, his anti-immigrant and anti-Catholic views were embedded in constitutional provisions in 37 or 38 states,[2] prohibiting public aid for "sectarian" schools. Those "Blaine amendment" provisions were used to prevent or strike down, among other things, school choice programs that included religious schools among the options.

In *Espinoza*, the Court held that a Blaine amendment, owing both to its bigoted pedigree and its discrimination on the basis of religious status, could not be applied to exclude religious schools and their patrons from a school-choice program. Such status-based discrimination, the Court ruled, violated the First Amendment guarantee of free exercise of religion.

* The author serves as a justice on the Arizona Supreme Court, a research fellow for the Hoover Institution, and an adjunct professor in constitutional law at the Arizona State University and University of Arizona law schools. Bolick cofounded and served as vice president for litigation at the Institute for Justice (1991–2004), president of the Alliance for School Choice (2004–2007), and vice president for litigation at the Goldwater Institute (2007–2016). The author thanks Emily Jordan, a second-year law student at Boston College Law School, for her outstanding research assistance.

[1] Espinoza v. Mont. Dep't. of Revenue, 140 S. Ct. 2246 (2020).

[2] *Id.* at 2259 (the majority counts 37); *id.* at 2269 (Alito, J. concurring) (counting 38).

I. Blaine's Legacy

Supreme Court decisions rarely provide detailed history lessons, but *Espinoza* does. In fact, it even includes a historical cartoon in a concurring opinion by the justice who surely would be voted the least likely to publish a cartoon: Justice Samuel Alito.

In the Founding era and the 19th century, governments at every level provided financial support for private, secular, and religious primary and secondary schools.[3] But late in the 19th century, immigration from predominantly Catholic nations, especially Ireland, alarmed nativist groups such as the Ku Klux Klan. One tactic designed to thwart Catholic influence was a proposed national constitutional amendment that would prohibit government aid to sectarian schools. The amendment was narrowly defeated, but nativists were much more successful in amending state constitutions or inserting an amendment into constitutions of newly admitted states in the west. The 1871 cartoon from *Harper's Weekly* presented in Justice Alito's concurrence depicts Catholic priests as crocodiles voraciously approaching schoolchildren while the public school crumbles in the background.[4]

Although "sectarian" today is considered synonymous with "religious," in the late 19th century it was considered a code word for Catholic, as well as Mormon, Jewish, and other denominations outside the mainstream. The campaign against funding for sectarian schools dovetailed with the common-school movement headed by Horace Mann, which was intended to inculcate mainstream Protestant values. Common-school advocates supported Blaine amendments and used them to maintain Protestant hegemony over public-school funding and to exclude Catholic schools.[5]

The language of the state Blaine amendments varies but has common denominators, such as prohibiting public funding for the "aid" or "benefit" of sectarian schools, sometimes both directly and indirectly. The Montana provision at issue in *Espinoza* is typical, stating that the state and its subdivisions "shall not make any direct or indirect appropriation . . . for any sectarian purpose or to aid any . . . school . . . controlled in whole or in part by any church,

---

[3] *Id.* at 2258 (majority op.).

[4] *Id.* at 2269–70 (Alito, J., concurring).

[5] *Id.* at 2271–72.

sect, or denomination."[6] The prohibition would not apply to public schools, even though they were Protestant in orientation, because they were controlled by the state rather than the church. Montana did not voluntarily adopt the Blaine amendment but rather was obliged to do so as a condition of statehood.[7]

Even after the Blaine amendments were adopted in dozens of states, the anti-immigration efforts persisted. In the early 20th century, those efforts grew even more overt, taking the form of state laws backed by the Ku Klux Klan that forbade instruction in foreign languages or required students to attend public rather than private schools. The laws were struck down by the Supreme Court in a series of decisions in the 1920s. In the most famous of these, *Pierce v. Society of Sisters* in 1925, the Court held "[t]he fundamental theory of liberty upon which all governments in the Union repose excludes any general power of the State to standardize its children by forcing them to accept instruction from public teachers only."[8] The Court declared that "[t]he child is not the mere creature of the State; those who nurture him and direct his destiny have the right, coupled with the high duty, to recognize and prepare him for additional obligations."[9]

The showdown between parental liberty and the Blaine amendments, however, would not come for nearly another century. While the nativists were unsuccessful in eradicating the immigrants' private schools altogether, their success in excluding them from school funding would loom large when efforts surfaced many decades later to provide public support for religious schools and those who patronize them.

II. The Long and Winding Road to *Espinoza*

In the 1970s, alarmed by the closure of inner-city Catholic schools, state legislators across the country devised programs to rescue them. Dubbed "parochiaid," programs in Pennsylvania, New York, and elsewhere funneled direct grants to private schools and provided

---

[6] Mont. Const. art. X, § 6(1).

[7] Espinoza, 140 S. Ct. at 2268–69 (Alito, J., concurring).

[8] 268 U.S. 510, 535 (1925).

[9] *Id.*

tuition assistance to parents.[10] These programs were challenged under the First Amendment's Establishment Clause, which provides that "Congress shall make no law respecting an establishment of religion." The Establishment Clause was applied to the states through the Fourteenth Amendment.

During the Warren Court era, in which liberals dominated the U.S. Supreme Court, the prohibition against religious establishment evolved into a more rigid separation of church and state. This evolution was reflected in a 1973 decision striking down parochiaid programs. In *Committee for Public Education v. Nyquist*, the Court reasoned that because the programs were limited to private schools, which were predominantly religious, they had the impermissible "primary effect" of advancing religion.[11] The Court struck down all forms of aid, including tuition assistance to parents and direct aid to the schools.

Nyquist appeared to kill the idea of school vouchers in its infancy. But the decision's reasoning seemed the leave the door open, if only a crack. It was grounded in a principle that would later take root in Establishment Clause jurisprudence: neutrality. The programs under review in *Nyquist* were tilted exclusively toward private schools. A footnote in the decision seemed to provide hope that a more neutral program might survive scrutiny. (A note to aspiring litigators: always read the footnotes!) In footnote 38, the Court expressly reserved the question of "whether the significantly religious character of the statute's beneficiaries might differentiate the present cases from a case involving some form of public assistance (e.g., scholarships) made available generally without regard to the sectarian-nonsectarian, or public-nonpublic nature of the institution benefited."[12]

When my colleagues and I at the Institute for Justice began working with school-choice activists in the 1990s to develop and defend programs to assist low-income children trapped in failing public schools, our goal was to drive an entire movement through that footnote. Fortunately, a 1983 decision in a case called *Mueller v.*

[10] See Clint Bolick, Voucher Wars: Waging the Legal Battle over School Choice 4–5 (2003). This book, published by the Cato Institute, chronicles the intense 12-year litigation battle between the enactment of the Milwaukee parental choice program in 1990 and the U.S. Supreme Court decision upholding Cleveland school vouchers in 2002.

[11] 413 U.S. 756 (1973).

[12] *Id.* at 782 n.38.

Allen—in which I wrote my first-ever amicus curiae (friend of the court) brief—seemed to vindicate our approach. By a 5-4 vote (the same no-margin-for-error vote that would characterize virtually every Supreme Court case involving school choice), the Court upheld a Minnesota program allowing families to deduct K–12 educational expenses, including tuition, from their state income taxes. The deduction was available to both private- and public-school families. The challengers pointed out that because public schools are free, nearly all of the deductions were claimed for private-school expenses. But the majority found that the program fit within *Nyquist*'s footnote 38 exception. "The historic purposes of the [Establishment] Clause," the Court ruled, "simply do not encompass the sort of attenuated financial benefit, ultimately controlled by the private choices of individual parents, that eventually flows to parochial schools from the neutrally available tax benefit at issue in this case."[13]

Those two principles—neutrality and private individual choices—would furnish the twin components of our strategy for designing and defending school-choice programs. Neutrality meant that religious schools were only one available option. The path of funding would characterize programs as either direct aid (the provision of funding or other assistance directly to religious schools) or indirect (religious schools benefit only through the independent choices of third parties). If choice programs were neutral and based on private choice, we believed, they satisfied the Establishment Clause.

The school-choice opponents, teacher unions and their allies, pursued a multibarreled approach. Their preferred strategy was to defeat school choice under the Establishment Clause. They hoped that Supreme Court appointments after *Mueller* would spell the demise for school choice. But the opponents also raised an array of state constitutional challenges, including Blaine amendments in states whose constitutions included them. This strategy gave the opponents two strategic advantages. First, they needed to win on only one of the theories they deployed to challenge the programs, whereas the defenders had to prevail on all of them. Second, they could secure a victory on "independent state grounds": a state supreme court's interpretation of its own constitution is the final word; if no federal

---

[13] 463 U.S. 388, 400 (1983).

constitutional or statutory issue is presented, it cannot be appealed to the U.S. Supreme Court.

Even during the earliest days of defending school-choice programs in the early 1990s, we were aware that if we lost a case on Blaine amendment grounds, we would have no recourse unless we could develop a federal constitutional challenge to the amendments. But, of course, our first priority was to successfully defend the programs. In that regard, our strategy was to conflate the Blaine amendment analysis with the federal constitutional argument. Even under the Establishment Clause, we believed, it is impermissible to "aid" religious schools; but these programs didn't aid schools, they aided children, whose families could use their funds wherever they chose. So, they satisfied not only Establishment Clause scrutiny but the Blaine amendments as well.

Our strategy paid off in the first two state supreme court decisions upholding school-choice programs under both the Establishment Clause and Blaine amendment. In sustaining the Milwaukee Parental Choice Program by a 4-3 vote, the Wisconsin Supreme Court ruled that, although its Blaine amendment was more "specific" than the Establishment Clause, the program did not violate it for the same reason it did not violate the Establishment Clause: "public funds may be placed at the disposal of third parties so long as the program on its face is neutral between sectarian and nonsectarian alternatives and the transmission of funds is guided by the independent decisions of third parties."[14]

At around the same time, the Arizona Supreme Court upheld, by a 3-2 vote, a program that provides tax credits to taxpayers who contribute to private-school scholarship funds. The court ruled that, because the program allowed taxpayers to keep their own money, the state's version of the Blaine amendment was not implicated given that the funds were never public.[15] The court went on, however, to conclude that because Arizona was granted statehood after most Blaine amendments were adopted, they shared no apparent historical connection with the Arizona provision. Were such a connection established, the court declared, "we would be hard pressed to

[14] Jackson v. Benson, 578 N.W.2d 602, 620–21 (Wis. 1998).
[15] Kotterman v. Killian, 972 P.2d 606, 618 (Ariz. 1999).

divorce the amendment's language from the insidious discriminatory intent that prompted it."[16]

Meanwhile, the U.S. Supreme Court was deciding numerous cases involving direct and indirect aid to religiously affiliated entities, some of them implicating Blaine amendments. In particular, in *Mitchell v. Helms* in 1999, the Court upheld against an Establishment Clause challenge the use of federal funds to lend educational materials and equipment to both public and private schools, overruling contrary prior decisions in the process. The plurality opinion by Justice Clarence Thomas held that "the religious nature of a recipient should not matter to the constitutional analysis, so long as the recipient adequately furthers the government's secular purpose."[17] The plurality buttressed its opinion by tracing the history of the Blaine amendments to demonstrate that "hostility to aid to pervasively sectarian schools has a shameful pedigree that we do not hesitate to disavow."[18] The plurality concluded, tantalizingly from the perspective of possible future challenges to Blaine amendments, that "nothing in the Establishment Clause requires the exclusion of pervasively sectarian schools from otherwise permissible aid programs, and other doctrines of this Court bar it. This doctrine, borne of bigotry, should be buried now."[19]

But that opinion received only four votes. The deciding votes were cast by Justices Sandra Day O'Connor and Stephen Breyer, concurring only in the judgment and emphasizing that a direct aid program like the one at issue is permissible only if no "public funds ever reach the coffers of religious schools" and could only be used for secular purposes.[20] As the usual swing vote, Justice O'Connor's divergence from the plurality cast her in doubt on the constitutionality of school choice, where public funds would ultimately enter religious school coffers, albeit only as a result of independent decisions by parents.

The suspense over which way the duo would go lasted only two years, as the Court in 2002 upheld the Cleveland school voucher program in *Zelman v. Simmons-Harris*, by a (you guessed it) 5-4 vote,

---

[16] *Id.* at 624.

[17] 530 U.S. 793, 827 (2000).

[18] *Id.* at 828.

[19] *Id.* at 829.

[20] *Id.* at 867 (O'Connor, J., concurring in the judgment).

with Justices O'Connor and Breyer parting company with each other. The program, designed to help low-income children escape a failing public-school system, was part of a broader array of school choices, including charter schools. The majority emphasized that the program involved "true private choice" and "is neutral in all respects toward religion." In particular, the program "confers educational assistance to a broad class of individuals defined without reference to religion."[21]

The dissents were histrionic. Justice David Souter echoed the views of his fellow dissenters, arguing that the Court should "ignore" the "severe educational crisis" in the Cleveland public schools, the "wide range of choices" available within the public-school system, and the "voluntary character of the private choice." Instead, he characterized the decision as "remov[ing] a brick from the wall that was designed to separate religion and government." He warned of "religious strife" akin to the Balkans, Northern Ireland, and the Middle East.[22]

Although those dire predictions of social upheaval would not come to pass, the difference in perspectives between the majority and dissenters could not be more profound. Those differences still persist 18 years later and manifested themselves in *Espinoza*.

III. Blaine Moves to the Forefront

Having lost what I characterized at the time as the Super Bowl for school choice, opponents doubled down on state constitutional challenges. Even before the *Zelman* decision, Robert Chanin, then-general counsel for the National Education Association and my constant litigation adversary, declared that if they lost on the Establishment Clause, they still had plenty in their state constitution "toolbox," especially Blaine amendments.[23]

The Blaine amendments were deployed not only in court but in the legislative arena. Even after *Zelman*, many school-choice opponents argued that although such programs might be permissible in other states, they would be unconstitutional in theirs because state constitutional provisions were more restrictive than the Establishment Clause.

[21] 536 U.S. 639, 653 (2002).

[22] *Id.* at 685–86 (Souter, J., dissenting).

[23] Bolick, *supra* note 10, at 156.

Despite strong opposition, several states passed school-choice programs following *Zelman,* and the programs inevitably faced challenges under state constitutional provisions. Many programs were upheld. Some were invalidated on state constitutional grounds other than the Blaine amendments. The Florida Supreme Court, for instance, struck down a voucher program holding that it violated the state constitutional guarantee of uniform public schools.[24]

Still others were struck down under Blaine amendments. The Arizona Supreme Court, which had upheld scholarship tax credits, invalidated school vouchers. But the court emphasized that Arizona's constitutional provision, unlike similar ones in other states, forbids aid to all private schools, secular and religious alike. The court considered the vouchers "aid" because private schools were the only possible destination for the money.[25] Likewise, the Colorado Supreme Court held in 2015 that a school district voucher program violated its Blaine amendment, writing that "this stark constitutional provision makes one thing clear: A school district may not aid religious schools."[26] The court rejected the district's invitation "to wade into the history of [the constitutional provision's] adoption and declare that the framers created [the provision] in a vulgar display of anti-Catholic animus,"[27] and held that the application of the Blaine amendment did not violate the First Amendment.

Meanwhile, at the national level, the Blaine amendment figured prominently in a Supreme Court case from Washington state. The case involved a state scholarship program that could be used at any college, public, private, or religious, and for any major—except studying for the ministry. That narrow exclusion, the state argued, was compelled by its Blaine amendment.

---

[24] Bush v. Holmes, 919 So. 2d 392 (Fla. 2006).

[25] Cain v. Horne, 202 P.3d 1178 (Ariz. 2009). Despite striking down the voucher program, the court stated that "[t]here well may be ways of providing aid to these student populations without violating the constitution." *Id.* at 1185. That suggestion helped give rise to the idea of education scholarship accounts, which place education funds at the disposal of families to use for a variety of educational purposes, including private-school tuition but public-school services as well. The Arizona Court of Appeals upheld that program under the same state constitutional provision. Niehaus v. Huppenthal, 310 P.3d 983 (Ariz. App. 2013).

[26] Taxpayers for Pub. Educ. v. Douglas County Sch. Dist., 351 P.3d 461, 470 (Colo. 2015).

[27] *Id.* at 471.

Joshua Davey, a student pursuing a divinity degree, argued that the exclusion, among other things, violated the free exercise clause. In a 7-2 decision authored by Chief Justice William Rehnquist,[28] the Court upheld the exclusion of training for the ministry from the aid program in *Locke v. Davey*. The Court invoked its oft-used metaphor that there is "'play in the joints'" between the two First Amendment religion clauses, meaning that "there are some state actions permitted by the Establishment Clause but not required by the Free Exercise Clause."[29] The majority concluded that, in the context of a scholarship program "that goes a long way toward including religion in its benefits," the narrow exclusion of theology students, by virtue of its state constitutional prohibition, did not evidence hostility toward religion.[30] The Court found "neither in the history or text" of Washington's Blaine amendment was there anything "that suggests animus toward religion." Indeed, state resources traditionally were excluded from supporting study for the ministry. Thus, the majority concluded that the state's "interest in not funding the pursuit of devotional degrees is substantial and the exclusion of such funding places a relatively minor burden" on the scholarship recipients.[31]

Justice Antonin Scalia, joined by Justice Thomas, dissented. In typically caustic fashion, Scalia disdained the "play in the joints" principle, remarking that "I use the term 'principle' loosely, for that is not so much a legal principle as a refusal to apply *any* principle when faced with competing constitutional directives."[32] Rather, the dissenters emphasized that the program discriminated on its face against religion, and argued that the supposed lightness of the burden, and the ostensible absence of religious animus, were either not true or insufficient to justify the discrimination.

---

[28] Rehnquist was reputedly a skillful and strategic chief justice. According to insider accounts, he would often vote with the majority against his own position (the chief justice votes last) in order to exercise his prerogative to assign the opinion to himself, whereupon he would write the narrowest possible decision. *Locke v. Davey* bears the hallmarks of that approach.

[29] 540 U.S. 712, 718–19 (2002) (quoting Walz v. Tax Comm'n of the City of New York, 397 U.S. 664, 669 (1970)).

[30] *Id.* at 724.

[31] *Id.*

[32] *Id.* at 728 (Scalia, J., dissenting) (emphasis in original).

Locke v. Davey gave both hope and worry to school choice supporters and opponents alike. On the one hand, two justices who had joined the plurality's veiled attack on Blaine amendments only four years earlier in *Mitchell v. Helms*, Chief Justice Rehnquist and Justice Anthony Kennedy, were now saying they saw no evidence of hostility toward religion in the text or history of Washington state's Blaine amendment. On the other hand, the majority emphasized the "relatively minor burden" on scholarship students, observing that the program otherwise included religious participants among its beneficiaries. The decision gave no clear indication of what would happen if a state invoked a Blaine amendment to exclude religious beneficiaries altogether from a neutral aid program.

It would take another 16 years to find out.

IV. False Hope

School-choice advocates attempted repeatedly to convince the Court to decide the question of a broader exclusion, unjustified by tradition, left open in *Locke v. Davey*. They thought they finally succeeded when the Court agreed to decide *Trinity Lutheran Church of Columbia, Inc. v. Comer.*

The facts were not the normal stuff of Supreme Court decisions. The plaintiff operated a preschool and daycare center that wanted to replace its pea gravel playground surface with scrap tire rubber. The state of Missouri had a program offering reimbursement to nonprofits that wanted to resurface playgrounds with recycled tires. But the state denied Trinity Lutheran's grant application because it was a church. The federal court of appeals held that although the Establishment Clause would not forbid such a grant, the Free Exercise Clause did not require the state to disregard the prohibition of aid to religious entities in its Blaine amendment.

When the Supreme Court granted review, anti-Blaine advocates were optimistic. The ruling striking down the church's exclusion from the program, by a surprising 7-2 vote, appeared at first glance to vindicate those hopes. Six members of the Court—Chief Justice John Roberts (who authored the opinion) along with Justices Kennedy, Thomas, Elena Kagan, Alito, and Neil Gorsuch—held that while programs that were neutral toward religion were upheld against free exercise challenges, "[w]e have been careful to distinguish such laws from those that single out the religious for disfavored treatment."[33] The state's policy of excluding religious nonprofits, the Court observed, "puts Trinity Lutheran to a choice: It may participate in an otherwise available benefit program or remain a religious institution."[34] Placing a religious institution in that dilemma, the Court held, triggered strict scrutiny, requiring the state to demonstrate a compelling interest served by the narrowest possible means.

On its face, the decision seemed like a decisive victory for anti-Blaine advocates. Seven votes were cast to strike down the discriminatory policy (although Justice Breyer concurred only in the result). The dissenting opinion by Justices Sonia Sotomayor and Ruth Bader Ginsburg lamented the apparent demise, or at least narrowing, of *Locke v. Davey*.[35] By a clear majority, the Court seemed to clear the way for Free Exercise Clause challenges to all manner of programs, including school choice, that excluded religious options. If it all seemed for anti-Blaine advocates too good to be true . . . it was.

Although the majority opinion was written in clarion terms, four justices (Roberts, Kennedy, Alito, and Kagan) joined in footnote 3, which declared, quite remarkably: "This case involves express discrimination based on religious identity with regard to playground resurfacing. We do not address religious uses of funding or other forms of discrimination."[36]

So, after years of anticipation, spirited arguments by both sides, reams of friend-of-the-court court briefs, and massive media attention, the case that was thought to be about the reach of the Blaine amendment turned out to be a case about playground resurfacing, and nothing more.

In an opinion concurring in part, Justices Gorsuch and Thomas argued for a broader application of the principles underlying the case. They worried that the majority was leaving open the possibility of a "distinction between religious *status* and religious *use*," which made no sense given that the First Amendment focuses on free *exercise* of religion.[37] They pointedly refused to join footnote 3, arguing that the

[33] 137 S. Ct. 2012, 2020 (2017).

[34] *Id.* at 2022.

[35] *Id.* at 2035–39 (Sotomayor, J., dissenting).

[36] *Id.* at 2024 n.3 (plurality op.).

[37] *Id.* at 2025 (Gorsuch, J., concurring in part) (emphasis in original).

neutrality principle on which the case was decided "do[es] not permit discrimination against religious exercise—whether on the playground or anywhere else."[38]

Resolving the question of whether states violate the Free Exercise Clause if they enforce their Blaine amendments to exclude religious choices in contexts beyond school playground resurfacing would have to await a case that squarely presented that broader question.

V. Blaine Vanquished

The tea leaves following *Trinity Lutheran* were fairly optimistic for school-choice supporters. Among the cases remanded in light of that decision was the Colorado Supreme Court ruling striking down school vouchers under the Blaine amendment.[39] But what were courts supposed to do given *Trinity Lutheran's* opaque language and extraordinarily narrow holding? And if the Supreme Court were to consider the Blaine amendment in a broader context, which way would the justices who joined footnote 3 go?

Following the retirement of Justice Kennedy and his replacement by Justice Brett Kavanaugh, the Court decided to revisit the issue in the school-choice context. *Espinoza* involved a Montana tax credit of up to $150 for contributions to student scholarship organizations. By the time the Court took the case, the program had only one participating organization, Big Sky Scholarships, which provided scholarships to families with financial hardships or disabled children to attend private schools of their choice. The legislature, however, also provided that the program be administered in accordance with the state's Blaine amendment, which forbade any "direct or indirect appropriation" of public funds "to aid any . . . school . . . controlled in whole or in part by any church."

After the program commenced, the Montana Department of Revenue, applying the no-aid provision, promulgated a rule forbidding the use of scholarship funds in religious schools. The state's attorney general disagreed with the department's action; he advised that the Blaine amendment did not require excluding religious schools from the program, and that doing so would "very likely" violate the

---

[38] *Id.* at 2026.

[39] Douglas County Sch. Dist. v. Taxpayers for Pub. Educ., 137 S. Ct. 2012 (2017).

federal Constitution by discriminating against religious schools and their students.

Three mothers whose children attended Stillwater Christian School challenged the department's rule excluding them from participation in the program. The trial court enjoined the rule, holding (as had the Arizona Supreme Court in *Kotterman v. Killian*) that the state constitution only forbade appropriations, not tax credits. The program commenced operation and delivered scholarships to dozens of students, including several attending Stillwater Christian School.

The Montana Supreme Court reversed the trial court.[40] It held that the program allowed public funds to flow to religious schools, a result incompatible with the state's Blaine amendment. Because of the direct financial support, the court concluded that the exclusion of religious schools from the program did not violate the Free Exercise Clause. Finally, the court ruled that the department lacked authority to rewrite the statute to allow secular but not religious private schools to participate; therefore, the proper remedy was to strike down the program entirely.

Such a remedy presented school-choice supporters with a conundrum. It is not uncommon in discrimination cases for courts to invalidate a program altogether rather than to extend benefits to everyone. Given that it is ordinarily a state's prerogative not to provide financial benefits at all, one could argue that such a remedy was the judicially moderate one. With such an outcome, school-choice advocates could "win" the case but lose the remedy, for the Court could conclude that the program violated the Free Exercise Clause yet defer to the Montana Supreme Court's judgment that the entire program should be struck down. Or it could find that by virtue of the Montana Supreme Court's remedy, there was no discrimination.

The Supreme Court issued its decision on June 30, 2020, the last regularly scheduled day of the Court's 2019-2020 term (although it would continue to issue decisions in July due to delays attributable to the COVID-19 pandemic). The Court returned to its predictable 5-4 conservative/liberal split that predominates in watershed Establishment Clause cases. But although the margin was slender and the case produced seven separate opinions, the opinion of the Court—as

---

[40] 435 P.3d 603 (Mont. 2020).

18 years earlier in *Zelman*—spoke with a single voice. As did the chief justice (Rehnquist) in *Zelman*, so too here did the chief justice (Roberts) take the helm in *Espinoza*, with considerably less equivocation than in *Trinity Lutheran*.

The majority noted that none of the parties questioned the allowance of the scholarship tax-credit program under the Establishment Clause. They focused instead on the Free Exercise Clause, asking whether it "precluded the Montana Supreme Court from applying Montana's no-aid provision to bar religious schools" from the program.[41] The majority answered yes.

The Court's opinion largely tracked the concurring opinion of Justices Gorsuch and Thomas in *Trinity Lutheran*. That opinion, the Court noted, distilled cases "into the 'unremarkable' conclusion that disqualifying otherwise eligible recipients from a public benefit 'solely because of their religious character' imposes 'a penalty on the free exercise of religion that triggers the most exacting scrutiny.'"[42] The Court concluded that Montana's no-aid provision bars religious schools from public benefits solely because of the religious character of the schools. The provision also bars parents who wish to send their children to a religious school from those same benefits, again solely because of the religious character of the school."[43] Hence, "the Montana Constitution discriminates based on religious status just like the Missouri policy in *Trinity Lutheran*."[44]

This focus on religious "status" as the basis for discrimination had worried Justice Gorsuch in *Trinity Lutheran*, for it seemed an artificial divide between types of government discrimination subject to the Free Exercise Clause. But the Court's opinion cohered around it in *Espinoza*. The majority acknowledged Justice Gorsuch's point that there is no "meaningful distinction between discrimination based on use or conduct and that based on status," but stated that it "need not examine it here" because the "no-aid provision discriminates based on religious status."[45]

---

[41] Espinoza, 140 S. Ct. at 2254 (majority op.).

[42] *Id.* at 2255 (citation omitted).

[43] *Id.*

[44] *Id.* at 2256.

[45] *Id.* at 2257.

Apparently recognizing the difficulty of squaring the result in *Espinoza* with that in *Locke v. Davey*, the Court turned to that issue. It first noted that Washington state had simply refused to fund a particular course of instruction and therefore had denied Davey a scholarship based on what he proposed to do. Montana's Constitution, however, does not "zero in" on any essentially religious course of instruction but rather bars all aid to a religious school, thus putting "religious families to a choice between sending their children to a religious school or receiving such benefits."[46] Since the language of the Washington and Montana provisions was similar, the Court seems to be saying that it is the *construction* of the provisions by courts or other governmental entities, leading to particular forms of discrimination, that matters.

The Court continued by noting that there was "a 'historic and substantial' state interest in not funding the training of clergy," while no such "tradition supports Montana's decision to disqualify religious schools from government aid."[47] Citing the *Mitchell* plurality, it traced the history of the Blaine amendment to anti-Catholic bigotry (which would have been true in the Washington state context as well), and remarked that the "no-aid provisions of the 19th century hardly evince a tradition that should inform our understanding of the Free Exercise Clause."[48]

Criticizing the dissenting opinions of Justices Sotomayor and Breyer, who would have taken a more case-by-case approach, the Court said that the rule it was applying was "straightforward": "When otherwise eligible recipients are disqualified from a public benefit 'solely because of their religious character,' we must apply strict scrutiny."[49] Citing *Pierce v. Society of Sisters* for the proposition that parents have the right to direct the upbringing of their children, the Court ruled that the state failed to meet its burden of a compelling interest achieved through narrowly tailored means. That led to the Court's core holding: "A State need not subsidize private education. But once a State decides to do so, it cannot disqualify some private schools solely because they are religious."[50]

[46] *Id.*

[47] *Id.* at 2257–58 (citation omitted).

[48] *Id.* at 2259.

[49] *Id.* at 2260.

[50] *Id.* at 2261.

That left the difficult question of remedy: expand the benefits or strike down the entire program? Here, the Court focused on the legislative details. The legislature had enacted a program that was open to all private schools and their students. Because the Montana Supreme Court had violated federal law by invalidating the program, the correct result was to restore the status quo ante, that is, restore the scholarship tax credit program.[51] School-choice supporters won the legal battle and preserved their program.

Although five justices joined the majority decision in full, several had more to say. Justice Thomas concurred, noting that although the case presented free exercise issues, the Establishment Clause remains a "'brooding omnipresence,' . . . ever ready to be used to justify the government's infringement on religious freedom."[52] Justice Thomas believes that, because the Establishment Clause does not protect individual rights, it is not incorporated against the states under the Fourteenth Amendment and therefore applies only to Congress. Thomas has made that argument in prior cases but here was joined by Justice Gorsuch. Applying that view of the Establishment Clause, Thomas took on *Locke v. Davey* and other precedents, concluding that "[r]eturning the Establishment Clause to its proper scope . . . will go a long way toward allowing free exercise of religion to flourish as the Framers intended."[53]

Justice Alito appeared to have the most fun in his concurring opinion, not only featuring the Blaine amendment cartoon but hoisting the dissenters on their own petard. In *Ramos v. Louisiana*, a successful challenge to Louisiana's use of nonunanimous juries to convict even in capital cases,[54] Alito had objected that the original invidious motivation for adopting such laws should not lead to their invalidation—they were re-adopted under different circumstances—but lamented that in that case "I lost." Thus, he concluded, "[i]f the original motivation for the laws mattered there, it certainly matters here."[55] Alito went on to document, in meticulous detail, the invidious discrimination

---

[51] *Id.* at 2261–63.

[52] *Id.* at 2263 (Thomas, J., concurring) (citing S. Pac. Co. v. Jensen, 244 U.S. 205, 222 (1917) (Holmes, J., dissenting)).

[53] *Id.* at 2267.

[54] See the article by Nicholas and Mitchell Mosvick covering the case in this volume.

[55] 140 S. Ct. at 2268 (Alito, J., concurring) (citing Ramos v. Louisiana, 140 S. Ct. 1390 (2019) (involving nonunanimous jury verdicts in criminal trials)).

underlying the Blaine amendments, citing a brief filed by the Cato Institute among others. He argued that even though the amendment was re-adopted in a 1972 constitution, it was not cleansed of its bigotry because the original language harking back to those origins was retained. Although public schools have evolved from those envisioned by Horace Mann, Alito wrote, "many parents of many different faiths still believe that local schools inculcate a worldview that is antithetical to what they teach at home."[56] The Montana scholarship tax credit, he concluded, "helped parents of modest means do what more affluent parents can do: send their children to a school of their choice."[57]

In his concurring opinion, Justice Gorsuch continued to criticize what he perceives as an artificial distinction between religious status and use. Here, the state effectively told parents, "You can have school choice, but if anyone dares to send the child to an accredited religious school, the program will be shuttered." He concluded that "[c]alling it discrimination on the basis of religious status or religious activity makes no difference: It is unconstitutional all the same."[58]

The Court's opinion drew three dissenting opinions. Justice Ginsburg, joined by Justice Kagan, found that the "essential component" of differential treatment was missing: "Recall that the Montana Supreme Court remedied the state constitutional violation by striking the scholarship program in its entirety."[59] That decision placed religious and secular private schools on an equal footing. "On that ground, and reaching no other issue," Justice Ginsburg dissented.

But Justice Kagan also joined Justice Breyer's dissenting opinion, in part. Breyer did not buy into the majority's distinction between religious status and use, characterizing the Court's opinion as holding "that the Free Exercise Clause forbids a State to draw any distinction between secular and religious uses of government aid to private schools that is not required by the Establishment Clause." That holding, he argued, risks "the kind of entanglement and conflict that the Religion Clauses are intended to prevent."[60]

---

[56] *Id.* at 2274.

[57] *Id.*

[58] *Id.* at 2278 (Gorsuch, J., concurring).

[59] *Id.* at 2295 (Ginsburg, J., dissenting).

[60] *Id.* at 2281 (Breyer, J., dissenting).

In the part of his dissent joined by Justice Kagan, Breyer likened the Montana program to the aid program in *Locke v. Davey*, an essentially religious endeavor a state could legitimately elect not to fund, rather than a church applying for a playground resurfacing grant as in *Trinity Lutheran*. So, for him, "the question in this case—unlike in *Trinity Lutheran*—boils down to what the schools would *do* with state support."[61] Because it would aid the schools' religious endeavors, Breyer concluded the program was impermissible. Dispensing with the circuit-breaker from *Zelman* of true parental choice, Breyer drew a bright-line rule: "If, for 250 years, we have drawn a line at forcing taxpayers to pay the salaries of those who teach their faith from the pulpit," he declared, "I do not see how we can today require Montana to adopt a different view respecting those who teach it in the classroom."[62] In the remaining part of his dissent not joined by Kagan (and seemingly in tension with the first part), Breyer argued for a case-by-case determination of cases within the play-in-the-joints intersection between the Free Exercise and Establishment Clauses, remarking that there is no test-related substitute for legal judgment.[63]

Justice Sotomayor combined elements of both Ginsburg's and Breyer's perspectives in her solo dissent and took them a step further. No discrimination resulted from the Montana Supreme Court's ruling, she observed, because the "tax benefits no longer exist for anyone in the State."[64] But her key concern was that the decision weakened the country's longstanding commitment to separation of church and state.[65] Echoing her *Trinity Lutheran* dissent, Sotomayor concluded that "it is no answer to say that this case involves 'discrimination,'" because it is the religion clauses themselves that make such distinctions relevant.[66] "Today's ruling is perverse," she declared. "Without any need or power to do so, the Court appears to require a State to reinstate a tax-credit program that the Constitution did not demand in the first place."[67]

---

[61] *Id.* at 2285 (emphasis in original).

[62] *Id.* at 2288.

[63] *Id.* at 2291.

[64] *Id.* at 2291 (Sotomayor, J., dissenting).

[65] *Id.* at 2292.

[66] *Id.* at 2297.

[67] *Id.*

VI. Questions After *Espinoza*

As in *Zelman*, the majority and dissenters in *Espinoza* remained far apart in their constitutional worldview. Indeed, it is not clear what the four dissenters would do if faced with the question of overturning *Zelman* in a case before a differently composed Court.

The Blaine amendments remain on the books, though they are no longer permitted to achieve their intended goal of excluding state aid to religious schools *if* the state has elected to provide such aid to private schools in the first place. But not all Blaine amendments are worded the same, or necessarily share the same origins or subsequent evolution, so courts will have to grapple with whether such differences are consequential.

And what remains of *Locke v. Davey*? The majority distinguished the case but did not overrule it (although Justices Thomas and Gorsuch apparently would do so). Is it limited to its very narrow facts of a state excluding otherwise available state aid to studying for the ministry? Or are there other uses, supported by historical tradition, where a state permissibly may exclude aid, either by policy choice or in perceived fealty to a Blaine amendment?

Speaking of religious "uses," Chief Justice Roberts clung tenaciously to a possible distinction between religious status and use. Like Justice Gorsuch, I find it difficult to clearly comprehend that distinction, but if the Court embraces such a distinction, lower courts will have to define it. Just as school choice advocates seized the *Nyquist* footnote to carve an exception that may have ended up swallowing the rule, so too will opponents surely seek to expand the religious use loophole, if indeed it turns out to exist.

One curious aspect of the majority holding was its use of the term "subsidize" to describe the relationship between the scholarship tax programs and the participating schools. The Court's verbiage here is interesting. From the start, school-choice proponents argued that vouchers and tax credits were *not* subsidies to religious schools. During my school-choice litigation days, if a court concluded that a school-choice program constituted a subsidy, our goose was cooked. *Zelman* was based on the proposition that school vouchers were a form of indirect aid guided by true private choice. And as the Arizona Supreme Court ruled in *Kotterman v. Killian*, scholarship tax credits are a further step removed from direct aid because the tax benefits go to contributors, not beneficiaries, and no state funds end up in religious school coffers. Yet the Supreme Court in *Espinoza* referred to such credits as a subsidy. Was the Court's shift in language here unintentionally loose, or was it signaling that more-direct forms of "subsidies," such as the type struck down in *Nyquist*, are permissible now?

And, of course, the remedy of extending benefits to all in *Espinoza* was a function of the specific legislative and judicial circumstances. Could a court in different circumstances find that a remedy invalidating the entire program was proper?

No sooner is the ink dry on a Supreme Court decision than creative minds begin to engage over the next one. *Espinoza*, in a very important sense, is the culmination of a long journey meant to make America safe for school choice. But Court opinions, especially those decided by a 5-4 vote, are rarely the final word unless future courts determine they are worthy of reverence. Whether *Espinoza* falls into that category is left to future judgment. But, for the moment, school-choice advocates have a victory to cherish.[68]

---

[68] I congratulate my former Institute for Justice colleague and dear friend of 35 years, Richard Komer, who came out of retirement to argue the case and finish the job he began so many years before.

The *Heller*-ization of Originalism: *Ramos v. Louisiana* and the Problem of Frozen Context

*Nicholas M. Mosvick & Mitchell A. Mosvick**

In *Ramos v. Louisiana*,[1] the Supreme Court rendered a series of opinions in response to Evangelisto Ramos's challenge to a Louisiana law that allowed nonunanimous jury verdicts for criminal convictions. The Court's only clear overlapping holding interpreted the Sixth Amendment to prohibit less-than-unanimous verdicts as violating the right to a "trial, by an impartial jury."[2] This holding therefore constrains states' police powers over their own court systems via the Court's "selective incorporation" doctrine under the Fourteenth Amendment. Such nonunanimous procedural rules are unconstitutional, said the Court, because the prevailing public meaning in 1791 of "trial by jury" always and everywhere meant only a *unanimous* jury verdict, based on "400 years" of English common-law practice, colonial agreement at ratification, some Founding-era state constitutions, and court practices at the time. *Ramos* ruled that a federal verdict supported by less than a unanimous vote in 1791 was not a jury verdict at all, and, under selective incorporation, it is not a constitutional verdict in a state court in 2020 either.

Justice Neil Gorsuch's opinion, joined in various parts by different groups of justices, is explicit that the methodology justifying this interpretation of the Sixth Amendment lies in seeking its "original

---

* Nicholas Mosvick is a senior fellow at the National Constitution Center; Mitchell Mosvick is an attorney and solicitor of England and Wales, practicing law in London. Both authors write solely in their personal capacities and not on behalf of any institution or organization.

[1] 140 S. Ct. 1390 (2020).

[2] For shorthand, we refer to the right to a "trial by jury" throughout.

public meaning."[3] And Justice Gorsuch's particular approach to pursuing that original public meaning bears a striking resemblance to Justice Antonin Scalia's majority opinion in *District of Columbia v. Heller*.[4] The striking resemblance of method as applied to the use of historical evidence for interpreting ambiguous text, however, does *Ramos* no favors. The history of criminal jury trials at English common law, the diversity of thinking on judge and juror conduct in the colonies over time, and American jurists' views of unanimity paint a far more complicated picture than Justice Gorsuch's opinion would indicate.

Heller had significant, albeit disputed, linguistic and grammatical arguments to make regarding the Second Amendment's text. The Court's holding in *Ramos*, by contrast, barely addresses the text of the Sixth Amendment. And its arguments from the historical context lend little support for the view that the Sixth Amendment's bare language guaranteeing a "trial by jury" required unanimity for all time.

Ramos's outcome is perhaps uncontroversial for the American public of 2020.[5] It is a puzzling decision, however, both as a matter of its grounding in American and English history and as a practical exposition of originalist constitutional theory in the *Heller* mode. The issue is not whether many prominent statesmen and jurists, as well as a number of state constitutions, viewed unanimous verdicts as important practices in 1791. Rather, the issue is whether the Sixth Amendment text clearly supports *constitutionalizing* the unanimity requirement. The lead opinion in *Ramos* is unconvincing in this respect, and barely addresses either the text or the contrary views of

---

[3] The opinions contain overlapping and underlapping concurrences and dissents. For example, on whether *Apodaca v. Oregon* was due precedential status under the doctrine of *stare decisis* (three justices say "no," five say "yes," arguably one, Justice Elena Kagan, absents herself entirely by not joining any parts of the opinions on the matter); the racist origins of some of the late 19th-century attempts to allow nonunanimity (all nine justices agree this was a historical factor in Louisiana's initial enactment in 1898, while none indicate that its modern advocacy is itself racist); the retroactivity of *Ramos* under *Teague v. Lane*; and finally, how incorporation under the Fourteenth Amendment should work (most justices accepting "selective incorporation" under the Due Process Clause of the Fourteenth Amendment, with Justice Clarence Thomas continuing his advocacy for incorporation under the Privileges or Immunities Clause).

[4] 554 U.S. 570 (2008).

[5] Of the amici curiae filing in *Ramos*, 10 briefs were filed on behalf of the petitioner, Ramos, and two were filed on behalf of the respondent, Louisiana.

prominent jurists and state legislatures on the subject throughout the period before, during, and after ratification of the amendment.

Textually it is not apparent why unanimity should be required. The phrase "unanimous verdict" does not appear in the Sixth Amendment, even though so many other specific rights and restrictions do appear there. We might ask why constitutionalization of unanimity would be more obviously critical to the definition of a "trial by jury" to the 1791 public than other time-honored practices of courts, judges, and juries that came with unanimity.[6] We should not assume that, because James Madison and many jurists in 1791 thought unanimity in criminal jury verdicts was critical, therefore "the public" would understand the plain meaning of a right to "trial by jury" could only mean a right to "trial by a jury, [whose verdict must be unanimous]."[7]

Historical evidence that the Sixth Amendment's text constitutionalized unanimity is wanting. Despite enthusiasm amongst jurists and legislators in 1791 and today for the policy values of mandating unanimity, such a view has never itself been unanimous among commentators—not in the 18th, 19th, 20th, or 21st centuries. There were movements to abandon unanimity throughout the 19th century,[8] the century that begat the Fourteenth Amendment and its Due Process Clause, which is the basis for constitutionalizing the

---

[6] Justice Gorsuch remarks that "[r]elatedly, the dissent suggests that, before doing anything here, we should survey all changes in jury practices since 1791." Ramos, 140 S. Ct. at 1409, n.47. He says it would make for "an interesting study—but not one that could alter the plain meaning of the Constitution or obliviate its undisputed unanimity requirement." *Id.*

[7] The right to trial by jury is the only right addressed in both the Constitution (art. III, § 2) and the Bill of Rights. Yet in neither instance did the Framers address the unanimity issue; nor did the Continental Congress or First Congress require unanimity in the extensive criminal procedure sections of either the Northwest Ordinance of 1787 or Judiciary Act of 1789.

[8] The late 19th century in particular saw interest in abandoning unanimity from a variety of sources across the United States, including state legislators, newspaper editorials, and an ex-president. See, e.g., Mineral Point Tribune, "The Jury System," Feb. 9, 1876, at 5 (Wisconsin bill introduced to state legislature allowing criminal jury verdicts by 11 of 12 jurors); San Francisco Morning Call, "Unanimous Juries," Dec. 20, 1893, at 6 (calling unanimity a "flagrantly illogical rule"); Sunday Herald (Utah), "The Jury System: Some Sensible Criticism on It by Ex-President Hayes," Nov. 17, 1889, at 1. (President Rutherford Hayes making similar criticisms).

juror unanimity requirement in *Ramos*.[9] And apart from the policy divergence amongst scholars, very few commentators anytime near the Founding stated that the Sixth Amendment constitutionalized the matter.

The Court would do better to maintain judicial humility in the face of the plain fact that the text of the amendment simply does not address unanimity.[10] The result in *Ramos* prevents legislators from enacting and experimenting with democratic changes to jury verdict procedures. Befitting its English common-law heritage and recognizing the broader context of trial practice at the Founding, the Court should pause before freezing such a practice against all future legislative change. This would follow then–Judge Benjamin Cardozo's warning that "[t]he half truths of one generation tend at times to perpetuate themselves in the law as the whole truths of another, when constant repetition brings it about that qualifications, taken once for granted, are disregarded or forgotten."[11]

* * *

In Part I, we first discuss the similarities in interpretive method between Justice Gorsuch's lead opinion in *Ramos*[12] and those made by Justice Scalia's majority opinion in *District of Columbia v. Heller*,

[9] Due to long-standing criticisms of forced unanimity by jurists, including its opportunity for corruption of juries, many jurisdictions descended from the English common law long ago abandoned requiring unanimity for all criminal verdicts, save for Australia and Canada (and now, post-*Ramos*, the United States). See Ethan J. Leib, A Comparison of Criminal Jury Decision Rules in Democratic Countries, 5 Ohio St. J. Crim. L. 629, 636–38 (2008). This includes England and Wales, the source of the common law, where after two hours' deliberation, a jury may report a majoritarian verdict of 10 to 2 or 11 to 1 if they cannot agree unanimously. See Juries Act 1974, s. 17.

[10] Beyond the scope of this article is the glaring fact that the original conditions for juries in 1791 included explicit limitation of jurors to property-holding, religious, white men. No advocate would contend that such clear original conditions define the original public meaning of the word "jury" in the Sixth Amendment so as to bind the legislatures of 2020. See Brief for States of Utah et al. as Amici Curiae Supporting Respondent at 18–19, Ramos v. Louisiana, 140 S. Ct. 1390 (2020) (No. 18-5924) (meaning of jury is not so "capricious" as to limit the jury pool to male freeholders); see also Albert W. Alschuler & Andrew G. Deiss, A Brief History of the Criminal Jury in the United States, 61 U. Chi. L. Rev. 867, 877 (1994).

[11] Allegheny Coll. v. Nat'l Chautauqua Bank, 159 N.E. 173, 174 (N.Y. 1927) (Cardozo, C.J.).

[12] We shall refer to Justice Gorsuch's opinion as a whole as the "lead opinion," as it sometimes commands a majority, plurality, or bare minority on different points.

the latter widely seen as the archetype for modern original-public-meaning judicial analysis. In Part II, we discuss whether, using the "*Heller* method" of originalism employed in *Ramos*, the historical context underlying the text of the Sixth Amendment was so abundantly clear that jury unanimity was the only way the 1791 public could read the words "trial by jury." We criticize each of the principal historical sources Justice Gorsuch relies on to support his claim that the context of the Sixth Amendment's textual guarantee requires unanimity as a *constitutional* matter. The fuller historical picture is richer, more complicated, and less supportive of Justice Gorsuch's absolutist statements concerning the "historical need for unanimity" as a piece of the "hard-won liberty" protected by the Sixth Amendment.[13]

In doing so, we necessarily ask whether the method outlined by the Court in *Ramos* appears to be guided by the original conditions of jury trials in criminal matters common in Georgian England and the colonies. The result is to retrospectively freeze a key aspect that the Court liked—unanimity—rather than the numerous other key elements of past jury trials they would rather not constitutionalize. We conclude by asking whether, in its approach to interpreting broad guarantees of rights (to "bear arms" or to a "trial by jury"), the *Ramos* Court (and perhaps *Heller* as well) ends up opening the door to the subjective scorekeeping of which historical conditions of 1791 "stick" from a constitutional perspective and which may be discarded as relics of a bygone era. This may lead unwittingly into the "original expectation" or "original application" interpretive trap that has been a particular target for critics of "new originalism."[14]

Part I: The *Heller*-Method in *Ramos*

It is difficult to read *Ramos* without noting the absolute assuredness of Justice Gorsuch's lead opinion. Justice Gorsuch writes that "the text and structure of the Constitution clearly suggest that the

[13] Ramos, 140 S. Ct. at 1403, 1408.

[14] See, e.g., Saul Cornell, Originalism on Trial: The Use and Abuse of History in District of Columbia v. Heller, 69 Ohio St. L.J. 625, 626 (referring to the methodology in *Heller* as nonneutral, "admittedly clever" but merely a "parlor trick" demonstrating that "plain meaning originalism has no coherent, historical methodology"); Patrick Charles, The Second Amendment in Historiographical Crisis, Why the Supreme Court Must Reevaluate the Embarrassing "Standard Model" Moving Forward, 39 Fordham Urb. L.J. 1727 (2012).

term 'trial by an impartial jury' carried with it *some* meaning about the content and requirements of a jury trial" and that "[w]herever we might look to determine what the term 'trial by an impartial jury' meant at the time of the Sixth Amendment's adoption[,] the answer is unmistakable and one of those requirements was unanimity."[15] The lead opinion notably does not discuss that the historic process leading to juror unanimity had many more inputs than merely protection of English rights, or that the American incorporation of some, but not all, aspects of the English common law was uncertain, contested, and geographically divergent.

Gorsuch discusses the text of the Sixth Amendment itself only to rebut Louisiana's textual arguments. First, Louisiana argued that the Sixth Amendment's language does not require unanimity nor address whether there is a voting requirement for jury verdicts at all. Second, Louisiana points out that the original draft by James Madison of the Sixth Amendment's text included the requirement that criminal trials "shall be by an impartial jury of freeholders of the vicinage, with the requisite of unanimity for conviction."[16] For reasons unexplained, "unanimity" was struck.[17] Gorsuch doesn't address Louisiana's first piece of evidence directly, save for his reply that the Sixth Amendment "surely meant *something.*"[18] Second, he criticizes Louisiana's argument for "invit[ing] us to distinguish between the historic features of common-law jury trials that (we think) serve 'important enough' functions to migrate silently into the Sixth Amendment and those that don't."[19] Ironically, this is an elegant

---

[15] Ramos, 140 S. Ct. at 1394. Gorsuch adds that "[i]f the term 'trial by an impartial jury' carried any meaning at all, it surely included a requirement as long and widely accepted as unanimity." *Id.* at 1395–96.

[16] 1 Annals of Cong. 435 (1789).

[17] Gorsuch cites Madison's letter to Edmund Pendleton to show what little evidence there is on why the Senate acted as it did. What he does not say is that Madison's letter, like the responses of Virginia senators Richard Henry Lee and William Grayson, show disappointment and outrage over the textual changes made by the Senate when it moved to strike language thought to be critical to criminal jury trials. Therefore, it would be perplexing to cite this evidence as showing that the altered text retained the meaning of the original proposed text. See James Madison to Edmund Pendleton, Sept. 14, 1789, in 5 The Writings of James Madison, 1787–1790 (Gaillard Hunt ed., 1904).

[18] Ramos, 140 S. Ct. at 1395.

[19] *Id.* at 1401–02.

description of the faults of Gorsuch's approach, as he does choose which features of 1791 jury trials are "important enough" to maintain without indicating which others he would retain, nor providing a basis for making such a distinction.

Justice Gorsuch reads the Sixth Amendment text to include those features of a criminal jury trial that he believes were part and parcel of the English common-law practice that the American colonists inherited and meant to preserve in the Sixth Amendment.[20] His historical sources, in their entirety, are these:

- The requirement for unanimity is part of old English common law, emerging in 14th-century England, first cited in passing in the 1367 *Anonymous Case*, and preserved over "400 years" of English practice preceding the Founding;[21]
- Six state constitutions prior to the ratification of the Sixth Amendment included an explicit unanimity requirement, 10 of the original 13 preserved a right to jury trial explicitly, and "state courts appeared to regard unanimity as an essential feature of the jury trial";[22]
- Blackstone's 1769 treatise on the English common law states that only a unanimous jury of 12 could convict in serious crimes;[23]
- Six "[i]nfluential, postadoption treatises" confirm the understanding that, "unanimity in the verdict of the jury is indispensable";[24] and
- Several Supreme Court decisions state, mostly in *dicta*, that unanimity is necessary for jury verdicts.[25]

Those sources are strong evidence that "the public" would read the words "trial by jury" in 1791 as requiring a unanimous jury verdict.

This use of history to support a contextual claim about the implicit meaning of a textual right's scope is very closely in line with

---

[20] *Id.* at 1395–97.

[21] *Id.* at 1395 & nn.11, 15.

[22] *Id.* at 1395 & nn.11–12, 14.

[23] *Id.* at 1395 & n.10.

[24] *Id.* at 1396 & nn.16–18.

[25] *Id.* at 1396–97 & nn.19–22.

Justice Scalia's approach in *Heller*.[26] *Heller* has been declared by some to be "the triumph of Originalism"[27] and the "finest expression" of original-public-meaning jurisprudence by the Court.[28] At a minimum, any deficiencies in Justice Gorsuch's historical approach in *Ramos* warrant close study if they are the hallmarks of an original-public-meaning jurisprudence rooted in *Heller*.

In *Heller*, Justice Scalia begins with a lengthy textual and grammatical discussion, consulting English and American dictionaries as to the meaning of key terms. Beyond the text, Justice Scalia relies upon the following sources for contextualizing the historical meaning of a right "to keep and bear arms":

- The history of the colonists in their struggle against the English and the need for normal people to have arms in this context, stating that "[b]y the time of the founding, the right to have arms had become fundamental for English subjects."[29] Scalia writes that "[i]n the tumultuous decades of the 1760's and 1770's, the Crown began to disarm the inhabitants of the most rebellious areas. That provoked polemical reactions by Americans invoking their rights as Englishmen to keep arms."[30]
- Blackstone's commentaries on the rights to "keep arms" and "bear arms," as "Blackstone, whose works, we have said,

---

[26] *Heller* has come under criticism for its historical approach. See, e.g., Robert W. Gordon, Taming the Past: Essays on Law in History and History in Law 370 (2017) ("The Court's actual opinion in *Heller* ignored all the evidence an originalist could be expected to find most useful, that of what the Founders' contemporaries thought the Amendment was designed to do, while drawing heavily upon evidence from much earlier English practice and much later nineteenth-century American practice. . . ."); Reva Siegel, Dead or Alive: Originalism as Popular Constitutionalism in Heller, 122 Harv. L. Rev. 191 (2008).

[27] Linda Greenhouse, "3 Defining Opinions," N.Y. Times, July 13, 2008, at WK4.

[28] Randy E. Barnett, "The Constitution Means What It Says," Wall St. J., June 27, 2008, at A13. See also David G. Savage, "Supreme Court Finds History Is a Matter of Opinions," L.A. Times, July 13, 2008, http://articles.latimes.com/2008/julh13/nation/na-scotusl3 ("This year the Supreme Court relied more than ever on history and the original meaning of the Constitution in deciding its major cases."); Cass R. Sunstein, Second Amendment Minimalism: Heller as Griswold, 122 Harv. L. Rev. 246 (2008) (declaring it "the most explicitly and self-consciously originalist opinion in the history of the Supreme Court").

[29] Heller, 554 U.S. at 593.

[30] *Id.* at 594.

'constituted the preeminent authority on English law for the founding generation,' cited the arms provision of the Bill of Rights as one of the fundamental rights of Englishmen."[31]

- The 1689 Declaration of Right, which enshrined that Protestants would never be disarmed by the Crown, as being pivotal to colonial notions about the importance of being able to keep and bear arms.[32]

- The fact that 9 of the original 13 state constitutions written before or immediately after 1791 included more specific rights to "bear arms in defense of themselves and the state" or "bear arms in defense of himself and the state."[33]

- Concurrent and postadoption treatises discussing the issue.[34]

The *Heller* approach to ascertain the "original public meaning" of the relevant amendment is parallel to the approach Justice Gorsuch follows in *Ramos*. Both look to the historical context of English rights, especially as crystallized in late 17th-century cases or Crown actions, Blackstone's views, the existence and number of state constitutional provisions with more specificity than the federal amendment at issue, and supportive statements in postadoption treatises.

Part II: The Unanimity Rule in English and American History

Each of Gorsuch's rationales for constitutionalizing unanimity listed in Part I is problematic, and the history is far less simple than portrayed. Although addressing all historical evidence in support

---

[31] *Id.* at 665–66 (quoting Alden v. Maine, 527 U.S. 706, 715 (1999)). As discussed *infra*, Blackstone was not nearly as widely influential or discussed in public or legal teachings until postadoption, beyond his obvious popularity with Madison and a few key Founders. Blackstone's writings on the English common law could therefore hardly have influenced the original "public meaning" of constitutional text to the "public" itself, though certainly it influenced the Framers' intent or, at a stretch, the original lawyers' meaning.

[32] *Id.* at 593–94.

[33] *Id.* at 584–85.

[34] Heller, 554 U.S. at 605–10. It is worth noting that *Heller*'s treatise citations were of more recent vintage than the sources cited by Justice Gorsuch in *Ramos*.

of unanimity is beyond this article's scope,[35] even if one accepts his strongest evidence, he essentially ignores the text itself, presses into permanence common-law conclusions meant to be in flux over time, and does not deal with the varied history of colonial jury practices. Following this logic would entail considering whether other important courtroom conditions and practices of 1791 should be included as part of the "jury trial" guarantee, as well as engaging with jurists' criticisms of unanimity throughout American history.

A. The Cutting-Room Floor and Textual Counterarguments in Ramos

Before even considering the historical context in 1791, it is critical to address the text itself. It is here that we see an immediate divergence between Justice Gorsuch's approach in *Ramos* and Justice Scalia's in *Heller*.

Both Justice Gorsuch in *Ramos* and Justice Scalia in *Heller* contend with textual objections to their contextualized original-public-meaning approach, albeit in contexts that point in different directions. In *Heller*, Scalia deals with dissenting Justice John Paul Stevens's objection that James Madison's original draft of the Second Amendment included *limiting* language on the Second Amendment right in question. In *Ramos*, Gorsuch deals with Louisiana's assertion that Madison's original draft of the Sixth Amendment included more *expansive* language requiring unanimity for criminal trials, but those words did not make it into the final text. In *Heller*, Justice Scalia wrote "[i]t is always perilous to derive the meaning of an adopted provision from another provision deleted in the drafting process."[36] Similarly, Justice Gorsuch in *Ramos* supplements this view with a cursory note that, "rather than dwelling on text left on the cutting room floor, we are much better served by interpreting the language Congress retained and the States ratified," and that anyway, "this snippet of drafting history could just as easily support

---

[35] For example, the history of the minority of state constitutional provisions guaranteeing unanimity at the Founding, paired with the rest who simply echoed or prefaced the federal guarantee of a right to "trial by jury" generally, is both beyond the scope of this article, but also perhaps the weakest among Justice Gorsuch's assembled rationales.

[36] 554 U.S. at 590.

the opposite inference."[37] Reva Siegel has pointed out in a similar context that this approach of waiving off such material "discounts evidence drawn from the amendment's drafting history, appearing to favor evidence remote in time over evidence proximate in time to the amendment's ratification."[38]

While it would be precarious to conclude that the omission of Madison's draft language simply means unanimity was rejected, Justice Gorsuch's implication that it actually supports the implied inclusion of unanimity in the right to "trial by jury" also goes too far. Where a legislature (including the First Congress) has shown it knows how to specifically address a topic in other parts of its legislation and chooses not to do so, at minimum it raises a presumption that they did not mean to include that specific language (even by implication).[39] Surely, the reverse of Gorsuch's concern that the right to an "impartial trial by jury" must "mean something" ought to raise the question of what the Sixth Amendment text already protects: (1) the rights belonging to "the accused"; (2) the right to a "trial" which must be (3) "speedy" and (4) "public"; (5) the trial being by a "jury"; (6) the jury being "impartial"; (7) the jury being "of the state and district wherein the crime shall have been [allegedly] committed," which (8) shall not be retroactively decided; (9) to be "informed of

---

[37] 140 S. Ct. at 1400. It is true that "deleted" provisions in drafts, "snippet[s] of drafting history," and "text left on the cutting room floor" may often cut both ways in terms of interpretive history. In *Heller*, Scalia found that the most natural interpretation of Madison's deleted text regarding "conscientious objectors" is that those opposed to carrying weapons for potential violent confrontation would not be "'compelled to render military service,' in which such carrying would be required." Heller, 554 U.S. at 590. Gorsuch, similarly, criticizes this use of drafting history: "Maybe the Senate deleted the language about unanimity, the right of challenge, and 'other accustomed prerequisites' because all this was so plainly included in the promise of a 'trial by an impartial jury' that Senators considered the language surplusage." Ramos, 140 S. Ct. at 1400. See also *supra* note 18.

[38] Siegel, *supra* note 26, at 197. See also Caleb Nelson, A Critical Guide to Erie Railroad Co. v. Tompkins, 54 Wm. & Mary L. Rev. 921, 954–55 (2005) (assuming significant changes by draftsmen to the text is stylistic and not substantive is unwarranted because "after all, legal draftsmen often change the language of a bill in order to alter its meaning, not to keep its meaning the same").

[39] See, e.g., Pac. Gas & Elec. Co. v. State Energy Res. Conservation & Dev. Comm'n, 461 U.S. 190, 220 (White, J., concurring) ("While we are correctly reluctant to draw inferences from the failure of Congress to act, it would, in this case, appear improper for us to give a reading to the Act that Congress considered and rejected.").

the nature and cause of the accusation"; (10) to confront witnesses against the accused; (11) to have "compulsory process" [right to issue subpoenas] to obtain witnesses; and (12) "to have the assistance of counsel" in defense. But for all this specificity, "unanimity" in verdicts is not included here, nor in Article III, nor in early legislation. From the drafting history it is clear that the Framers knew the precise language for how they might include it if they had wanted to, but it was left on the cutting-room floor, in Gorsuch's words.

B. The English Common-Law Connection

It is striking that both Justice Gorsuch in *Ramos* and Justice Scalia in *Heller* rely heavily on English common-law sources and history for their interpretations of constitutional text. Scalia argues that there was a deeply felt need for the colonists to protect their freedom to keep and bear arms as *against* the English Crown, while Gorsuch contends that there was a deeply felt need for the colonists to jealously protect a centuries-long tradition as Englishmen subject to criminal trials requiring unanimous jury verdicts.[40] And though the context is quite different, both cases involve rights alleged to be critically important due to the depredations of the Crown at the time of the Founding.[41]

Yet pinning so much interpretive value on the state of the English common law in 1791 as determinative of an American constitutional provision is a flawed enterprise. As Justice Byron White wrote in *Williams v. Florida*, "relevant constitutional history casts considerable doubt on the easy assumption in our past decisions that, if a given feature existed in a jury at common law in 1791, then it was

[40] See Bernadette Meyler, Toward a Common Law Originalism, Cornell Law School Research Paper 06-022, 1–8 (2006) (the common law was "far from a unified field at the time of the Founding, nor was it so conceived" to be a place of determinacy or fixation).

[41] To be fair, while the constitutional literature was replete with encomiums about the right to trial by jury, and the importance of juror independence, very little of that literature implicated the importance of the unanimity of jury verdicts in such trials. Among the complaints against the Crown listed in the Declaration of Independence was "[d]epriving us in many cases, the benefits of trial by jury." Two years earlier, in 1774, the Continental Congress resolved that colonies were entitled to "the great and estimable privilege of being tried by a jury of their peers in the vicinage." Declaration and Resolves of the First Continental Congress (Oct. 14, 1774). Neither refers to unanimity.

necessarily preserved in the Constitution."[42] White was critical of past Court decisions which had assumed "every feature of the jury as it existed at common law—whether incidental or essential to that institution—was necessarily included in the Constitution wherever that document referred to a 'jury.'"[43]

Justice Gorsuch cites *Patton v. United States* for the maxim that "the Sixth Amendment affords a right to 'a trial by jury as understood and applied at common law, . . . includ[ing] all the essential elements as they were recognized in this country and England when the Constitution was adopted.'"[44] This rationale, however— that "all the essential elements" from the jury trials of the 1791 common law are constitutionalized—was agreed to by only four justices of the eight considering the case.[45] According to Justice Gorsuch's own analysis in Part IV(A) of *Ramos*'s overruling of *Apodaca v. Oregon*, Justice George Sutherland's opinion in *Patton* recognizing unanimity as an "essential element" of the Sixth Amendment is without precedential value and interesting only as *dicta*.[46] As noted, in *Williams v. Florida*, an actual majority of the Court held the opposite: not "every feature of the jury as it existed at common law—whether incidental or essential to that institution—was necessarily included in the Constitution wherever that document referred to a 'jury.'"[47]

---

[42] 399 U.S. 78, 92 (1970).

[43] *Id.* Cf. State v. Gann, 254 Or. 549, 557 (1969) ("An accident of English history is not a firm foundation for a cornerstone of American constitutional law; nevertheless, a majority of the United States continued to search English legal history to determine the scope of the American constitutional guarantee of trial by jury.").

[44] Ramos, 140 S. Ct. at 1397 (quoting Patton v. United States, 281 U.S. 276, 288 (1930)) (alterations original). Justice Scalia had previously articulated a similar view that whatever the merits of the common law's evolutionary approach, its conclusions circa 1791 were to be frozen as background for interpreting the Bill of Rights. See Crawford v. Washington, 541 U.S. 36 (2004).

[45] Chief Justice Charles Evans Hughes did not participate, and Justices Louis Brandeis, Oliver Wendell Holmes, and Harlan Stone all concurred only as to the result and did not join the reasoning of Justice Sutherland's plurality opinion.

[46] Justice Gorsuch argues in Part IV(A) of his opinion that essentially no part of Justice Lewis Powell's *Apodaca* opinion has precedential force. Only three members of the Court (including Gorsuch) joined that part of his opinion.

[47] 399 U.S. at 91.

The approach in *Ramos* and *Heller*, in contrast, risks treating the ever-changing, adaptable English common law as being closer to a mere statute, freezing its constitutional meaning in 1791. Yet the nature of English common law was and is based in incremental evolution, with judges slowly amending concepts over time to apply to a changing world. As Bernadette Meyler observes:

> Although insisting that the common law stemmed from a time beyond memory, jurists like Sir Edward Coke and Sir Matthew Hale, whose work was received in America and lauded by members of the Founding era, implicitly developed the theory that the common law was open to alteration through suggesting that, in law, history could be strategically deployed rather than only factually invoked.[48]

As an example of where this kind of reasoning could quickly go astray, Louisiana's *Ramos* brief observed that if every common-law feature of a jury trial were required, it would go beyond unanimity. The size would be fixed at 12, the trial must be held in the "vicinage" where the crime occurred, and the jury pool would be limited to male "freeholders," among many other things.[49] In fact, in 18th-century England and the American colonies that imitated it, jurors were chosen or excluded based on their property-holding status, class, general intelligence, prior experience on juries, and—of course—their gender and race.[50]

Justice Oliver Wendell Holmes wrote that "[t]he law embodies the story of a nation's development through many centuries, it cannot be dealt with as if it contained only the axioms and corollaries of a book of mathematics."[51] Yet, for Gorsuch, the axiom of "jury unanimity" is a star fixed according to the common law in 1791, constitutionally mandated and unmoveable over centuries during which it has been questioned repeatedly.

---

[48] Meyler, *supra* note 40, at 7.

[49] Brief of Respondent at 13, Ramos v. Louisiana, 140 S. Ct. 1390 (2020) (No. 18-5924) (citing 4 William Blackstone, Commentaries on the Laws of England *344).

[50] See *supra* note 10.

[51] Oliver Wendell Holmes, Jr., The Common Law 1 (1881).

C. The English and Colonial History of Juror Unanimity

The American colonies did not even follow the English common law consistently before 1791, however. Gorsuch states in a footnote that "[t]o be sure, a few of the Colonies had relaxed (and then restored) the unanimity requirement well before the founding . . . [using Carolina's 1669 Constitution permitting majority verdicts as an example]. But, as Louisiana admits, by the time of the Sixth Amendment's adoption, unanimity had again become the accepted rule."[52] This omits quite a bit of colonial history involving far more experimentation with jury verdicts and adjudication generally, but more fundamentally it misses the point: Common-law jurists fluctuate in their view of doctrines over time, and freezing what appears to be a consensus practice in 1791 mistakes a dynamic history for a static legal monoculture.

Over the arc of the colonies' pre-Revolution history, many experimented with majoritarian jury verdicts or non-jury trials altogether before moving towards a norm of enforced unanimity.[53] Experimentation by colonies ranged from the near-absence of juries in noncapital criminal cases to using majoritarian jury verdict systems.[54] In fact, in the early period, while juries were more widely used in noncapital trials juries in New England, Pennsylvania, West Jersey, and North Carolina, they were not initially used in Maryland, New Netherland, and Virginia.[55]

---

[52] Ramos, 140 S. Ct. at 1396 n.15.

[53] See Mary Sarah Bilder, The Transatlantic Constitution: Colonial Legal Culture and the Empire 186 (2004) (arguing that the American Revolution had ended the "transatlantic constitution" in 1776, but that it proved more difficult to erase transatlantic legal culture in which the colonies had "grown to maturity as part of a conversation about when the laws of England applied"); *id.* at 45. See also Paul Samuel Reinsch, The English Common Law in the Early American Colonies, in 1 Select Essays in Anglo-American Legal History 367, 415 (1907) ("Of Course, the more simple, popular, general parts of the English common law were from the first of great influence on colonial legal relations. This is, however, very far from declaring the common law of England a subsidiary system in actual force from the beginning of colonization. On the contrary, we find from the very first, originality in legal conceptions, departing widely from the most settled theories of the common law, and even a total denial of the subsidiary character of English jurisprudence.").

[54] Reinsch, *supra* note 53, at 18.

[55] Alschuler & Deiss, *supra* note 10, at 871 n.17 (noting that criminal jury trials in America became more frequent in the 18th century than they had been in the 17th century, but, particularly early on, American colonies varied greatly in their use of criminal juries and despite formal declarations that the right to jury trial extended "to all persons in Criminall cases").

Examples of experimentation abound. For instance, under the Duke of York's laws of 1665, proceedings of the earliest courts in the New York, New Jersey and Pennsylvania colonies were informal and the "major part of this jury could give a verdict."[56] Under the 1661–62 Virginia Code, the law of juries was written with "special carefulness and precision," yet it departed from the English requirement that the jurors shall come from the immediate neighborhood of the place where the act was committed.[57] And while Gorsuch mentions Carolina's 1669 Constitution and its nonunanimous provision, he fails to mention its profoundly influential drafter—John Locke.[58]

New England saw even greater experimentation. In Massachusetts, for a brief period, trial by jury was abolished and, even once restored, colonial magistrates had considerable powers over the jury.[59] In Connecticut, "a majority of the jury could decide the issue," and if the jury failed to agree, or in the case of equal division, the magistrate had a casting vote.[60] At the time, Connecticut was independent of England in legal matters and thus, like Massachusetts, could depart far from the common law in its system of popular courts and in the "absence or radical modification of the jury trial."[61] Separately, the New Haven colony (later merged principally into the Connecticut colony) initially did not even utilize the institution of jury trial due to its theocratic system

---

[56] Reinsch, *supra* note 53, at 38. The Duke's Law stated: "A verdict shall be so esteemed when the major part of the jury is agreed, and the minor shall be concluded by the major without allowance of any protest by any of them to the contrary; except in case of life and death where the whole jury is be unanimous in their verdict." Charter to William Penn and Laws of the Province of Pennsylvania, Passed Between the Years 1682 and 1700, Preceded by Duke of York's Laws in Force from the Year 1676 to the Year 1682, with an Appendix Containing Laws Relating to the Organization of the Provincial Courts and Historical Matter 34 (1879).

[57] Reinsch, *supra* note 53, at 47. This had changed by the 18th century, as by 1750, "juries held a less conspicuous position in Virginia than any other mainland province, mattering mostly in trials for life." See John M. Murrin & A.G. Roeber, Trial by Jury: The Virginia Paradox, in The Bill of Rights: A Lively Heritage 109–29 (John Kukla ed., 1987).

[58] "Every jury shall consist of twelve men; and it shall not be necessary they should all agree, but the verdict shall be according to the consent of the majority." The Fundamental Constitutions of Carolina, March 1, 1669, Avalon Project, https://avalon.law .yale.edu/17th_century/nc05.asp.

[59] Reinsch, *supra* note 53, at 47.

[60] *Id.* at 26.

[61] *Id.*

of laws—although it did allow appeal to the local church elders.[62] In Rhode Island, a modified form of jury trial was instituted in the late 17th century and the laws of the colony were seen as "very unmethodical" and "very arbitrary and contrary to the laws" of England.[63] While consensus did grow over the course of the 18th century towards unanimity, it happened largely after English authorities in the 1690s moved to secure colonial compliance with the laws of England.[64]

D. The Reality of 18th-Century English and Colonial Criminal Jury Trials

Insistence on juror unanimity, on the premise that it was a guarantor of juror independence and the rights of the accused, was of relatively recent vintage at the time of the Founding. The far muddier history of how unanimity worked in practice in the centuries leading up to the Founding era is not treated at all in Justice Gorsuch's opinion. Unanimity prior to *Bushell's Case* in 1670 was routinely achieved by coercion, torture, the threat thereof to jurors, and not by their freely given, independent deliberation. Even after *Bushell's Case*, the practices of English, colonial, and early state juries were still extremely coercive toward jurors, and nearly all aspects of judicial and juror procedure were vastly different than modern practices in ways that showed jurors to be far less independent and far more subject to threats and overbearing judicial control than American courts in 2020 would tolerate.

English Lord Chief Justice Alexander Cockburn described the practice of forced unanimity in stark terms:

> Our ancestors insisted on unanimity as the essence of the verdict, but were unscrupulous how that unanimity was obtained. . . . It was a contest between the strong and the weak, the able-bodied, and the infirm, as to who best could bear hunger and thirst, and all the discomforts incident to the confinement [of jurors].[65]

---

[62] *Id.*; Judge Jon C. Blue, The Case of the Piglet's Paternity: Trials from the New Haven Colony, 1639–1663, 16 (2015).

[63] Reinsch, *supra* note 53, at 29.

[64] Bilder, *supra* note 53, at 56–57 (discussing the creation of new royal charters during the period which required the submission of laws for review by the Privy Council, which allowed for "divergence" but not "repugnance" to the laws of England).

[65] Maximus A. Lesser, The Historical Development of the Jury System 194–95 (1894). Cockburn was lord chief justice of the Courts of England and Wales from 1859 to 1875.

During the 14th century, when unanimity became the rule, jurors were harshly regulated. Jurors were allowed and sometimes expected to investigate the case themselves ahead of any trial they would be involved in, but, by the 1370s, it was treated as an irregularity to communicate with jurors once sworn in. If jurors were spoken to by either party or given food or drink, the verdict could be quashed in favor of a new trial.[66]

In his 1730 second edition of *State Trials*, a compendium of trials from King Richard II to George I, Sollom Emlyn observed that the history of forced verdicts convinced him that the rule of unanimity should be abandoned, rather than celebrated:

> The law requires that the twelve men, of which a jury consists, shall all agree before they give in a verdict; if they don't, they must undergo a greater punishment than the criminal himself. They are to be confined in one room without meat, drink, fire or candle, till they are agreed. . . . To what end therefore are they to be restrained in this manner? It may indeed force them to an outward seeming agreement against the dictates of their consciences, but can never be a means of informing their judgment or convincing their understanding. . . . [S]uppose it should be thought requisite that two-thirds should be of a mind, and if so many could agree to find the prisoner guilty, he should be convicted, and if they did not, he should be acquitted. Would not this be a sufficient security for innocence? Sure it would be much better to make a provision in case of non-agreement, than by forcible methods to extort the appearance of one, for it is all one to the prisoner, whether he be convicted without the concurrence of all or by a concurrence which is sincere, but forced.[67]

For most of the jury's common-law history, English courts allowed a mechanism whereby a writ of attaint would allow a second jury to be impaneled to review a "false" verdict given by the first jury. "False" verdicts were thought to come from corruptness or false-swearing (as by coming to the "false" conclusion while under oath,

---

[66] 3 William Blackstone, Commentaries on the Laws of England 375–76 (Edward Christian ed., 12th ed. 1794).

[67] 1 Complete Collection of State Trials and Proceedings for High-Treason, and Other Crimes and Misdemeanours: From the Reign of King Richard II to the End of the Reign of King George I, vi-vii (2d ed. 1730).

jurors were essentially engaging in perjury). Jurors subject to attaint would be fined, imprisoned, or both.[68] In 1670, this method of controlling juries by fine or imprisonment was declared illegal in *Bushell's Case*,[69] and the writ of attaint and punishment of the jury for a wrongful verdict became at least formally unlawful.[70]

Thus, unanimity prior to 1670, and for the bulk of Gorsuch's "400 years" of unbroken practice, was routinely achieved by coercion, torture, and even judicial threats to jurors and not by their freely given independent deliberation.[71] Although *Bushell's Case* represented a judicial attempt to prohibit some of the most egregious practices applied to juries to create unanimity, coercive practices continued thereafter—including in the early American states after ratification of the Sixth Amendment.[72]

In the Founding era, checks on judicial control of juries were limited. Lawyers were rarely present in court and judges played a significant role in conducting trials, though this would change rapidly in the early 19th century:

> During the eighteenth century, since lawyers were rarely present, judges played a major role in conducting trials. . . . Judges examined witnesses and the accused and summed up

[68] 4 William Blackstone, Commentaries on the Laws of England *338.

[69] The practice of attaintment was judicially abolished in 1670 by *Bushell's Case*, where a juror, by writ of habeas corpus, sought his release from prison after acquitting the Quaker William Penn of unlawful assembly despite clear evidence he violated the law. (1670) 124 Eng. Rep. 1006. Formal abolishment of attaintment did not occur in England until the Juries Act of 1825.

[70] William Searle Holdsworth, A History of English Law 388 (1903); William Forsyth, History of Trial by Jury 146–47 (1852).

[71] See John B. Langbein, The Criminal Trial Before the Lawyers, 45 U. Chi. L. Rev. 263, 299 n.107 (1978) (citing J.B. Thayer, Sir Matthew Hale, and Alfred Havighurst as authorities recounting cases where jurors were fined for disobeying judicial orders to bring a unanimous verdict of guilt).

[72] See Renico v. Lett, 559 U.S. 766, 780 (2010) (Stevens, J., dissenting) ("At common law, courts went to great lengths to ensure the jury reached a verdict. Fourteenth-century English judges reportedly loaded hung juries into oxcarts and carried them from town to town until a judgment 'bounced out.' . . . Well into the 19th and even the 20th century, some American judges continued to coax unresolved juries toward consensus by threatening to deprive them of heat, sleep, or sustenance or to lock them in a room for a prolonged period of time."); People v. Sheldon, 156 N.Y. 268 (1898) (citing numerous state court decisions overturning verdicts compelled by coercion and citing Blackstone, Coke, and Emyln).

> the case at the end of the trial, often clearly stating their own views on the merits of the prosecution. Although, following *Bushell's Case* (1670), judges were no longer allowed to fine or otherwise punish juries who failed to come up with the verdict they wanted, they could still put pressure on juries, demanding, for example, why they had reached a particular conclusion, or asking them to reconsider their verdict. . . . The increasing participation of lawyers altered the role of the judges. They continued to exercise supreme authority in the courtroom, but during the nineteenth century their role gradually shifted to one of arbitrating the adversarial contest between barristers, settling any arguments over the law and summing up for the jury.[73]

A good portrait of the power of the trial judge to control juries in this post–*Bushell's Case* era comes from the account given by Judge Ryder. His extensive notes on his time as a criminal court judge of the Old Bailey in London in the 1750s and 1760s gives perhaps the most accurate portrait of the type of judge-jury relationship in English criminal cases with which the Founding generation would have been familiar. In numerous cases Judge Ryder recounts summing up the case for the jury and suggesting his view of the merits and what their decision should be. Although, if it were for acquittal, he sometimes seemed to permit the Crown to call a rebuttal witness—*against the Judge's stated view on the merits*—before the jury made its decision. Citing one case among many, Judge Ryder recounted how, in a case where one drinking companion accused another of highway robbery, "I told the jury I thought there was no ground to find [the accused] guilty on this single evidence [a he-said, he-said, as it were], and the jury found him Not Guilty."[74] In this period, jurors barely had time to deliberate in any event, even after being tipped by the judge as to what their verdict should be. Cases in England were heard at a

---

[73] Trial Procedures, The Proceedings of the Old Bailey, 1674–1913, https://www.oldbaileyonline.org/static/Trial-procedures.jsp.

[74] John H. Langbein, Shaping the Eighteenth-Century Criminal Trial: A View from the Ryder Sources, 50 U. Chi. L. Rev. 1, 23 (1983) (quoting and citing from the aforementioned accounts of his life conducting trials in mid-18th-century England).

fantastically fast pace, with minimized procedures, best characterized as hyper-expedited trials.[75]

Notably, under English practice at the Founding, while the prosecution could be represented by counsel, felony defendants had only
been allowed to be represented by defense counsel beginning in the
1730s.[76] This meant that judges often acted as chief enquirer, questioning witnesses, and thereby shaping the jury's view of the facts,
with the accused left to attempt their own defense.[77] In England, it
was not until the 1836 Prisoners' Counsel Act that defense counsel
was even allowed the right to address the jury directly at all. Prior
to that time, judicial discretion was required for defense counsel to
examine and English courts varied greatly in granting it.[78] Other judicial powers beyond those mentioned by Judge Ryder existed in the
American colonies and early states and compounded the evidentiary
deficiencies created by the neutering of defense counsel. If a trial
judge thought the jury was heading toward the "wrong" conclusion,
he could provisionally terminate the case before it went to verdict,
allowing the prosecution or defense to have a retrial and pick a new
jury.[79] If the case reached deliberations, but the jury returned with
the "wrong" verdict in the judge's view, the judge could send them
back to deliberate further. Astonishingly, even after the jury rendered its preliminary verdict, it continued to remain open "to the
judge to reject a proffered verdict, probe its basis, argue with the

[75] Langbein, *supra* note 71, at 277–78 (in the early 18th century, "[o]rdinary criminal
trials took place with what modern observers will see as extraordinary rapidity."); see
also *id.* at 274 ("in the 1730s a single session lasted several days and processed fifty
to one hundred cases of felony (plus a handful of serious misdemeanors)," and two
juries of 12 men, "[t]he one London jury and the one Middlesex jury tried all these
cases").

[76] *Id.* at 282.

[77] See *id.* at 284–300 (judicial dominance and jury subordination continued in the
65 years after *Bushell's Case* and thus the case made no practical difference to the conduct of criminal procedure for a century).

[78] *Id.* at 313–14 n.80 (recounting historical development of defense counsel participation, noting that "[t]he prohibition upon defense counsel addressing the jury in sum-
mation continued to be enforced until it was abolished by statute in 1836," and citing
an example of a prosecutor objecting to defense counsel's request to cross-examine a
witness in 1741).

[79] *Id.* at 287–88.

jury, give further instruction, and require redeliberation."[80] There-fore the fact that "the jury would lightly disclose the reasoning for a verdict became especially important . . . because it enabled the court to probe the basis of the proffered verdict, hence to identify the jury's 'mistake' and to correct it.'"[81]

Thus, unanimity in jury verdicts has historically often been trum-peted as an individual right against oppression, but, for much of its history, *forced unanimity* was the rule. As we have recounted, this was often forced toward the judge's view as to the correct outcome, and serious punishments awaited jurors who wished to exercise their "independence." Further, unanimity in 1791 and earlier was also very much a *protection of the Court's judgment* against appeal and of the judiciary against criticism.[82] The illiberal nature of trial procedures, lack of effective counsel, and judicial control of juries bequeathed by the English common law and practiced in the Ameri-can states were part and parcel of the system within which juror unanimity practically operated. All of this suggests that there were many other critical elements to the history and practice of unanim-ity and jury deliberation in the Founding era rather than a single-minded fixation on unanimity alone. This fuller story should give the Court pause about plucking the unanimity concept out of its his-torical context and importing it into the Sixth Amendment.

E. The Postadoption Treatises and Unaddressed Critics of Unanimity

If the history of jury practices leading up to the Founding was much more diverse than the *Ramos* decision imagines, what support remains for constitutionalizing unanimity? Justice Gorsuch's final

---

[80] *Id.* at 291–95.

[81] *Id.* at 294–95.

[82] See Sir Matthew Hale, The History of the Common Law 293 (4th ed. 1792) (com-menting that the unanimity requirement granted "a great weight, value and credit" to a verdict); John P. Dawson, A History of Lay Judges 126 (1960) (relating that unanimity was embraced by English judges so that they could "divest themselves of any duty to assemble or appraise the evidence. The fact-finding function was imposed instead on groups of laymen, whose ignorance was disguised by a group verdict and whose sources of knowledge the judges refused to examine."); John v. Ryan, Less than Unani-mous Jury Verdicts in Criminal Trials, 58 J. Crim. L., Criminology & Police Sci. 212 (1967) (recounting historical theory of the development of English juror unanimity that, "[t]o shift the pressure from themselves, the [English] judges originated the una-nimity rule") (citations omitted).

major turn is to postadoption (of the Sixth Amendment) treatises, mirroring Justice Scalia's similar mustering in *Heller*. In *Ramos*, Gorsuch omits discussion of any disagreeable postadoption views on juror unanimity. Such views, however, were expressed by prominent Anglo-American scholars and jurists, including influential members of the Founding generation and later widely known jurists.

Of the jurists Gorsuch does rely on, none stands out more than William Blackstone. Just as Justice Scalia did in *Heller*, Gorsuch takes Blackstone's views to be critical to his originalist enterprise, and he is the only jurist that Gorsuch quotes in the body of his opinion. Gorsuch invokes Blackstone for the proposition that "no person could be found guilty of a serious crime unless 'the truth of every accusation . . . should . . . be confirmed by the unanimous suffrage of twelve of his equals and neighbors'" and that a "'verdict, taken from eleven, was no verdict' at all."[83]

Recent scholarship has cautioned that the Court may sometimes accord exaggerated prominence to Blackstone in discerning original public meaning.[84] The reception of Blackstone's *Commentaries* among both the drafters of the Constitution and the ratifying public in 1791 was far more middling than the Court assumes. It is true that in the immediate postratification period Blackstone gained traction as the preeminent teacher of the English "common law" to American lawyers.[85] However, "[w]hile instructors may have embraced his works by 1800, he seems not to have occupied any privileged position in the minds of instructors in the decades preceding the Constitutional Convention."[86] There is less reason, therefore, to assume the ratifying public was relying on Blackstone's view on jury unanimity in its reading of the Sixth Amendment text. And any member of "the public" with any knowledge of the history of colonial experimentation with nonunanimity would not necessarily have found Blackstone to be obviously right in his view that a verdict rendered by a less-than-unanimous jury was "no verdict at all."

---

[83] Ramos, 140 S. Ct. at 1396 (some internal quotations omitted).

[84] Martin Minot, The Irrelevance of Blackstone: Rethinking the Eighteenth-Century Importance of the Commentaries, 104 Va. L. Rev. 1359 (2018); Davison M. Douglas, Foreword: The Legacy of St. George Tucker, 47 Wm. & Mary L. Rev. 1111, 1112–13 (2006).

[85] Minot, *supra* note 84, at 1384 (noting that the works of Sir Edmund Coke, Sir Matthew Hale, and Matthew Bacon were more commonly read by the Founders).

[86] *Id.* at 1383.

Nor are Blackstone's own views on the application of English common law to the colonies necessarily helpful to Gorsuch's reliance on importing the English common law. Blackstone, in his 1765 *Commentaries*, rejected the notion that the American colonies were automatically subject to the English common law:

> [If] an uninhabited country be discovered and planted by English subjects, all the English laws then in being, which are the birthright of every subject, are immediately there in force. . . . But in conquered or ceded countries, that have already laws of their own, the king may indeed alter and change those laws; but, till he does actually change them, the ancient laws of the country remain, unless such as are against the law of God, as in the case of an infidel country. Our American plantations are principally of this latter sort; being obtained in the last century, either by right of conquest and driving out the natives (with what natural justice I shall not at present enquire) or by treaties. And therefore the common law of England, as such, has no allowance or authority there[.][87]

Beyond Blackstone, the jurists critical of unanimity often expressed an alternative view that majoritarian voting requirements were superior to unanimity or endorsed unanimity only with serious misgivings regarding the coercion involved in producing it. This is largely consistent with Justice Gorsuch's sources. Outside of Joseph Story's *Commentaries* and Thomas Cooley's Reconstruction-era commentaries,[88] the sources Gorsuch cites do not relate the criticality and importance of unanimity to *the Sixth Amendment itself*

---

[87] 1 Blackstone, Commentaries on the Laws of England 107 (4th ed. 1770). See also Bilder, *supra* note 53, at 39 (writing that Blackstone's *Commentaries* reveal that among English legal commentators there was uncertainty over the application of English common law to the colonies right up to the Revolution, while for colonial attorneys and crown officers, the "relationship between English law and the colonies was an evolving set of arguments, not a simple rule").

[88] Thomas M. Cooley, Constitutional Limitations 319–20 (1871) ("wherever the right of this trial [by jury] is guaranteed by the constitution without qualification or restriction, it must be understood as retained in all those cases which were triable by jury at the common law, and with all the common-law incidents to a jury trial, so far, at least, as they can be regarded as tending to the protection of the accused").

as many of the cited sources are taken out of context.[89] Yet even Cooley goes on to qualify his support that the Sixth Amendment guarantee of a jury trial requires unanimity; he notes that "this is a very old requirement in the English Common law, and it has been adhered to, notwithstanding very eminent men have assailed it as unwise and inexpedient," citing critics such as John Locke, William Forsyth, Francis Lieber, and Jeremy Bentham.[90] All other treatises Gorsuch cites state a normative view that the rule of unanimity is how jury trials *should* be conducted, not that the Bill of Rights compels them to be as a constitutional matter.

Early American jurists who criticized unanimity included the influential Founder and Supreme Court justice James Wilson. In his *Lectures of Law* in 1792, Wilson discussed at length the illiberal history of producing unanimity by restraint and coercion. He ultimately supported the rule of unanimity as good policy on "popular sovereignty" grounds.[91] But Wilson was also harshly critical of the history of the rule:

> Unanimity produced by restraint! Is this the principle of decision in a trial by jury? Is that trial, which has been so long considered as the palladium of freedom—Is that trial brought to its consummation by tyranny's most direful engine—force upon opinion—upon opinion given under all the sanctions and solemnities of an oath?[92]

---

[89] Gorsuch cites Nathan Dane's *Digest of American Law* as stating the Constitution required unanimity. But Dane appears to be referring to the original 17 amendments submitted by James Madison to the Senate in September 1789, which included the "unanimity" language later discarded by the Senate as discussed in Part I. 6 Nathan Dane, Digest of American Law 226 (1824) (". . . By the 10th article of said amendments, the jury in *criminal* matters must be unanimous"). In a different volume not cited by Gorsuch, Dane does say that the federal Crimes Act of 1790 would require a unanimous jury verdict for capital or infamous crimes under the act because "trial by jury" was "fully declared in all our constitutions, and repeatedly in our laws." 7 Nathan Dane, Digest of American Law 335 (1824).

[90] Cooley, *supra* note 88, at 320 n.1.

[91] That is, the state or society was always a party to criminal prosecutions and thus, under the social contract, the party injured transferred the right of punishment to the state that was represented through the medium of the selected jury. Thus, a unanimous sentiment of 12 jurors was necessary to convict a citizen. Mark David Hall & Kermit L. Hall eds., 2 Collected Works of James Wilson 985 (2007).

[92] *Id.* at 975.

Wilson recited the long history of English compulsion of jurors and remarked that, "[e]very other agreement produced by duress is invalid and unsatisfactory: what contrary principles can govern this?"[93] Wilson suggested that instead a verdict should be the sum of 12 different opinions reduced to an average result to form a "useful and satisfactory" verdict and that would not cause men to "counterfeit" the verdict by forming "disingenuous" unanimity.[94] Contemporaneous to Wilson's lectures, English barrister and Cambridge professor Edward Christian, in his 1794 edition of Blackstone's *Commentaries*, likewise deemed the unanimity principle "repugnant to all experience of human conduct, passion and understanding," which "could hardly in any age have been introduced into practice by the deliberate act of a legislature."[95] And in 1801, then-New York Supreme Court justice James Kent called the doctrine of compelling a jury to unanimity by hunger and fatigue "a monstrous doctrine" that was "altogether repugnant to a sense of humanity and justice."[96]

Similarly, while concluding for jurisprudential reasons that criminal trials should retain a unanimity requirement, the towering 19th-century jurist William Forsyth also expressed doubts about the provenance of unanimity. In his 1852 book *History of Trial by Jury*, Forsyth recognized the same history of forced unanimity noted by both Wilson and Blackstone, writing that it was "impossible to deny there are strong reasons to be urged against the [unanimity] requirement" because in many cases the unanimous verdict was "apparent and not real . . . purchased at the sacrifice of truth."[97] Significantly, he quotes at length from the English commissioners appointed in 1830 to report upon the Courts of Common Law, who said,

> It is difficult to defend the justice or wisdom of the [principle of unanimity]. It seems absurd that the rights of a party,

---

[93] *Id.* at 974–75.

[94] *Id.* at 989–90.

[95] Blackstone (Edward Christian ed.), *supra* note 66, at 376 n.20.

[96] People v. Olcott, 2 Johns. Cas. 301, 309 (N.Y. 1801) (such a verdict could not "receive the sanction of public opinion").

[97] William Forsyth, History of Trial by Jury 205–06 (1852) (noting that the "marvel" of juries was that they should agree at all, because the truth was that "verdicts are often the result of the surrender or compromise of individual opinion" as one or more jurymen "find themselves in a minority, and many causes concur to render them less tenacious of their opinion than we might expect").

in questions of a doubtful and complicated nature, should depend upon his being able to satisfy twelve persons that one particular state of facts is the true one. . . . [There seems little reason] why the present principle of keeping them together till unanimity be produced by a sort of duress of imprisonment, should be retained. *And the interests of justice seem manifestly to require a change of law upon this subject.*[98]

Like Wilson, Forsyth concluded that unanimity should still be required in criminal cases, but only after carefully considering the history of the practice.

In both the antebellum and Reconstruction periods, widely respected 19th-century German-American jurist and Columbia constitutional law professor Francis Lieber publicly advocated a move toward a majority rule for jury verdicts. He had previously taken the position in 1853, in his treatise *On Civil Liberty and Self-Government*, noting that John Locke himself opposed the unanimity rule by writing a majority requirement into Carolina's 1669 Constitution.[99] Lieber proposed to the New York Constitutional Convention of 1867 that the unanimity requirement be replaced with the rule that, "each jury shall consist of twelve jurors, the agreement of two-thirds of whom shall be sufficient for a verdict, in all cases, both civil and penal, except in capital cases, when three-fourths must agree to make a verdict valid."[100] In the proposal, Lieber observed that nowhere but in England and the United States is unanimity required to make a verdict, despite its origins in the "strange logic of hunger, cold and darkness."[101] He further argued that the practice of retrying a case after a jury was hung due to a nonunanimous verdict resulted in an implicit violation of the protection against double jeopardy.[102] Finally, Lieber declared that juror unanimity was "merely accommodative

---

[98] *Id.* at 251–52 (emphasis added).

[99] Francis Lieber, On Civil Liberty and Self-Government 238 (1853) ("The jury trial has been mentioned here as one of the guarantees of liberty, and it might not be improper to add some remarks on the question whether the unanimous verdict ought to be retained, or whether a verdict as the result of two-thirds or a simple majority of jurors agreeing ought to be adopted. . . . It is my firm conviction, after long observation and study that the unanimity principle ought to be given up, would be of no value.").

[100] Francis Lieber, The Unanimity of Juries, 15 Am. L. Reg. 727, 730 (1867).

[101] *Id.* at 728–29.

[102] *Id.* at 731.

unanimity" and not "an intrinsically truthful one" since any refractory juror could "defeat the ends of justice by holding out."[103]

Other later treatise writers, like Maximus Lesser, noted the innumerable policy reasons for eliminating unanimity, primarily that it would make corruption "less practicable."[104] And John Norton Pomeroy, whose 1864 work Gorsuch cites as an influential post-adoption treatise confirming the unanimity requirement, wrote that while it was "a long and widely accepted" practice,

> the force of the argument against the practice of requiring unanimity in juries is overwhelming; no other deliberative bodies, whether legislative or judicial, follow it, and strenuous endeavors have been made by the best judicial writers in England to bring this national institution in a conformity with reason but as yet all attempts at a reform have proved unavailing.[105]

None of these points contrary to unanimity, made by scholars from the Founding era and onward, are cited or discussed. The numerous "postadoption treatises" Gorsuch cites simply do not present strong support for the idea that the Sixth Amendment itself constitutionalizes unanimity, much less show an overwhelming consensus that unanimity was the only permissible answer to how to conduct a common-law trial.

Conclusion

The concept of mandatory unanimity in jury verdicts has been contested throughout American history.[106] Underlying Justice Gorsuch's view is the premise that we must freeze some conditions existing in

---

[103] *Id.* at 730.

[104] Lesser, *supra* note 65, at 194–95.

[105] John Norton Pomeroy, An Introduction to Municipal Law §135, 78 (1864). Pomeroy goes on to note the English jury has historically been "generally, almost uniformly" a "passive instrument in the hands of judges and prosecuting officers, and have blindly registered their decrees." *Id.* at §136, 79.

[106] We do not discuss those post-Reconstruction advocates for nonunanimity who did so on the basis of racism. Many scholars, jurists, courts, and legislators advocated majoritarian verdict rules on jurisprudential grounds without mention of race. Indeed, whether racism animated Louisiana's 1898 supermajority jury verdict procedure, there is no evidence that its advocacy for preserving its majoritarian verdicts in 2020 was so animated. See Ramos, 140 S. Ct. at 1454 (Alito, J., dissenting).

1791 with respect to the Anglo-American practice of criminal jury trials. This logically leads to the question whether other critical and accepted trial conditions from 1791 were meant to be likewise preserved for all time by the bare language of the Sixth Amendment. The American people of 2020 would find the routine processes of jury trials in the Founding era, which occurred alongside the unanimity mandate, deeply unsettling and surprising.[107] Justice Gorsuch's paeans to the ancient "English" right to a unanimous jury verdict also ring a bit less sonorously once one understands that 1791 juries were often deprived of light, warmth, food, and water, and exhorted toward reaching the "right" verdict by powerful trial judges confining them until they agreed to a unanimous verdict.

A more textual approach would consider that Madison's original draft of the Sixth Amendment included "unanimous" only to have the Senate strike it before proceeding to a vote before the Congress of 1791. The majority opinion in *Heller* saw a somewhat analogous challenge in the deletion from the Second Amendment of language regarding "standing armies," conscientious objectors, and the division between the military and civil power. But, as noted earlier, the Second Amendment's final text created potential uncertainty over whether the militia clause limited the "right to bear arms." There is no such grammatical complexity in the Sixth Amendment—it simply does not mention unanimity or verdict rules. Madison's original draft of the Sixth Amendment would clearly have made unanimity integral to the guarantee of an "impartial trial by jury." The final text does not, and we cannot say for certain why that is.

It is worth questioning whether the methodology of *Ramos*, broadly following *Heller* in interpreting the historical context of the Bill of Rights, is sensible for the Court in interpreting vague constitutional guarantees like the right to "trial by jury." There are other, more modest approaches to solving this problem consistent with original public meaning. The Court need not conclude that something which was proclaimed as critical in 1791, out of its context, simply must

---

[107] Compare *supra* Part II(C) (discussing English and early American procedure whereby a trial judge could cut off proceedings midstream, prior to verdict, allowing the prosecution or defense to have a retrial and pick a new jury) with United States v. Jorn, 400 U.S. 470, 487 (1971) (barring retrial of criminal case where first judge acted "abruptly" by cutting off prosecutor "in midstream" and discharged the jury without giving the parties an opportunity to object).

be found in the Constitution, notwithstanding a textual vacuum. Sometimes "original conditions" and "original public meaning" may dovetail; at other times they may not. If the public's reading of the words "trial by jury" could *not* plausibly be read to refer to majoritarian, nonunanimous trials by juries in Carolina in the late 1600s, in Scottish trials in 1791 (allowing a majority verdict), or in a 10-2 verdict from a jury of 12, as in Ramos's trial, then there should be convincing historical evidence. There is not. With the text indeterminate and the history mixed, the better *historical* answer may be that unanimity simply is not constitutionalized by the Sixth Amendment. That *Ramos* determined otherwise anchors criminal procedure to 1791 standards unmoored from context and therefore places unanimity outside the legislative power of Congress or state legislatures.[108]

The justices should be more cautious about not only the use of history and the import of the English common law, but the underlying historical conditions for trial procedure they are freezing in 1791. In constitutionalizing the rule of unanimity, *Ramos* risks damaging "original public meaning" as an interpretive method, making it seem reducible to a process of finding historical evidence for a common view at the time of ratification. This is problematic when the 2020 *Ramos* Court treats that common view as fundamental while the 1972 *Apodaca* Court did not, with precisely the same history to draw on and no change to the original understanding during those 48 years. Ultimately, this is problematic for an originalism that seeks original understandings and not merely original conditions.

---

[108] See Gordon Van Kessel, Adversary Excesses in the American Criminal Trial, 67 Notre Dame L. Rev. 403, 408 (1992) (noting that a major barrier to American criminal procedure reform lies in "[a] legal system of fixed rules made impervious to significant modification by Supreme Court decisions constitutionalizing or otherwise federalizing the rules of criminal procedure"); Albert W. Alschuler, Implementing the Criminal Defendant's Right to Trial: Alternatives to the Plea Bargaining System, 50 U. Chi. L. Rev. 931, 995–98 (1983) (remarking on the unlikelihood that incorporation of the Sixth Amendment would be used to preclude state experimentation with trial procedures including different jury and lay adjudication methods, and stating "[i]t would be strange and unfortunate if the federal Constitution were read to preclude states from seeking workable alternatives to our existing regime of criminal justice—a regime so costly").

Looking Ahead: Déjà Vu at the Supreme Court

Anastasia Boden*

If there were ever a time that people wanted to look ahead, it's now. After wrapping up a hot-button Supreme Court term, the country is locked down in the middle of a global pandemic and anticipating a fierce and polarizing election. Many people simply want to look to the future and hope 2020 passes as quickly as possible along with the coronavirus, murder hornets, cancel culture, and civil-rights violations that came with it.

And yet, for Supreme Court watchers, looking forward will necessarily entail looking back. Next term the Court will hear a slew of cases that were scheduled for argument last term but were rescheduled after COVID-19 forced the marble palace to temporarily close. Cases concerning whether the Religious Freedom Restoration Act (RFRA) authorizes money damages, a law that limits the political affiliation of state supreme court judges, and due process limits on personal jurisdiction over out-of-state defendants were all originally slated for last term but will be heard in the upcoming term instead.

One case in particular should instill an acute sense of déjà vu: In *California v. Texas*, the Court will once again consider the constitutionality of the Affordable Care Act's requirement that every person obtain health insurance, also known as the "individual mandate." No, it's not Groundhog Day; it's the October 2020 Supreme Court term.

Even the Court's new docket forces us to look back. In *Edwards v. Vannoy*, the Court will consider whether its decision last term in *Ramos v. Louisiana* (incorporating against the states the Sixth Amendment's guarantee of a unanimous jury verdict) applies retroactively. In *Facebook Inc. v. Duguid*, which was put on hold last term while the Court decided

---

* Anastasia Boden is a senior attorney at the Pacific Legal Foundation (PLF), where she specializes in constitutional litigation. The views expressed herein are those solely of the author, not of PLF or its clients.

the constitutionality of a federal robocall ban, the Court will consider the reach of that same act. In *Collins v. Mnuchin*, involving the president's ability to remove the director of the Federal Housing Finance Agency (FHFA), the Court will decide virtually the same question it answered last term in *Seila Law v. Consumer Financial Protection Bureau*, just in the context of a different agency.

Looking back is, of course, inherent to the institution. The Supreme Court is a court of final review, and it carefully considers precedent. But the fact that COVID-19 required cases to be rescheduled heightens the sensation of looking back.[1]

One difference between the coming term and last term is that we can expect this one to be a bit quieter. Big terms, like October 2019–2020, are usually followed by more discreet ones. In addition to that rule of thumb, Chief Justice John Roberts has demonstrated a commitment to preserving the image of the Court as independent from politics, and those instincts may be heightened during an election year. And, if the leaks are accurate, Justice Brett Kavanaugh is eager to "avoid certain thorny dilemmas" in the wake of his contentious confirmation hearing.[2] It stands to reason that the justices will select a less eventful docket this term. That being said, 2020 has been thoroughly unpredictable. All bets are off.

I. The Affordable Care Act

Ever since the Affordable Care Act's (ACA) passage, in more Supreme Court terms than not, there's been a case challenging some aspect of its validity. From *NFIB v. Sebelius*[3] in the October 2011 term

---

[1] Speaking of COVID-19, the Court so far has declined to weigh in on various pandemic-related measures, including shut-down orders, voting rules, and prisoner policies. Given the Court's refusal to grant emergency relief in *Calvary Chapel Dayton Valley v. Sisolak*, a case involving a Nevada order that prohibited churches from admitting more than 50 persons for services but that permitted casinos to operate at 50 percent capacity, it's clear the Court is reluctant to wade into the debate about the unprecedented restrictions on personal liberties that followed in the wake of the pandemic. As long as the outbreak continues, petitions will undoubtedly continue to be filed, including a petition from Calvary Chapel once the lower courts decide the case on the merits. Perhaps the longer the orders stay in force, the more likely the justices will see fit to resolve the constitutional disputes wrought by the government's response to the outbreak.

[2] Joan Biskupic, "How Brett Kavanaugh Tried to Sidestep Abortion and Trump Financial Docs Cases," CNN, July 29, 2020, https://cnn.it/3gzVepd.

[3] 567 U.S. 519 (2012).

(challenging the individual mandate and Medicaid expansion), to *Burwell v. Hobby Lobby*[4] in 2012 (challenging the employer contraception mandate under RFRA), to *King v. Burwell*[5] in 2014 (challenging the IRS's authority to extend tax credits to federal health insurance exchanges), to *Zubik v. Burwell*[6] in 2015 (challenging the contraception mandate as applied to religious organizations), to *Health Options v. United States*[7] and *Little Sisters of the Poor v. Pennsylvania*[8] this past term (challenging the government's refusal to reimburse insurers for losses suffered due to the ACA and agency authority to exempt religious organizations from the contraception mandate, respectively), nary a term has gone by without an Obamacare challenge. The October 2020 term will be no different, as the Court reconsiders the constitutionality of the individual mandate in light of Congress's decision to reduce the "tax" for noncompliance to $0.[9]

As most Court watchers will remember, in 2012 the Court upheld the ACA's requirement that individuals purchase health insurance (the so-called individual mandate) on the theory that it was a legitimate exercise of Congress's taxing power. Despite the fact that Congress itself described the fee for noncompliance as a penalty, the chief justice used a "saving construction" to rule that the mandate was a tax on the failure to maintain coverage. He reasoned that though the fee was not explicitly called a tax, it had familiar hallmarks of a tax: it generated revenue, was paid by taxpayers to the treasury, and was assessed by the IRS. Chief Justice Roberts wrote that while his view was not "the most natural interpretation," it was a "fairly possible" one.[10]

In an unsigned dissent, Justices Antonin Scalia, Anthony Kennedy, Clarence Thomas, and Samuel Alito argued that the "tax" was designed as a penalty for violating the law rather than a forced contribution to raise revenue. And because Congress itself called the fee a "penalty," the monetary assessment for failing to maintain health insurance was not a tax. According to the dissenters, the majority

---

[4] 573 U.S. 682 (2013).

[5] 135 S. Ct. 2480 (2015).

[6] 136 S. Ct. 1557 (2016).

[7] 140 S. Ct. 1308 (2020).

[8] 140 S. Ct. 2367 (2020).

[9] California v. Texas, 140 S. Ct. 1262 (2020) (cert. granted).

[10] NFIB, 567 U.S. at 563.

had effectively rewritten the statute in order to save it. "We have never held that any exaction imposed for violation of the law is an exercise of Congress' taxing power—even when the statute calls it a tax, much less when (as here) the statute repeatedly calls it a penalty," the dissenters wrote.[11] When Congress "adopt[s] the criteria of wrongdoing" and then imposes a penalty as the "principal consequence on those who transgress its standard," it has created a penalty, not a tax.[12]

The dissenters further reasoned (and on this point Chief Justice Roberts agreed) that the penalty could not be justified as a use of Congress's commerce power. Congress may regulate economic activity that, in the aggregate, has a substantial effect on interstate commerce. But rather than regulating activity, the mandate regulated *in*activity—that is, the failure to purchase health insurance.[13] And "[i]f all inactivity affecting commerce is commerce, commerce is everything."[14] Using such reasoning, there would be no limit on the federal government's ability to compel activity in order to regulate it.

Fast forward several years and Congress has reduced the ~~penalty~~ tax to zero. While both the mandate and the "shared responsibility payment" for failure to comply remain on the books, Congress in 2017 set the payment at the lesser of "zero percent" of a person's household income and "$0."

Two individuals and 18 states[15] filed a lawsuit arguing that the "tax" is now an unconstitutional mandate under the Court's decision in *NFIB*. The tax is no longer a tax, they claim, because it generates no revenue, an essential prerequisite for any tax. They further argue that the mandate is not severable from the rest of the act and so the entire thing must fall.

---

[11] *Id.* at 662.

[12] *Id.* at 662–63.

[13] Leaks and certain clues within the dissenting opinion, including the fact that it refers to the plurality's concurring opinion as "the dissent," drew speculation that Chief Justice Roberts changed his vote to uphold the mandate as a tax at the last minute, thus saving Obamacare. See, e.g., *id.* at 658.

[14] *Id.*

[15] Texas, Alabama, Arizona, Arkansas, Florida, Georgia, Indiana, Kansas, Louisiana, Mississippi, Missouri, Nebraska, North Dakota, South Carolina, South Dakota, Tennessee, Utah, and West Virginia brought suit. Wisconsin was originally a plaintiff state, but later sought dismissal from the appeal.

For their part, the federal defendants agree that the mandate is unconstitutional, but they disagree that it's not severable from the rest of the law. Based on the defendants' unwillingness to defend the mandate on the merits, 20 states and the District of Columbia have intervened to argue that the mandate should be upheld.[16]

The district court held that the mandate was unconstitutional and not severable from the rest of the act and struck down the entire statute (though it stayed its judgment, pending appeal). On appeal in the Fifth Circuit, the U.S. House of Representatives intervened to defend the ACA.

In an opinion by Judge Jennifer Elrod, the Fifth Circuit affirmed, ruling that "[n]ow that the shared responsibility payment amount is set at zero" a "saving construction is no longer available."[17] The tax no longer raises revenue, is no longer paid into the treasury, and is no longer determined by factors like taxable income. It is simply no longer a tax, and, as a mandate, it cannot be upheld under the commerce power given the opinion of a majority of justices in *NFIB v. Sibelius*. The Fifth Circuit remanded to the district court to determine severability.

The House and the state intervenors petitioned the Court for review and the justices agreed to hear the case. We'll finally find out whether the chief justice meant what he said when he ruled that the ACA does not mean what it says. If the "individual mandate" was not a mandate at all but a "tax," what happens when the "tax" goes away?

There's also an interesting standing question that asks whether the individual plaintiffs are injured by the mandate and have standing to challenge it, given that they suffer no penalty if they merely choose not to buy health insurance. The Fifth Circuit ruled that they did in fact have standing, based on their statements that they would follow the law because *it is the law* and will suffer an injury (lost money) by purchasing insurance. The defendants contend that such an injury is self-inflicted since the plaintiffs would have suffered no harm if they had just flouted the law and declined to buy insurance.

---

[16] Those states are California, Colorado, Connecticut, Delaware, Hawaii, Illinois, Iowa, Kentucky, Massachusetts, Michigan, Minnesota, Nevada, New Jersey, New York, North Carolina, Oregon, Rhode Island, Vermont, Virginia, and Washington.

[17] Texas v. United States, 945 F.3d 355 (5th Cir. 2019).

It's an interesting question that often comes up when the government issues guidance or imposes a regulation that affects a person's rights or responsibilities and then argues that, because the agency has not explicitly directed the would-be plaintiffs to do anything, or penalized them directly, they are therefore barred from challenging the requirement in court.[18] Arguably, rule-of-law considerations weigh in favor of permitting plaintiffs to challenge laws that purport to regulate their behavior, even if the government claims they are free to ignore the law as written.

If the mandate is indeed struck down, and, depending on severability, this may be the Obamacare litigation to end all Obamacare litigation. Or, history might repeat itself, and we'll see the act at the Court in a future term in a Nietzschean cycle of eternal return.

II. Religious Liberty

A. Free Exercise

In *Fulton v. City of Philadelphia*,[19] the justices will consider whether to overturn a case that tops many religious freedom lawyers' list of most reviled court opinions: *Employment Division v. Smith*.[20] *Fulton* concerns Philadelphia's decision to exclude religious agencies from participating in the city's foster system on the basis that they had refused to refer same-sex couples as potential parents. Catholic Social Services (CSS), an adoption agency, and longtime foster parent

---

[18] See, e.g., Owner-Operator Indep. Drivers Ass'n v. Fed. Motor Carrier Safety Admin., 656 F.3d 580, 586 (7th Cir. 2011) (finding it "odd that the Agency is arguing that it must have a strict rule now to get [its objects] to be more compliant with [the agency's] rules, but at the same time it is asserting that these rules are not meant to change anyone's immediate behavior enough to confer standing to challenge that regulation"); Stilwell v. Office of Thrift Supervision, 569 F.3d 514, 518 (D.C. Cir. 2009) (finding that "it is more than a little ironic that [the government] would suggest [the plaintiff] lack[s] standing and then, later in the same brief, label [the plaintiff] as a prime example [of] . . . the very problem the Rule was intended to address"); Contender Farms, L.L.P. v. U.S. Dep't of Agric., 779 F.3d 258, 265 (5th Cir. 2015) (rejecting the government's argument that private participants in the horse industry lacked standing to challenge a regulation requiring organizations to enforce industry standards against them); Duarte v. City of Lewisville, 759 F.3d 514 (5th Cir. 2014) (holding that family members had standing to challenge ordinance regulating where their immediate relative could live).

[19] 140 S. Ct. 1104 (2020) (cert. granted).

[20] 494 U.S. 872 (1990).

Sharonell Fulton, alleged that the city's policy violated their free-exercise rights, the Establishment Clause, Pennsylvania's Religious Freedom Protection Act, and their right to free speech.

When children enter foster care, the city of Philadelphia largely relies on private agencies to find them homes. In 2018, there were 30 such agencies operating in the city. One such agency, CSS, had placed thousands of children with parents and over 40 children with Fulton. But CSS's participation was halted in 2018 after a reporter from the *Philadelphia Inquirer* notified officials that two Catholic agencies would not recommend same-sex couples as foster parents. There was no evidence that a same-sex couple had ever been turned away or had even approached CSS. Nevertheless, the city ended its contract with the group.

After CSS and Fulton sued, the district court and the Third Circuit upheld the policy on the basis that it was a neutral act of general applicability under *Employment Division v. Smith*. Both courts further ruled that there was no free speech problem with conditioning a foster organization's use of government funds on implementing an anti-discrimination policy.

In *Smith*, the plaintiff had sought an exemption from a state drug law that prevented him from using peyote in a Native American religious ceremony. The Court rejected the plaintiff's First Amendment claims and ruled that "the right of free exercise does not relieve an individual of the obligation to comply with a valid and neutral law of general applicability on the ground that the law proscribes (or prescribes) conduct that his religion prescribes (or proscribes)."[21] Writing for the majority, Justice Scalia wrote that the government could not regulate a religious ceremony qua religious ceremony, but to make people's obligation to obey a generally applicable law contingent on their religious beliefs would "permit every citizen to become a law unto himself."[22]

Smith has been widely loathed by religious freedom advocates since the day it was issued, and it was the impetus for RFRA, which restores the "compelling interest" test for laws that burden free-exercise rights. CSS and Fulton argue that the Free Exercise Clause requires affirmative freedom from government interference, not

[21] *Id*. at 879 (cleaned up).

[22] *Id*.

freedom from nondiscriminatory laws. They therefore urge the Court to apply strict scrutiny to any government action that infringes exercises of faith. But there are other routes the Court could take, apart from overturning *Smith*. In addition to arguing that *Smith* should be abandoned, CSS and Fulton also argue that the Third Circuit incorrectly applied *Smith* and that the city's policy places an unconstitutional condition on their free speech rights.

Religious liberty is one area where the Court has been consistently active in vindicating constitutional rights. But here it's being asked to strike a balance between protecting that freedom and allowing the government to pursue its interest in anti-discrimination laws. It remains to be seen whether it will disturb the holding in *Smith*, as it's been asked many times before, or whether it will find some other middle ground.

B. RFRA Money Damages

In *FNU [First Name Unknown] Tanzin v. Tanvir*, the Court will consider whether RFRA permits money damages in cases against federal officials in their individual capacity.[23] The plaintiffs are a group of Muslim men, all of whom are U.S. citizens or lawful permanent residents, who allege that senior government officials placed them on the "no fly" list as retaliation for refusing to become FBI informants. At least one of the men had been banned from traveling by plane for years despite presenting no threat to aviation safety, causing him to lose his trucking job and depriving him of the ability to visit his family in Pakistan. Because the men refused the officials' overtures to act as informants at least in part because of their sincerely held religious beliefs, they sued the officials under RFRA.

The district court dismissed the case on the basis that RFRA does not permit money damages against government officials. The Second Circuit, however, reversed. As a separation-of-powers matter, the legislature is generally responsible for policy considerations, such as whether to confer indemnity or immunity, and courts are responsible for applying the law and fashioning the appropriate remedy. To preserve that balance, the Second Circuit declined to read Congress's intent into the statute. Instead, it applied a presumption that all remedies are available to a court unless Congress expressly

[23] 140 S. Ct. 550 (2019) (cert. granted).

says otherwise. Finding no indication that Congress sought to exclude money damages, the court ruled that they were available under RFRA.

Money damages are an important remedy for plaintiffs who seek to vindicate their constitutional rights in court. Where people have been injured and injunctive or declaratory relief is impractical or unavailable, damages often are the only way to make the person whole. And even when they are not the *only* remedy, they are important means of imposing accountability. The government argues, however, that there are good policy reasons for withholding damages as a remedy, because they may purportedly dissuade officials from vigorously performing their duties. The government further argues that it would threaten the separation of powers to allow damages when they are not clearly authorized. Interestingly, both parties argue that the case presents separation-of-powers concerns, but they each think those concerns weigh in their own favor.

III. The Administrative State

A. Separation of Powers

Following its decision in *Seila Law* last term, in which Chief Justice Roberts wrote an opinion deeming the Consumer Financial Protection Bureau's (CFPB) structure unconstitutional, the Court will consider in *Collins v. Mnuchin* whether the structure of the FHFA presents similar concerns.[24]

The claim in both cases is that restrictions on the president's removal power violate the Constitution's promise of separation of powers. Administrative agencies often wield the power of all three branches, and, as Justice Kavanaugh observed as a judge on the D.C. Circuit, they exercise "huge policymaking and enforcement authority" that can "greatly affect the lives and liberties of the American people."[25] Yet these agencies are largely unaccountable to the executive, who is elected by the public and is charged by the Constitution with "tak[ing] care that the laws be faithfully executed." Both the CFPB and FHFA, for example, are led by a single director, removable

---

[24] Seila Law LLC v. Consumer Fin. Prot. Bureau, 140 S. Ct. 2183 (2020); Collins v. Mnuchin, 938 F.3d 553 (5th Cir. 2019), cert. granted, No. 19-422 (U.S. July 9, 2020).

[25] In re Aiken County, 645 F.3d 428, 442 (D.C. Cir. 2011) (Kavanaugh, J., concurring).

only for "inefficiency, neglect or malfeasance."[26] In order for the president to discharge his duties and for these agencies to be truly accountable, the argument goes, the president must be able to remove these executive officers at will.

In *Seila Law,* the Court declined to overturn its decision in *Humphrey's Executor v. United States* (1935), which allows Congress to restrict the president's authority to remove executive officers in some instances.[27] Whether *Humphrey's* is in jeopardy is hard to say, but the Court refused to extend it to the stark circumstances of the CFPB, "an independent agency that wields significant executive power and is run by a single individual who cannot be removed by the president unless certain statutory criteria are met."[28] Chief Justice Roberts concluded that the CFPB's scheme is "incompatible with our constitutional structure," which "scrupulously avoids concentrating power in the hands of any single individual."[29]

Given that the Court so recently declined to overturn *Humphrey's* in *Seila Law,* it's unclear if the case will go any further in *Collins,* but it is likely to at least restore *some* accountability to the FHFA and the so-called fourth branch of government.[30]

B. The Anti-Injunction Act

In *CIC Services v. Internal Revenue Service,*[31] the justices will decide whether the Anti-Injunction Act (AIA), which bars lawsuits brought to stop the collection of taxes, bans a lawsuit against an Internal Revenue Service reporting requirement merely because the violation of that requirement carries a tax penalty. [32] If so, the Court would make

---

[26] Establishment of the Bureau of Consumer Financial Protection, 12 U.S.C. § 5491 (2010); 12 U.S.C. § 4512 (2008) (establishing the director of the FHFA).

[27] 295 U.S. 602 (1935).

[28] Selia Law, 140 S. Ct. at 2192.

[29] *Id.* at 2202.

[30] See FTC v. Ruberoid Co., 343 U.S. 470, 487 (1952) (Jackson, J., dissenting) (noting that administrative agencies "have become a veritable fourth branch of the Government, which has deranged our three-branch legal theories").

[31] CIC Servs., LLC v. IRS, 925 F.3d 247 (6th Cir. 2019), cert. granted, No. 19-930 (U.S. May 4, 2020).

[32] The Anti-Injunction Act provides that, generally speaking, "no suit for the purpose of restraining the assessment or collection of any [federal] tax shall be maintained in any court by any person." 26 U.S.C. § 7421 (2018).

it more difficult for plaintiffs to challenge allegedly illegal rules when they have some tax consequence.

In 2016, the IRS issued new record-keeping and reporting require-ments, mandating that taxpayers report certain transactions that purport to be insurance but that the IRS concluded did not actually qualify. Noncompliance subjected taxpayers to penalties. CIC Services, a taxpayer adviser firm, challenged the requirements on the theory that the IRS had not undergone the necessary notice-and-comment rulemaking process under the Administrative Procedure Act. The IRS then moved to dismiss the case based on the AIA, which requires plaintiffs to wait until a tax has been collected to challenge its validity.

The Sixth Circuit ruled that, because violations of the IRS require-ments carry a tax penalty, the AIA barred a pre-enforcement chal-lenge to them. That conclusion conflicts with a previous Supreme Court decision interpreting the AIA's sister statute, the Tax Injunc-tion Act.[33] It also stretches the underlying policy of the AIA, which is to facilitate the collection of taxes. The result is to bar lawsuits not just against tax impositions, but against rules that have any tax implication.

CIC moved for rehearing en banc, which the Sixth Circuit de-nied. But several judges dissented from denial, including Judges Amul Thapar, Raymond Kethledge, John Bush, Joan Larsen, John Nalbandian, Chad Readler, and Eric Murphy. Judge Jeffrey Sutton, who was the deciding vote, concurred in the denial of rehearing. He believed that the dissenting opinion by Judge Nalbandian "seems to be right as an original matter," because it's doubtful the AIA was intended to ban a suit "whenever the IRS enforces a regulation with a penalty that it chooses to call a tax."[34] He concluded, however, that "reading between the lines of Supreme Court decisions is a tricky business," and "poses fewer difficulties for the Supreme Court than it does for us."[35] He thus suggested it was the Supreme Court's mess to clean up, and the Court has taken up his invitation to do so.

The case has the potential to significantly broaden or narrow the abil-ity of plaintiffs to seek pre-enforcement review of purportedly illegal

---

[33] Direct Mktg. Ass'n v. Brohl, 575 U.S. 1 (2015).

[34] CIC Servs., LLC v. IRS, 936 F.3d 501, 504 (6th Cir. 2019) (Sutton, J., concurring in denial of rehearing en banc).

[35] *Id.* at 505.

rules. On the one hand, as CIC noted in its petition, "[p]re-enforcement review is the lifeblood of administrative law."[36] It's what allows "a law-abiding citizen [to] challenge illegal regulations in court, without having to violate the regulation first and then raise its invalidity as a defense to an enforcement action."[37] On the other hand, the Court has affirmed the government's interest in securing its revenues.

Even in this case, the specter of Obamacare haunts the Court once again. In *NFIB v. Sebelius*, the Court ruled that the individual mandate was not a tax for purposes of the AIA, which meant that the suit could move forward, even though it was a tax for purposes of Congress's taxing power. The Court is thus forced, once again, to determine if a "penalty" is a tax for purposes of the AIA.

IV. Nominal Damages and Mootness

Constitutional lawsuits sometimes have the effect of inducing the government to change its policy before the litigation is complete. That's generally a happy outcome for the plaintiff, except that, in the absence of a court opinion, the government may choose to resume its policy at a later date. Nonetheless, when plaintiffs get what they asked for, like getting rid of an unconstitutional policy, courts will usually rule that the case is "moot" and that they no longer have jurisdiction to hear the case. Next term, in *Uzuegbunam v. Preczewski* (pronounced Oo-zah-BUN-um versus Preh-SHEV-skee), the Court will resolve the deep circuit split concerning whether such mootness can be defeated by bringing a claim for nominal damages.[38]

In 2016, Chike Uzuegbunam was stopped by campus police from distributing religious literature in an outdoor plaza at Georgia Gwinnett College (GGC), where he was a student. The officer explained that no one could distribute writings of any kind at that location, in accordance with the school's (ironically titled) "Freedom of Expression Policy." Instead, students were permitted to engage in expression only if they reserved one of two designated "speech

---

[36] Petition for Writ of Certiorari at 2, CIC Servs. v. IRS, No. 19-930 (U.S. May 4, 2020).

[37] *Id.*

[38] Uzuegbunam v. Preczewski, 781 Fed. Appx. 824 (11th Cir. 2019), cert. granted, No. 19-968 (U.S. July 9, 2020). Plaintiffs typically seek nominal damages when their constitutional rights have been violated but money damages are nonexistent or difficult to calculate. They thus stand as a symbol in litigation for the violation of the plaintiff's rights.

zones" which occupied a small part of campus and were open just 18 hours a week.

Uzuegbunam dutifully reserved a zone, only to be approached by a member of campus police yet again, who told him there had been complaints about his speech and subsequently asked him to stop speaking. The officer explained that Uzuegbunam's reservation did not include permission to engage in "open-air speaking," and that his speech qualified as "disorderly conduct" under GGC's "Student Code of Conduct."[39]

After this second encounter, Uzuegbunam sued university officials under the First Amendment, asking for declaratory and injunctive relief and nominal damages. Thereafter, GGC revised its policy to permit speech everywhere without a permit except in limited circumstances and changed its code of conduct. It then moved to dismiss the lawsuit as moot. The district court granted the motion based on mootness, ruling that the college had changed its policies, there was "no reasonable basis to expect that it would return to them," and the nominal damages could not save the suit from being moot.

The Eleventh Circuit affirmed, ruling that the plaintiffs' "abstract" constitutional injury, represented by the nominal damages claim, was not sufficient to keep the case live.[40] A claim for nominal damages will defeat mootness, it said, only where the plaintiffs have also pleaded a claim for compensatory damages and there is an ongoing dispute as to that claim.[41] Maintaining jurisdiction in Uzuegbunam's case, however, where there was no claim for compensatory damages, "would serve no purpose other than to affix a judicial seal of approval to an outcome that has already been realized."[42]

Represented by Alliance Defending Freedom, Uzuegbunam asked the Court to review the Eleventh Circuit's decision and to resolve

---

[39] The code forbade "disturb[ing] the peace and/or comfort of person(s)." See Petition for Writ of Certiorari at 4, Uzuegbunam v. Preczewski, No. 19-968 (U.S. July 9, 2020).

[40] Uzuegbunam, 781 Fed. Appx. at 829.

[41] The court noted that a claim for nominal damages may present a live case or controversy where it is the only appropriate remedy. For example, in boundary disputes, landowners sometimes request nominal damages for trespass when seeking a court order regarding the boundary. Or, in libel lawsuits, plaintiffs sometimes ask for nominal damages to vindicate their reputation when seeking a judicial determination that the libel is false. It contrasted those situations with a case where the plaintiff seeks both nominal damages and declaratory or injunctive relief and the defendant subsequently changes its policy.

[42] Uzuegbunam, 781 Fed. Appx. at 830.

the resulting split between the six circuits that hold that the government's policy change does not moot nominal damages claims, the two circuits that hold such claims moot only if the government changes a policy it has never enforced against the plaintiff, and the Eleventh Circuit, which held that such claims are always moot unless there is an accompanying compensatory damages claim. They argue that nominal damages claims represent a constitutional injury and entitle a plaintiff to an adjudication on the merits in the same way that claims for compensatory damages do.

A diverse array of groups filed amicus briefs in support of certiorari, demonstrating the broad interest among organizations that litigate in the public interest. Amici include atheist, Jewish, Catholic, and Muslim groups, the Foundation for Individual Rights in Education, and student groups like Young Americans for Liberty.[43] As the American Humanist Society observed, "[o]rderly society requires proper vindication of constitutional rights," including claims for nominal damages.[44] Such awards "are necessary to ensure scrupulous observance of the Constitution."[45]

---

[43] Americans for Prosperity (AFP) wrote a particularly interesting amicus brief arguing that the Eleventh Circuit's decision would exacerbate the problems wrought by qualified immunity doctrine. It noted that, "[s]tudent plaintiffs can only overcome qualified immunity in a §1983 case and be heard against individual defendants if there is well-established precedent on point. But precedent cannot be developed" when claims are routinely dismissed, either for qualified immunity reasons itself, or because of mootness problems. Brief for Ams. for Prosperity as Amici Curiae Supporting Petitioners at 4, Uzuegbunam v. Preczewski, No. 19-968 (U.S. July 9, 2020). AFP went on to quote Judge Don Willett, who described a qualified immunity conundrum:

> Section 1983 meets Catch-22. Plaintiffs must produce precedent even as fewer courts are producing precedent. Important constitutional questions go unanswered precisely because no one's answered them before. Courts then rely on that judicial silence to conclude there's no equivalent case on the books. No precedent = no clearly established law = no liability. An Escherian Stairwell. Heads government wins, tails plaintiff loses.

Id. (quoting Zadeh v. Robinson, 928 F.3d 457, 474, 480 (5th Cir. 2019), petition for cert. filed, No. 19-676 (U.S. Nov. 22, 2019)). More permissive mootness doctrines, AFP concluded, present yet another obstacle to the development of the body of law necessary to overcome qualified immunity.

[44] Brief for Am. Humanist Ass'n as Amici Curiae Supporting Petitioners at 8, Uzuegbunam v. Preczewski, No. 19-968 (U.S. July 9, 2020).

[45] *Id.* at 11.

The case presents an important question that is of interest to any individuals who might assert their constitutional rights in court, particularly in contexts—like schools—where the case may be mooted quickly (for instance, because the plaintiff graduates). Not only do litigants seek a full vindication of their constitutional rights in court but—so long as there is no adjudication on the merits—the government may resume their conduct at a later date, which leaves constitutional rights in peril.

V. The Criminal Docket

A short note on the criminal docket. The Court will hear at least three criminal cases relating to the Fourth, Sixth, and Eighth Amendments. In *Jones v. Mississippi*, the Court will consider whether the Eighth Amendment's prohibition on cruel and unusual punishment requires a judge to make an affirmative finding that a minor is "permanently incorrigible" before imposing a sentence of life without parole.[46] The facts are enough to make a mother cry. The juvenile in the case stabbed his grandfather to death during an altercation when he was 15 years old. The boy, who suffered from depression and other mental health conditions for which he was medicated, had come to live with his grandparents to escape his "troubled" household. His father was a violent alcoholic, his stepfather was abusive, and his mother abused alcohol and suffered from various mental disorders. The boy testified that he stabbed his grandfather in self-defense, but the jury rejected that defense and sentenced him to life without parole, which was the mandatory penalty at the time.

Following the Supreme Court's 2012 decision in *Miller v. Alabama*, which ruled mandatory life imprisonment without parole for minors unconstitutional, the Supreme Court of Mississippi instructed the state circuit court on remand to take into account various "characteristics and circumstances" when considering a new sentence.[47] At the hearing, the state offered no new evidence, while the defense offered testimony from several witnesses, including his grandmother (the widow of his grandfather). Nevertheless, the court imposed the same sentence. The question for the Supreme Court is whether *Miller* requires an affirmative finding that the minor is permanently incorrigible before imposing life without parole.

[46] 140 S. Ct. 1293 (2020) (cert. granted).
[47] 567 U.S. 460 (2012).

In *Edwards v. Vannoy*,[48] the Court will decide whether its decision last term in *Ramos v. Louisiana*,[49] which incorporated against the states the Sixth Amendment's right to a unanimous jury verdict applies retroactively to cases that have already made their way through the state courts and are now on federal collateral review. Thedrick Edwards was sentenced to life in prison after committing a series of robberies and a rape in 2006. One person on the jury voted to acquit Edwards on each count, but, because Louisiana did not then require a unanimous verdict, Edwards was found guilty. Before *Ramos*, only two states did not require unanimous juries, Oregon and Louisiana (Louisiana voters changed the law before the Court heard *Ramos* but did so too late to be of help to Mr. Ramos). Edwards would not have been convicted if he had been prosecuted in any one of the 48 other states (or by the federal government). The Supreme Court granted certiorari to decide whether *Ramos*, which now requires a unanimous verdict, applies to Edwards and others whose cases are on federal collateral review.

Last, in *Torres v. Madrid*, the Court will consider whether a seizure occurs any time the government uses physical force, even if that force is not successful at subduing the target.[50] The plaintiff, Roxanne Torres, sued police officers for excessive force after they shot her while she was sitting in her car in a parking lot. The officers, who were waiting to serve an arrest warrant on another person, approached Torres's car, which startled her. Torres claimed she did not identify the two officers as members of the police and she thus attempted to flee. In response, the police shot at her. Despite being shot, Torres was able to elude capture and drove to a hospital. In her excessive force suit, the district court ruled (and the Tenth Circuit affirmed) that no Fourth Amendment "seizure" occurred because an officer's application of physical force is not a seizure if the person is able to evade apprehension. The Court granted certiorari to resolve the resulting circuit split, and its decision will have far-reaching applications for plaintiffs who challenge uses of force that may injure, but not detain them.

---

[48] No. 19-5807 (U.S. May 4, 2020) (cert. granted).

[49] 140 S. Ct. 1390 (2020).

[50] 140 S. Ct. 680 (2020) (cert. granted).

VI. Impeachment

It is a truth universally acknowledged that a court in possession of a caseload must be asked to hear cases related to purported misconduct by President Trump. Next term, the Supreme Court will hear a case involving the attempts by members of Congress to secure materials from Special Counsel Robert Mueller's investigation into possible Russian interference in the 2016 election for use in its impeachment investigations. Last year, Mueller submitted a report to Attorney General William Barr, and Barr later released a redacted version to the public. The House Judiciary Committee then sought a court order requiring the disclosure of the redacted portions of the report, in addition to grand jury transcripts and other materials, in connection with its impeachment investigations. The committee cited a federal rule of criminal procedure that allows a court to authorize disclosure of otherwise confidential grand jury materials "in connection with a judicial proceeding."

The district court ruled that impeachment is a "judicial proceeding" under the rule and granted the committee's request to access the materials. The D.C. Circuit affirmed,[51] and the Supreme Court blocked the release of the grand jury materials pending its review of that decision. Notably, unless the justices expedite the oral argument, they will not hear the case until after Election Day.

VII. Severability

Last term revealed a deepening disagreement among the justices about how to handle the issue of severability, that is, whether or how to strike unconstitutional provisions from a larger act. In *Barr v. American Association of Political Consultants*,[52] Justices Kavanaugh and Neil Gorsuch had a lively exchange about what the remedy should be in a lawsuit challenging a federal ban on robocalls, even though both agreed that a portion of the ban was unconstitutional. The plaintiffs in that case, a group that sought to make robocalls with political content, argued that the law's exemption for calls related to government debt rendered the law unconstitutional under the First Amendment. Both Justice Kavanaugh (writing for the majority) and

[51] U.S. House of Representative v. U.S. Dep't of Justice, 951 F.3d 589 (D.C. Cir. 2020).
[52] 140 S. Ct. 2335 (2020).

Justice Gorsuch (writing a concurrence) agreed that the exemption was a content-based restriction on speech that failed strict scrutiny. Justice Kavanaugh, however, ruled that the exemption was severable from the remainder of the act.[53] He therefore struck down the exemption and left a total ban in place. Justice Gorsuch, joined by Justice Thomas, would have entered an injunction preventing the government from enforcing the ban at all against the plaintiffs.[54]

Both the majority opinion and the concurrence accused the other of overreach. Justice Kavanaugh wrote that he was adhering to the traditional severability analysis, which seeks to determine Congress's intent and which yields a far more modest result than Justice Gorsuch's approach. He noted that Justice Gorsuch would have invalidated an entire statute (at least, as applied to the plaintiffs) based on one sliver of it being unconstitutional. Justice Kavanaugh, by contrast, was merely getting rid of that one unconstitutional sliver—a result that he believed Congress would have preferred.

Justice Gorsuch argued that it was the majority that was acting contrary to Congress's intent by effectively rewriting the statute. "Just five years ago," he said, "Congress expressly allowed robocalls" for some purposes.[55] By reinstating a total ban on all robocalls, the majority contradicted Congress's deliberate steps to restrict less speech. Moreover, such a remedy left the plaintiffs with no practical relief because the ban remained in effect, just without an exemption for other groups. "What is the point of fighting this long battle," he asked, "if the prize for winning is nothing at all?"[56] He also indicated that severability doctrine should be revisited.

To this, Justice Kavanaugh quipped: "Justice Gorsuch suggests . . . that severability doctrine may need to be reconsidered. But when and how? As the saying goes, John Marshall is not walking through that door."[57] This constitutional lawyer, for one, has never heard of such a saying. But after an extended trip down a Google rabbit hole, it appears the justice was referring to a press conference some years ago when Rick Pitino, then-coach of the Boston Celtics said, "Larry Bird is not

---

[53] *Id.* at 2352–55.

[54] *Id.* at 2365–67 (Gorsuch, J., concurring in part and dissenting in part).

[55] *Id.* at 2366.

[56] *Id.*

[57] *Id.* at 2356.

walking through that door."[58] Coach Pitino's message was that Boston fans should focus on the present rather than yearning for the past. In other words, the quip appears to be Justice Kavanaugh's way of saying "stare decisis" with regards to severability doctrine.[59]

This same debate made an appearance in *Seila Law*, except with Chief Justice Roberts writing the majority opinion and adhering to the traditional severability analysis and Justice Thomas advocating for enjoining the law as to the plaintiffs. There, Chief Justice Roberts described severability as "a scalpel rather than a bulldozer."[60] Justice Kavanaugh later used almost identical language in *Barr*, when he said: "The Court's precedents reflect a decisive preference for surgical severance rather than wholesale destruction."[61]

We can expect the debate to resurface next term in the Affordable Care Act litigation if the Court rules that the mandate is

[58] JazzBasketball1, Rick Pitino – "Walking Through That Door" Press Conference, YouTube (July 2, 2011), https://bit.ly/3fEzKGe. Thanks to Josh Blackman for the pointer. See Josh Blackman, "Part III: Barr v. AAPC and Stare Decisis," Reason: The Volokh Conspiracy, July 7, 2020, https://bit.ly/2Pw8krw.

[59] One could argue that Coach Pitino's quote favors abandoning precedent in favor of current conditions. His full quote was:

> Larry Bird is not walking through that door, fans. Kevin McHale is not walking through that door, and Robert Parish is not walking through that door. And if you expect them to walk through that door, they're going to be gray and old. What we are is young, exciting, hard-working, and we're going to improve. People don't realize that, and as soon as they realize those three guys are not coming through that door, the better this town will be for all of us because there are young guys in that (locker) room playing their asses off. I wish we had $90 million under the salary cap. I wish we could buy the world. We can't; the only thing we can do is work hard, and all the negativity that's in this town sucks. I've been around when [baseball player] Jim Rice was booed. I've been around when [baseball player] Yastrzemski was booed. And it stinks. It makes the greatest town, greatest city in the world, lousy. The only thing that will turn this around is being upbeat and positive like we are in that locker room . . . and if you think I'm going to succumb to negativity, you're wrong. You've got the wrong guy leading this team.

Pitino, *supra* note 58. Arguably, Coach Pitino might take Justice Gorsuch's side in the severability debate, and not rely on doctrines of the past where they do not meet the conditions of today.

[60] Seila Law, 140 S. Ct. at 2210.

[61] Barr, 140 S. Ct. at 2350–51.

unconstitutional. Or, the Court may address it in *Carney v. Adams*, which challenges a Delaware law that limits the political makeup of state courts.[62] In that case, the Third Circuit invalidated a state constitutional provision that requires judges who are not members of the majority political party on the court to be members of the other "major political party." The court not only struck down that provision but deemed it inseverable from a separate requirement mandating that no more than a "bare majority" of judges on any one court be composed of the same political party. Severability is one of the key questions before the Supreme Court.

For now, it seems that Chief Justice Roberts and Justice Kavanaugh are firmly in the majority when it comes to severability. But even if the doctrine does not change, we may get more quips and colorful language out of the dispute.

Conclusion

The Court's term begins on October 5, and, at least to start, the cases will be familiar because we expected to hear them argued months ago. While likely a quieter term than the last, we will still see some fireworks. From the (never-ending) ACA litigation, to friction between religious liberty and anti-discrimination law, to a case related to impeachment, the Court will be unable to wholly escape controversy despite Chief Justice Roberts's efforts to keep the Court free of politics. But who knows what goes on in that oak-paneled room where it happens? Supreme Court terms are always quiet following bigger years, until . . . they *aren't*. It's 2020. Nothing is certain, except maybe death, taxes, and the likelihood of seeing Obamacare before the Court in a future term.

[62] 140 S. Ct. 602 (2019) (cert. granted).

Contributors

Jonathan H. Adler is the inaugural Johan Verheij Memorial Professor of Law and director of the Coleman P. Burke Center for Environmental Law at Case Western Reserve University School of Law, where he teaches courses in environmental, administrative and constitutional law. Adler is the author or editor of seven books, including *Rebuilding the Ark: New Perspectives on Endangered Species Act Reform* (2011) and *Business and the Roberts Court* (2016), as well as over a dozen book chapters. His articles have appeared in publications ranging from the *Harvard Environmental Law Review* and *Yale Journal on Regulation* to the *Wall Street Journal* and *USA Today*. He has testified before Congress on several occasions, and his work has been cited by the Supreme Court. Adler is a contributing editor to *National Review Online* and a regular contributor to the popular legal blog *The Volokh Conspiracy*. A regular commentator on constitutional and regulatory issues, he has appeared on numerous radio and television programs, including *PBS Newshour* and NPR's *Talk of the Nation*. Adler is a senior fellow at the Property & Environment Research Center in Bozeman, Montana. He also serves on the NFIB Small Business Legal Center Advisory Board, the academic advisory board of the *Cato Supreme Court Review*, the board of the Foundation for Research on Economics and the Environment, and the Environmental Law Institute's *Environmental Law Reporter*. In 2018, Professor Adler was elected a member of the American Law Institute. Before joining Case Western, Adler clerked for Judge David B. Sentelle on the District of Columbia Circuit Court of Appeals. Adler also worked at the Competitive Enterprise Institute, where he directed its environmental studies program. He holds a B.A., *magna cum laude* from Yale and a J.D. *summa cum laude* from George Mason University School of Law.

Tanner J. Bean is an associate at the Salt Lake City–based law firm of Fabian VanCott, where he focuses on employment, litigation, and appellate matters. Before joining the firm, Tanner clerked for

Judge Molly J. Huskey on the Idaho Court of Appeals. Tanner has particular experience in religion– and LGBT–based discrimination in employment, housing, public accommodations, and education. Tanner received his J.D., with honors, from Brigham Young University J. Reuben Clark Law School, where he served as president of the Trial Advocacy Team, symposium editor of the *BYU Law Review*, and research fellow and student management board member of the International Center for Law and Religion Studies. Tanner also received his B.A. from Brigham Young University, majoring in English. Tanner serves on the J. Reuben Clark Law Society's Young Lawyers/Student Chapters and Religious Freedom committees and is the founder of the Workplace Religious Accommodations Database (WRAD) Pro Bono Project.

Anastasia Boden is a senior attorney at the Pacific Legal Foundation's Economic Liberty Project, where she challenges anti-competitive licensing laws and laws that restrict freedom of speech. Boden represents entrepreneurs and small businesses challenging bureaucratic impediments to free business practices. These include challenges to competitor's veto laws, which require startups have permission from established competitors before opening their doors. In addition to litigating, Boden testifies before legislatures on the impact of occupational licensing on entrepreneurship. Her writings on all matters of law and liberty have been featured in the *Washington Post, Chicago Tribune, Forbes,* and more. In 2015, Boden was selected to join the Claremont Institute's prestigious John Marshall Fellowship. Prior to joining PLF, she worked at the Cato Institute's Robert A. Levy Center for Constitutional Studies and at the Washington Legal Foundation. Boden earned her B.A., with honors, from the University of California, Santa Barbara, and her J.D. from Georgetown University Law Center.

Clint Bolick is an associate justice of the Arizona Supreme Court, serving since 2016. Before joining the court, Bolick co-founded the Institute for Justice, where he was vice president and director of litigation until 2004. From 2007 until his appointment to the Arizona bench, Bolick served as the vice president for litigation at the Goldwater Institute. Before then, he was the president and general counsel of the Alliance for School Choice. Before co-founding the Institute for Justice, Bolick was a staff attorney for the Mountain

States Legal Foundation and served in the Reagan administration's Equal Employment Opportunity Commission. Bolick's writings include articles in *BYU Law Review*, *Oklahoma City University Law Review*, *Arizona State University Law Journal*, and several books on law and public policy, including *Voucher Wars: Waging the Legal Battle Over School Choice* (2003), *Leviathan: The Growth of Local government and the Erosion of Liberty* (2004), *David's Hammer: The Case for an Activist Judiciary* (2007), and *Immigration Wars: Forging an American Solution* (2013), the latter of which he co-wrote with former Florida governor Jeb Bush. Bolick has served on the boards of several education and public service organizations, including BASIS Schools, Great Hearts Academies, the Arizona Charter Schools Association and the Arizona State Advisory Committee of the U.S. Commission on Civil Rights. He also served as commissioner of the Industrial Commission of Arizona. Bolick's honors and awards include the Women's Freedom Foundation's "Second Annual Leadership Award" (1997), the Thomas J. Szasz Award for Outstanding Contributions to the Cause of Civil Liberties (1999), *American Lawyer*'s "Nation's 3 Lawyers of the Year" (2002), *Legal Times*'s "90 Greatest DC Lawyers in the Past 30 Years" (2008), and Drew University's "Alums Who Move the World" (2014). Bolick received his B.A., *magna cum laude*, from Drew University, where he majored in political science, and his J.D. from the University of California, Davis.

Trevor Burrus is a research fellow in the Cato Institute's Robert A. Levy Center for Constitutional Studies and editor-in-chief of the *Cato Supreme Court Review*. His research interests include constitutional law, civil and criminal law, legal and political philosophy, legal history, and the interface between science and public policy. His academic work has appeared in journals such as the *Harvard Journal of Law and Public Policy*, the *New York University Journal of Law and Liberty*, the *New York University Annual Survey of American Law*, the *Syracuse Law Review*, and many others. His popular writing has appeared in the *Washington Post, New York Times* (online), *USA Today, Forbes, Huffington Post*, and others. Burrus lectures regularly on behalf of the Federalist Society, the Institute for Humane Studies, the Foundation for Economics Education, and other organizations, and he frequently appears on major media outlets. He is also the co-host of "Free Thoughts," a weekly podcast that covers topics in libertarian theory, history, and philosophy. He is the editor of *A Conspiracy against Obamacare* (2013) and *Deep Commitments: The Past, Present, and Future of Religious Liberty* (2017), and holds a B.A. in philosophy from the University of Colorado at Boulder and a J.D. from the University of Denver Sturm College of Law.

Judge Thomas M. Hardiman has served on the United States Court of Appeals for the Third Circuit since his appointment by President George W. Bush in 2007. Before this, Hardiman was a judge of the United States District Court for the Western District of Pennsylvania. Prior to joining the federal bench, Hardiman was a litigator for Skadden Arps in their Washington, D.C. office, and for Reed Smith in Pittsburgh. Hardiman is a member of the American Law Institute, a master of the University of Pittsburgh chapter of the American Inns of Court, and chair of the Committee on Information Technology of the Judicial Conference of the United States. Hardiman received his B.A. from the University of Notre Dame, and his J.D. from the Georgetown University Law Center, where he was an editor for the *Georgetown Law Journal* and a moot court semi-finalist.

Paul J. Larkin Jr is the John, Barbara, and Victoria Rumpel senior legal research fellow at the Heritage Foundation's Meese Center for Legal and Judicial Studies, Institute for Constitutional Government, where his work focuses on criminal justice, drug, and regulatory policies. Before joining Heritage, Paul was assistant general counsel for Verizon Communications, a special agent for criminal enforcement and then acting director of the Environmental Protection Agency's Criminal Investigation Division. Prior to these roles, he served as counsel to the Senate Judiciary Committee. Earlier, Paul was an assistant solicitor general in the Department of Justice, arguing over two dozen cases before the Supreme Court. His scholarly works have appeared, among other places, in the *Harvard Journal of Law and Public Policy*, the *Journal of Law and Policy*, the *Washington and Lee Law Review*, the *Georgetown Journal of Law and Public Policy*, the *Federalist Society Review*, and the *Journal of Criminal Law and Criminology*. Paul clerked for the Honorable Robert Bork of the United States Court of Appeals for the District of Columbia Circuit. He holds a B.A., *summa cum laude*, in philosophy from Washington and Lee University, an M.A. in public policy from George Washington University, and a J.D.

from Stanford Law School, where he was a published member of the *Stanford Law Review.*

Peter Margulies is a professor of law at the Roger Williams University School of Law in Bristol, Rhode Island, where he teaches immigration law, national security law, and professional responsibility. Margulies has filed amicus briefs in several high-profile cases before the Supreme Court and is frequently cited for his legal expertise in the *New York Times, National Law Journal,* and other media. In addition to his academic work, Margulies has used his deep knowledge of immigration law to assist Haitian refugees in various legal matters and has engaged in community legal service outreach. Margulies has written articles in a number of law reviews, including the *Georgetown Immigration Law Journal, Florida Law Review, Fordham Law Review, Indiana Journal of Global Legal Studies,* and *International Law Studies.* Margulies's books include *Law's Detour, Justice Displaced in the Bush Administration* (2010), as well as chapters in *Enron and Other Corporate Fiascos: The Corporate Scandal Reader* (2009) and *Counterinsurgency Law: New Directions in Asymmetric Warfare* (2013). Margulies received his B.A. from Colgate University, and his J.D. from Columbia University.

Mitchell A. Mosvick is the international legal counsel for a multinational corporation. Previously, Mosvick practiced appellate and international law at a law firm in Washington, D.C., including in cases before the United States Supreme Court. Mosvick worked on briefs in numerous Supreme Court cases including the Sixth Amendment case *Padilla v. Kentucky,* and he represented the Cato Institute as its counsel of record in its amicus brief in *Lee v. United States.* Mosvick is an attorney in the United States as well as a solicitor of England and Wales, and has advised parties on constitutional, international, administrative, and all forms of corporate and commercial legal matters. He served as law clerk to the Honorable Judge Jackson L. Kiser of the Western District of Virginia and earned his J.D. at the University of Virginia School of Law. He currently resides in London.

Nicholas M. Mosvick is a senior fellow at the National Constitution Center. He received his PhD in American history from the University of Mississippi, where his research focused on the constitutional arguments over conscription during the Civil War.

He received his J.D. and M.A. from the University of Virginia School of Law's joint law and history program. Before receiving his PhD, Mosvick was a legal associate at Cato's Robert A. Levy Center for Constitutional Studies. He is currently working on a book related to his dissertation, as well as projects on Justice Stanley Matthews and the use of the Militia Clause in antebellum constitutional discourse regarding the militia and federalism.

Jennifer J. Schulp is the director of Financial Regulation Studies at the Cato Institute's Center for Monetary and Financial Alternatives, where she focuses on the regulation of securities and capital markets. Before joining Cato, Schulp was a director in the Department of Enforcement at the Financial Industry Regulatory Authority (FINRA), representing FINRA in investigations and disciplinary proceedings relating to violations of the federal securities laws and self-regulatory organization rules. Prior to this she worked in private practice at Gibson Dunn. Schulp clerked for Judge E. Grady Jolly on the Fifth Circuit Court of Appeals. She received her J.D. from the University of Chicago Law School, where she was awarded the Karl Llewelyn Cup and the Thomas R. Mulroy Award for Excellence in Appellate Advocacy. She holds a B.A. in political science from the University of Chicago.

Ilya Shapiro is director of the Robert A. Levy Center for Constitutional Studies at the Cato Institute, where he previously served as a senior fellow and editor-in-chief of the *Cato Supreme Court Review*. Before joining Cato, he was a special assistant/advisor to the Multi-National Force in Iraq on rule-of-law issues and practiced international, political, commercial, and antitrust litigation at Patton Boggs and Cleary Gottlieb. Shapiro is the co-author (with David H. Gans) of *Religious Liberties for Corporations? Hobby Lobby, the Affordable Care Act, and the Constitution* (2014). He has contributed to many academic, popular, and professional publications and regularly provides media commentary—including an appearance on the *Colbert Report*—and is a legal consultant to CBS News. Shapiro has testified before Congress and state legislatures and, as coordinator of Cato's amicus brief program, has filed more than 300 "friend of the court" briefs in the Supreme Court. He lectures regularly on behalf of the Federalist Society, was an inaugural Washington Fellow at the National Review

Institute and a Lincoln Fellow at the Claremont Institute, and has been an adjunct professor at the George Washington University Law School and University of Mississippi School of Law. In 2015 *National Law Journal* named him to its list of "rising stars" (40 under 40). Before entering private practice, Shapiro clerked for Judge E. Grady Jolly of the U.S. Court of Appeals for the Fifth Circuit. He holds an A.B. from Princeton, an M.Sc. from the London School of Economics, and a J.D. from the University of Chicago (where he became a Tony Patiño Fellow). His latest book, *Supreme Disorder: Judicial Nominations and the Politics of America's Highest Court*, is out this September.

Stephen I. Vladeck is the A. Dalton Cross Professor in Law at the University of Texas School of Law and a nationally recognized expert on the federal courts, constitutional law, national security law, and military justice. Vladeck has argued multiple cases before the Supreme Court and the lower federal courts. He has served as an expert witness both before federal and foreign tribunals and has been repeatedly recognized for his influential and widely cited legal scholarship and his service to the legal profession. Vladeck is co-host, with Professor Bobby Chesney, of the popular and award-winning *National Security Law Podcast*. He is the Supreme Court analyst for *CNN* and a co-author of Aspen Publishers' leading national security law and counterterrorism law casebooks. He is co-editor-in-chief of the *Just Security* blog and a senior editor at *Lawfare*. Before joining Texas Law, Vladeck taught at the University of Miami School of Law and American University Washington College of Law. He is an elected member of the University of Texas Faculty Council, an elected member of the American Law Institute, and a distinguished scholar at the Robert S. Strauss Center for International Security and Law. He is the Supreme Court Fellow at the Constitution Project and a member of the Advisory Committee to the ABA Standing Committee on Law and National Security, the Board of Academic Advisors of the American Constitution Society, and serves on the advisory boards of the Electronic Privacy Information Center, the National Institute of Military Justice, and the RAND History of U.S. Military Policy. A graduate of Yale Law School, Vladeck clerked for Judge Marsha S. Berzon on the Ninth Circuit Court of Appeals and for Judge Rosemary Barkett on the Eleventh Circuit Court of Appeals. While in law school, he was executive editor of the *Yale Law Journal* and the student director of the Balancing Civil Liberties & National Security Post-9/11 Litigation Project. He was also awarded the Harlan Fiske Stone Prize for Outstanding Moot Court Oralist and shared the Potter Stewart Prize for Best Team Performance in Moot Court. He earned a B.A. *summa cum laude* with highest distinction from Amherst College, majoring in history and mathematics.

Keith E. Whittington is William Nelson Cromwell Professor of Politics in the Department of Politics at Princeton University. He is the author of many books, including *Repugnant Laws: Judicial Review of Acts of Congress from the Founding to the Present* (2020), *Speak Freely: Why Universities Must Defend Free Speech* (2018), *Judicial Review and Constitutional Politics* (2015), *Political Foundations of Judicial Supremacy: The Presidency, the Supreme Court, and Constitutional Leadership in U.S. History* (2009), *Constitutional Construction: Divided Powers and Constitutional Meaning* (2001), and *Constitutional Interpretation: Textual Meaning, Original Intent, and Judicial Review* (1999). He is co-editor of *Congress and the Constitution* (2005) and *The Oxford Handbook of Law and Politics* (2008). Whittington is also the editor of *Law and Politics: Critical Concepts in Political Science* (2015). He has published widely on American constitutional theory and development, federalism, judicial politics, and the presidency, including co-authoring multiple volumes of the epic *American Constitutionalism* series. He has served as a John M. Olin Foundation Faculty Fellow, on the American Council of Learned Societies Junior Faculty Fellow, National Center for Free Speech and Civic Engagement Fellow, and was a visiting scholar at the Social Philosophy and Policy Center and a visiting professor at the University of Texas School of Law and Harvard Law School. Whittington is a member of the American Academy of the Arts and Sciences. He is currently completing *Constitutional Crises, Real and Imagined* and *The Idea of Democracy in America, from the American Revolution to the Gilded Age*. His work for a general audience has appeared in the *Washington Post, Wall Street Journal, New York Times, The Atlantic, Reason*, and the *Lawfare* and *Volokh Conspiracy* blogs. Whittington earned his B.A. and B.B.A. from the University of Texas and his M.A. and PhD from Yale University.

Ilan Wurman is an associate professor at the Sandra Day O'Connor College of Law at Arizona State University, where he teaches administrative law and constitutional law. He writes on administrative law, separation of powers, and constitutionalism, and his academic writing has appeared or is forthcoming in the *Yale Law Journal*, the *Stanford Law Review*, the *University of Chicago Law Review*, the *University of Pennsylvania Law Review*, the *Duke Law Journal*, and the *Texas Law Review* among other journals. He has also authored *A Debt Against the Living: An Introduction to Originalism* (2017), and *The Second Founding: An Introduction to the Fourteenth Amendment* (2020). Wurman is also writing a casebook, *Administrative Law Theory and Fundamentals: An Integrated Approach* (forthcoming 2021). Before joining ASU, Wurman was a fellow at the Stanford Constitutional Law Center and an associate at the firm of Winston & Strawn. Prior to this he clerked for Judge Jerry E. Smith on the Fifth Circuit Court of Appeals. Wurman earned his B.A., *magna cum laude*, from Claremont McKenna College, where he majored in government and physics, and his J.D. from Stanford Law School, where he was an editor for the *Stanford Law Review* and for the *Harvard Journal of Law and Public Policy*, the latter in a cross-institutional role.